Digital Cartography

Robert G. Cromley
University of Connecticut

Prentice Hall, Englewood Cliffs, New Jersey 07632

Library of Congress Cataloging-in-Publication Data

Cromley, Robert G.
Digital cartography / Robert G. Cromley.
p. cm.
Includes bibliographical references and index.
ISBN 0-13-710930-X
1. Digital mapping. I. Title.
GA139.C76 1992
526--dc20 91-16455
CIP

Editorial/production supervision: *Brendan M. Stewart*
Prepress buyer: *Kelly Behr*
Manufacturing buyer: *Susan Brunke*
Acquisition editor: *Michael Hays*
Editorial assistant: *Dana Mercure*

A Simon & Schuster Company
Englewood Cliffs, New Jersey 07632

The publisher offers discounts on this book when ordered in bulk quantities. For more information, write: Special Sales/Professional Marketing, Prentice Hall, Professional & Technical Reference Division, Englewood Cliffs, NJ 07632.

Printed in the United States of America
10 9 8 7 6 5 4 3 2 1

ISBN 0-13-710930-X

Prentice-Hall International (UK) Limited, *London*
Prentice-Hall of Australia Pty. Limited, *Sydney*
Prentice-Hall Canada Inc., *Toronto*
Prentice-Hall Hispanoamericana, S.A., *Mexico*
Prentice-Hall of India Private Limited, *New Delhi*
Prentice-Hall of Japan, Inc., *Tokyo*
Simon & Schuster Asia Pte. Ltd., *Singapore*
Editora Prentice-Hall do Brasil, Ltda., *Rio de Janeiro*

To Ellen

Table of Contents

Chapter 5 - Generalization: Classification and Simplification **175**

Chapter 6 - Two-Dimensional Display **227**

Preface

The advent of computer technology has revolutionized the way cartographers produce maps and even more fundamentally redefined what a map is. Digital cartographic procedures are not merely automated manual ones, but require a different organization of functions. Digital approaches to mapmaking have compelled researchers to rethink cartographic practices and become more rigorous in the development of cartographic theory. In this trend, the concern is more for generalization of the cartographic process and as this generalization process continues the boundaries that separate cartography from other disciplines are vanishing.

Digital Cartography is designed to be both an advanced text and a reference book on digital mapmaking procedures. The eight chapters proceed from basic concepts through the different stages of the cartographic process to the role of digital cartography in decision-making. Each chapter includes maps and figures necessary to illustrate key concepts. A list of references follows each chapter. Algorithms are also given for solving the cartographic problems presented; algorithms rather than source code or programs are emphasized as the text is not designed to teach existing software.

It is always difficult to structure the subject material of any field that has many interrelationships into a sequential list as necessitated by the form of a text; there are many cross-references in this text. The first chapter introduces the reader to the many forms and functions of maps including those unique to the computer environment. Chapter One provides an historical background for the symbiosis between hardware developments and numerical procedures for cartographic display. It also establishes the relationship between digital cartography and the field of lined. In this process, one object--a raw data set--is converted into a sequence of other objects by means of various cartographic functions and transformations. Subsequent chapters are organized around stages in the digital cartographic design sequence.

Chapter Two is also an introductory chapter because it discusses the many computational primitives that form the basis for subsequent algorithms. This chapter shows the relationship between digital cartography and the field of analytic geometry; such a chapter is essential for understanding how the computer can "see" numerically what humans see visually. It also demonstrates that numerical procedures can replicate the functions of many analog devices such as the measuring stick and compass.

Chapter Three discusses the many ways of organizing digital cartographic information into a digital database that is a central concern in digital cartography. It first examines the topological relations that underlie data organization. Next, the basic approaches to file structures are outlined followed by a description of topological cartographic objects and data structures for storing them. Finally, linear indexing methods are presented for the sequencing of two-dimensional objects in a linear list.

Chapter Four covers various aspects of data acquisition and preprocessing. First, the relationship between geographic scale and measurement is examined. Next, digital remote sensing techniques are presented for collecting geographic data directly through instrumentation followed by the different approaches for encoding geographic base file from existing map documents. These include manual and automated techniques that are dependent on the desired structure of the resulting digital representation. Finally, different preprocessing procedures are presented for manipulating the original encoded data for storage and display including searching and sorting techniques for establishing spatial order.

Chapter Five presents different spatial generalization and analytical models that are used in conjunction with maps. A series of background topics ranges from spatial central tendency measures to those of dispersion, orientation and spatial autocorrelation. These concepts are then applied to cartographic operators such as attribute classification and point and line simplification.

Chapter Six covers different aspects of two-dimensional cartographic display. First, some background is presented on the nature of symbolism operators. Next, the procedures and problems associated with the planar display of discrete geographic surfaces. Next the problems and procedures associated with the planar display of continuous geographic surfaces. The discussion centers on the differences between grid and triangulation approaches to isarithmic mapping. Finally, the concepts windows and viewports are discussed for final display on a hardware device.

Chapter Seven discusses the problems and procedures associated with the two-dimensional perspective of a three-dimensional surface. These topics include viewing projections and hidden line and surface removal.

Finally, Chapter Eight examines how digital maps are used in decision-making processes. The first section presents the concept of cartographic overlay - a set operator frequently used in conjunction with maps. A section on thematic compositing discusses the problems and procedures associated with overlaying different attribute coverages for the same geographic domain. Next is a discussion of how maps are used in map analysis procedures as variables within the context of a map algebra. The final section introduces the reader to the important subject of geographic information systems in which mapping becomes one component of a total system for the storage, retrieval, modelling, display, and analysis of spatial data for decision-making.

I would like to acknowledge Alex Bothel, John Diniz, Beatriz Milne and the University of Connecticut Research Foundation for their part in preparing the graphics for this book. I would also like to thank Marc Armstrong, Nick Chrisman, Dean Hanink, Tim Nyerges and other anonymous reviewers for their many helpful comments and insights on earlier versions of this manuscript. Any remaining omissions or errors are the responsibility of the author alone. Finally, I wish to thank Ellen, Gordon, and Edwin (who came aboard in midstream) for their support and perseverance through the dog days and nights of this project.

Chapter 1
Introduction

The development of computer technology and its application to graphics have had a profound effect on cartography. Over the past two decades, the computer has been an instrument for replicating traditional manual procedures for constructing map products. Many terms such as "automated cartography," "computer-aided cartography" and "computer-assisted cartography" [Rhind, 1977, 1980; Boyle, 1979] describe these developments but they do not reflect the significance of the revolution. Marble [1987] contends that the introduction of the computer into cartography has finally revolutionized the way cartography is perceived as well as practiced. At the same time that the computer has affected the way professional cartographers view their discipline, it has made preparation of map products easier for others. Anyone who possesses a mapping software package and the appropriate hardware can make a map or map-like product. Indeed mapping routines have become regular options in general purpose statistical analysis programs (for example, the SAS/GRAPH procedure within the Statistical Analysis System [SAS Institute, 1987]).

Although the computer has provided the impetus for a reformulation of cartographic practices, computer-assisted procedures by themselves do not necessarily represent a new paradigm. Instead the computer is the professional cartographer's assistant and its peripheral devices the instruments of a new cartography that we are calling *digital cartography.*

1.1 THE DEVELOPMENT OF COMPUTER-ASSISTED CARTOGRAPHY

It is difficult to separate computer technology from the practice of digital cartography. The design of many algorithms for solving problems and even theoretical developments have been strongly influenced by the available technology. Morrison [1980] has divided the development of computer-assisted cartography into three stages: 1) the period of the early 1960s when cartographers had a "wait-and-see" attitude; 2) the period of the late 1960s and 1970s when cartographers replicated products which were done manually by a previous technology; and 3) the post 1980s when there was a full implementation of new products.

At the beginning of the computer age in cartography, specialized graphical peripheral devices were rudimentary or did not exist. The basic computing system as configured in Figure 1.1 consisted of a central processing unit (CPU), peripheral storage devices such as hard disk drives and tape drives, an input device such as a card reader and a line printer output device. Cards, hard disks, and tapes formed the basic storage units of the system. The CPU was used to perform all of the manipulation operations. All data input originally was punched onto a card using a key punch machine and then entered into the system via a card reader. Output from the system could go directly in machine readable code onto disk, tape, paper tape or punch card or onto a printed page.

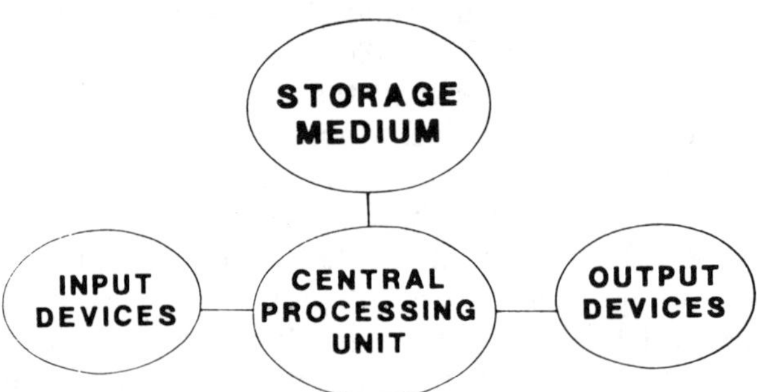

Figure 1.1 A Basic Computing System.

Early mapping programs such as SYMAP, developed at the Harvard Laboratory for Computer Graphics and Spatial Analysis [Schmidt and Zafft, 1975], and CMAP [Scripter, 1969] were developed to utilize the line printer as a display device. However, the size of a standard print cell was one sixth (or one eighth) of an inch by one tenth of an inch and not well suited for graphical displays requiring greater precision. Additionally, if the original spatial information was encoded as areal boundaries, it had to be converted into rectangular cells for printing. SYMAP included algorithms to handle this conversion efficiently. At this stage, the computer-assisted process was more manual than automated. The input of maps into the system was primarily a manual process; only operations within the CPU and the display transformations were automated.

Teletype terminals reduced the number of steps required to enter data into the processing system. A keyboard enabled users to enter data directly into the system, bypassing the key punch step, and cards began to become obsolete. Teletype terminals also facilitated the development of interactive systems in which the same unit could be used for both input and output. However, teletype terminals only permitted hardcopy output. Video display terminals brought the next significant change because images could be displayed on a screen (softcopy) and greater flexibility was achieved because the screen could be reused repeatedly to display new images without producing hardcopy until necessary.

The awareness that computing systems could be used to handle spatial information generated the need for specialized devices. Printers were developed with special print trains that varied in size and symbolism. Drum and flatbed plotters were created to produce hardcopy line drawings. Storage tube and refresh cathode ray terminals enabled maps and other graphic images to be displayed on graphic screens. The technology of storage tube terminals meant that the entire image had to be redrawn whenever a portion of the image changed. Refresh technology permitted alteration to an image so that animation could be performed although refresh systems never had enough memory for many cartographic applications. Animation on a storage tube device could only be done by photographing a frame at a time from the screen and displaying the result on a movie projector [Moellering, 1973].

These improvements in display, however, failed to significantly advance the automation of cartographic information processing; they only improved the quality of the output although it still barely matched poor-quality manual work. The introduction of digitizing tablets and scanners greatly reduced the effort associated with data input. Electromechanical digitizers permit the recording of point locations by successively positioning a light pen or the crosshairs on a cursor over each point and depressing the recording mechanism. Optical scanners convert a hardcopy image into a table of digital values by measuring the intensity of reflected light. Both of these developments permit hardcopy maps to be transformed into digital images.

While hardware improved, software developed at a slower pace but at a rate sufficient to have produced a plethora of mapping programs by the late 1970s [see Brassel, 1977; Harvard University, 1979; Marble *et al.*, 1981]. Much research was conducted and many software packages were produced, but there were few attempts to integrate the body of knowlege that developed [some exceptions are Tomlinson, 1972; Tomlinson, Calkins and Marble, 1976]. Some information on computer-assisted mapping has been integrated into traditional cartography texts [see Robinson *et al.*, 1984; Dent, 1985], but few texts have been solely devoted to computer-assisted procedures and programs [see Peucker, 1972; Monmonier, 1982.] In the 1980s, the microcomputer and lasers are changing the technology of mapping again, and a new wave of mapping software is being generated by this new technology [see Carter, 1984].

More importantly, the computer and related digital hardware including optical scanners and electromagnetic sensors have opened the display and analysis of spatial distributions to other disciplines with related interests. Allied fields such as digital image processing and computational geometry have arisen in the domain of civil engineering, computer science, applied mathematics and environmental sciences. The traditional boundaries between these fields have blurred and cartographers are no longer the only or even the major players in the spatial display and analysis arena [Burrough, 1986]. Cartography and digital cartography themselves are becoming subsumed within the emerging framework of geographic information systems (see Chapter 8) that analyze map data for information to be used in decisionmaking. The form and function of a map and the process of mapmaking has been reevaluated.

1.2 THE MAP AS A DATA MODEL

Dent [1985] describes maps as graphic representations of the cultural and physical environment; he also assumes that a map is tangible. Visibility and tangibility are characteristics of traditional map products that the computer has forced us to reconsider. To be tangible, a map must have permanence. But what must be the half-life of a map to be tangible: years for paper or thirty seconds for the screen of a CRT? Does something need to be "seen" to be a map? Does a printed document inside an atlas become a map only once the atlas is opened by a human and its information retrieved by visual inspection? With respect to visibility, is a *digital image* stored on a diskette any less a map given its contents can be inspected on a virtual display?

These characteristics of traditional maps have led Moellering [1980] to propose four classes of map based on the attributes of visual and tangible reality (see Table 1.1). A *real map* is any cartographic product that is directly viewable and permanent. Real maps would include most traditional map products. A (type I) *virtual map* is directly viewable as a cartographic image but has only a transient tangible reality; map displays on a CRT would be in this category. A (type II) virtual map has a permanent reality but cannot be directly viewed as a cartographic object. Spatial data recorded on a hard copy medium like paper but not as a cartographic image would constitute a type II map. Finally, a (type III) virtual map has neither visual nor tangible reality. A digital image on magnetic disk or tape would fall into this class.

Table 1.1 Classification of Map Products[a]

	Permanent	Not Permanent
	Real Maps:	Type I Virtual Maps:
	Conventional Sheet Map	CRT Map Image
	Globe	a) Refresh
Directly	Orthophoto Map	b) Storage Tube
Viewable	Machine Drawn Map	c) Plasma Panel
	Plastic Relief Map	Cognitive Map (two-dimensional image)
	Block Diagram	
	Type II Virtual Maps:	Type III Virtual Maps:
	Gazetteer	Digital Memory (data)
Not	Anaglyph	Magnetic Disk or Tape (data)
Directly	Traditional Field Data	Video Animation
Viewable	Hologram (stored)	Digital Terrain Model
	Fourier Transform (stored)	Cognitive Map (relational geographic data)
	Laser Disk Data	

[a]Source: Moellering (1980).

In addition to form, another characteristic of a map is function. To be valid, a map must communicate *information* to the map reader. Information instructs the reader to distinguish something "new" or "different" from something that is "ordinary" [see Peucker, 1972, p.2]. When producing a map, the cartographer must sort the available data, or pieces of fact, in order to glean information from redundant facts.

In this view, then, maps are cartographic abstractions of the environment. The abstraction process includes the *selection*, *classification*, *simplification*, and *symbolization* of cartographic information [Dent, 1985]. The selection of information is determined by the purpose of the map. Classification places objects in groups having identical or similar attributes. Simplification eliminates unnecessary detail. Symbolization replaces the form of real world objects with a cartographic representation.

In the most general sense, a map is a *data model.* Peuquet [1984] defines a data model as "a general description of specific groups of entities and the relationships between these groups of entities." The function of a model is performed through a variety of media [Harvey, 1969]. *Iconic models* replicate reality with only a change in *scale* such as engineering models of shoreline erosion. The attempt is made to retain all the elements of the real world but to reduce the size so that laboratory conditions can be met for various simulations. *Analog models* also involve a reduction in scale but represent real world features with look-alike features. *Symbolic models* are a highly idealized representation of reality in which a *language* is substituted for the real world objects. Real maps generally are a combination of analog and symbolic models. For example, traditional *thematic map*s consist of two important components: a *geographic base map* representing the spatial attributes and a *thematic overlay* representing some non-spatial attribute of the features being mapped (Figure 1.2). In such a map, the geographic base map is an analog model because the cartographic forms are similar to their real world partners but different in scale. The thematic overlay is a symbolic model because this information is represented by an abstract language such as graduated circles or shade patterns.

A major impact of computer technology with respect to the map data model has been the further abstraction of the geographic base map into a digital image as a symbolic model. The realm of the computer has no "look alike" features for representing the cultural and physical environment, only binary codes that can be manipulated by executing a program.

1.3 MAPS AND DATA PROCESSING SYSTEMS

The processing of cartographic information is a special form of general data processing. Early in the development of digital approaches to cartography, Tobler [1959] analyzed the relationship between maps and data processing systems. A data processing system consists of data gathering, data manipulation, data storage, and data utilization (Figure 1.3a). Data manipulation can be further refined into the components of input, memory, arithmetic, and control (Figure 1.3b). Within this framework, traditional maps are a data storage medium because they are a depository of information in much the same manner as books. Maps also can be input or output with respect to data manipulation. Data processing output provides information for reading and interpretation during data utilization.

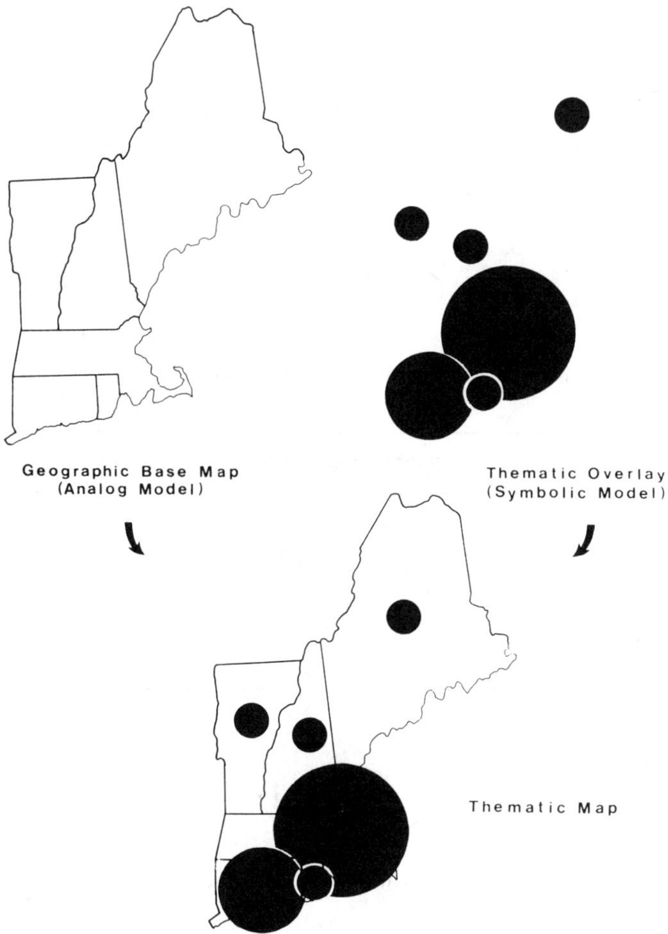

Figure 1.2 The Thematic Map Model.

Muehrcke [1972] has defined a cartographic information processing system as a sequence of transformations where one form is converted into another. The process begins with the transformation of data collection where the whole of experience is filtered into the selection of raw data; these data are in turn converted into a map by a mapping transformation. Finally, the map is interpreted by the map reader and transformed into a mental image. Moellering [1980] has noted that this system must be modified to include the different classes of map products and the "inter-transformations" among these groups.

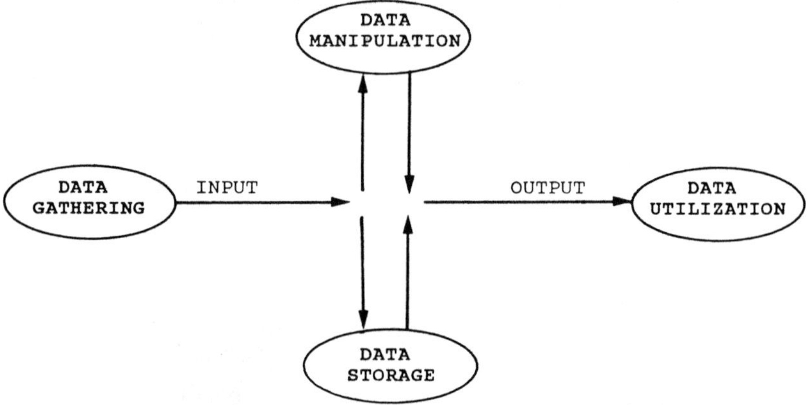

(a) a general data processing system

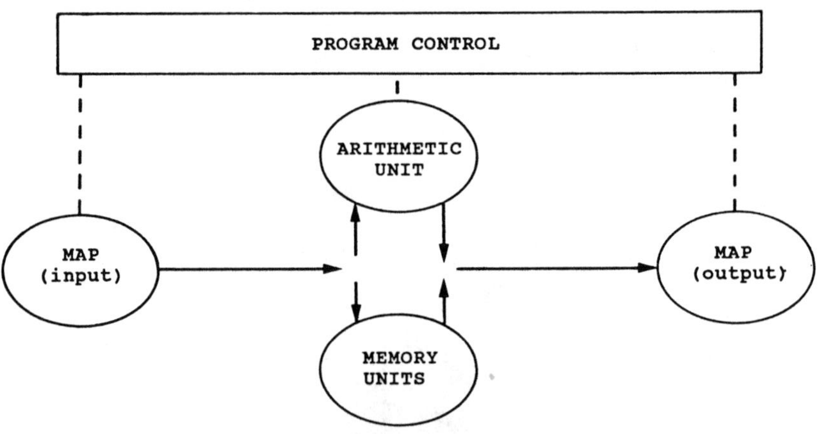

(b) the data manipulation stage

Figure 1.3 A Stylized Data Processing System.
(after Tobler, 1959)

In its simplest version, a *digital cartographic information processing system* would replace the traditional map with a *digital map* (type III virtual), a *softcopy map* (type I virtual) and a *hardcopy map* (real map) (see Figure 1.4). Raw data is extracted from the real world by data acquisition and is then converted into a digital map by the process of data organization. Software display operators can then either generate a softcopy map on a virtual display screen or a hardcopy map directly on a plotter. If softcopy map exists on a screen, firmware (instructions that are built directly into the circuits of the device) can create a hardcopy map of it on an attached hardcopy unit (*e.g.*, an inkjet printer).

Another significant impact that computer technology has had on cartography has been a greater separation of functions within the data processing system [Marble and Peuquet, 1983; Marble 1987.] The separation of storage (the digital map) and display (the virtual map display) has greatly facilitated storage and updating. It has also permitted the separation of geographic base map information regarding the spatial attributes of features from thematic information concerning their non-spatial attributes in storage. Cartographers have greater control over the abstraction process because they can evaluate alternative classifications, simplifications, or symbolisms without having to produce a hardcopy map.

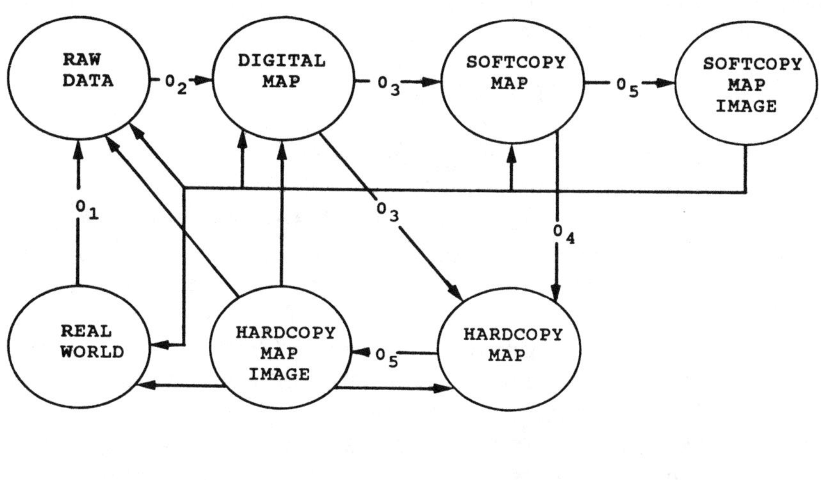

o_1 - Data Collection

o_2 - Data Organization

o_3 - Software Display

o_4 - Firmware Display

o_5 - Map Reading

Figure 1.4 A Digital Cartographic Information Processing System. (modified from Moellering, 1980)

The opportunity for incorporating new strategies in data manipulation is as important as the increased flexibility in cartographic generalization. First, digital systems have permitted human/machine interaction whereby the knowledge of experts embodied in the system can instruct the user in the construction of map products [Freeman and Ahn, 1984]. Secondly, maps are more than just descriptive data models of geographic information. They are also *normative models* for spatial analysis. A normative model in cartography is concerned with the "ideal state" of a cartographic information system for an accurate and efficient display and interpretation of information. Digital procedures include theory and techniques from statistics, operations research, database management, graph theory and other fields of mathematics and computer science to produce the optimal or "best" storage and presentation of cartographic features.

Finally, the digital framework has enabled cartographers to rethink cartographic practices and replace descriptive and ideographic approaches to problem analysis with a nomothetic concern for generalization and theory building. Instead of remaining an art, digital cartography is becoming a science. Using the scientific method of deduction, maps are not viewed as unique objects where individual situations are the rule and experience the guide but rather the underlying unity of maps and mapping processes are examined. This approach relies on the formal relationship between maps and the deductive logic of geometry.

1.4 MAPS AND GEOMETRY

The practice of digital cartography requires the development of a conceptual framework for handling the distribution of objects and events in space. Nystuen [1963] has identified three fundamental spatial concepts that are properties of spatial distributions. *Direction* is the orientation associated with the line of sight from a point. Directional relationships are important because they give a frame of reference between objects. *Distance* is the physical separation between points in space. Distance relationships are important in geographical analysis because spatial interaction usually declines with distance. *Connectiveness* or *relative location* is the contiguity or adjacency that exists among cartographic objects. A *neighborhood* exists around any object that contains other elements that are in some way connected to it. Neighborhood relationships are important in spatial analysis because events at one object will influence events at neighboring objects. To these three properties should be added the property of *absolute location.* Absolute location is the physical position of a point defined by a metric that is irrespective of the location of any other point.

Maps are a medium for the expression of these spatial concepts and as such they represent a spatial language; maps then have a parallelism with geometry, which is the language of space [Harvey, 1969]. Although the foundations of geometry date at least to the Hyksos period (1700 B.C.) of ancient Egypt [Borsuk and Szmielew, 1960], the first systematic treatment of geometry as a means of interpreting reality was in Euclid's twelve elements. Euclid established not only the axiomatic method of proofs but also the foundation for *algorithm* construction [Preparata and Shamos, 1985]. An algorithm is the decomposition of a task such as a problem solution into a finite sequence of steps. Algorithms are crucial to digital cartography because Turing's theorem states that any algorithm can be automated [Peucker, 1972], although it may not be practical to do so. One research focus is to find practical algorithms for cartographic tasks.

Euclidean geometry remained intact for nearly two thousand years and held a strong influence over not only cartography and geography but mathematics as well. In the 19th century the Hungarian Bolyai and the Russian Lobachevski independently proposed a new geometry based on the negation of Euclid's parallel postulate [Borsuk and Szielew, 1960]. This new geometry, called hyperbolic geometry, permitted more than one line passing through a point to be parallel to a line not containing the point. Soon other geometries were discovered and a hierarchy of geometries was formulated (Figure 1.5).

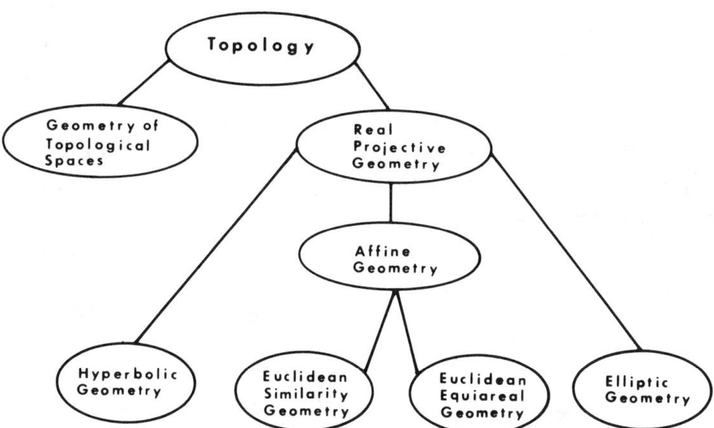

Figure 1.5 A Hierarchy of Geometries.
(after Harvey, 1969)

Understanding the relationships between these geometries requires a formal definition based on set theory. A set **X** is a collection of **n** objects denoted as $\mathbf{X} = \{x_1, x_2, x_3, \ldots, x_n\}$. An object **x** is either an element of the set **X**, denoted as $x \in X$, or it is not. For example, we could define **X** as the set of all New England states, **X = {Connecticut, Maine, Massachusetts, New Hampshire, Rhode Island, Vermont}**. **Vermont** is an element of X although **Delaware** is not. A special set called the *null set*, denoted as ø, is known as the empty set because it has no elements. Elements of a set are sets themselves; for example, **Connecticut** itself is a set consisting of one element. **Connecticut** can also be a collection of other objects such as the points that define its area. Very frequently in cartography, a feature that is represented by a single element at one scale will be represented by a collection of elements at another scale.

If every element of **X** is also an element of the set **Y**, then **X** is a subset of **Y**, denoted as $\mathbf{X} \supseteq \mathbf{Y}$. If **Y** is the set of all states in the United States, then **Connecticut, Maine, Massachusetts, New Hampshire, Rhode Island,** and **Vermont** are also elements of **Y**; therefore, the set **X** representing New England is a subset of the set **Y** representing the United States.

The *intersection* of two sets, denoted as $(\mathbf{X} \cap \mathbf{Y}) = \{\mathbf{x} \mid \mathbf{x} \in \mathbf{X} \textbf{ and } \mathbf{x} \in \mathbf{Y}\}$, are those members of set **X** that are also members of set **Y**. This time let **X** be the set of all points that comprise the outline of Canada on a map; let **Y** be the set of all points that comprise the corresponding outline of the United States on the same map. The intersection of these two sets, $\mathbf{Z} = (\mathbf{X} \cap \mathbf{Y})$, is the set of all points that comprise the common points shared by the United States and Canada on the map (this will be discussed in greater detail in Chapter 3).

The *union* of two sets, denoted as $(\mathbf{X} \cup \mathbf{Y}) = \{\mathbf{x} \mid \mathbf{x} \in \mathbf{X} \textbf{ or } \mathbf{x} \in \mathbf{Y}\}$, is all members of both sets. It should be noted that any element that is a member of both **X** and **Y** is listed only once in their union; the union then is also defined as $(\mathbf{X} \cup \mathbf{Y}) = (\mathbf{X} + \mathbf{Y} - (\mathbf{X} \cap \mathbf{Y}))$. If **X** is the set of all points that comprise the surface area of Canada and **Y** is the set of all points that comprise the surface area of the United States, then the union of these two sets, $\mathbf{Z} = (\mathbf{X} \cup \mathbf{Y})$, is the set of all points that comprise the surface area of Anglo-America.

Finally, the *difference* of two sets, denoted as $(\mathbf{X} - \mathbf{Y}) = \{\mathbf{x} \mid \mathbf{x} \in \mathbf{X} \textbf{ and } \mathbf{x} \notin \mathbf{Y}\}$, are all elements that are members of the first set but not members of the second. The difference of two sets then is the remainder of the first set once its intersection with the second set is removed. If **X** now is the set of all points comprising the surface area of the North American continent and **Y** is the set of all points comprising the surface area of the cultural region known as Latin America, then the difference of these two sets, $\mathbf{Z} = (\mathbf{X} - \mathbf{Y})$, is the set of all points comprising the surface area of Anglo-America minus the United States-Mexican border.

Assume that all sets under consideration are subsets of some fixed universal set **E**. For example, **E** could be the set of all points in a plane. Any point, line or area would be a subset of **E**. The set **X** and **Y** are *disjoint* in **E** if their intersection **(X ∩ Y)** equals the null set (see Figure 1.6a). For example, if **E** is the set of all U.S. states, then the set of New England states and the set of Pacific Coastal states are disjoint as no state is common to both sets. Next, the sets **X** and **Y** are *complements* of each other in **E** if and only if **(X ∪ Y) = E** and **(X ∩ Y) = ø** (see Figure 1.6b). Frequently, the complement of the set **X** will be denoted as **X′**. If **E** is the set of all U.S. incorporated urban places having a population greater than 2500 in 1980 and **X** is the set of all Ohio incorporated urban places having a population greater than 2500, then the complement of **X**, **X′**, is the set of all incorporated urban places in the remaining forty-nine states.

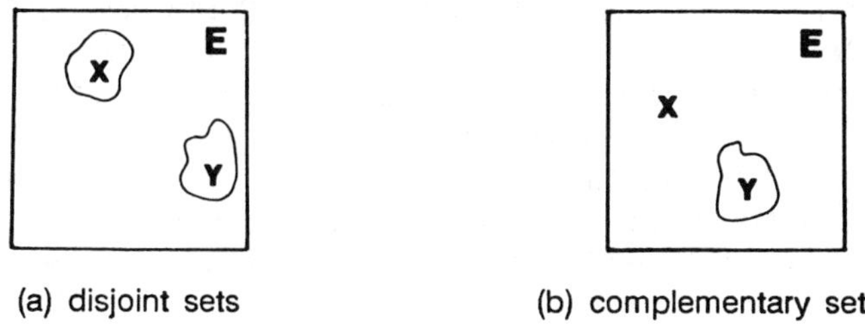

(a) disjoint sets (b) complementary sets

Figure 1.6 Disjoint Sets and Complements.

Given two sets **X** and **Y**, a new set called the *Cartesian product* of **X** and **Y**, denoted as **X*x*Y = {(x,y) | x ∈ X and y ∈ Y}**, consists of all *ordered pairs* **(x,y)** such that **x** is an element of **X** and **y** is an element of **Y**. The first term is **x** and the second term is **y** [Cairns, 1961]. For example, let **X** be the set of all New England states and **Y** be the set of all Middle Atlantic states, then **Z = XxY = {(Connecticut, Delaware), (Connecticut,Maryland),..., (Vermont, Pennsylvania)}** is the set of all state pairs where the first element of each pair is a New England state and the second element is a Middle Atlantic state.

A subset **R** of the cartesian product of **X** on itself is called a *relation* on the set **X**. A *binary relation* is a set of ordered pairs **(x,y)** that belong to **X*x*X** that satisfy some condition. For example, let **X** be the set of all United States states; let **X*x*X** represent the set of all origin-destination pairs of states. The binary relation **R = {(x,y) | more than 1000 people moved from origin x to destination y during the 1980s}**. The set of those **x** for which there is a **y** in the relation is called the *domain* of relation **R**; the set of **y** for which there is an **x** is called the *range* of relation **R**. For example, assume that **R = {(Alabama,Mississippi),**

(Alabama, Arkansas), (Florida,Michigan), (Oklahoma,Iowa), (Texas,New York), (Texas, Arkansas), (Utah, Michigan), (Washington,Florida), (Wyoming,Florida)}. The domain of **x = {Alabama, Florida, Oklahoma, Texas, Utah, Washington, Wyoming}**. The range of **y = {Arkansas, Florida, Iowa, Michigan, Mississippi, New York}**. A relation represents a *many-to-many* relationship between the elements of the domain and elements of the range as each element in the domain can have more than one associated element in the range and *vice versa*.

A relation is *reflexive* if and only if **(x,x)** ∈ **R** for all **x** ∈ **X**; the relation **R** above is not reflexive as no pair has the same origin and destination value. A relation is *symmetric* if and only if **(x,y)** ∈ **R** implies that **(y,x)** ∈ **R**; the relation **R** is not symmetric as **(New York,Texas)** for instance is not included although **(Texas,New York)** is included. A relation is *transitive* if and only if **(x,y)** ∈ **R** and **(y,z)** ∈ **R** implies that **(x,z)** ∈ **R**. Again relation **R** is not transitive because although **(Wyoming, Florida)** and **(Florida,Michigan)** are elements of **R**, **(Wyoming,Michigan)** is not. Relations that are reflexive, symmetric, and transitive in the set **X** are called *equivalences*. Given that **X*x*X** represents the set of all origin-destination pairs of states, an example equivalence relation would be **Y** = **{(x,y) | x and y have state capitals}**. This relation is reflexive, symmetric, and transitive as every state has a capital.

A *function* is a relation in which for every element in the domain there exists just one unique element in the range. Therefore, each functional relationship can be denoted as **y** = **f(x)**. Suppose that **X** is the set of all U.S. states; let the relation $\mathbf{R_1}$ = **{(x,y) | state x shares a border with state y}**. The domain of **x** and the range of **y** are all states that border another state; **Alaska** and **Hawaii** do not belong to either the domain or the range because, although they have borders, they do not share a border with another U.S. state. This relation is symmetric but is not transitive or reflexive. This relation also is not a function, as any state in the domain may have more than one bordering state. However let **X** be the set of all U.S. settlements; the relation **F** = **{(x,y) | y is the capital of the state containing settlement x}** is a function because each state can have only one capital although it can have many towns. A function represents a *many-to-one* relationship between the elements of the domain and elements of the range. An element in the range can be paired with many elements in the domain but an element of the domain has only one corresponding element in the range. Every function is a relation but not every relation is a function.

A *biunique function* is a relation in which for every element in the domain there exists only one unique element in the range and for every element in the range there exists only one element in the domain. A biunique function is also called a *transformation*. Although the relation **F** is a function, it is not a transformation as each state has more than one town associated with it. If **X** is again the set of all settlements, then the relation **T** = **{(x,y) | x is settlement having the largest population in each state and y is the capital of the state containing x}** is a transformation as each state has only one largest settlement and one capital. Any transformation **T** of a set **X** onto itself is an exact correspondence under which each element **x** corresponds to a unique element **y**. For example, if point **a** on a plane is matched with only one unique point **b** on the plane through some function, then this would be a transformation of the plane.

If the entities of a pair coincide such that these entities remain unchanged, then the entity is called *invariant*. A transformation where every entity is invariant is called the *identity* transformation, denoted as **I**. For example, if any number is multiplied by the number one, its value remains the same or is invariant. If the product of two transformations is the identity transformation, then one transformation T^{-1} is the *inverse* of the other, $(T \circ T^{-1}) = I$. For example, if **T** = **{(x,y) | y = m · x, where m is any real number not equal to zero}**, then the inverse transformation T^{-1} = **{(x,y) | y = (1/m) · x, where m is any real number not equal to zero}**.

A *group* is a set **G** in which a binary operator $\circ$ is defined such that:

For all x, y $\in$ G, then $(x \circ y) \in G$;

For all x, y, z $\in$ G, then $((x \circ y) \circ z) = (x \circ (y \circ z))$;

For all x $\in$ G, there exists an identity element i $\in$ G, such that $x \circ i = x$;

For all x $\in$ G, there exists an inverse element $x^{-1} \in G$, such that $x \circ x^{-1} = i$.

A non-empty set of one-to-one transformations of a set onto itself forms a *transformation group*.

Felix Klein defined geometry as the study of those properties of a set of points that remain invariant when the elements of the set are subjected to a transformation group [Smart, 1988]. The spatial properties of maps that are invariant differ then according to the transformation group to which they are subjected [Taylor, 1977]. In equiarea Euclidean geometry, the length of a line (and thus the area of any region) is preserved by its transformation group. The equiarea transformation group is the most restrictive, permitting only translation and rotation (Figure 1.7). In this geometry, direction, distance and connectiveness are all invariant.

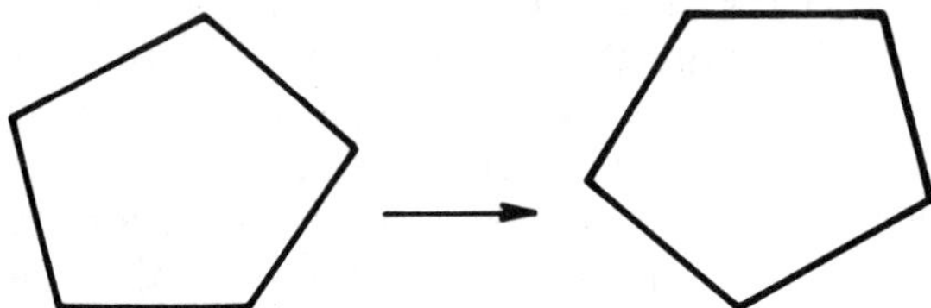

Figure 1.7 An Equiarea Transformation.

The transformation group for similarity geometry also includes scaling, so that distance is no longer invariant (Figure 1.8). However while one cannot measure distance, angle measures are preserved so that direction remains invariant. Thus the shapes of objects remain constant and familiar cartographic objects are easily recognizable.

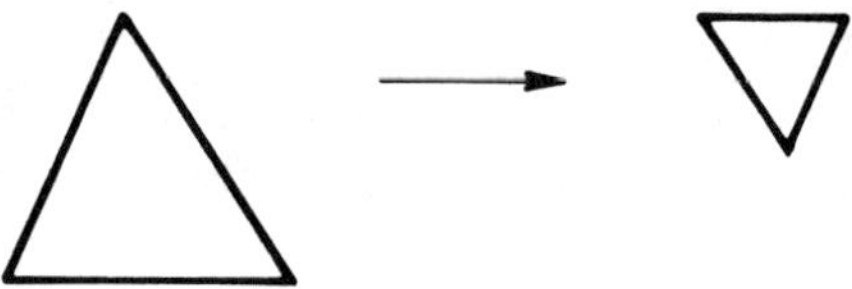

Figure 1.8 A Similarity Transformation.

In affine geometry, neither distance nor angles are preserved, but parallelism and linearity remain invariant. Direction is altered but remains consistent (Figure 1.9). Affine transformations are used in the rectification of satellite imagery to ground truth and in many digitizing applications (see Chapter 4).

Figure 1.9 An Affine Transformation.

In projective geometry, neither distance, angles nor parallelism is invariant. Thus both the area and the shape of an object can be distorted by a projective transformation (Figure 1.10). This geometry is used in map projections, and the different families of geodesic projections from a sphere to a plane require trade-offs between the properties of area and shape (Harvey, 1969, 203-205). An equiarea projection may do a poor job of maintaining shape, while a conformal projection retains shape but distorts area. In either case, the property of connectiveness between regions is preserved.

Figure 1.10 A Projective Transformation.

Finally, in almost all maps, regardless of how distorted distance and direction are, the connectivity among objects is retained. In the geometry of topology, only connectedness or neighborhoods are preserved (Figure 1.11). Traditional sheet maps preserved the topology of the entities displayed. One of the major stumbling blocks in the development of early digital maps was the initial neglect of a map's topology with respect to regions (see Chapter 3). This lack of attention greatly restricted the flexibility of digital images and reduced the effectiveness of the corresponding digital cartographic processing system.

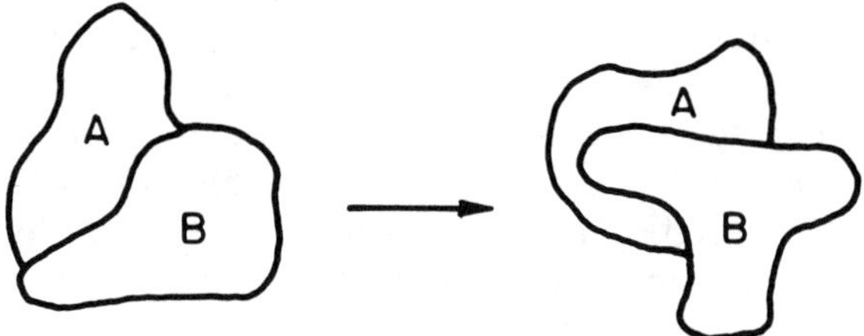

Figure 1.11 A Topological Transformation.

A definition of a map is now given based on the above concepts. A *cartographic entity* is an element that exists in the real world [National Committee for Digital Cartographic Data Standards (NCDCDS), 1988]. The representation of that entity in either symbolic or analog form is a *cartographic object*. A *digital cartographic object* is the representation of an entity in symbolic form in digital storage [adapted from NCDCDS, 1988]. A *cartographic feature* is the generic term for either a cartographic entity or its corresponding object [NCDCDS, 1988]. A *map* is a set of cartographic features that have some physical or cultural manifestation on the surface, subsurface, or suprasurface of a celestial sphere. This definition encompasses all four of Moellering's categories of real and virtual maps.

A *cartographic relation* is a binary relation in which each element of the domain of map **X** has one or more corresponding elements in the range of map **Y** and *vice versa.* A *cartographic function* is a binary relation in which each element of the domain of map **X** has one corresponding element in the range of map **Y**. A *cartographic transformation* is a binary relation in which there exists a one-to-one correspondence between each element of the domain of map **X** and the range of map **Y**. Cartographic functions are not as strong as cartographic transformations because the inverse of a cartographic function does not exist. The process of cartographic generalization is a cartographic function rather than a transformation as it involves many-to-one relationships between elements. For example, once a group of objects has been classified, it is impossible to retrieve the original values through an inverse operation.

Normative cartography is the study of those properties of the spatial and non-spatial attributes of cartographic objects that should remain invariant when the elements of the map are subject to the cartographic relations of some relation set. Digital cartography provides the medium within which objects and their relations are studied. This is similar to Tobler's transformational view of cartography [Tobler, 1979]. As noted above, there are occasions when we can study those properties of maps that do remain invariant when subjected to the transformations of some transformation group; however as we shall examine here, in digital cartography, many cartographic operations result in a many-to-many or a many-to-one correspondence rather than a one-to-one correspondence. The term "should" precedes "remain invariant" because digital cartography is not deterministic science and probably never will be; there will remain some subjectivity in the production of a map. There should always be an attempt however to replace relations with functions and functions with transformations whenever possible, as the informational content of a transformation is higher [Knopfli, 1982]. The cartographic information processing system will be viewed in the context of this geometry. Within this framework, the digital map or image has the most important position as all relations, functions and transformations into this state and out of it are determined by its structure. It is important at this stage to define more fully what digital cartographic objects comprise this space.

1.5 POSITIONAL CARTOGRAPHIC OBJECTS

The nature of digital cartographic objects is determined by the mode of digital image compilation. Maps can be transformed into digital images based on either a *vector* or *raster* data model of space. In a vector model, space in a plane is a continuous set of points, while in raster model, space is filled by a discrete set of points called a two-dimensional *lattice* (Figure 1.12). A raster organization of space is also referred to as a *lattice* or *tessellation* model. A tessellation is an infinitely repeatable pattern over space [Coxeter, 1961].

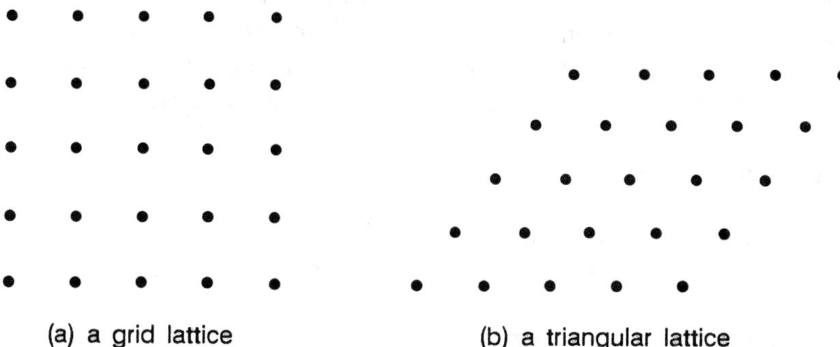

Figure 1.12 Different Lattices.

Secondly in a vector model, the basic unit of observation corresponds to a line on a map, while in a raster model the basic unit is a unit of space within a mesh. Another way of examining the difference between the two modes is that vector objects identify the linear features that separate areas while raster objects identify the areal features separated by linear ones. Thus in the former approach, area is bounded by lines, while in the latter lines are identified by the break between areas. This does not mean that the vector model cannot deal with points and areas – just that a point is a degenerate line and that area is a closed line.

The National Committee for Digital Cartographic Data Standards has established several requirements for the definition of digital cartographic objects [NCDCDS, 1988]. First, objects can combine the spatial properties of absolute location and relative location. The committee uses the terms geometry and topology instead of absolute and relative location. This is somewhat misleading because topology is a geometry. Second, objects must be modular so that lower dimensional objects can be used to define higher dimensional objects. Third, the objects explicitly recognize that the entities they represent can be studied in planar, hyperbolic, and elliptic geometry. This implies that a variety of planar and spherical coordinate systems can be used. Finally, a set of cartographic objects must be able to be expanded at a later date if new theories and technologies warrant it.

The following set of cartographic object definitions is adapted from the committee's report and only includes for now objects that define position in space and possess the property of absolute location. Because the objects are modular and hierarchical with respect to their dimensionality, all two-dimensional objects are composed of zero- and one-dimensional objects, and one-dimensional objects are composed of zero-dimensional objects. Lower dimensional objects contained in the definition of a higher dimensional object will also possess the property of relative location with respect to other objects of the same dimension that are also contained within the same higher dimensional object.

Zero-Dimensional Objects

point - a zero-dimensional object that specifies an absolute location in a two-dimensional space.

endpoint - a point that marks the terminus of a one-dimensional positional object.

lattice point - a zero-dimensional object that specifies an absolute location in a tessellation of two-dimensional space.

One-Dimensional Objects

line - a locus of points that forms a nonintersecting curve in a two-dimensional space terminating at two endpoints (see Figure 1.13a).

outline - a line whose two endpoints have the same absolute location (see Figure 1.13b).

straight line segment - a locus of points that does not change its orientation in a two-dimensional space terminating at two endpoints. alias: line segment (see Figure 1.13c).

string - a sequence of line segments that intersect once and only once at each line segment endpoint excluding two segment endpoints that form the endpoints of the string (see Figure 1.13d).

ring - a sequence of line segments that intersect once and only once at each line segment endpoint (see Figure 1.13e).

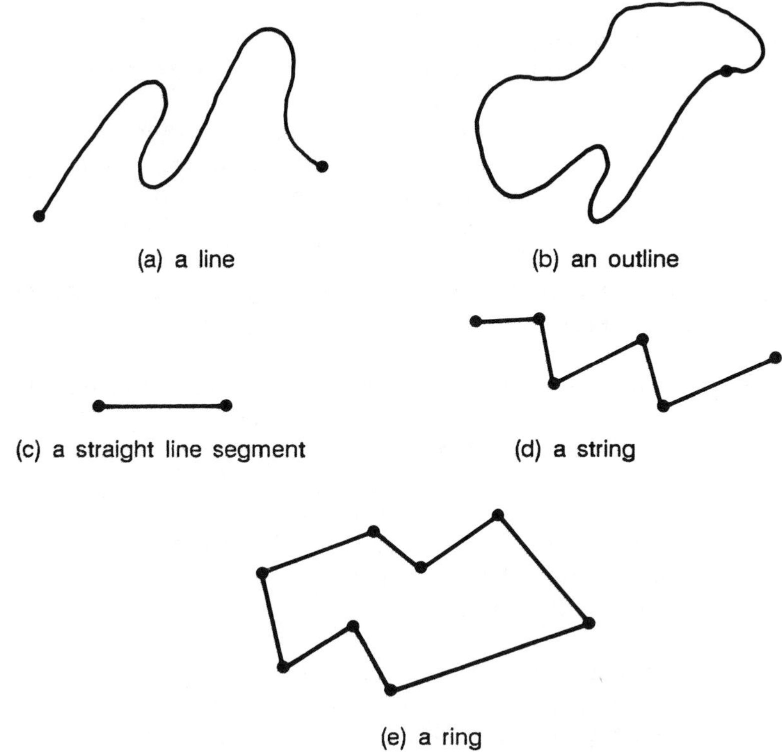

Figure 1.13 One-Dimensional Objects.

All one-dimensional objects can be *directed* or *undirected*. Directed one-dimensional objects imply movement from one endpoint of the object to the other endpoint. In a directed object one endpoint is the *start point* and the other one is the *terminus point* (for a ring these points have the same absolute location). The direction of this movement along an object is represented by an arrowhead (see Figure 1.14). Direction of movement also creates a left and right side for the object.

Figure 1.14 The Direction of Movement Along a One-Dimensional Object.

Two-Dimensional Objects

area - the interior of a continuous two-dimensional object (may include inner rings) (see Figure 1.15a).

region - an area having one or more outer outlines and zero or more nonintersecting inner outlines (see Figure 1.15b).

background region - an area having one or more inner outlines and zero or more nonintersecting outer rings that is the complement to the set of all regions (see Figure 1.15c).

polygon - an area bounded by one outer ring and zero or more nonintersecting inner rings (see Figure 1.15d).

background polygon - an area having no outer ring and one or more nonintersecting inner rings that is the complement to the set of all polygons (see Figure 1.15e).

pixel - a regularly shaped two-dimensional picture element that is the smallest nondivisible element of an image.

cell - a two-dimensional object that represents an element of a regular tessellation of space. The most common cells are rectangles, squares, triangles, and hexagons (see Figure 1.16).

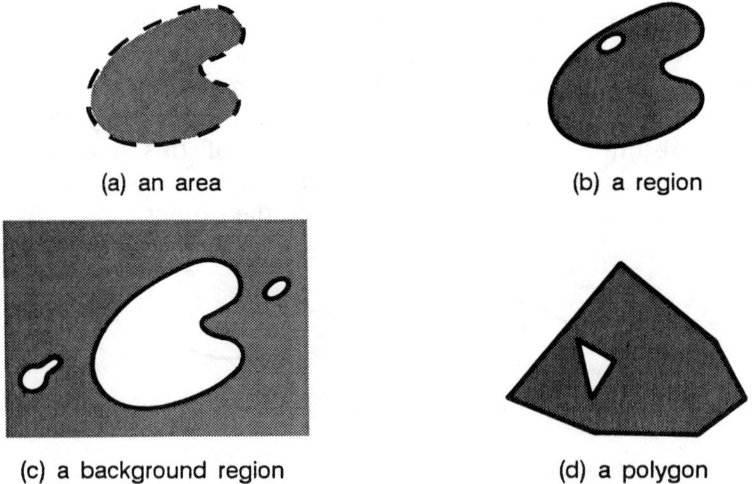

Figure 1.15 Two-Dimensional Objects.

(e) a background polygon

Figure 1.15 Two-Dimensional Objects (continued).

The concept of a background region (polygon) is needed to exhaust two-dimensional space. The *body of a map* generally refers to the domain of the cartographic entities. On a planar surface, the body of a map abruptly ends at a boundary. Where the body of the map ends, the background begins. In other words, the background is the complementary set to the body of the map. Their union exhausts two-dimensional space. It is not always necessary to define a background for the two-dimensional surface of a sphere as it closes on itself. A background region (polygon) then is the complement of the set of regions (polygons) that comprise the body of a map. As such, regions (polygons) represent holes within the background region (polygon.)

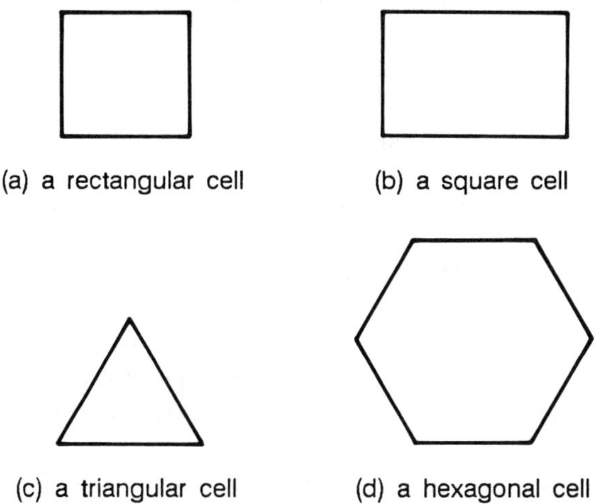

(a) a rectangular cell (b) a square cell

(c) a triangular cell (d) a hexagonal cell

Figure 1.16 Different Shaped Cells.

1.6 SUMMARY

These notions of digital cartographic objects form the primitives for more complex map objects that together form a display. The remainder of this book proceeds from basic concepts of organizing and manipulating these objects through the different stages of the digital cartographic process to the role of digital cartography in decisionmaking.

1.7 REFERENCES

Borsuk, K. and W. Szmielew. [1960]. **Foundations of Geometry**, Amsterdam: North Holland Publishing Co.

Boyle, A.R. [1979]. "Automated Cartography," **World Cartography**, 15, 63-70.

Brassel, K. [1977]. "A Survey of Cartographic Display Software," **International Yearbook of Cartography**, 17, 60-77.

Burrough, P.A. [1986]. **Principles of Geographical Information Systems for Land Resources Assessment**, Oxford: Clarendon Press.

Carter, J.R. [1984]. **Computer Mapping: Progress in the '80s**, Resource Publications in Geography, Washington, D.C.: Association of American Geographers.

Coxeter, H.S.M. [1961]. **Introduction to Geometry**, New York: John Wiley & Sons, Inc.

Dent, B.D. [1985]. **Principles of Thematic Map Design**, Reading, Massachusetts: Addison-Wesley Publishing Co.

Freeman, H. and J. Ahn [1984]. "Autonap – An Expert System for Automatic Map Name Placement," **Proceedings**, First International Symposium on Spatial Data Handling, 544-69.

Harvard University. [1979]. **Mapping Collection: Mapping Software and Cartographic Data Bases**, Vol. 2, Cambridge, Massachusetts: Laboratory for Computer Graphics and Spatial Analysis.

Harvey, D. [1969]. **Explanation in Geography**. New York: St. Martins Press.

Knopfli, R. [1982]. "Generalization – A Means to Transmit Reliable Messages through Unreliable Channels," **International Yearbook of Cartography**, 12, 83-91.

Marble, D.F. [1987]. "The Computer and Cartography," **The American Cartographer**, 14, 101-103.

Marble, D.F. and D.J. Peuquet [1983]. "The Computer and Cartography: Some Methodological Comments," **The Professional Geographer**, 35, 343-44.

Marble, D.F., H.W. Calkins, D.J. Peuquet, K. Brassel, and M. Wasilenko [1981]. **Computer Software for Spatial Data Handling**, (3 Vol.), Ottawa: International Geographical Union, Commission on Geographical Data Sensing and Processing.

Moellering, H. [1973]. "The Computer Animated Film: A Dynamic Cartography," **Proceedings**, Association for Computing Machinery, 64-69.

Moellering, H. [1980]. "Strategies of Real Time Cartography," **The Cartographic Journal**, 17, 12-15.

Monmonier, M.S. [1982]. **Computer-Assisted Cartography: Principles and Prospects**, Englewood Cliffs, New Jersey: Prentice-Hall.

Morrison, J.L. [1980]. "Computer Technology and Cartographic Change," **Progress in Contemporary Cartography**, 1, 5-23.

Muehrcke, P. [1972]. **Thematic Cartography**, Commission on College Geography Resource Paper No. 19, Washington, D.C.: Association of American Geographers.

National Committee for Digital Cartographic Standards [1988]. "The Proposed Standard for Digital Cartographic Data," **The American Cartographer**, 15.

Nystuen, J.D. [1963]. "Identification of Some Fundamental Spatial Concepts," **Papers of the Michigan Academy of Science, Arts, and Letters**, 48, 373-84.

Peucker, T.K. [1972]. **Computer Cartography**, Commission on College Geography Resource Paper No. 17, Washington, D.C.: Association of American Geographers.

Peuquet, D.J. [1984]. "A Conceptual Framework and Comparison of Spatial Data Models," **Cartographica**, 21, 66-113.

Preparata, F.P. and M.I. Shamos [1985]. **Computational Geometry: An Introduction**, New York: Springer-Verlag.

Rhind, D.H. [1977]. "Computer-Aided Cartography," **Transactions**, Institute of British Geographers, 2, 71-97.

Rhind, D.H. [1980]. "The Nature of Computer-Assisted Cartography," **Progress in Contemporary Cartography**, 1, 25-37.

Robinson, A., R.D. Sale, J.L. Morrison, and P.C. Meuchrke [1984]. **Elements of Cartography**, (Fifth Ed.), New York: John Wiley & Sons, Inc.

SAS Institute [1987]. **SAS/GRAPH User's Guide**, (Fifth Ed.), Cary, North Carolina: SAS Institute, Inc.

Schmidt, A.H. and W.A. Zafft [1975]. "Programs of the Harvard University Laboratory for Computer Graphics and Spatial Analysis," in **Display and Analysis of Spatial Data**, J.C. Davis and M.J. McCullagh (eds.), New York: John Wiley & Sons, Inc.

Scripter, M. [1969]. "Choropleth Maps on Small Digital Computers," **Proceedings**, Association of American Geographers, 1, 133-36.

Smart, J. [1988]. **Modern Geometries**, (Third Ed.), Pacific Grove, California: Brooks/Cole Publishing Co.

Taylor, P.J. [1977]. **Quantitative Methods in Geography: An Introduction to Spatial Analysis**, Boston: Houghton Mifflin Co.

Tobler, W.R. [1959]. "Automation and Cartography," **Geographical Review**, 49, 526-34.

Tobler, W.R. [1979]. "A Transformational View of Cartography," **The American Cartographer**, 6, 101-06.

Tomlinson, R.F. [1972]. **Geographical Data Handling**, Ottawa: International Geographical Union Commission of Geographical Data Sensing and Processing.

Tomlinson, R.F., Calkins, H.W., and D.F. Marble [1976]. **Computer Handling of Geographic Data**, Geneva: UNESCO.

Chapter 2
Basic Analytic Geometry

How can we program the computer to "see" numerically what the cartographer sees visually? This is a fundamental challenge for digital cartography. The drawing of geometric shapes which for centuries have been constructed manually by skilled practitioners using drafting tools such as compass and straight edge must be converted into a set of instructions to activate and regulate the mechanical pens or electronic beams of graphic output devices such as plotters and CRTs. This is accomplished by replacing the synthetic geometry of Euclid in which the proof of a problem solution is deduced by logical argument form, already proven theorems and axioms, with analytic geometry in which the geometric aspects of the problem are translated into algebraic terms [Rosenbaum, 1963]. Algebraic operations take the place of their manual counterparts.

The benefits of this conversion go beyond the mere replication of map products. In digital cartography the restrictions of visual experience are removed. Three dimensional surfaces of temperature, atmospheric pressure, or income that have no natural manifestation in our visual reality can be given a geometric form. Similarly, numerical forms like mathematical functions can be converted into a geometric one.

Just as cartographic objects are modular so that primitive objects form the foundation for more complex objects, cartographic operations are modular and the more complex operations presented in later chapters are the composite of many primitive operations. This chapter is an introduction to the basics of analytic geometry which form the primitives for many algorithmic tasks in digital cartography. The limitations of coordinates as representations of location have been noted [Dutton, 1989] but coordinates underlie vector models of space. The discussion begins with concepts in planar (two-dimensional) geometry. Most traditional map products depict a two-dimensional space. Chapter Seven will cover extensions for three-dimensional surfaces.

2.1 CARTESIAN COORDINATES

The simplest geometric object is the cartographic point. The simplest algebraic one is a *real number* or *scalar*. The set of all real numbers can be represented geometrically by a linear feature called a *number scale* (Figure 2.1). Each real number is represented by a point on the scale. The number scale establishes the relationship between a geometric system of points and an algebraic one of numbers. Each point **p** of the number scale is the graphical expression of a real number **r**, while for each real number **r** there exists a unique point **p**. There is a one-to-one correspondence between real numbers and points on the number scale (Figure 2.2), or the number scale is a transformation of geometric points into algebraic numbers.

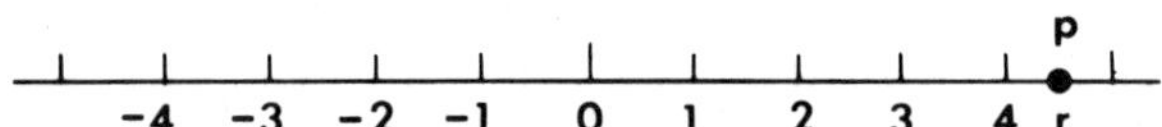

Figure 2.1 A Number Scale.

Any real number can be written as an unending decimal expression. Therefore, there are an infinite number of real numbers. An important subset of real numbers is *integers*, which are whole numbers having only repeating zeroes to the right of the decimal in a decimal expression. As single values within an interval, integers represent discrete values within a continuum of real numbers.

On the number scale, the point corresponding to the number zero is called the *origin*. Although the location of the origin is arbitrary, it acts as the reference point for all other points (real numbers). The point corresponding to the number one is called the *unit point*. The length between the origin and the unit point is the metric for measuring one unit of distance on the scale. If **x** is a real number represented by a point on the number scale, then the number of distance units between this point and the origin are called the *absolute value* of **x** and are denoted by the symbol **|x|**. The absolute value of a number gives only its distance from the origin, not its direction to the left or right of the origin. The distance between any two points on the number scale is equal to the absolute value of the difference of the corresponding numbers. For example, the distance between points **-3** and **+5** is **|(-3)-(+5)|** or **|-8|** or **8**. The absolute value is never negative, as distance is always positive.

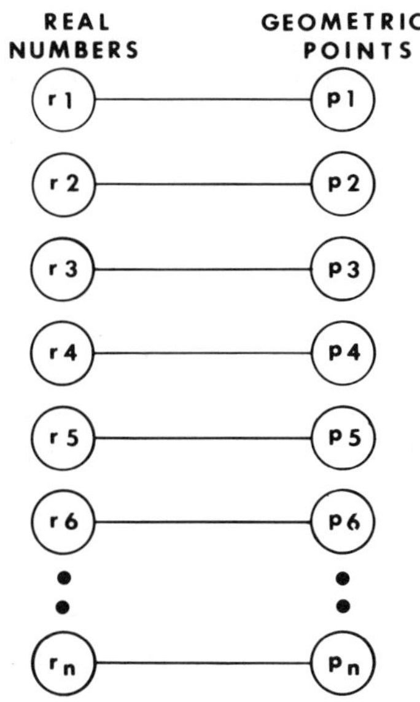

Figure 2.2 The Correspondence Between Geometric Points and Algebraic Numbers.

The number scale effectively represents any one-dimensional object. However, most cartographic objects are two dimensional. Therefore, the concepts of number scales and real numbers need to be expanded to two-dimensional space. If **R** is the set of real numbers, then **R**x**R** (generally denoted as $\mathbf{R}^2$) is the cartesian product of **R** with itself. If two number scales are drawn at a right angle with respect to each other, then these two number scales are called *coordinate axes*. By convention, the horizontal one is the X-axis and the vertical one is the Y-axis (Figure 2.3). Any point in two-dimensional Euclidean space (a *plane*) can be represented by a pair of real numbers, each associated with an axis (or dimension). The value of each number is found by the intersection of each axis with a line emanating from the point at a right angle to the respective axis (see Figure 2.3). The value for the X-axis is usually given first. In general, the pair of numbers **(x,y)** is the cartesian coordinate associated with any point **p**. This equivalence is also written as **p(x,y)**. In the cartesian coordinate system, the **x** value is called the *abscissa* and the **y** value is the *ordinate*. The intersection of the two axes is the origin point whose corresponding coordinate is **(0,0)**.

Some final comments regarding number scales, cartesian coordinate systems, and computing hardware should be made. The two axes divide the coordinate plane into four quadrants **(I, II, III, and IV)** (Figure 2.4). In the first quadrant, both **x** and **y** values are positive; in the second quadrant, only **y** is positive while **x** is negative. In the third quadrant, both **x** and **y** are negative; in the fourth, **x** is positive and **y** is negative.

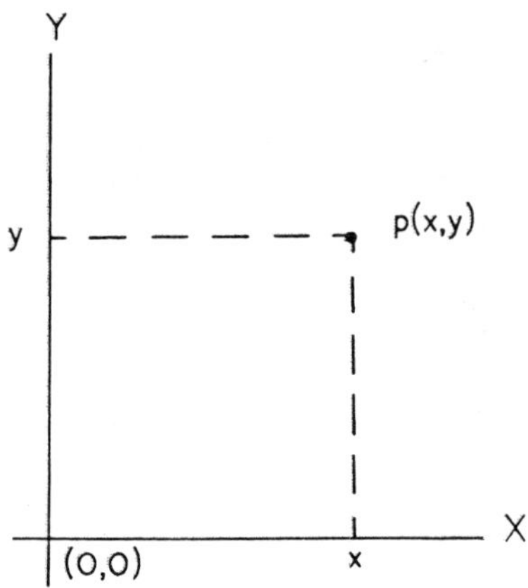

Figure 2.3 The Cartesian Coordinate Plane.

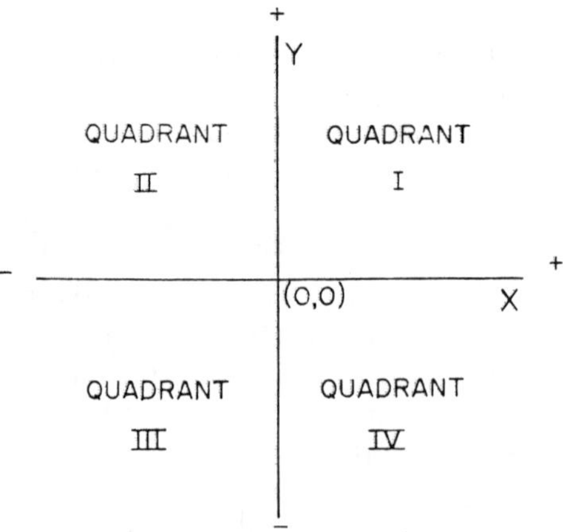

Figure 2.4 The Partition of the Plane into Four Quadrants.

Because the location of the origin is arbitrary, in many applications only the first quadrant (positive quadrant) is needed to encode and display cartographic features. The *hardware space* of many display devices often only recognizes this quadrant. In Section 2.3, we will see how any feature in another quadrant can be shifted into the first quadrant. This partitioning of two-dimensional space into quadrants is also fundamental to raster representation of features as quad-trees (see Chapter Three). Secondly, in the SYMAP coordinate system, positive ordinate values lie below the origin because line printers can only advance in a downward direction with respect to an output page.

In theory, any interval on a number scale can be successively subdivided into smaller intervals to find points that represent real numbers with additional non-zero digits to the right of the decimal. The number line is a continuum of points. The *user space* arbitrarily defined by the practitioner to position the location of points conforms to this theoretical concept. On digital computing machines, however, there exists a limit to the number of digits that can be used by the machine to represent any real or integer number. The *resolution* of any machine is the number of digits beyond which all real numbers in a given interval will have the same numerical representation.

Similarly, for all graphic output devices, there exists some limit to the precision of the display geometry. On any display, a true continuum of points does not exist; instead only a finite number of points can be referenced over a fixed interval. Only a discrete lattice of points exists in hardware space. Thus integers are used to reference the basic element of a graphic device, either a pixel on a raster device or a dot point on a vector device. All graphic display devices also have a certain resolution beyond which two points in user space are indistinguishable. Any user space defined by a practitioner must be transformed into the referencing units of the output device before display. While the original user space may be a continuum of real numbers in the abstract, the machine display area is a discrete array of points. A one-to-one correspondence or transformation between real numbers and points cannot occur in practice; instead a many-to-one or a functional relation between numbers and points exists (see Figure 2.5). In general, point resolution then is the precision at which a transformation becomes a functional relation. Numerically, *precision* is the number of significant digits that may be stored; graphically, it is the number of cells per metric unit that may be stored. This has important implications for the scale at which any object is encoded versus the resolution of the scale at which it is displayed because many coordinates can reference the same point on the display device. Finite representation also results in rounding or overflow errors that give inconsistent answers to simple problems [see Douglas, 1984]. Secondly, greater coordinate precision may improve the aesthetic quality of the object being represented but not necessarily its positional *accuracy* [White, 1984]. Accuracy is a measure of how close a representation is to reality.

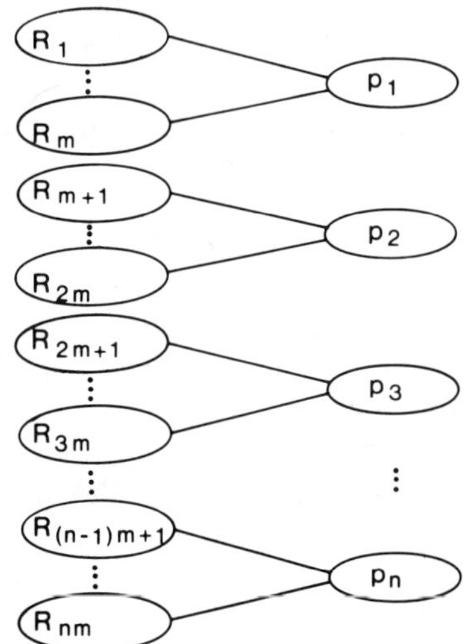

Figure 2.5 The Functional Relationship Between Numbers and Points in Hardware Space.

2.2 VECTORS AND MATRICES

A *vector* is an **n** dimensional force emanating from an origin point and having a direction and a fixed length or magnitude. The discussion here is confined to two-dimensional vectors. Vectors are graphically portrayed by lines connecting their origin points to their respective endpoints (Figure 2.6). An arrowhead is added to denote the direction of the vector. A directed line segment (see Chapter One) is a vector. If a vector were infinitely long (see Figure 2.7), it would partition the plane into two halfplanes. The *clockwise halfplane* is defined as the halfplane that lies to the right of the vector with respect to its direction; the *counter-clockwise halfplane* is the halfplane to the left.

Alternatively, a vector is expressed numerically as a row or column array of components. The value of each component is the length of the projection that the vector would make on each axis when viewed from a position that is perpendicular to that axis (Figure 2.8). These values are calculated by subtracting the respective coordinate values of the origin point from those of the endpoint:

$$\begin{pmatrix} x \\ y \end{pmatrix} = \begin{pmatrix} x_2 - x_1 \\ y_2 - y_1 \end{pmatrix}. \tag{2.1}$$

Vector **a** in Figure 2.8 starts at point **(1,2)** and ends at point **(2,4)**. It has an **x** component value of **(2 - 1)** or **1** and a **y** component value of **(4 - 2)** or **2**.

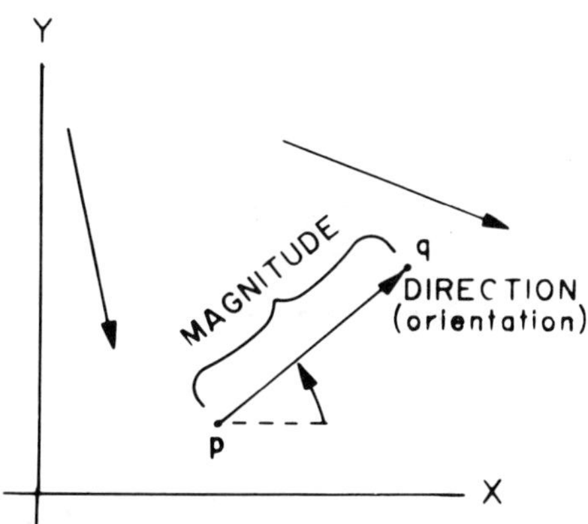

Figure 2.6 Some Example Vectors.

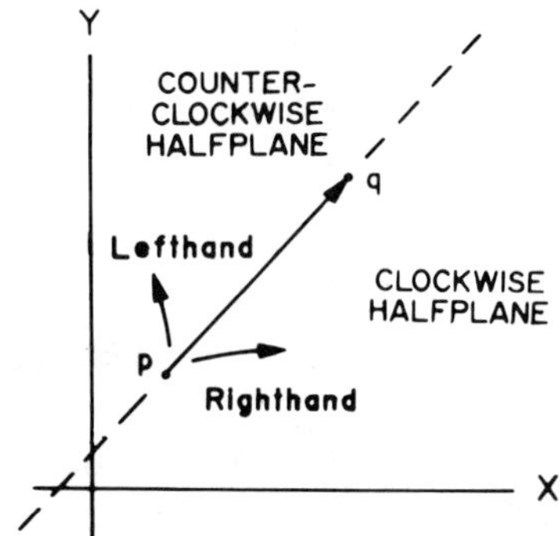

Figure 2.7 The Halfplane Partition of a Plane.

Any point **p** in a plane can be represented by a vector that starts at the origin and ends at **p** (Figure 2.9). The origin is also referenced by a special vector known as the *zero vector*. All components of this vector are equal to zero. This means that the zero vector is the only vector that has an indeterminate direction and no length. One-dimensional vectors are *scalars*. Scalars have all the properties of real numbers.

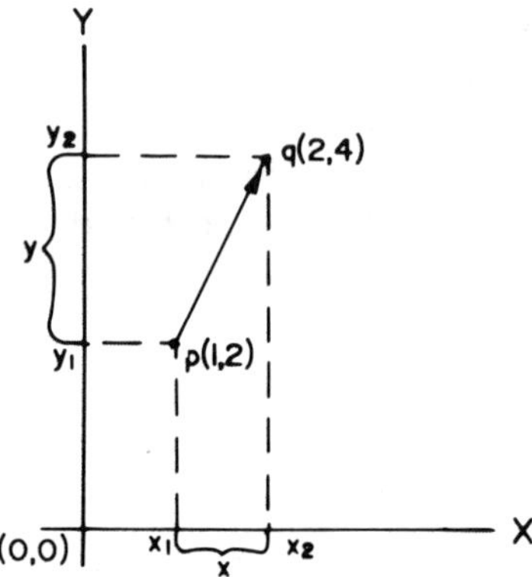

Figure 2.8 The Component Projection of a Vector.

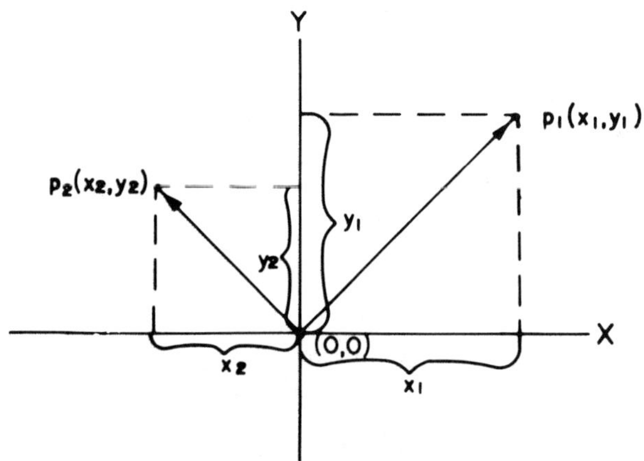

Figure 2.9 The Representation of Cartesian Coordinates as Vectors.

The magnitude of a vector, denoted as |**a**|, is defined as the square root of the sum of the squares of its components:

$$|a| = (x^2 + y^2)^{1/2} . \qquad (2.2)$$

For example, if **a** = **(1,2)**, then its magnitude is **a** = **(1 + 4)**$^{\frac{1}{2}}$ or **(5)**$^{\frac{1}{2}}$. The distance between any two points **p**(x_1,y_1) and **q**(x_2,y_2) in a plane is equal to the magnitude of a vector connecting **p** and **q**. The distance is calculated as:

$$|p - q| = [(x_1 - x_2)^2 + (y_1 - y_2)^2]^{1/2} . \qquad (2.3)$$

Two vectors having the same number of components can be "added" or "subtracted." Vector addition is performed by adding the respective component values of each vector. For example, if **a** = **(2,3)** and **b** = **(1,4)**, the addition of **a** and **b** is a new vector **a+b** = **(2+1,3+4)** or **(3,7)**. Geometrically, the addition of two vectors forms a vector that corresponds to the middle diagonal of a parallelogram formed by the two original vectors (Figure 2.10). The result of vector addition is always a vector of the same dimension as the original two vectors.

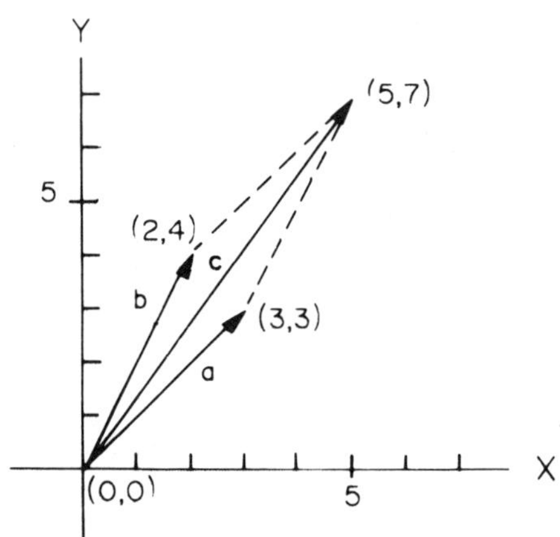

Figure 2.10 The Addition of Two Vectors.

Similarly, one vector can be subtracted from another vector of the same dimension by subtracting the component values of the second vector from the respective component values of the first. The vector **a-b** is **(2-1,3-4)** or **(1,-1)**. Geometrically, the subtraction of two vectors is a vector corresponding to the cross diagonal of the parallelogram formed by **a** and **b** (Figure 2.11). However, while vector **a+b** is equal to vector **b+a**, the vector **a-b** is not equal to the vector **b-a**. In the example, **b-a** equals **(1-2,4-3)** or **(-1,1)**. The direction of **a-b** is always opposite that of **b-a** but the magnitude of each is the same. The operation of vector addition is commutative and that of vector subtraction is not.

A vector with any number of components can be multiplied by a scalar, **h**. Scalar multiplication is performed by multiplying the respective components of a vector by the scalar. For example, if **h** = **(2)** and **a** = **(2,3)**, the resulting scalar multiplication, **ha**, is **(2·2,2·3)** or **(4,6)**. The multiplicaton of a vector by a positive scalar forms a vector having the same direction as the original vector but a magnitude that is a multiple of the magnitude of the original vector (Figure 2.12.) The magnitude of vector **(4,6)** is $\sqrt{52}$ or $2\sqrt{13}$, which is twice as large as $\sqrt{13}$, the magnitude of vector **(2,3)** (Figure 2.12). Multiplying a vector by a negative scalar will change the vector direction **180°**.

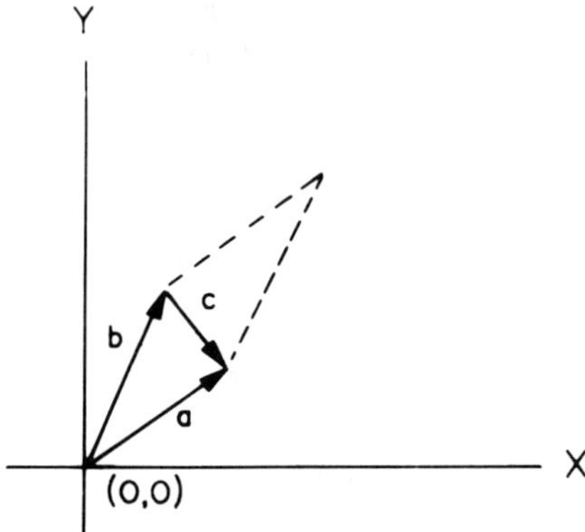

Figure 2.11 The Subtraction of Two Vectors.

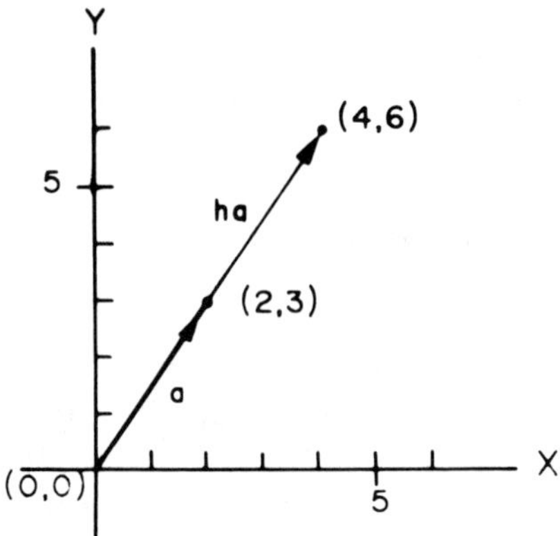

Figure 2.12 Scalar Multiplication.

A *normal vector* has a magnitude equal to one. Any vector **a** = **(x,y)** can be normalized, **a′** = (x′,y′), by dividing its respective components by its magnitude:

$$\begin{pmatrix} x' \\ y' \end{pmatrix} = \begin{pmatrix} x/|a| \\ y/|a| \end{pmatrix} \quad . \tag{2.4}$$

Two vectors having the same number of components can also be multiplied. The result of this vector multiplication is a scalar known as the *inner product* of the two vectors. Vector multiplication is defined as the sum of the product of the respective components. If vector **a** = $(\mathbf{x_1},\mathbf{y_1})$

and vector **b** = **(x_2,y_2)**, the inner product of these two vectors is written as:

$$a \cdot b = x_1x_2 + y_1y_2 \ . \tag{2.5}$$

For example, if **a = (2,3)** and **b = (1,4)**, then **a b = (2)(1)+(3)(4)**. The magnitude of a vector is merely the square root of the inner product of the vector with itself.

The inner product of two vectors is also directly related to the angle between them, denoted by α (see Figure 2.13). The inner product can also be calculated as:

$$a \cdot b = |a| \ |b| \cos \theta \ . \tag{2.6}$$

Alternatively, the cosine of the angle between two vectors is found by:

$$\cos \theta = a \cdot b \ / \ |a| \ |b| \ . \tag{2.7}$$

The cosine of the angle between two vectors having the same or directly opposite direction will have a value of one or negative one respectively. Two vectors are *orthogonal* or perpendicular to each other if their inner product is zero; in this case, the value of α is **90°** or a right angle.

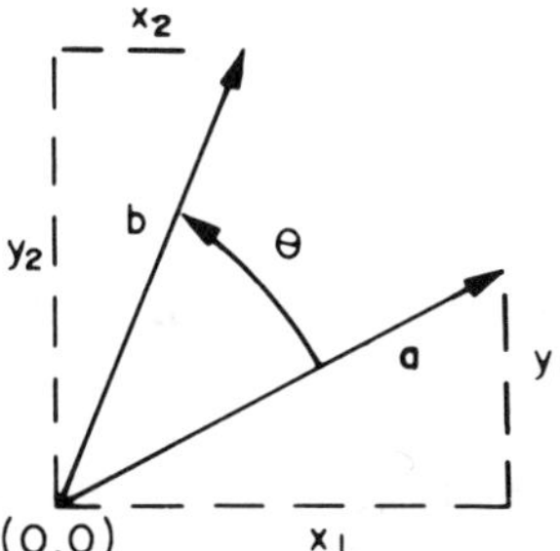

Figure 2.13 The Angle Between Two Vectors.

A *matrix* is a rectangular array of numbers (referred to as elements) arranged in rows and columns. In general notation, a matrix **A** is written as:

$$\mathbf{A} = \begin{bmatrix} a_{11} & a_{12} \\ a_{21} & a_{22} \end{bmatrix} . \tag{2.8}$$

Each matrix having **m** rows and **n** columns is an **m x n** matrix (called m by n); each row corresponds to an **n**-dimensional vector, while each column corresponds to an **m**-dimensional vector. Any vector is a single row or single column matrix. The double subscript of each element is used to define its location in the array; the first subscript denotes its row location and the second its column location. An alternative symbolism is to write the elements of the matrix in terms of its vectors:

$$A = \begin{bmatrix} x_1 & x_2 \\ y_1 & y_2 \end{bmatrix} . \tag{2.9}$$

In this case, the subscript refers to individual vectors while the letter refers to similar components of each vector. In equation (2.9), x_1 refers to the x component of the first column vector. Two matrices are the same size if they have the same number of rows and columns.

Similar to vectors, matrices can be "added" and "multiplied." Matrix addition is defined for matrices of the same size. The sum of two matrices is obtained by adding the respective elements of each matrix. For example, if

$$A = \begin{bmatrix} 4 & 5 \\ 2 & 3 \\ 1 & 2 \end{bmatrix} \quad \text{and} \quad B = \begin{bmatrix} 3 & 6 \\ 0 & 3 \\ 2 & 2 \end{bmatrix}$$

then,

$$A+B = \begin{bmatrix} 7 & 11 \\ 2 & 6 \\ 3 & 4 \end{bmatrix} .$$

In matrix addition, the order of operation is not important. It obeys the commutative and associative laws: **A+B = B+A**, and **(A+B) + C = A + (B+C)**.

The product **AB** of two matrices **A** and **B** is defined if and only if the number of columns in **A** is equal to the number of rows in **B**. If **A** is an **m x p** matrix and **B** is a **p x n** matrix, the resulting product matrix **C** is an **m x n** matrix. Each element of **AB** is defined as the inner product of the **i**th row of **A** and the **j**th column of **B**. Each element is calculated as:

$$c_{ij} = a_{i1}b_{1j} + a_{i2}b_{2j} + \ldots + a_{ip}b_{pj} . \tag{2.10}$$

For example, if

$$A = \begin{bmatrix} 4 & 5 \\ 2 & 3 \\ 1 & 2 \end{bmatrix}$$

and

$$B = \begin{bmatrix} 3 & 0 & 2 \\ 6 & 3 & 2 \end{bmatrix},$$

then,

$$AB = \begin{bmatrix} (4)(3)+(5)(6) & (4)(0)+(5)(3) & (4)(2)+(5)(2) \\ (2)(3)+(3)(6) & (2)(0)+(3)(3) & (2)(2)+(3)(2) \\ (1)(3)+(2)(6) & (1)(0)+(2)(3) & (1)(2)+(2)(2) \end{bmatrix}$$

$$= \begin{bmatrix} 42 & 15 & 18 \\ 24 & 9 & 10 \\ 15 & 6 & 6 \end{bmatrix}.$$

In this example, **AB** is defined but **BA** does not exist. Even if both **AB** and **BA** exist, matrix multiplication does not obey the commutative law: **AB** *does not necessarily equal* **BA**. However, matrix multiplication does obey the associative and distributive laws: **(AB)C** = **A(BC)** and **A(B+C)** = **AB** + **AC**.

A number of special matrices can now be defined. The *zero matrix* is any matrix whose elements are all zeroes. A *square matrix* is any matrix having as many rows as columns. The products **AB** and **BA** exist only if **A** and **B** are both square matrices. A very important square matrix is the *identity matrix*, denoted as **I**. It is defined as a square matrix whose diagonal elements are all ones and all other elements are zeroes. Each row and column of **I** is a unit coordinate vector. The identity matrix has the following properties: **IA** = **AI** = **A**. The *transpose* of a matrix **A**, denoted as $\mathbf{A}^T$, is formed by interchanging the rows and columns of **A** such that row i of **A** becomes column i of $\mathbf{A}^T$ and column j of **A** becomes row j of $\mathbf{A}^T$. Finally, a *symmetric matrix*, **S**, is a square matrix whose elements $s_{ij} = s_{ji}$. The transpose of a symmetric matrix, $\mathbf{S}^T$, is equal to **S**.

An important scalar associated with square matrices is the *determinant*. The determinant of a **2 x 2** square matrix is found as the difference between the cross product of its diagonal elements. Let vector **a** = (x_1,y_1) and vector **b** = (x_2,y_2); matrix **C** is defined as:

$$C = \begin{bmatrix} x_1 & x_2 \\ y_1 & y_2 \end{bmatrix}.$$

The determinant of **C**, denoted as | **C** | , is ascertained as:

$$| C | = (x_1y_2 - x_2y_1) . \qquad (2.11)$$

The absolute value of the determinant of a **2 x 2** matrix also measures the area of a parallelogram formed by the two column vectors of the matrix (Figure 2.14). In Figure 2.14, the area of the shaded area between vectors **(2,3)** and **(5,1)** is **|2·1-3·5| = |2-15| = |-13| = 13**. The value of the determinant is also related to the value of the inner product between two vectors: the value of the determinant of a matrix formed by two non-zero vectors will be zero if and only if the value of the inner product between equals one or negative one. In this case, the two vectors lie in the same or directly opposite direction and there is no area between them.

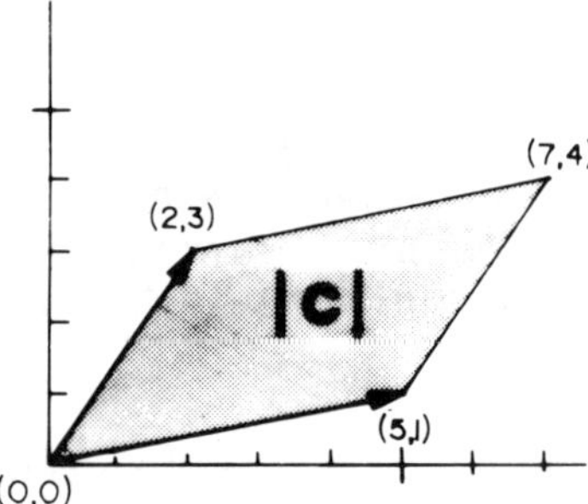

Figure 2.14 The Area of a Parallelogram Formed by Two Vectors.

The determinant can also be used to ascertain whether one vector lies to the left or right of another. Using the first vector to divide the plane into two halfplanes, the second vector will lie in the clockwise (right) halfplane of the first if the value of the determinant is negative. If the second vector lies in the counter-clockwise (left) halfplane of the first, the value of the determinant will be positive. In Figure 2.14, the value of the determinant was negative because vector **(5,1)** was in the clockwise halfplane of vector **(2,3)**. This result is important because it enables the machine to determine visual relationships numerically. The machine can tell if one vector lies to the left or right of another by calculating the determinant of the matrix formed by the two vectors.

2.3 HOMOGENEOUS COORDINATES AND POINT TRANSFORMATIONS

Homogeneous coordinates are the extension of cartesian coordinates from any dimension into the next higher dimension. The homogeneous representation of a two-dimensional point **(x,y)** is **(hx,hy,h)** where **h** is any non-zero scalar. Any two-dimensional vector **(x,y)** can be converted into a homogeneous vector **(x,y,1)** by adding a third component where **h=1**. Any three-dimensional point **(a,b,c)** can be converted into the following two-dimensional point **(a/c,b/c)**. The homogeneous transformation of **(x,y)** then is the trace of a ray emanating from the origin passing through the point **(x,y,1)** (see Figure 2.15.) Multiplying a three dimensional homogeneous vector by a non-zero scalar constant does not change its two dimensional representation. If **m** is a non-zero scalar, then the vectors **(a,b,c,)** and **(ma,mb,mc)** are both equal to **(a/c,b/c)**.

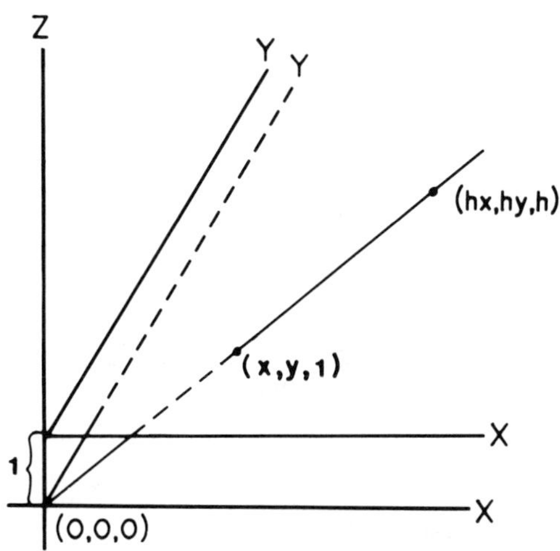

Figure 2.15 The Homogeneous Representation of a Plane.

The homogeneous representation of coordinates is necessary to perform the two-dimensional point transformations of *translation*, *rotation*, and *scaling*. Point transformations are used to manipulate cartographic objects in space. The movement of an object from one location to another, its movement at a location, or its enlargement or reduction is the result of one of these various point transformations. Each transformation is used to generate a "new" point **(x′,y′)** from the original point **(x,y)**.

Translation is used to offset the origin of the coordinate system. Because the origin is arbitrary, it is possible to reset its location whenever the need arises. The translation transformations are:

$$x' = x + T_x ;$$

and

$$y' = y + T_y . \tag{2.12}$$

When the translation factor T_x is positive, the origin is shifted to the left (see Figure 2.16) and when it is negative the origin is shifted to the right. When the translation factor T_y is positive, the origin is shifted downward, and when it is positive it is shifted upward (see Figure 2.16). In this manner, translation can be used to simulate the movement of an object from one location to another location by the redefinition of user space.

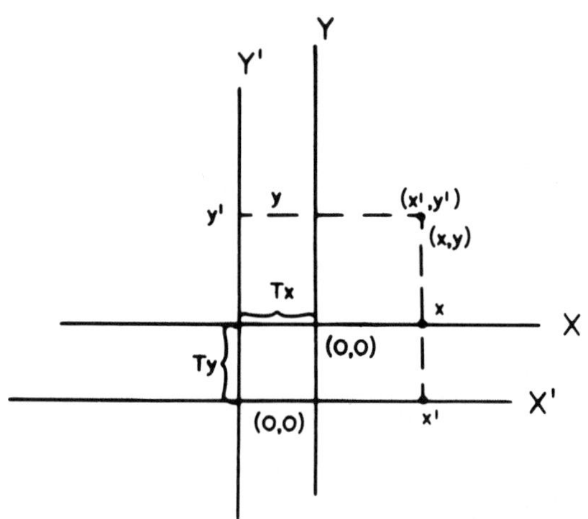

Figure 2.16 The Translation Transformation.

The translation procedure can be written in matrix notation as:

$$(x' \ y' \ 1) = (x \ y \ 1) \begin{bmatrix} 1 & 0 & 0 \\ 0 & 1 & 0 \\ T_x & T_y & 1 \end{bmatrix} . \qquad (2.13)$$

The matrix notation is used to separate the transformation operator from the coordinates.

The rotation transformation is used to rotate the original coordinate system about the origin by some angle θ measured in a counter-clockwise direction from the X-axis (see Figure 2.17.) The rotation transformations are defined as:

$$x' = x \cos \theta + y \sin \theta$$

and

$$y' = -x \sin \theta + y \cos \theta . \qquad (2.14)$$

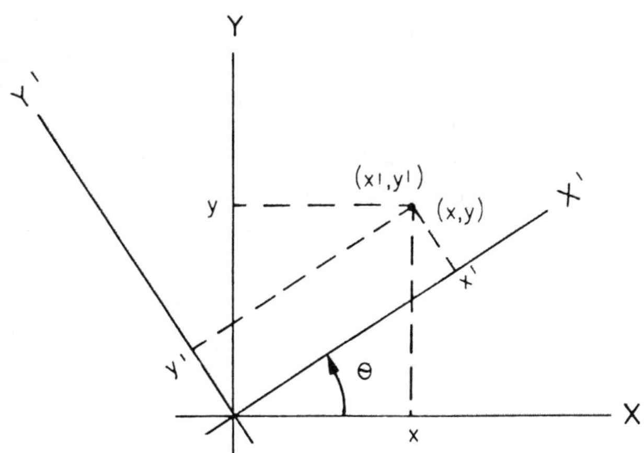

Figure 2.17 The Rotation Transformation.

In matrix notation, this procedure is written as:

$$(x' \; y' \; 1) = (x \; y \; 1) \begin{bmatrix} \cos\theta & -\sin\theta & 0 \\ \sin\theta & \cos\theta & 0 \\ 0 & 0 & 1 \end{bmatrix} . \quad (2.15)$$

In Figure 2.17, the value of **x** is the projection of point **p** on the original X-axis; the value of **x′** is the projection of the same point on the rotated X′-axis. The process of rotation permits us to turn a geometric object around by changing its orientation. This process is especially important for the viewing of three-dimensional surfaces.

As discussed in Chapter One, both translation and rotation preserve the property of distance during the transformation of two-dimensional space. Scaling is used to change the unit distance metric of the coordinate system. The scaling transformations are:

$$x' = S_x \cdot x ;$$

and

$$y' = S_y \cdot y . \quad (2.16)$$

The scaling procedure in matrix notation is written as:

$$(x' \; y' \; 1) = (x \; y \; 1) \begin{bmatrix} S_x & 0 & 0 \\ 0 & S_y & 0 \\ 0 & 0 & 1 \end{bmatrix} . \quad (2.17)$$

The process of scaling has the effect of elongating or reducing the vector associated with the original coordinate **(x,y)**. In Figure 2.18 the coordinate **(6,8)** is reduced along the ray connecting it to the origin to the new point **(3,4)** by the scaling factors S_x = **.5** and S_y = **.5**. Whenever the scaling factors S_x and S_y are less than one, the geometric object is reduced; whenever they are greater than one, the object is enlarged. Whenever S_x equals S_y, scaling preserves the property of orientation during the coordinate transformation. If S_x does not equal S_y, then the object is distorted and stretched in one dimension or the other (see Figure 2.19.)

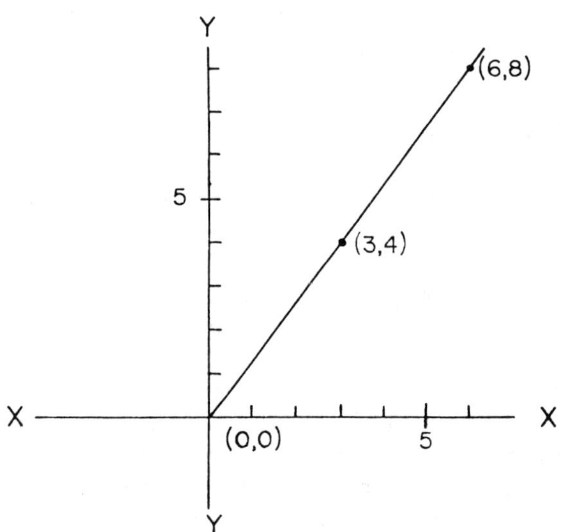

Figure 2.18 The Scaling Transformation.

Very often it is necessary to perform a sequence of point transformations known as *concatenation*. The matrix form of point transformation facilitates this process as the series of transformations can be multiplied in order and stored in a single matrix that represents the whole transformation. In this process, the sequence of the transformations is very important. Given a translation matrix **T**, and a scaling matrix **S**, a new point **p′** defined as **p·T·S** is not necessarily equal to the point **p″** defined as **p·S·T** as matrix multiplication does not obey the commutative law. In the former instance, the point **p** is first translated and then scaled, while in the latter case, the same point is scaled first and then translated. Thus the concatenated matrix **C** = **T·S** would be defined as:

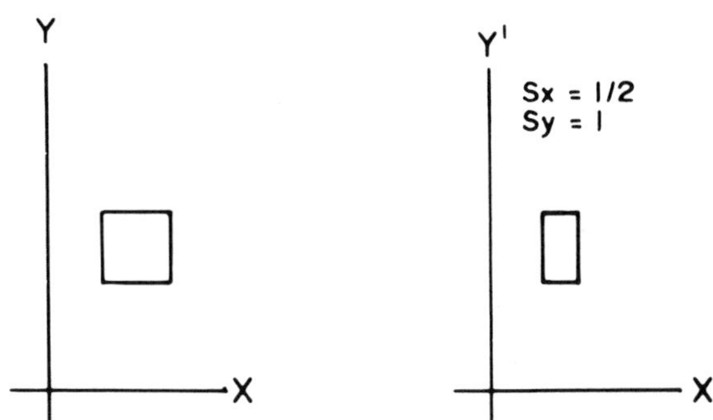

Figure 2.19 Distortion During Scaling.

$$\begin{bmatrix} 1 & 0 & 0 \\ 0 & 1 & 0 \\ T_x & T_y & 1 \end{bmatrix} \begin{bmatrix} S_x & 0 & 0 \\ 0 & S_y & 0 \\ 0 & 0 & 1 \end{bmatrix} = \begin{bmatrix} S_x & 0 & 0 \\ 0 & S_y & 0 \\ T_xS_x & T_yS_y & 1 \end{bmatrix} . \qquad (2.18)$$

Alternatively, the concatenated matrix $\mathbf{C} = \mathbf{S}\cdot\mathbf{T}$ would be defined as:

$$\begin{bmatrix} S_x & 0 & 0 \\ 0 & S_y & 0 \\ 0 & 0 & 1 \end{bmatrix} \begin{bmatrix} 1 & 0 & 0 \\ 0 & 1 & 0 \\ T_x & T_y & 1 \end{bmatrix} = \begin{bmatrix} S_x & 0 & 0 \\ 0 & S_y & 0 \\ T_x & T_y & 1 \end{bmatrix} . \qquad (2.19)$$

In practice, most map displays involve a concatenation of point transformations to move a coordinate from user space into the appropriate hardware space. A final note: if the translation factors are equal to zero, and the scaling factors are equal to one and the angle of rotation is zero, then the respective transformation matrices are identity matrices and any concatenation of these matrices would also be an identity matrix.

2.4 POINT AND LINE RELATIONSHIPS

Many cartographic functions utilize point and line relationships. A *straight line*, **L**, is a locus of points in the same orientation (Figure 2.20). However there are many mathematical expressions for representing a straight line. For instance, a straight line can be defined algebraically as the set of coordinates in $\mathbf{R}^2$ that satisfies the relation $\mathbf{Ax + By + C = 0}$ (the linear equation form); this is denoted as:

$$L = \{(x,y) \mid x \in R,\ y \in R, \text{ and } Ax + By + C = 0\} . \qquad (2.20)$$

A straight line in vector notation is the following inner product:

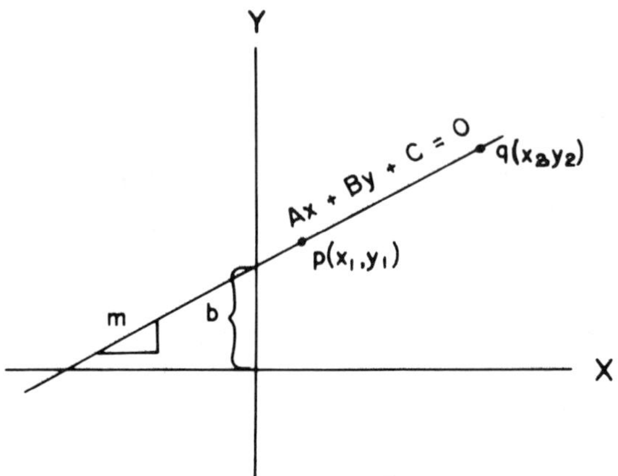

Figure 2.20 A Straight Line.

$$\begin{pmatrix} A \\ B \\ C \end{pmatrix} (x \ y \ 1) = 0 . \tag{2.21}$$

The parameters of this equation **A, B, and C** are scalars that define the positional properties of the line. The *slope* of a line, **m**, is defined as **(-A/B)** and is the change in the value of **y** for a unit change in the value of **x**. Two straight lines are parallel if they have the same slope. The *y-intercept*, **b**, is defined as **(-C/B)** and is the location where the straight line intersects the Y-axis. The *x-intercept* is defined as **(-C/A)** and is the location where the straight line intersects the X-axis. The equation for a straight line relation is alternatively given in slope-intercept form as:

$$y = mx + b . \tag{2.22}$$

In digital cartography, the relation expressed in equation (2.20) is preferred to that in equation (2.22) to represent straight lines because the slope of a line is undefined whenever **B** is equal to zero and cannot be represented in a digital computer. Secondly, the direction of the line is not preserved by equation (2.22). The parameters for the line connecting point $\mathbf{p}(x_1,y_1)$ to point $\mathbf{q}(x_2,y_2)$ in vector notation are:

$$\begin{pmatrix} A \\ B \\ C \end{pmatrix} = \begin{pmatrix} y_1 - y_2 \\ x_2 - x_1 \\ y_2 x_1 - y_1 x_2 \end{pmatrix} . \tag{2.23}$$

Conversely, the parameters for the line connecting point **q** to point **p** are:

$$\begin{bmatrix} A \\ B \\ C \end{bmatrix} = \begin{bmatrix} y_2 - y_1 \\ x_1 - x_2 \\ y_1x_2 - y_2x_1 \end{bmatrix} . \tag{2.24}$$

The parameters **A** and **B** relate to the parameters of the vector **v** between **p** and **q**; the ratio of the **y** component to the **x** component in equation 2.23 equals the slope, **(-A/B)** of the line. The value $(A^2+B^2)^{\frac{1}{2}}$ is the magnitude of the vector connecting **p** and **q**. The **C** parameter represents the area of the parallelogram formed by the two coordinate vectors **p** and **q** (Figure 2.21a.) If the two coordinates form vectors in the same or opposite directions, **C** will have a value of zero (Figure 2.21b) and the line will pass through the origin.

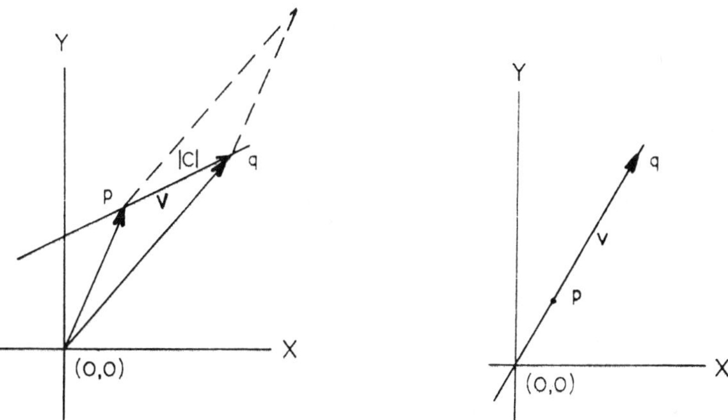

(a) a line not passing through the origin (b) a line passing through the origin

Figure 2.21 The Area Defined by the C Parameter.

The two endpoints of a line segment can also define the straight line passing from **p** to **q** in a point-vector form:

$$L = \{(x_1,y_1) + h\ (x_2-x_1,y_2-y_1)\ |\ h \in R\} . \tag{2.25}$$

The vector (x_2-x_1,y_2-y_1) connecting **p** to **q** is also expressed as **(A,-B)** using the parameters from the linear equation form. The point-vector form preserves the direction of the line and has the additional property that for any point lying on the line segment between **p** and **q**, the value of **h** will be in the closed interval [0,1]. This has important implications for operations involving line segments rather than lines. The form used to represent straight lines will depend on the operation.

A straight line, **L**, is normalized by dividing its respective parameters by the magnitude of the vector between **p** and **q**, $(A^2+B^2)^{\frac{1}{2}}$:

$$\begin{bmatrix} A' \\ B' \\ C' \end{bmatrix} = \begin{bmatrix} A/(A^2+B^2)^{\frac{1}{2}} \\ B/(A^2+B^2)^{\frac{1}{2}} \\ C/(A^2+B^2)^{\frac{1}{2}} \end{bmatrix} . \tag{2.26}$$

A normalized straight line has the same direction and position as its unnormalized counterpart but the magnitude of the vector connecting the scaled coordinate vectors, **p′** and **q′** , has a unit length (see Figure 2.22.) The point-vector form can also be normalized but it would lose its line segment property in the process.

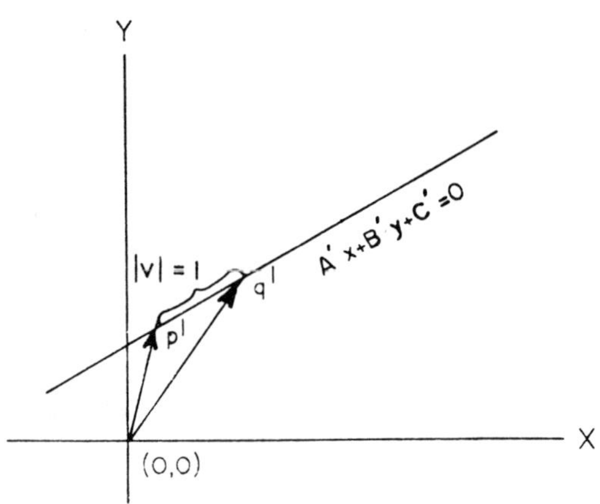

Figure 2.22 A Normalized Straight Line.

For any point $t(x_t,y_t)$ on the plane, its position with respect to the line **L** connecting **p** to **q** is found by calculating the scalar **s**:

$$s = Ax_t + By_t + C . \tag{2.27}$$

If **s** is less than zero, **t** lies in the clockwise halfplane of **L**; if **s** is greater than zero, **t** lies in the counter-clockwise halfplane; and, if **s** equals zero, **t** lies on **L**. For example, the equation of the line connecting points **(2,2)** and **(4,5)** is **-3x + 2y + 2 = 0** (Figure 2.23). The point **(6,3)** lies in the clockwise halfplane of this line as **(-3)(6)+(2)(3)+2 = -10.** Conversely, the point **(0,5)** lies in the other halfplane as **(-3)(0)+(2)(5)+2 = 12.** This is important becauses it again permits the machine to numerically assess the relative position of points with respect to straight lines.

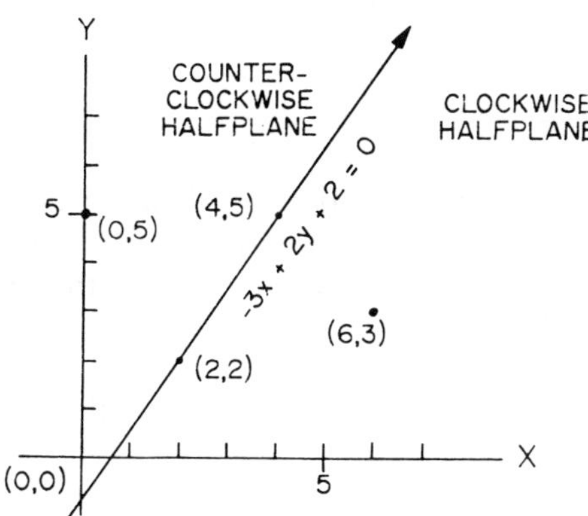

Figure 2.23 Relative Position of Points to a Straight Line.

All points on a straight line, **L′** , that is parallel to **L**, will have the same value of **s**. For example in Figure 2.24, the point **(4,0)** lies on a straight line parallel to the line **-3x + 2y + 2 = 0** that also passes through the point **(6,3)**. The value of s for point **(4,0)** is **(-3)(4)+(2)(0)+2** which also equals **-10**. In general, if the relation for **L** is **Ax + By + C = 0** and the relation for **L′** is **Ax + By + C′ = 0**, then the value of **s** for any point on **L′** with respect to **L** is **(C-C′)**. In the above example, the value of **C′** for **L′** was **12**; thus the value of **s** for all points on **L′** with respect to **L** is **(2-12)**.

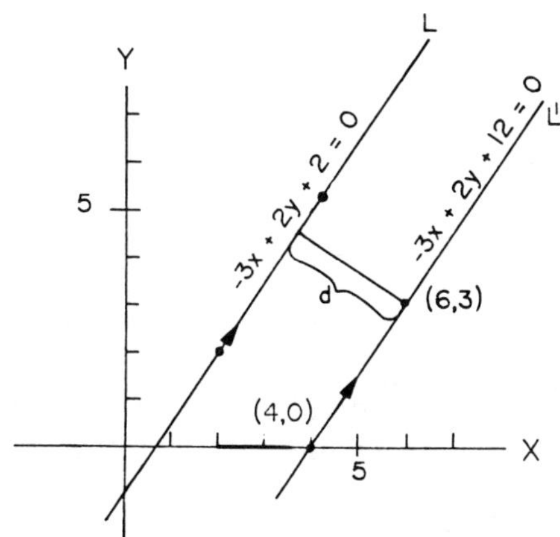

Figure 2.24 The Perpendicular Distance Between a Point and a Straight Line.

The perpendicular distance, **d**, between point **t** and line **L** (see Figure 2.24) is:

$$d = | s/(A^2+B^2)^{1/2} | . \tag{2.28}$$

In the above example, the perpendicular distance between point **(6,3)** and the straight line **-3x + 2y + 2 = 0** equals $|-10/(9+4)^{\frac{1}{2}}|$ or $10/\sqrt{13}$. If two parallel straight lines are normalized, then the perpendicular distance between these lines is $|C-C'|$.

The *midpoint*, $r(x_r,y_r)$, of the line connecting $p(x_1,y_1)$ and $q(x_2,y_2)$ (Figure 2.25) is:

$$\begin{pmatrix} x_r \\ y_r \end{pmatrix} = \begin{pmatrix} (x_1 + x_2)/2 \\ (y_1 + y_2)/2 \end{pmatrix} . \tag{2.29}$$

The midpoint between points **(2,2)** and **(6,9)** in Figure 2.25 is **(8/2,11/2)**.

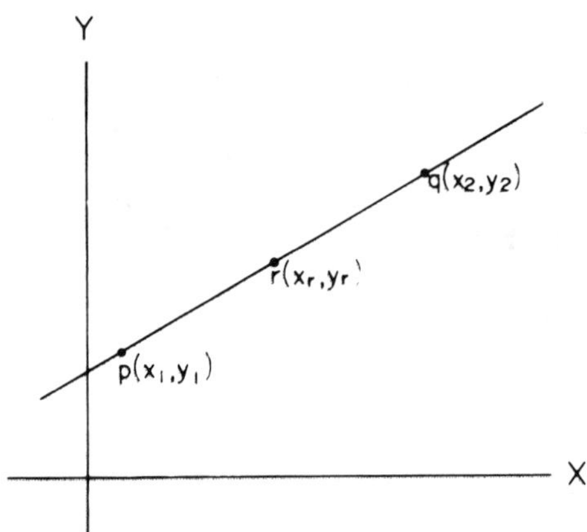

Figure 2.25 The Midpoint Between Two Points.

A *perpendicular bisector*, **P**, is a straight line perpendicular to the straight line connecting $p(x_1,y_1)$ and $q(x_2,y_2)$ that passes through its midpoint (Figure 2.26). The perpendicular bisector divides the plane into two halfplanes such that all points to one side of **P** are closer to **p** and those on the other side of **P** are closer to **q**. If **q** is in the clockwise halfplane of **P**, the parameters of **P** are:

$$\begin{pmatrix} A \\ B \\ C \end{pmatrix} = \begin{pmatrix} x_1 - x_2 \\ y_1 - y_2 \\ \frac{1}{2}[(x_2^2+y_2^2)-(x_1^2+y_1^2)] \end{pmatrix} . \tag{2.30}$$

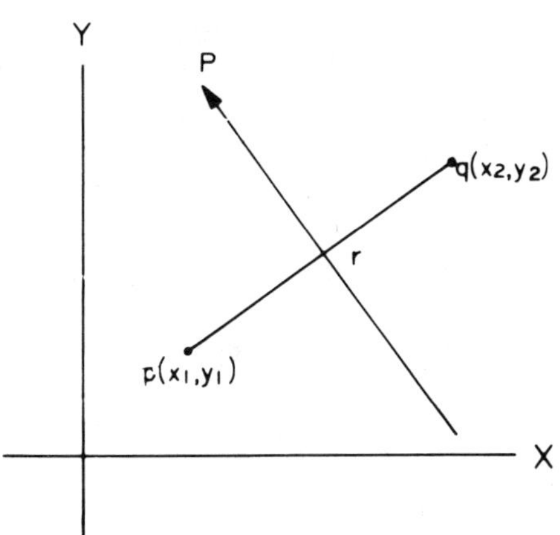

Figure 2.26 The Perpendicular Bisector Between Two Points.

The parameters for the perpendicular bisector between the points **(2,2)** and **(4,5)** in Figure 2.26 are:

$$\begin{bmatrix} A \\ B \\ C \end{bmatrix} = \begin{bmatrix} 2 - 5 \\ 2 - 4 \\ \tfrac{1}{2}[(4^2+5^2)-(2^2+2^2)] \end{bmatrix} .$$

Next, the *intersection*, $\mathbf{i(x_i,y_i)}$, of two lines, **Ax + By + C = 0** and **Ex + Fy + G = 0**, is:

$$\begin{bmatrix} x_i \\ y_i \end{bmatrix} = \begin{bmatrix} (GB-FC)/(FA-EB) \\ (CE-AG)/(FA-EB) \end{bmatrix} . \qquad (2.31)$$

In Figure 2.27, the intersection of straight lines **-3x + 2y +2 = 0** and **2x + 4y - 28 = 0** is:

$$\begin{bmatrix} x_i \\ y_i \end{bmatrix} = \begin{bmatrix} [(-28)(2)-(4)(2)]/[(4)(-3)-(2)(2)] \\ [(2)(2)-(-3)(-28)]/[(4)(-3)-(2)(2)] \end{bmatrix}$$

$$= \begin{bmatrix} (-64)/(-16) \\ (-80)/(-16) \end{bmatrix} .$$

If the two lines are parallel, the value **(FA-EB)** will equal zero and the intersection will not exist.

However, many problems arise if one is looking for the existence of intersections between two line segments rather than two lines. The linear equation form requires a two-step process requiring consideration of different special cases; first, the line intersection is calculated and then checks are made to determine if this point lies on each line segment. Douglas [1984] has noted the variety of cases that can occur in this situation. These concerns are eliminated or at least reduced using the point-vector form [Saalfeld, 1987]. For two segments, **S** and **S′** connecting points (x_1,y_1) to (x_2,y_2) and (x_1',y_1') to (x_2',y_2') respectively, their intersection is determined by solving for $h=D_1/D$ and $h'=D_2/D$, where

$$D = (x_2'-x_1')(y_1-y_2) - (x_2-x_1)(y_1'-y_2') ;$$

$$D_1 = (x_2'-x_1')(y_1'-y_1) - (x_1'-x_1)(y_2'-y_1') ; \qquad (2.32)$$

$$D_2 = (x_2-x_1)(y_1'-y_1) - (x_1'-1)(y_2-y_1) .$$

D equals **(FA-EB)**. The line segments are parallel and do not intersect if $D=0$ and either D_1 or D_2 are nonzero (or both are nonzero). If D, D_1 and D_2 all equal zero, then the line segments are collinear (they lie on the same line) and their endpoints are compared to determine if the segments overlap or intersect at an endpoint. Finally, if both **h** and **h′** are in the closed interval **[0,1]** then the two segments intersect at the position defined by either **h** or **h′**. This closed interval can be extended by an epsilon tolerance in either direction to find "near" intersections that may be associated with digitizing error [Saalfeld, 1987] (see Chapter Four).

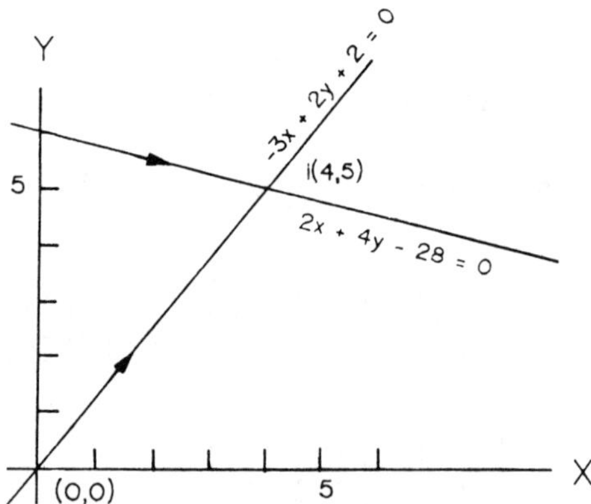

Figure 2.27 The Intersection of Two Straight Lines.

If two lines do intersect, there also exists a straight line, **Q**, that passes through their intersection and bisects the angle, θ , between them (Figure 2.28). If the equation for this line is $Rx + Sy + T = 0$, its parameters are calculated as the sum of the respective normalized components of the original intersecting lines:

$$\begin{bmatrix} R \\ S \\ T \end{bmatrix} = \begin{bmatrix} A' + E' \\ B' + F' \\ C' + G' \end{bmatrix} . \qquad (2.33)$$

where, **A′**, **B′**, **C′**, **E′**, **F′** and **G′** are the respective normalized parameters of the orginal two lines.

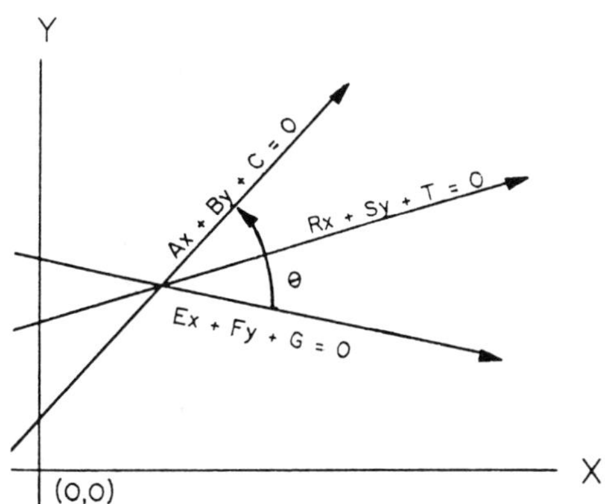

Figure 2.28 The Angle Bisector Between Two Lines.

For example, the parameters of the angle bisector between lines **-3x +4y + 2 = 0** and **12x + 5y + 9 = 0** are:

$$\begin{bmatrix} R \\ S \\ T \end{bmatrix} = \begin{bmatrix} (-3)/5 + 12/13 \\ 4/5 + 5/13 \\ 2/5 + 9/13 \end{bmatrix} .$$

If the direction of one of the intersecting lines changes, then the new angle bisector will be a straight line that is perpendicular to the first angle bisector (compare Figures 2.29a and 2.29b.) If both intersecting lines change direction, then the new bisector will have the opposite direction of the first bisector (compare Figures 2.29a and 2.29c.)

2.5 LINE AND AREA MEASUREMENT

The basic measurement for any line is its length; if the line is closed and forms the outline of a region, an area is enclosed. The length of this outline is the *perimeter* of the region. Because lines in digital computers are approximated by a straight line segment sequence, the length of the resulting string is the sum of the magnitudes of all the vectors (line segments) that comprise it. The length of a string having **n** segments is:

$$\text{Length} = \sum_{i=1}^{n} [(x_{i+1}-x_i)^2 + (y_{i+1}-y_i)^2]^{1/2} \; ; \qquad (2.34)$$

where, (x_i,y_i) are the coordinate endpoints of the respective segments.

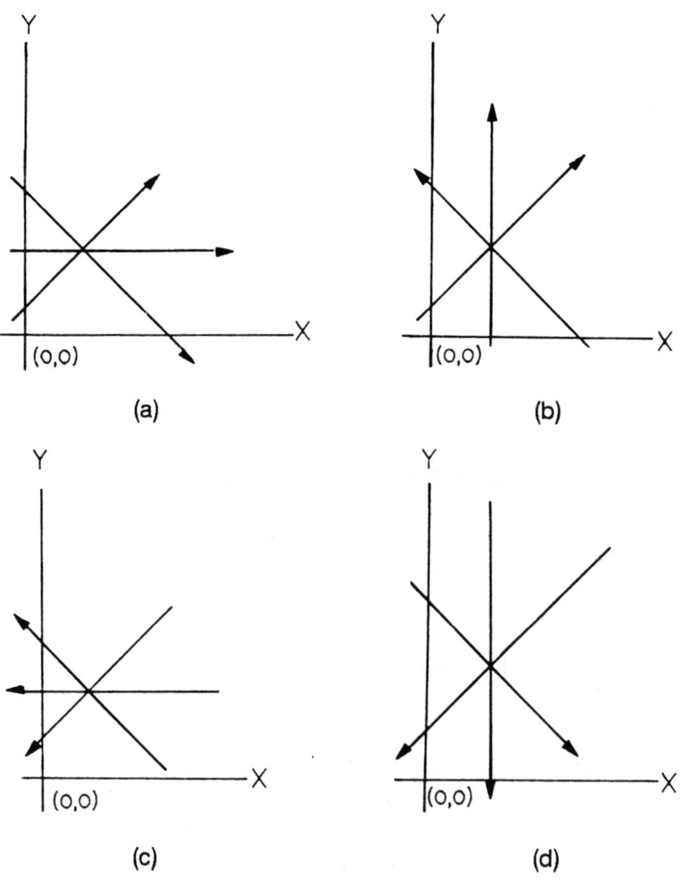

Figure 2.29 The Different Angle Bisectors Depending on the Direction of the Intersecting Lines.

The second basic measurement is the area of any enclosed polygon. As discussed in section 1.5, a polygon can consist of a series of interior and exterior outlines or rings. It is assumed here that the coordinates that comprise the exterior outline of any polygon are always given in a clockwise sequence around the polygon; the coordinates comprising an interior outline are always given in a counter-clockwise sequence. In this manner the polygon will always lie to the right of any line segment in its boundary. This convention will be retained in all further discussions.

The area enclosed by each ring of a polygon can be calculated either as the sum of its triangular or trapezoidal parts (see Figure 2.30). In the former approach, the sum of the area of a triangle formed by two successive coordinate vectors of the ring with any origin (see Figure 2.30a) is one-half the area of the parallelogram formed by these vectors. This value then is just one-half the value of the determinant of the matrix formed by the pair of coordinate vectors (refer back to equation 2.11 and Figure 2.14.) The total area enclosed by a ring having **n** segments is calculated as:

$$\text{Area} = -(1/2) \sum_{i=1}^{n} (x_i y_{i+1} - x_{i+1} y_i) \; . \qquad (2.35)$$

where (x_i, y_i) are the coordinate endpoints of the respective segments.

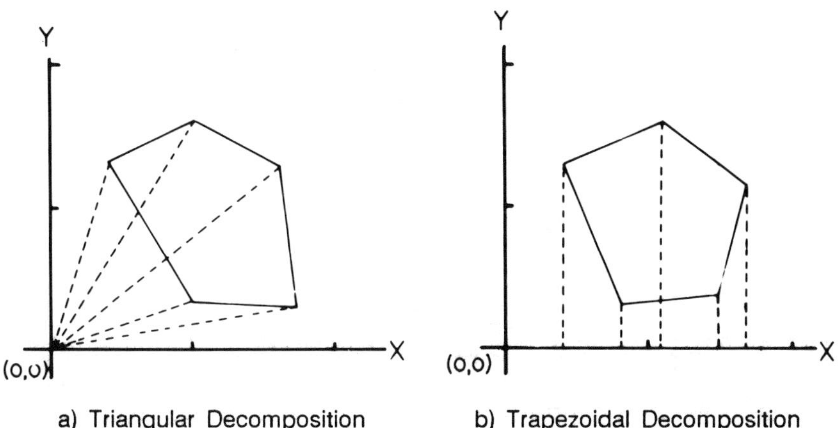

Figure 2.30 Alternative Polygon Decompositions for Area Measurement.

Using the clockwise convention for exterior rings, the area of any triangle where the *(i+1)st* vector lies in the clockwise halfplane of the *ith* vector will be positive; conversely, if the *(i+1)st* vector is in the counter-clockwise halfplane, the area of the resulting triangle will be negative. In this manner, the portions of triangles that lie outside the ring will be deleted and the area enclosed by the exterior ring will be positive. The reverse is true for interior rings; their area will be negative. The total area of any complex polygon is found by adding the areas associated with each ring.

For example, the exterior ring of the complex polygon given in Figure 2.31 consists of the point set **{(4,1), (2,3), (4,7), (6,6), (6,2), (4,1)}** and the interior ring consists of the point set **{(3,3), (5,4), (4,5), (3,3)}**. The area enclosed by the exterior ring is:

$$-(1/2)\ [(4\cdot3-1\cdot2)+(2\cdot7-3\cdot4)+(4\cdot6-7\cdot6)+(6\cdot2-6\cdot6)+(6\cdot1-2\cdot4)] = -(1/2)\ [(10)+(2)+(-18)+(-24)+(-2)] = 16\ .$$

The area enclosed by the interior ring is:

$$-(1/2)\ [(3\cdot4-3\cdot5)+(5\cdot5-4\cdot4)+(4\cdot3-5\cdot3)] = -(1/2)\ [(-3)+(9)+(-3)] = -(3/2)\ .$$

The total area of the polygon is **[(16)+(-3/2)]** or **14.5**.

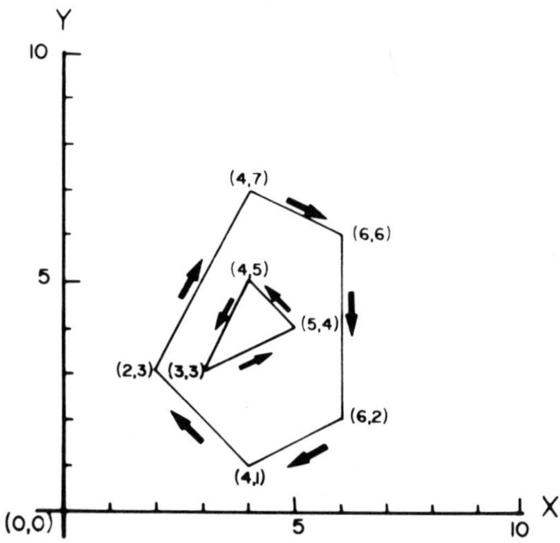

Figure 2.31 An Example Complex Polygon.

In the latter approach, the areas of trapezoids formed by the segments of the ring perimeter and X-axis are calculated and combined (Figure 2.30b). The area enclosed by a ring having **n** segments is calculated using the formula:

$$\text{Area} = 1/2 \sum_{i=1}^{n} (x_{i+1}-x_i)(y_{i+1}+y_i)\ ; \qquad (2.36)$$

where (x_i,y_i) are the coordinate endpoints of the ring segments.

Any trapezoid associated with an exterior line segment where x_{i+1} is less than x_i will have a negative area and its value will be subtracted from the total; the reverse would be true for interior segments. The reader can easily show through the expansion and simplification of equations (2.35) and (2.36) that both methods are identical.

Finally, it is also possible to calculate the area of any simple polygon measured in some basic areal unit whose vertices are lattice points in some tessellation of two-dimensional space (see Figure 2.32). This area is found using Pick's theorem (Coxeter, 1961):

$$\text{Number of Areal Units} = (1/2)\ b + c - 1\ . \qquad (2.37)$$

where **b** is the number of lattice points on the polygon boundary and **c** is the number of lattice points contained in the interior.

In Figure 2.32a, there are **12** points on the polygon boundary and no points inside; the area of this polygon is **(6 - 1)** or **5** units. In Figure 2.32b, there are **13** exterior vertices and **2** interior points; the area of this polygon is **(13/2 + 2 - 1)** or **7.5** units. The basic areal unit in Figure 2.32a is a unit square and the corresponding unit in Figure 2.32b is a parallelogram.

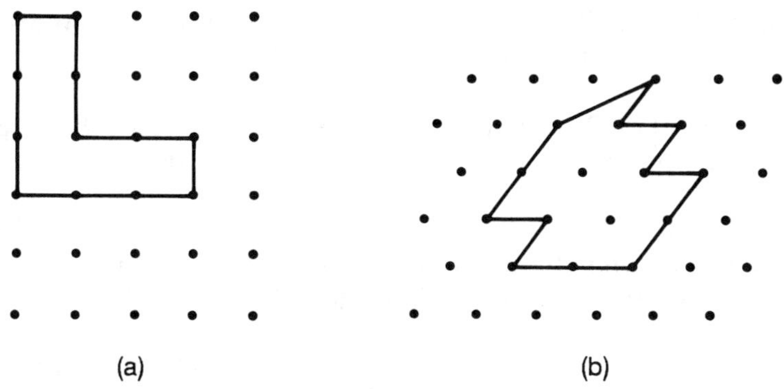

Figure 2.32 Area Calculation in a Tessellation of Space.

2.6 SUMMARY

This chapter has focused on the basics of analytical geometry that comprise the primitive tasks within more complex algorithms in digital cartography. However, the emphasis has been on the coordinate properties of maps as absolute locations and not their relative position within a digital image. In Chapter Three, the data organization of digital maps is discussed and topological properties are added to the locational ones.

2.7 REFERENCES

Coxeter, H.S.M. [1961]. **Introduction to Geometry**, New York: John Wiley & Sons, Inc.

Douglas, D. [1984]. "It makes me so CROSS," in **Basic Readings in Geographic Information Systems**, D. Marble, H. Calkins, and D. Peuquet (eds.), New York: SPAD Systems Ltd.

Dutton, G. [1989]. "The Fallacy of Coordinates," in **Multiple Representations: Scientific Report for the Specialist Meeting**, B. Buttenfield (ed.), Santa Barbara, California: National Center for Geographic Information and Analysis, 44-48.

Fisher, R.C. and A.G. Ziebur [1965]. **Calculus and Analytic Geometry**, Englewood Cliffs, New Jersey: Prentice-Hall.

Foley, J.D. and A. Van Dam [1984]. **Fundamentals of Interactive Computer Graphics**, Reading, Massachusetts: Addison-Wesley Publishing Co.

Harrington, S. [1983]. **Computer Graphics: A Programming Approach**, New York: McGraw Hill, Inc.

Monmonier, M.S. [1982]. **Computer-Assisted Cartography: Principles and Prospects**, Englewood Cliffs, New Jersey: Prentice-Hall.

Mudur, S.P. [1986]. "Mathematical Elements for Computer Graphics," in **Advances in Computer Graphics I**, G. Enderle, M. Grave, and F. Lillehagen (eds.), London: Springer-Verlag, 53-134.

Newman, W.M. and R.F. Sproull [1973]. **Principles of Interactive Computer Graphics**, New York: McGraw Hill Book Co.

Nordbeck, S. and B. Rystedt [1972]. **Computer Cartography: Point-in-Polygon Programs**, Lund: Studentlitterature.

Penna, M.A. and R.R. Patterson [1986]. **Projective Geometry and its Applications to Computer Graphics**, Englewood Cliffs, New Jersey: Prentice-Hall.

Rosenbaum, R.A. [1963]. **Introduction to Projective Geometry and Modern Algebra**, Reading, Massachusetts: Addison-Wesley Publishing Co.

Saalfeld, A. [1987]. "It doesn't make me nearly so CROSS: Some Advantages of the Point-Vector Representation of Line Segments in Automated Cartography," **International Journal of Geographical Information Systems**, 1, 379-86.

White, M. [1984]. "How Mathematics Can Help in Cartography," **Cartographica**, 5, 45-49.

Chapter 3
Data Structures

The central object in a digital cartographic processing system is the digital representation (see Chapter One). This object is intermediate between raw data and any type of map display. In Chapter Two, we saw how geometric objects can be translated into numerical ones measured by coordinates and learned a set of primitive operations that will form the basis for many higher level algorithms. In the design of these algorithms, however, it is impossible to separate the set of operators from the underlying structure of the data that are being transformed [Tarjan, 1983].

In the process of cartographic abstraction, a number of stages is involved in the design of the final cartographic database, moving from a very abstract to very concrete representation of cartographic objects. The real world (or at least our image of it) is transformed into a data model at a fairly high level of abstraction using various generalization operators such as selection and simplification. This abstraction of the real world in turn must be converted into a more specific data structure and finally into a file structure. In database design, the data structure is a representation of the data model in terms of diagrams, lists and arrays that can be integrated into an algorithmic design [Peuquet, 1985.] Data structures form the basis of software design. File structures are representation of the objects in hardware storage.

In this chapter, the basic concepts and forms of cartographic data organization are discussed. Few topics have had a more fundamental impact on the theory and practice of digital cartography than data organization. Therefore, it is important to discuss data organization before discussing either data collection or data display functions, as the algorithm design of these functions is very intertwined with the structure of the digital image.

3.1 BASIC TOPOLOGICAL CONCEPTS

In contrast to the algebraic relations of analytic geometry, data structures are based in the relations of topology. A topological space is a set of objects, **T**, together with a collection of open subsets of **T**, denoted as {**t**}, called a topology on **T**, that satisfy the following axioms [Cairns, 1961]:

1) the intersection of any finite collection of open subsets is open;

2) the union of any collection of open subsets is open.

The null subset, ϕ , and **T** itself are open subsets and form the trivial topology on **T**. For example, let **T** be the set of United States counties. One topology of this set would be the individual subsets containing the counties belonging to each state. Because each subset of state counties is open, the intersection of any finite collection of these subsets is either the null set when two different subsets like Oregon and Ohio are intersected, because no county belongs to more than one state, or an open subset itself as when Ohio is intersected with Ohio. The union of any collection of states would also be an open subset including the entire set of the United States.

A subset **S** is a neighborhood of any object, **s**, that is an element of the set **T**, if there is a member **R** that is an element of {**t**} such that **s** is an element of **R** and **R** is a subset of **S**. For example, Kentucky is a member of the topology for the set of United States counties; it is also a neighborhood for Leslie County (a county in Kentucky) as Leslie County is an element of Kentucky and Kentucky is a subset of itself.

In Euclidean $\mathbf{R}^n$ space, a subset **S** is a special neighborhood of the point **p** called an *ϵ-ball* if all points of $\mathbf{R}^n$ within an epsilon distance (a very small distance) of **p** are contained in **S** [McCarty, 1961]. An ϵ-ball associated with any point in Kentucky would also only contain points that are part of Kentucky. The concept of an ϵ-ball has been used by Perkal [1966] to generalize lines and to measure their length (Chapter Four.)

The complement S′ of any open subset S is closed; the closure S^- of a subset S is the intersection of all closed subsets that contain S (see Figure 3.1b). The interior of a subset S, denoted as S° , is the set of all the elements of S for which S is a neighborhood (Figure 3.1c). The boundary of a subset S, denoted as ∂S, is the set of all points in the intersection of the closure of S and the closure of its complement S′ (Figure 3.1d). For example, let the earth be an open subset of the solar system; its closure would be a subset that abruptly stopped at its surface. All elements of the earth whose neighborhood are completely self-contained by the earth are part of the earth's interior. The earth's surface where the earth and sky meet forms the boundary of the earth.

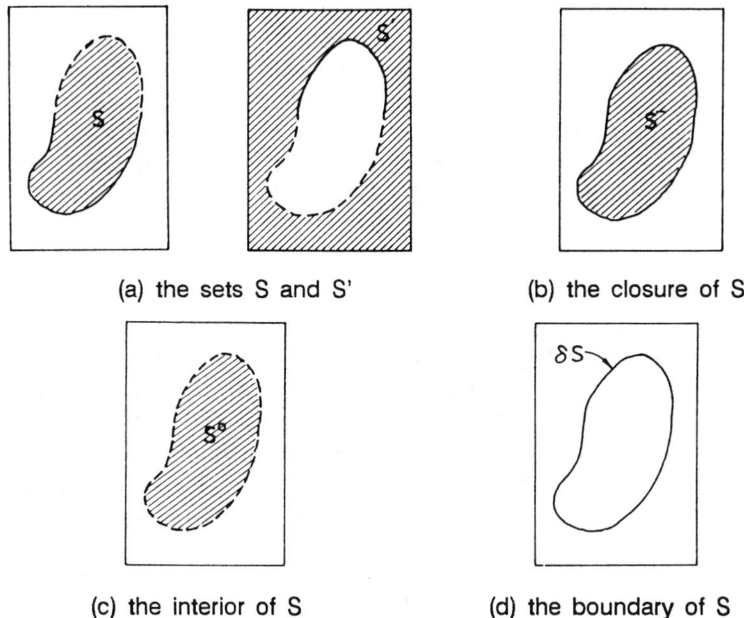

(a) the sets S and S'   (b) the closure of S

(c) the interior of S   (d) the boundary of S

Figure 3.1 The Closure, Interior, and Boundary of a Set.
(A solid line denotes points that are elements of a set, while a dashed line denotes points that are not elements.)

A set S is connected if and only if it cannot be expressed as the union of two mutually disjoint open subsets. For example, in Figure 3.2a S is the union of the mutually disjoint open subsets **X** and **W**. In this case, S is a disconnected set. In Figure 3.2b, S cannot be the union of two such sets; **X** and **W** overlap (their intersection is not equal to the null set).

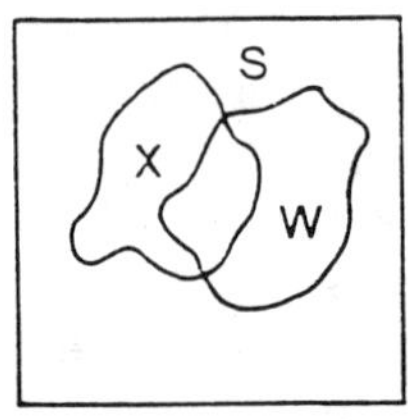

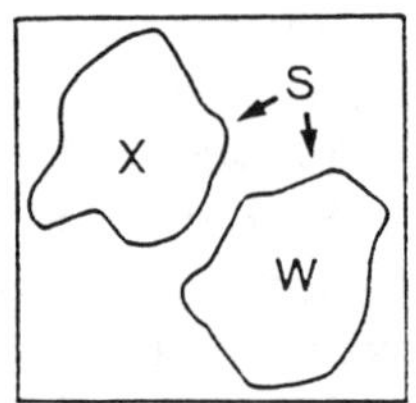

(a) disconnected subsets (b) connected subsets

Figure 3.2 Connected and Disconnected Subsets.

Many different cartographic objects can be represented as disconnected or connected sets. The geographic area of the United States is a disconnected set as the Hawaiian Islands, Alaska, and the contiguous forty-eight states are mutually disjoint subsets of a two-dimensional surface (Figure 3.3a). Alternatively, the subset of New England states (highly generalized to include no islands) would be a connected subset (Figure 3.3b).

Connected subsets are also called cells. In a two-dimensional surface, the primary connected subsets are 0-cells (points), 1-cells (lines) and 2-cells (areas) (see Corbett [1979] for a thorough discussion of topological cells). A pair of these objects having different dimensions is incident with each other if their intersection is not a null set. The higher dimensional object is said to be *bounded* by the lower dimensional object and the lower dimensional object is said to *cobound* the higher dimensional object. To say that object **A** cobounds object **B** is equivalent to saying that object **A** "is on the boundary of" object **B** [White, 1984]. A map is a collection of 0-cells, 1-cells and 2-cells in which every 2-cell is *bounded* by 1-cells, every 1-cell is bounded by 0-cells, every 0-cell cobounds some 1-cell and every 1- cell cobounds some 2-cell [White, 1979]. For example in Figure 3.3b, the state of Connecticut is bounded by the Massachusetts-Connecticut border and this border cobounds the state of Connecticut. Two objects of the same dimension are *adjacent* to each other if they share a bounding object. The state of Connecticut is adjacent to the state of Massachusetts because the two states share a common border.

Pairs of incident cells also have a symmetry in their structure known as *duality*. In duality, every occurrence of a *primal* object or relation can be replaced by its corresponding *dual* object or relation. The primal object can be thought of as the original object and the dual object as its counterpart although which object is designated as which is arbitrary. For example, boundary and coboundary are dual aspects of an incidence relation [Corbett, 1979]. Also, a 0-cell is a dual to a 2-cell and a 1-cell is a dual to a 1-cell. These relationships can be seen in the diagram in Figure 3.4; the primal objects are formed by the solid lines while the corresponding dual objects are formed by the dashed lines. The 2-cell **A** in the primal diagram is a 0-cell in the dual. In Figure 3.4, **(a,A)** is a primal incident pair in which the 1-cell **a** bounds the 2-cell **A** and **A** cobounds **a**. In the dual incident pair **(a,A)** the 1-cell **a** cobounds the 0-cell **A** and **A** bounds **a**. Duality illustrates the orientability of two-dimensional manifolds. When moving "from" 0-cell **1** "to" 0-cell **4**, 2-cell **A** is to the "right" and 2-cell **B** is to the "left". This orientation is interchanged in the dual. When moving "from" 0-cell **A** "to" 0-cell **B**, 2-cell **1** is to the "left" and 2-cell **4** is to the "right". This geometrical symmetry is used later in this chapter as the basis of the DIME system.

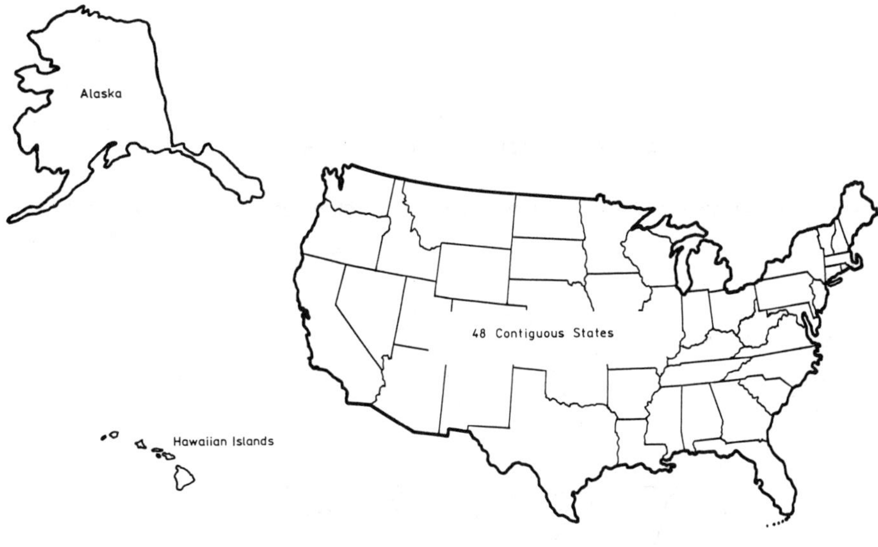

(a) the United States (a disconnected set)

Figure 3.3 Disconnected and Connected Cartographic Objects.

Diagrammatically, each subset (or object), s_i, and the set, **S**, that contains them are represented by open circles; the adjacency relation between each element, s_i, and the set **S** is represented by a straight line connecting the set object to each subset object (Figure 3.5a). Any adjacency relation between subset objects is also represented by a link (Figure 3.5b).

(b) New England (a connected set)

Figure 3.3 Disconnected and Connected Cartographic Objects (continued).

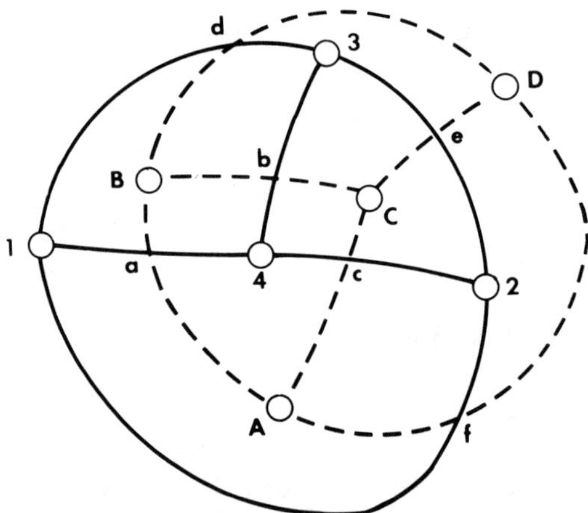

Figure 3.4 A Primal Set of Objects and Its Dual.

For a connected set **S**, if each subset, s_i, is only adjacent to at most two other subsets, then the collection of these subsets, $\{s_i\}$, forms a path topology on the connected set **S** (Figure 3.6). If two subsets are only adjacent to one other subset, then it is an open path topology (Figure

3.6a); if each subset is adjacent to exactly two other subsets, then it is a closed path topology (Figure 3.6b). A line or a string (defined in Section 1.5) is an example of the former; a line is a connected set for which each point is adjacent to at most two other points and two points only are adjacent to one other point and a string is a connected set for which each line segment is a subset that is adjacent to at most two other line segments and two segments are only adjacent to one other. An outline and a ring are examples of the latter; in an outline each point is adjacent to two other points and in a ring each line segment is adjacent to exactly two other segments.

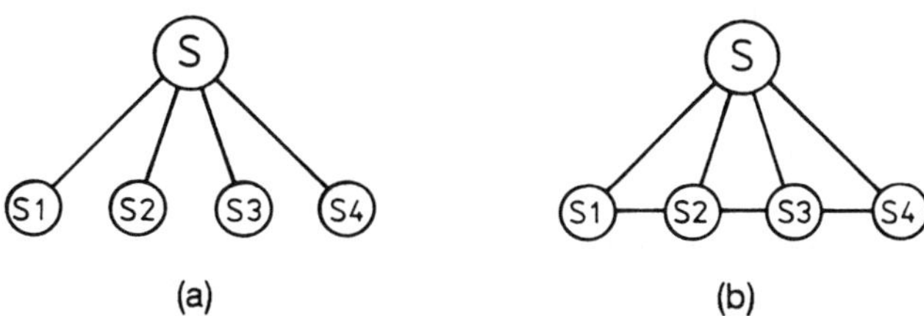

Figure 3.5 The Diagrammatic Representation of Cobounding Relations.

For a connected set **S**, if one subset is adjacent to three or more other subsets, then the collection forms a network topology on the set **S** (Figure 3.7). The New England states presented in Figure 3.2 are an example of a network topology.

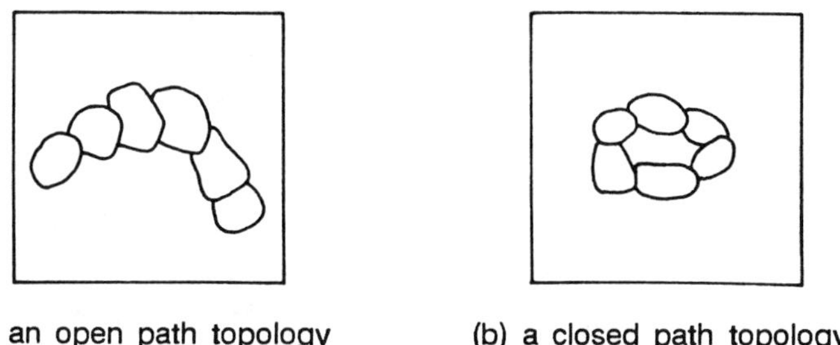

Figure 3.6 Path Topologies.

Any disconnected set can be decomposed into a set of connected subsets. The path or network topology for each of these subsets can be defined and then linked together through the adjacency relations between subsets and the set. For example in Figure 3.8a, the set **S** is composed of two mutually disjoint subsets **X** and **Y**. Each of these subsets though is connected. The connected subsets of **X** form a network topology and the connected subsets of **Y** form an open path topology (Figure 3.8b).

These topologies are then linked together by the adjacency relations (Figure 3.8c).

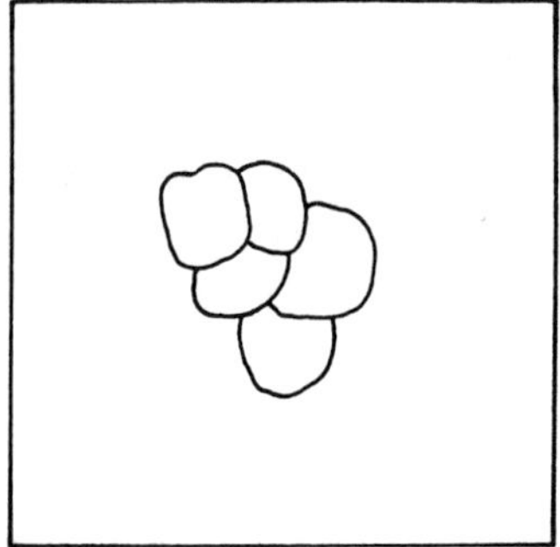

Figure 3.7 A Network Topology.

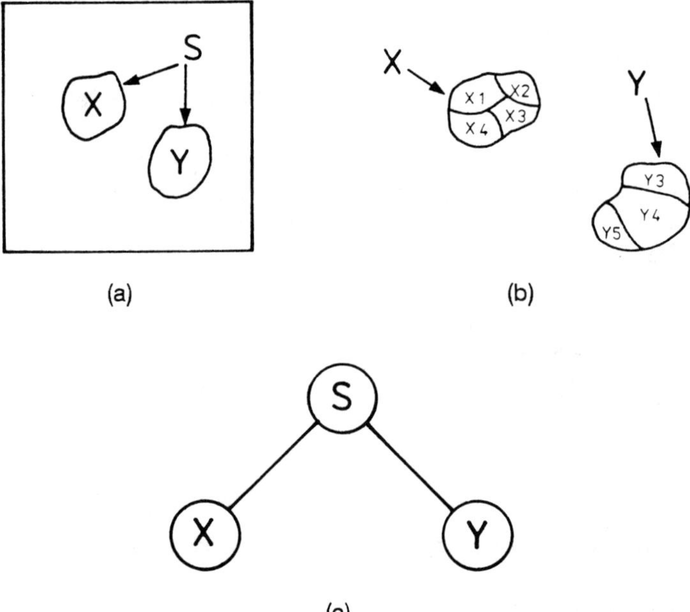

Figure 3.8 The Decomposition of a Disconnected Set into Connected Subsets.

The arrangement of objects within a data structure is based in part on the bounding, cobounding and adjacency relations that exist between pairs of objects in a set.

3.2 FILE STRUCTURES

3.2.1 List Structures

As mentioned at the beginning of this chapter, file structures are the concrete representation of objects in hardware storage. In data management, different file structures have been proposed for expressing the interrelationships between data elements based on their topological and metric properties. Each object is referred to as a *vertex*. Each vertex consists of a set of attributes or fields that define certain characteristics of the object. For example, let the objects be American cities. Each vertex would refer to an individual city. Its attributes or fields might include characteristics such as its population, unemployment rate, latitude or longitude. As discussed in Chapter One, topological transformations are those that preserve the property of neighborhood. If no object is in the neighborhood of another, the objects are just independent members of a disconnected set S. Such sets are called *unordered lists*. Although such sets can exist at the more abstract levels of data models and data structures, they do not exist at the very concrete level of file structures. In a file structure, all vertices are stored at some physical location on a storage medium in linear memory. In a computing machine, vertices are stored at positions referenced by an *address*. The objects of any set stored in a machine are implicitly connected by their address attribute (this is independent of any geographical connection between objects). The set that contains the objects as vertices is denoted as the *root vertex*.

A *linear list* is a set of vertices that have an open path topology expressed by their relative position in the list. The first vertex in the list is called the *head* or top of the list, while the last vertex in the list is called the *tail* or bottom of the list. Vertex **j** in the list is a neighbor of vertex **(j-1)** and vertex **(j+1)**. Vertex **(j-1)** is the *predecessor* of vertex **j** and vertex **(j+1)** is the *successor* of vertex **j**. The first vertex in a list has no predecessor, while the last vertex has no successor. The set itself is again the root vertex of the list. In Figure 3.9, the vertices of set **S** are now connected according to their positions in the list. Vertex **L** is first, followed in order by vertices **B**, **K**, **X**, **E**, and **C**.

The following set of operations can be performed on lists [Knuth, 1973]:

a) Access to the **jth** vertex of the list to retrieve or alter the contents of its attributes;
b) Search the list for a vertex with a certain value for some attribute;

c) Determine the number of vertices in the list;
d) Make a copy of the list;
e) Insert a new vertex before the **jth** vertex of the list;
f) Delete the **jth** vertex of the list;
g) Merge two or more lists into one list;
h) Split a list into two or more lists;
i) Sort the vertices into ascending order based on the values of a certain attribute.

Operations a-d do not involve any change in the relative positions of the vertices in the list (topology preserving), while operations e-i will usually alter the relative position of vertices in the list.

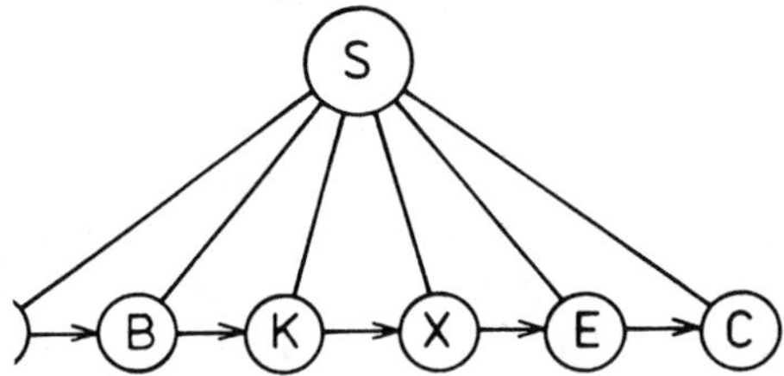

Figure 3.9 A Linear List.

Special lists where insertions, delections, and access always occur at the first or last vertex are known as *stacks*, *queues*, and *deques*. A stack is a list where all insertions and deletions occur at one end of the list (Figure 3.10a). A queue is a list where all insertions are made at one end of the list and all deletions are made at the other end (Figure 3.10b). A deque is a list where all insertions and deletions are made at either end (Figure 3.10c). Output-restricted deques permit deletions only at one end, while input-restricted deques permit insertions only at one end of the list.

Lists can be stored either as a *sequential allocation*, a *random access allocation*, or a *linked allocation* of space. In a sequential allocation, the vertices are stored in locations contiguous to one another; vertices and their addresses are inseparable. For example, the set **S** consists of the following list of vertices: **L**, **B**, **K**, **X**, **E**, and **C**. The address of the root vertex is the base address **s**. The address of the first vertex is **s+n** where **n** is the storage size for the contents of each vertex; the address of the second vertex is **s+2n**, *et cetera*. The contents of an attribute are processed directly as an array of values; in Figure 3.11, the attribute values represent the population of each vertex.

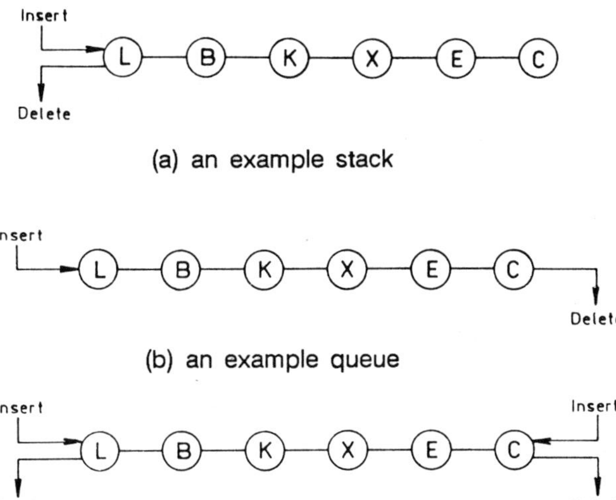

Figure 3.10 Stacks, Queues, and Deques.

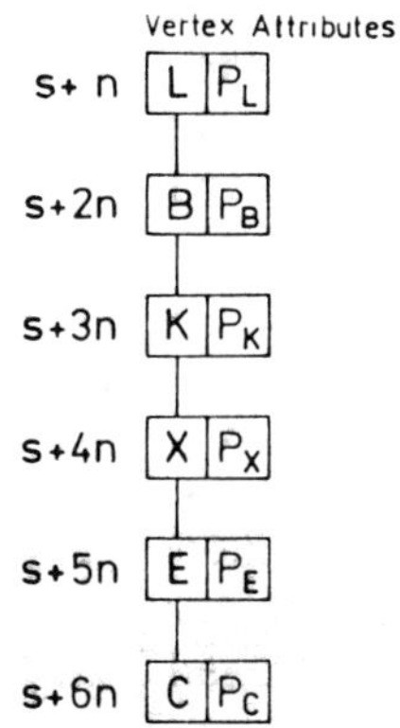

Figure 3.11 A List Stored in a Sequential Allocation.

In a random access allocation, the location of the vertices is randomly distributed in storage. An index array is kept in a sequential allocation; the values of this array are the addresses of the respective vertices. For example, let the respective addresses of the vertices be **l**, **b**, **k**, **x**, **e**, and **c**. In Figure 3.12, these values are then stored at the array addresses **s+n**, **s+2n**,..., **s+6n** respectively. The contents of an attribute are retrieved in a two-step process where the address of the vertex containing the attribute is first retrieved and this value in turn is used to retrieve the attribute value itself.

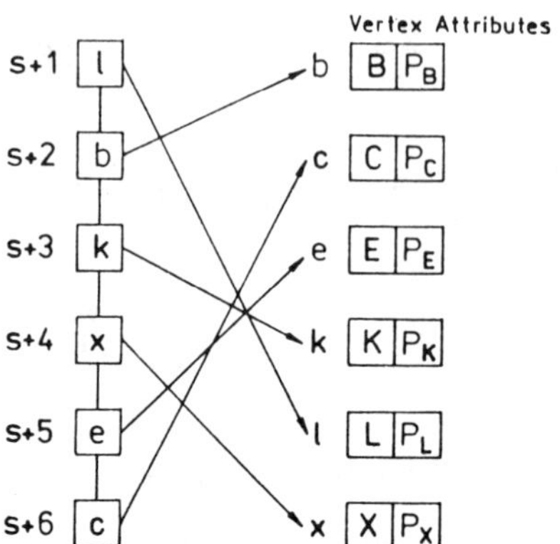

Figure 3.12 A List Stored in a Random Access Allocation.

In a linked allocation, the address of the first vertex in the list is found in the contents of the address of the root vertex (Figure 3.13). Among the contents of the address of the first vertex is the address of the next vertex in order. This sequence continues until at the address of the last vertex, a null address is encountered; the null address signifies that no further vertex can be encountered. In this approach, the address of the next vertex explicitly becomes another vertex attribute. This structural information should be distinguished from the other thematic attributes of the vertex.

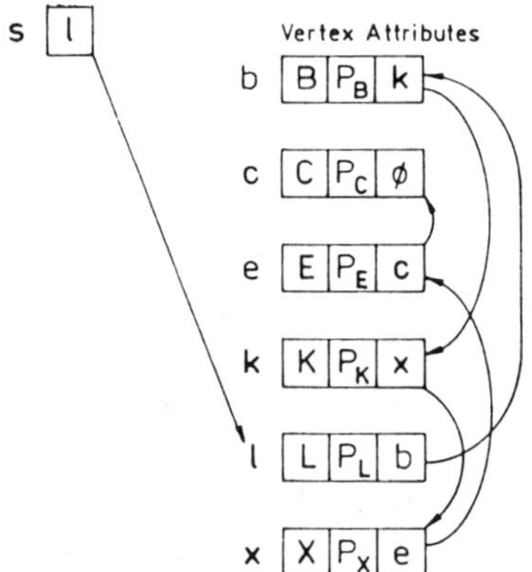

Figure 3.13 A List Stored in a Linked Allocation.

Linked allocations offer advantages over sequential and random access ones for certain list operations. It is easier to perform any operation that alters the absolute position of any vertex. Although a vertex's absolute position in the list is changed, its physical position in storage can remain unchanged. Only the contents of an attribute at a vertex is altered. Random access allocation also allows the storage position of the vertex to remain the same but the storage position of the pointer is changed. For example, if vertex **H** is inserted before node **X** in the list, the locations of **X**, **E**, and **C** must be moved in storage in a sequential allocation (Figure 3.14a). In a random access allocation, the locations of **x**, **e**, and **c** must be moved instead (Figure 3.14b). In a linked allocation, only the address attribute at vertex **K** is updated to **h** and the address value for vertex **H** is **x** (Figure 3.14c).

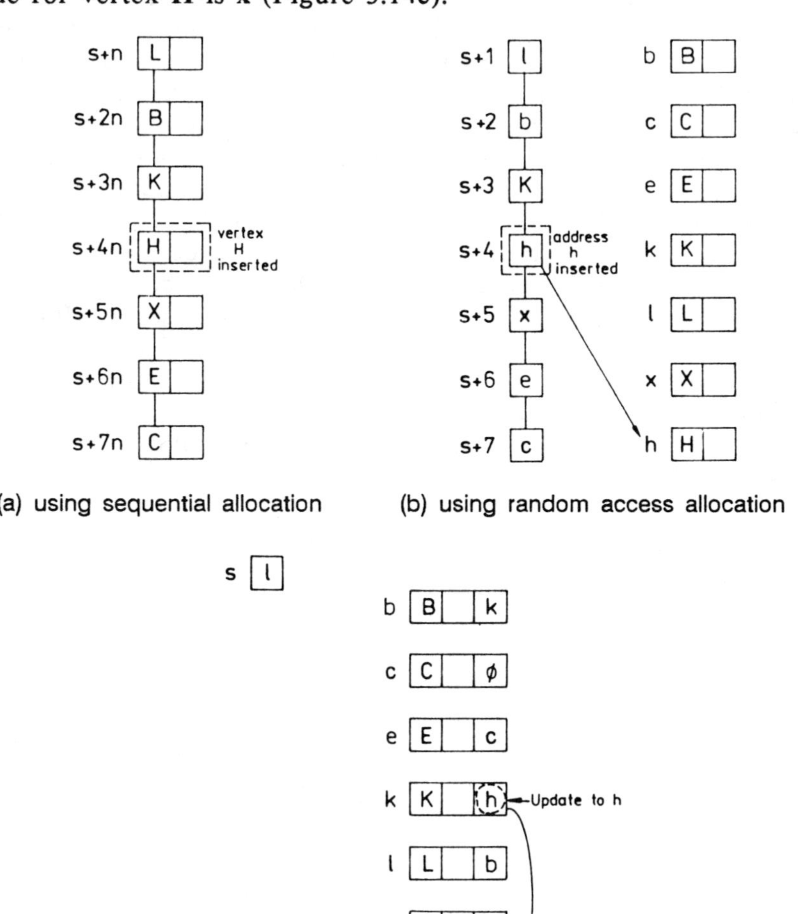

Figure 3.14 An Insertion Operation.

On the other hand, sequential and random access allocations offer advantages when performing any operation that does not change the absolute position of any node in the list. It is easier to search a list or gain access to the **jth** node if it is stored in either sequential or random access allocation. More will be discussed regarding search procedures in Chapter Four.

Two extensions of linear lists are *circular lists* and *double lists.* A circular list is a set of vertices that have a closed path topology. A circular list is stored in sequential allocation by repeating the first vertex as the last vertex of the array (Figure 3.15a). It is stored in a random access allocation by repeating the address of the first vertex as the address of the last vertex (Figure 3.15b). Finally, a circular list is most easily represented in a linked allocation by merely changing the null value of the address attribute for the last vertex to the address value of the first vertex (Figure 3.15c). The entry vertex (first vertex) for a circular list is generally very arbitrary. Double lists can be either linear or circular; in a double list one can move either forward or backward through the list of vertices. In a sequential or random access allocation, no modifications are necessary with respect to storage; movement can just occur in either direction in the array. In a linked allocation, a extra address pointer is necessary to denote the location of the predecessor vertex and the contents of the root vertex must also contain the address of the last vertex (Figure 3.16a).

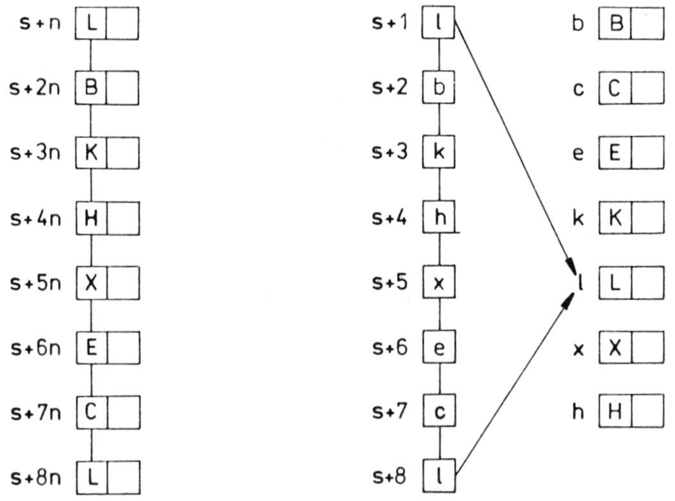

Figure 3.15 Representations of a Circular List.

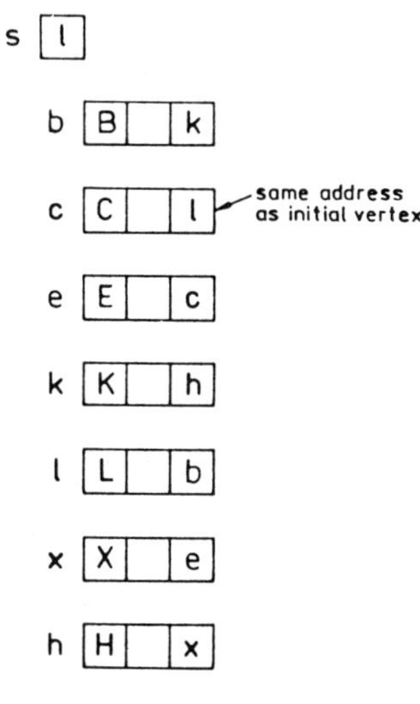

Figure 3.15 Representations of a Circular List (continued).

The deletion operation is easily performed using a double list in a linked allocation structure. If one knows which vertex is to be deleted, it is not necessary to search the list to find its position; one simply updates the forward vertex attribute of its predecessor to the address of its successor and the backward vertex attribute of its successor to the address of its predecessor. For example, if vertex **X** in Figure 3.16a is to be deleted, the successor vertex address for vertex **H** becomes **e** and the new predecessor vertex address for vertex **E** is **h** (Figure 3.16b). Although vertex **X** remains in its location, it is not an element of the list because it has no connection to any other element of the list.

3.2.2 Graphs and Trees

In a data structure, it is also possible for vertices to have more than one predecessor and successor vertex. A graph is a set of vertices that have a network topology. For example, any geographic base map can be represented by a graph. The vertices represent the regions of the base map and each pair of regions that share a common border are connected by a link (see Figure 3.17). The adjacency relations between vertices in a graph are symmetric and the link is represented diagrammatically by a line segment.

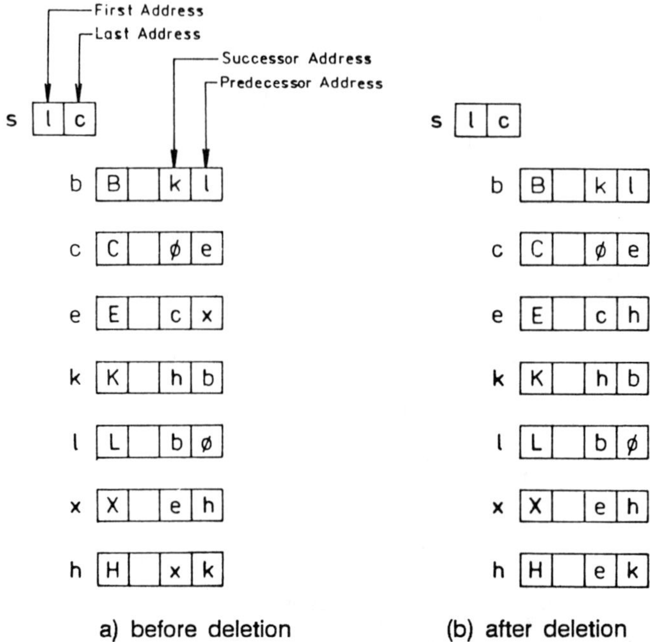

Figure 3.16 Double Lists and the Deletion Operation.

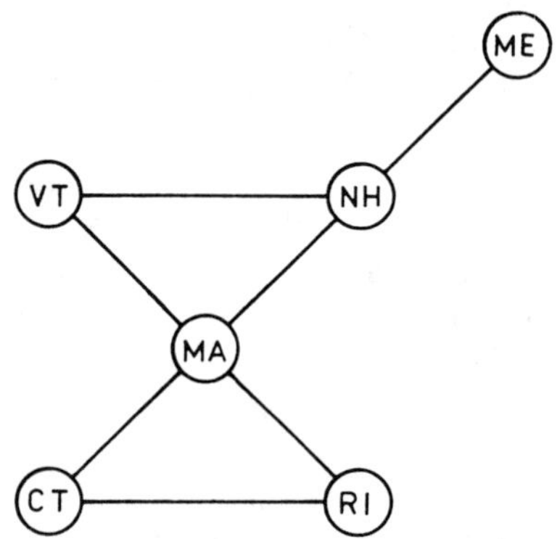

Figure 3.17 A Graph Representation of a Geographic Base Map.

In a directed graph, adjacency relations are potentially asymmetric. An arrowhead is added to denote the direction of the relationship. If vertex **A** is adjacent to vertex **B** but vertex **B** is not adjacent to vertex **A**, the arrowhead points from vertex **A** to vertex **B** (Figure 3.18). If the two vertices are mutually adjacent, arrowheads are given in both directions.

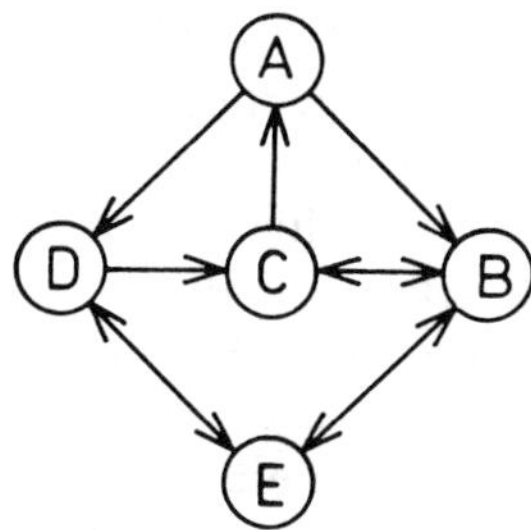

Figure 3.18 Directed Graph Relationships.

A *path* between two vertices, V_1 and V_2, is a list of the vertices that connect the first vertex to the last vertex given that each vertex in the list is distinct. Vertex V_1 is the head of the list and vertex V_2 is the tail of the list. In Figure 3.17, one path between vertex **A** and vertex **D** is the list {**A**, **B**, **C**, **E**, **D**}. A *minimal path* between two vertices is a list of vertices that minimizes some attribute with respect to the links of the path. A minimal path between vertex **A** and vertex **D** that minimizes the number of links is the list {**A**, **D**}.

A graph is *fully connected* if a path exists between every pair of nodes. A *cycle* is a path where the head and tail vertices are the same and no intermediate vertex is repeated. A fully connected graph that contains no cycles is known as a *tree*. In a tree there exists only one path between two vertices. In a rooted tree, there exists a root vertex that represents the higher order set that contains all the objects of the tree. Trees are usually organized hierarchically where one vertex is at the top and other vertices are at lower levels (Figure 3.19a). In this organization, each vertex of the tree has only one connection to a vertex at a higher level. The higher level vertex is again known as the predecessor vertex. A vertex can have more than one connection to vertices at a lower level; these nodes are again known as the successor nodes. At any level, vertices that have the same predecessor are known as *siblings*. In any tree diagram, we can denote the leftmost node of any set of siblings as the eldest sibling. The next leftmost node is the next younger sibling. The tree can be represented in storage in a link allocation as by the predecessor, eldest successor, and next younger sibling of each vertex (Figure 3.19b). In the overall hierarchy, a tree is a special subset of a graph and a list is a special subset of tree.

3.3 CARTOGRAPHIC OBJECTS AND THEIR NEIGHBORHOODS

In this chapter, the 0-cell, 1-cell, and 2-cell objects of a map were discussed in terms of their topological properties. This section defines the corresponding analog and digital cartographic representations of these objects and their respective neighborhoods. An *area* (an open 2-cell) is an open set of points on a manifold having a graph topology. A *region* (a closed 2-cell) is the closure of this set of points. The point neighborhood for a given point in a region is its ϵ-ball on a two-dimensional surface. An *interior region point* is one whose neighborhood is completely contained within the region (Figure 3.20); an *exterior region point* or *boundary point* is a point whose neighborhood lies partially outside the region (see Figure 3.20). An *exterior outline* then is a circular list of boundary points on the outer extremity of the region; an *interior outline* is a circular list of boundary points on an inner extremity of the region.

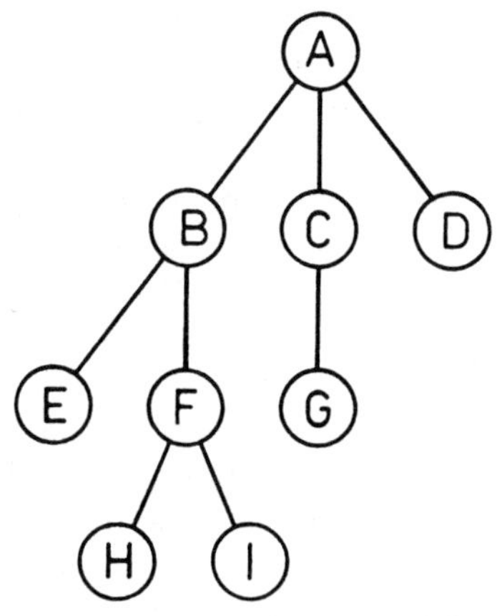

(a) diagram representation

VERTEX	PREDECESSOR	ELDEST SUCCESSOR	NEXT SIBLING
A	Ø	B	Ø
B	A	E	C
C	A	G	D
D	A	Ø	Ø
E	B	Ø	F
F	B	H	Ø
G	C	Ø	Ø
H	F	Ø	I
I	F	Ø	Ø

(b) linked allocation

Figure 3.19 A Tree Structure.

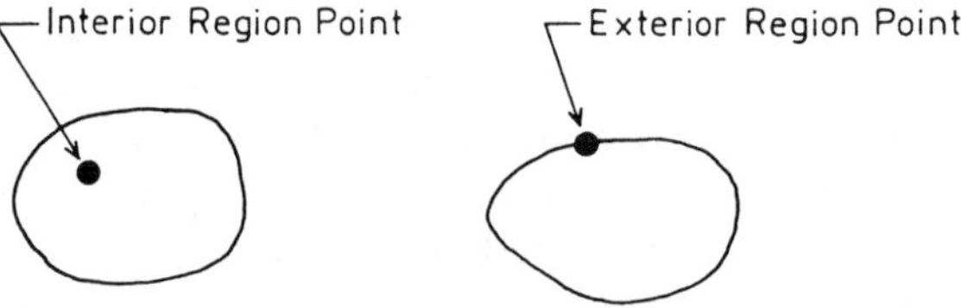

Figure 3.20 Interior and Exterior Region Points.

An *arc* (a 1-cell) is the list of exterior points formed by the nonempty intersection of two regions (Figure 3.21). An arc bounds two regions. A point neighborhood for a given point on an arc is the open interval containing the points that lie to either side of it on the line. An *interior arc point* is one whose neighborhood is completely contained in the domain of the arc (Figure 3.21); an *exterior arc point* is one whose neighborhood lies partially outside the domain of the arc. An exterior arc point is more commonly called a *node* (Figure 3.22). Arcs are bounded then by nodes.

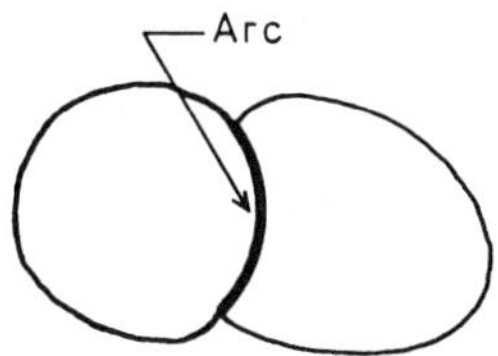

Figure 3.21 An Arc.

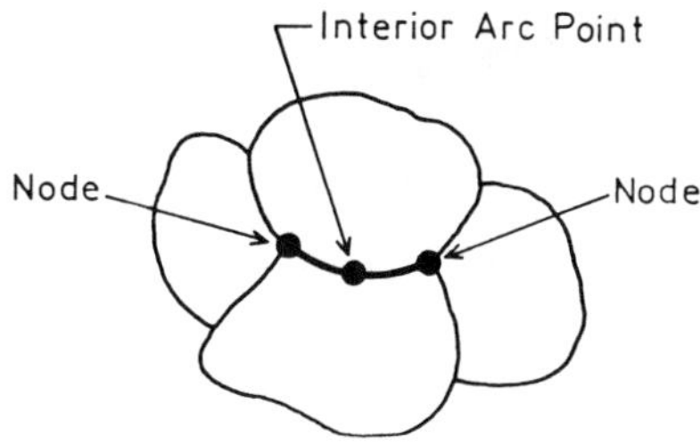

Figure 3.22 Interior Arc Points and Nodes.

If one region completely surrounds another region or regions, the surrounded region(s) is called an *island* (Figure 3.23). If the island consists of only one region, the arc formed by the intersection of the adjacent regions is a circular list; the head of this list is completely arbitrary. Although all points are interior arc points, the head of this list must be designated as an artifical node so that the arc will have a beginning and an end (Figure 3.24).

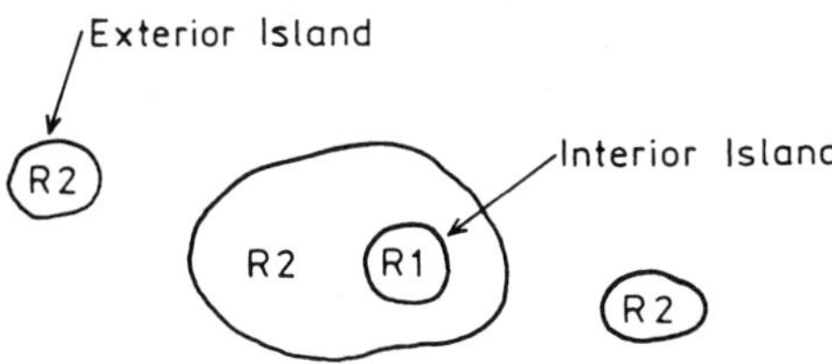

Figure 3.23 Islands.

Because there are an infinite number of points in an arc, an arc is caricaturized in digital representation a finite list of line segments called a *chain* (Figure 3.25). Chains are also frequently referenced by the list of points formed by the segment intersections (Figure 3.25). The nodes of a chain are the head and tail elements of the list, while all other elements are simple points of the chain.

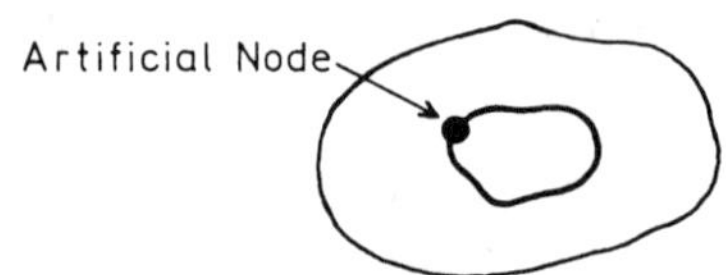

Figure 3.24 A Designated Artifical Node.

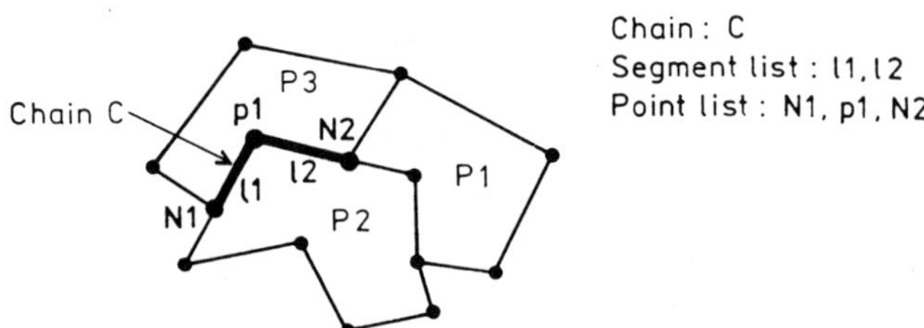

Figure 3.25 A Chain.

Finally, the caricaturized representation of a region is called a polygon (see Section 1.5). The boundary points of a polygon will consist of at least one exterior ring and zero or more interior rings and will be adjacent to other polygons (Figure 3.26). Figure 3.27 summarizes the transformation between analog cartographic objects and digital ones.

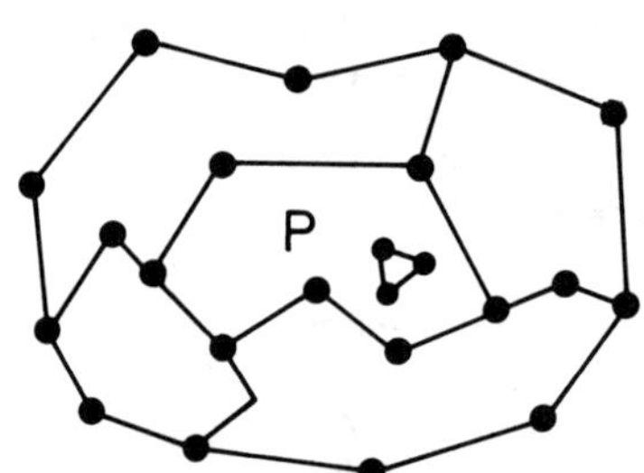

Figure 3.26 A Polygon.

The cobounding and adjacency relations between pairs of cartographic objects are now defined. A simple point **p** is equivalent to the coordinate **(x,y)** and is contained within chain **C**. It is also cobounded by a predecessor line segment **pL** and a successor segment **sL** (Figure 3.28). A node **N** is cobounded by a circular list of chains that can be sequenced in a counter-clockwise direction around it (Figure 3.29). (Note: an artificial node is contained in only one chain.) For each chain $\mathbf{C_i}$, node **N** is cobounded by a line segment $\mathbf{L_i}$ and is adjacent to node $\mathbf{N_i}$.

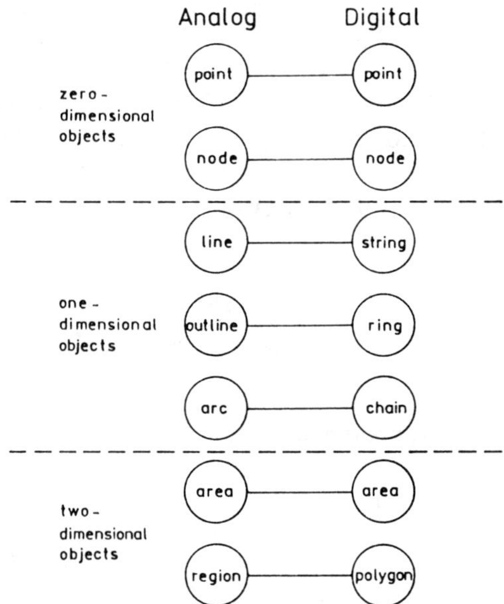

Figure 3.27 The Analog/Digital Transformation of Cartographic Objects.

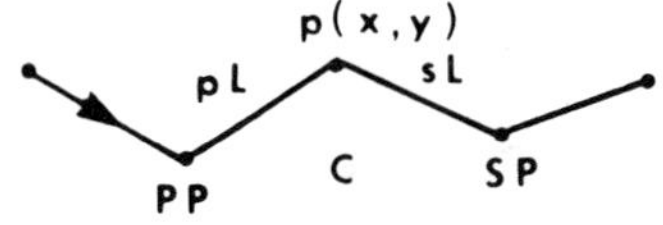

Figure 3.28 Point Cobounding Relations.

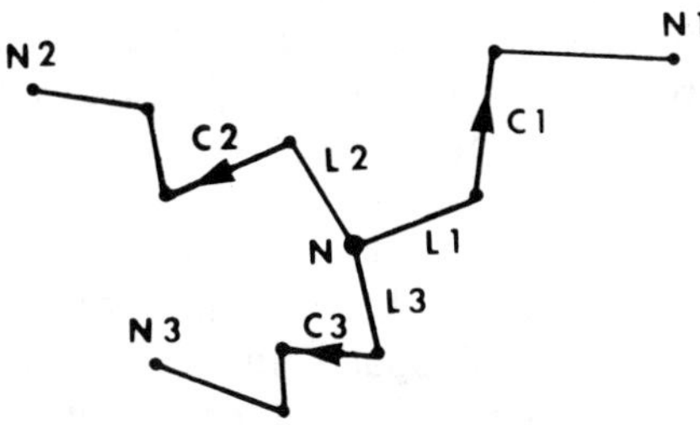

Figure 3.29 Node Neighborhood Relations.

A line segment **L** is contained within chain **C**. It is also cobounded by a predecessor segment **pL** and point **PP** and a successor segment **sL** and point **SP** (Figure 3.30). A chain **C** is alternatively equivalent to a list of line segments or a list of points. It is bounded by a predecessor node **pN** and a successor node **sN**. Given a direction of movement along chain **C** from node **pN** toward node **sN**, polygon **rP** is adjacent to **C** on the right and polygon **lP** is adjacent to it on the left (Figure 3.31). Additionally, chain **C** is cobounded by chain **rC** that is the next counter-clockwise chain around node **sN** and by chain **lC** that is the next counter-clockwise chain about node **pN** (Figure 3.31). If one moved clockwise around polygon **rP**, chain **rC** would be the next chain in order after chain **C**; similarly if one moved clockwise around polygon **lP**, chain **lC** would be the next chain in order after chain **C** (Figure 3.31).

Figure 3.30 Line Segment Neighborhood Relations.

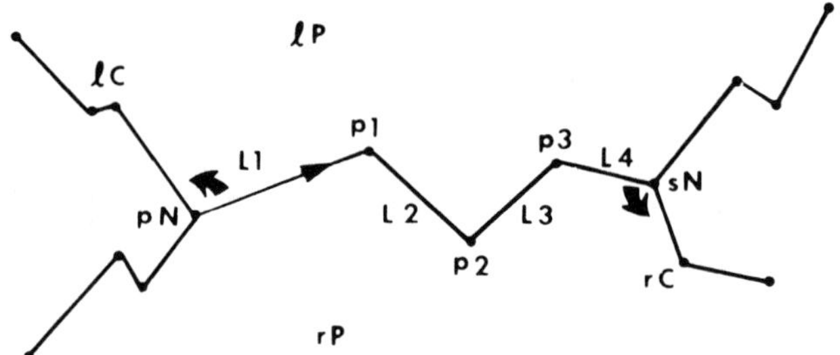

Figure 3.31 Chain Neighborhood Relations.

Next, a ring **R** bounds polygon **P**; as one moves either clockwise or counter-clockwise along ring **R**, polygon **P** always lies to its right (Figure 3.32). Ring **R** is comprised of a circular list of chains, a circular list of line segments or a circular list of points (Figure 3.32). Finally, a *complex* polygon is comprised of an unordered list of rings that contain its boundary points.

These cartographic objects and their topological relations form the basis for the representation of space in different vector data models. These data models are translated into data structures for organizing the data elements of a geographic base map in a machine environment (see Peucker and Chrisman, 1975; Peuquet, 1984; and Burrough, 1986). The following section examines alternative topological models and their corresponding data structures.

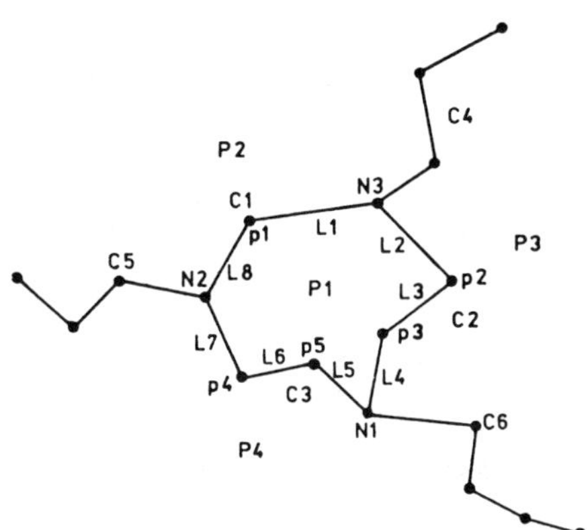

Figure 3.32 Polygon Neighborhood Relations.

3.4 TOPOLOGICAL DATA MODELS AND STRUCTURES

A major distinction among different vector data models is between those that have used a path topological approach versus those that have used a graph topological approach. In computer-assisted cartography, the latter are generally referred to as topological models while the former are called nontopological or geometric models. This distinction is misleading as the former focuses on the topology of boundaries or one-dimensional features as isolated entities while the latter focuses on the topology of regions or two-dimensional features in a coherent network. Today most vector models are a hybrid of both as path topological models became a subcomponent of the other.

3.4.1 Path Topological Models

One of the earliest path topological models came to be known as the *spaghetti model* [Chrisman, 1977]. In this model, the boundaries between areal units are recorded as strings of coordinates. There is not necessarily any correspondence between these strings and the boundary of individual polygons. For example, string **S1** in Table 3.1 traces portions of the boundaries belonging to polygons **P6**, **P4**, **P3**, **P2** and **P1** in Figure 3.33. Although base map outlines can be easily retrieved from this data model, it is difficult to perform any polygon operations with this structure.

Table 3.1 A Spaghetti Model Representation of New England

String	Coordinate List
S1	$(x_1,y_1),(x_2,y_2),(x_3,y_3),(x_4,y_4),(x_5,y_5),(x_6,y_6),(x_7,y_7),(x_8,y_8),(x_9,y_9),(x_{10},y_{10}),(x_{11},y_{11}),(x_{12},y_{12})$
S2	$(x_1,y_1),(x_{13},y_{13}),(x_{14},y_{14}),(x_{15},y_{15}),(x_{50},y_{50}),(x_{16},y_{16}),(x_{17},y_{17}),(x_{18},y_{18}),(x_{19},y_{19}),(x_{20},y_{20}),(x_{21},y_{21}),(x_{22},y_{22})$
S3	$(x_4,y_4),(x_{23},y_{23}),(x_{24},y_{24}),(x_{25},y_{25}),(x_{26},y_{26}),(x_{16},y_{16})$
S4	$(x_{23},y_{23}),(x_{27},y_{27}),(x_{28},y_{28}),(x_{15},y_{15})$
S5	$(x_{22},y_{22}),(x_{29},y_{29}),(x_{30},y_{30}),(x_{31},y_{31}),(x_{32},y_{32}),(x_{33},y_{33}),(x_{34},y_{34}),(x_{35},y_{35}),(x_{36},y_{36}),(x_{37},y_{37}),(x_{38},y_{38}),(x_{39},y_{39}),(x_{40},y_{40}),(x_{41},y_{41}),(x_{42},y_{42}),(x_{12},y_{12})$
S6	$(x_9,y_9),(x_{43},y_{43}),(x_{35},y_{35})$
S7	$(x_5,y_5),(x_{44},y_{44}),(x_{45},y_{45}),(x_{46},y_{46}),(x_{34},y_{34})$
S8	$(x_{44},y_{44}),(x_{47},y_{47}),(x_{48},y_{48}),(x_{49},y_{49}),(x_7,y_7)$

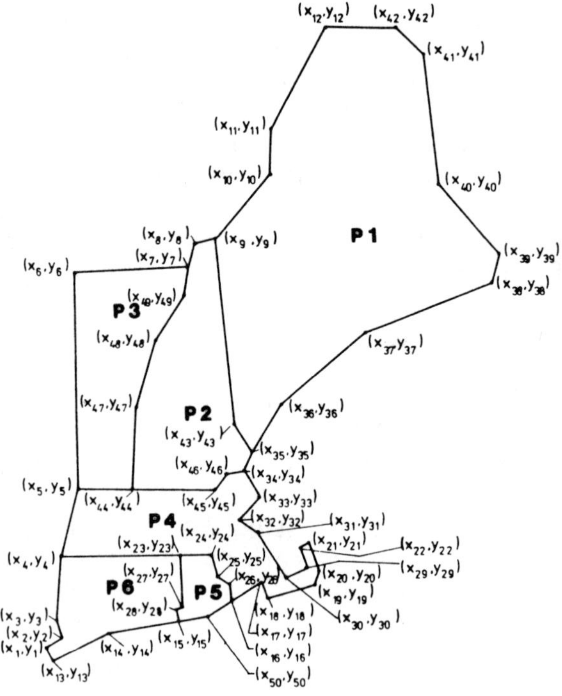

Figure 3.33 A Vector Caricature of the New England States.

To facilitate polygon operations, the *polygon model* records and stores the outline of each polygon independently as a circular list(s) of coordinates comprising its outline (Table 3.2). While the structure of this digital representation allows each entity to be easily identified in processing, the storage requirements are increased as the coordinates between polygons must be stored twice; and the editing of the digital image is more difficult as it is easy to mismatch the common string of points between two polygons. This latter phenomenon results in overlaps of gaps between polygons known as *slivers* [Peucker and Chrisman, 1975] (see Figure 3.34). Additionally, when all polygons are portrayed on a real map, the adjacency relations between polygons are also implicitly defined by the relative storage position of each polygon on the map. However, in a digital image, only the storage functions of a real map are present, nothing is visually implicit and the adjacency relations among polygons are difficult to reconstruct. Each adjacency can be identified by searching the polygon outline lists to find matching coordinate strings between two polygons.

Table 3.2 The Polygon Model Representation of New England (see Fig. 3.33)

Polygon	Coordinate List
P1	$(x_9,y_9),(x_{10},y_{10}),(x_{11},y_{11}),(x_{12},y_{12}),(x_{42},y_{42}),(x_{41},y_{41}),(x_{40},y_{40}),(x_{39},y_{39}),(x_{38},y_{38}),(x_{37},y_{37}),(x_{36},y_{36}),(x_{35},y_{35}),(x_{43},y_{43}),(x_9,y_9)$
P2	$(x_7,y_7),(x_8,y_8),(x_9,y_9),(x_{43},y_{43}),(x_{35},y_{35}),(x_{34},y_{34}),(x_{46},y_{46}),(x_{45},y_{45}),(x_{44},y_{44}),(x_{47},y_{47}),(x_{48},y_{48}),(x_{49},y_{49}),(x_7,y_7)$
P3	$(x_5,y_5),(x_6,y_6),(x_7,y_7),(x_{49},y_{49}),(x_{48},y_{48}),(x_{47},y_{47}),(x_{44},y_{44}),(x_5,y_5)$
P4	$(x_5,y_5),(x_{44},y_{44}),(x_{45},y_{45}),(x_{46},y_{46}),(x_{34},y_{34}),(x_{33},y_{33}),(x_{32},y_{32}),(x_{31},y_{31}),(x_{30},y_{30}),(x_{29},y_{29}),(x_{22},y_{22}),(x_{21},y_{21}),(x_{20},20),(x_{19},y_{19}),(x_{18},y_{18}),(x_{17},y_{17}),(x_{16},y_{16}),(x_{26},y_{26}),(x_{25},y_{25}),(x_{24},y_{24}),(x_{23},y_{23}),(x_4,y_4),(x_5,y_5)$
P5	$(x_{15},y_{15}),(x_{28},y_{28}),(x_{27},y_{27}),(x_{23},y_{23}),(x_{24},y_{24}),(x_{25},y_{25}),(x_{26},y_{26}),(x_{16},y_{16}),(x_{50},y_{50}),(x_{15},y_{15})$
P6	$(x_{23},y_{23}),(x_{27},y_{27}),(x_{28},y_{28}),(x_{15},y_{15}),(x_{14},y_{14}),(x_{13},y_{13}),(x_1,y_1),(x_2,y_2),(x_3,y_3),(x_4,y_4),(x_{23},y_{23})$

In general, effective editing procedures (see Chapter Four) and efficient display algorithms (see Chapter Six) are limited by these data structures. Besides the lack of any adjacency information between polygons, these first two models ignore the cobounding relations between zero- and one-dimensional objects.

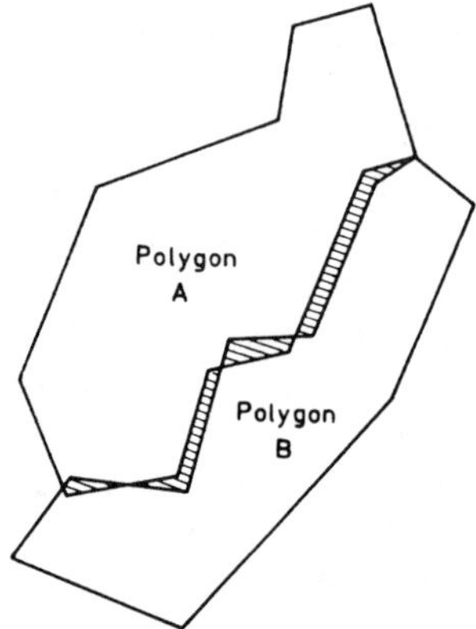

Figure 3.34 The Slivering Problem.

A marginal improvement over the earlier path topological models is the *point dictionary model*; in a point dictionary, the transformation between points and numerical coordinates is incorporated (Figure 3.35). All coordinate pairs are numbered sequentially and stored in a random access allocation. Each polygon is stored as a circular list of the point identification (ID) values that act as the address for accessing the appropriate coordinate (Table 3.3).

Table 3.3 The Point Dictionary Representation of New England

Polygon	Point List
P1	p9,p10,p11,p12,p42,p41,p40,p39,p38,p37,p36,p35,p43,p9
P2	p7,p8,p9,p43,p35,p34,p46,p45,p44,p47,p48,p49,p7
P3	p5,p6,p7,p49,p48,p47,p44,p5
P4	p4,p5,p44,p45,p46,p34,p33,p32,p31,p30,p29,p22,p21,p19, p18,p17,p16,p26,p25,p24,p23,p4
P5	p15,p28,p27,p23,p24,p25,p26,p16,p50,p15
P6	p1,p2,p3,p4,p23,p27,p28,p15,p14,p13,p1
Point	**Coordinate**
p1	(x_1,y_1)
p2	(x_2,y_2)
.	.
p50	(x_{50},y_{50})

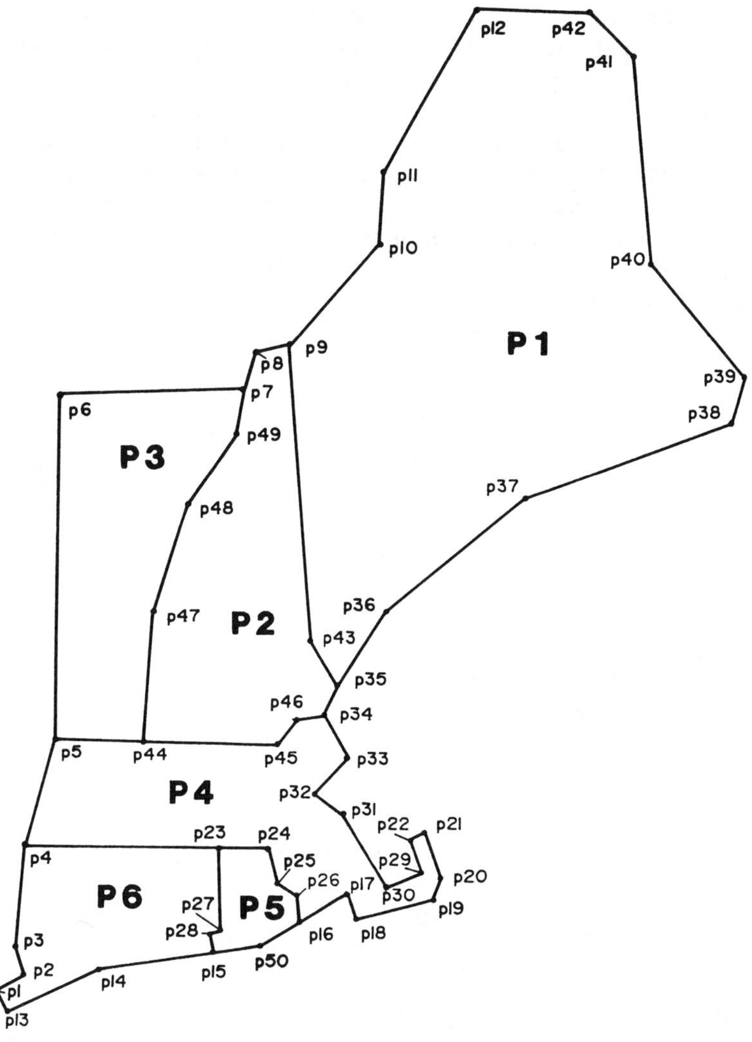

Figure 3.35 The Points Representing New England.

Any polygon display function now involves a composite retrieval operation as point ID values are first retrieved from the polygon list and in turn are used to retrieve the respective coordinates. In this approach, the storage requirements are slightly reduced as (x,y) pairs are stored only once in the point dictionary. However, each point ID is still recorded twice for common boundaries. Editing also is marginally improved as it is easier to detect the mismatch of point IDs rather than (x,y) pairs. This model retains the line retracing and adjacency problems of the polygon model.

The problems arising from the retracing of polygon rings are due to the improper identification of the elementary objects in a map [White, 1984]. Only one common boundary exists between two polygons; this shared boundary is the chain that bounds the two polygons. A further extension of path topological models incorporates the bounding and cobounding relations between polygons and chains (see Figure 3.36) and between chains and points (nodes are not recognized as being distinct from points). In the *chain/point dictionary model*, each polygon is now given as a circular list of chains and each chain in turn is a list of points (see Table 3.4).

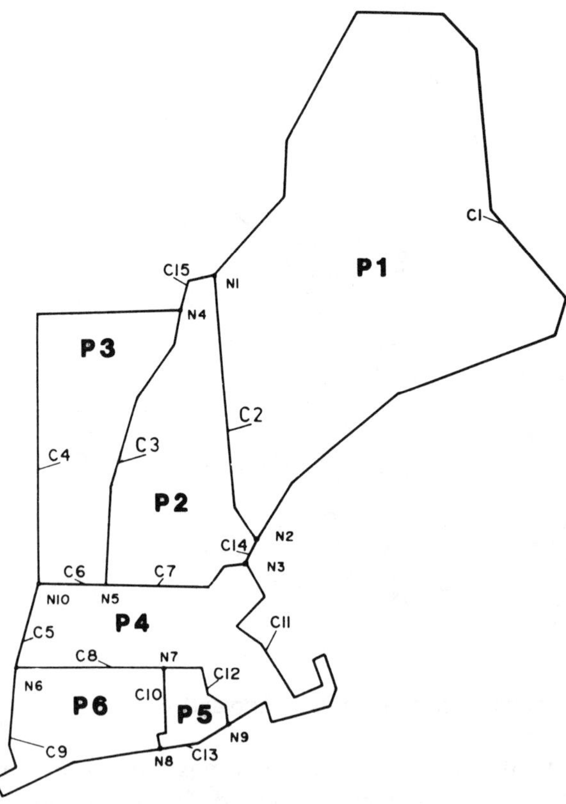

Figure 3.36 The Chains Representing New England.

The retrieval of a polygon outline is now a three-step process as chain ID values are first retrieved from the polygon list and in turn are used to retrieve the appropriate point IDs and finally the corresponding coordinates. The slivering problem is now eliminated if the same point

ID is given as the ending point for all chains that intersect at that common location.

Table 3.4 The Chain/Point Dictionary Representation of New England

Polygon	Chain List
P1	C1,C2
P2	C3,C15,C2,C14,C7
P3	C4,C3,C6
P4	C5,C6,C7,C11,C12,C8
P5	C10,C12,C13
P6	C9,C8,C10
Chain	**Point List**
C1	p9,p10,p11,p12,p42,p41,p40,p39,p38,p37,p36,p35
C2	p9,p43,p35
C3	p44,p47,p48,p49,p7
C4	p5,p6,p7
C5	p4,p5
C6	p5,p44
C7	p44,p45,p46,p34
C8	p4,p23
C9	p4,p3,p2,p1,p13,p14,p15
C10	p23,p27,p28,p15
C11	p16,p17,p18,p19,p20,p21,p22,p29,p30,p31,p32,p33,p34
C12	p23,p24,p25,p26,p16
C13	p15,p50,p16
C14	p34,p35
C15	p7,p8,p9

None of these models recognizes the difference between cartographic points and nodes; zero-dimensional objects are indistinguishable. More importantly, polygons are viewed as being independent objects. No neighborhood relationships between polygons are identified because the bounding function of chains has been omitted; no areal association that can be visualized in an analog map can easily be computed from any of these digital models.

3.4.2 Graph Topological Models

An early vector model that incorporated adjacency relations between polygons was the DIME (Dual Independent Map Encoding) file. The DIME file was developed by the U.S. Bureau of the Census for digitally storing the linear block faces of the Standard Metropolitan Statistical Areas (now called Metropolitan Statistical Areas) of the United States [Cooke and Maxfield, 1968]. The DIME file was an outgrowth of the ACG (Address Coding Guide) system whereby the Bureau of the Census could match a street address with a geographic location in a metropolitan area. This enabled the Bureau to use mailed census returns in 1970.

The basic unit of the DIME file is a DIME segment (Figure 3.37). A DIME segment is a straight line segment representing a portion of a street, political boundary, water feature, or railroad track. For each segment, the point IDs of the two endpoints are recorded as the "from" and "to" points giving direction to the segment. Given this direction the polygon IDs for the area to the right and left of the segment are recorded accordingly. More than one left and right area ID is attached to each segment as areas are organized hierarchically. The lowest areal unit is the block, followed by the block group and census tract, up to the state level. Therefore the left and right polygon IDs are the same if the segment is internal to an area; for example, if the segment is a portion of a street that lies inside an census tract, the left and right tract ID will be the same.

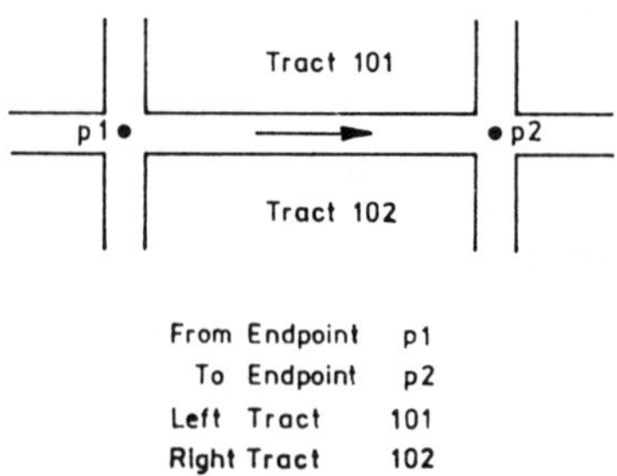

Figure 3.37 A DIME Segment.

It must be noted that the Census Bureau refers to the endpoints of a DIME segment as nodes but this definition is not consistent with the definition of a node given in this text. Although an endpoint bounds a segment, it is still an internal point of the chain bounding two adjacent polygonal units (with the exception of the block). Figure 3.38 identifies the corresponding DIME segments for the map of New England; the resulting DIME model for this map is presented in Table 3.5. The DIME data structure has certain advantages over the path topological models. Adjacency information between polygons can be readily accessed. Editing a base file with a DIME organization is facilitated by the dual relationship between the "from" and "to" point and right and left polygons.

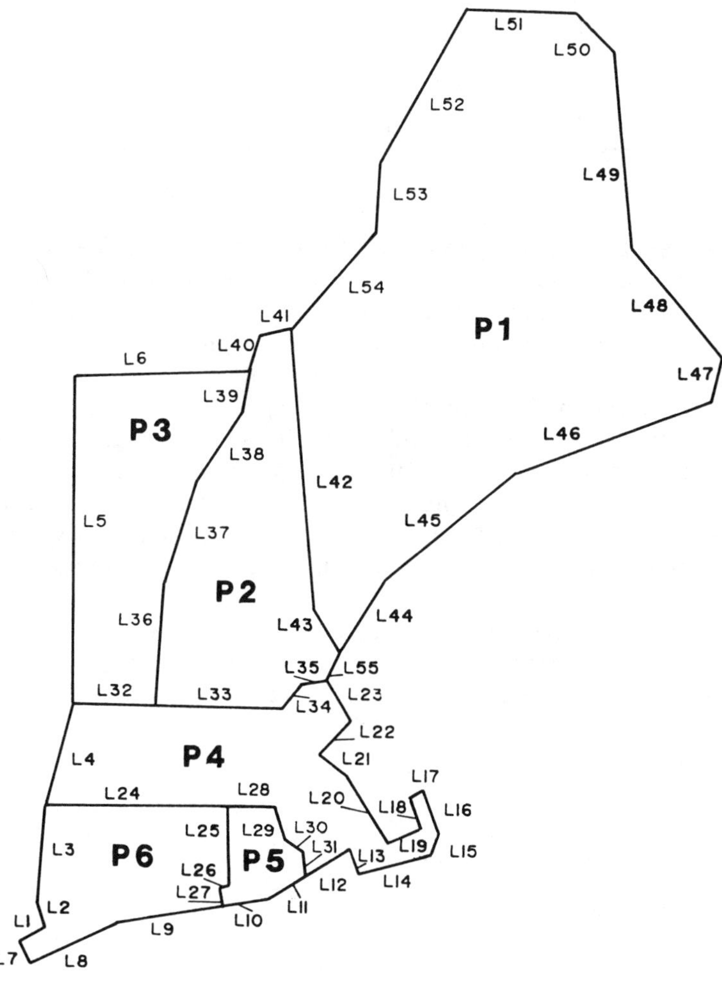

Figure 3.38 The Segments Representing New England.

Table 3.5 The DIME Representation of New England[a]

Line Segment	From Point	To Point	Left Polygon	Right Polygon
L1	p1	p2	P7	P6
L2	p2	p3	P7	P6
L3	p3	p4	P7	P6
.	.	.	.	.
L25	p23	p27	P5	P6
.	.	.	.	.
L54	p9	p10	P7	P1

[a]P7 denotes the background polygon

The retrieval of a polygon outline is more complicated because the path topology of these linear features is not explicitly defined. In stage one, an exhaustive search must be made to retrieve all segments for which a given polygon lies either to the right or left (but not both). For example, Table 3.6 presents the list of segments belonging to the boundary of polygon **P3**. In the next stage, these segments are ordered into a circular list so that the "to" endpoint of one segment is the "from" endpoint of the next segment (the endpoint of the last segment is the first node of the head segment in the list) (see Table 3.6). In this process, the "from" and "to" endpoint IDs are be switched when necessary so that the polygon always lies to the right of each segment.

Table 3.6 Extraction of a Polygon Outline from a DIME Model

Stage 1 - Retrieve all segments belonging to P3

L5	p5	p6	P7	P3
L6	p6	p7	P7	P3
L32	p5	p44	P3	P4
L36	p44	p47	P3	P2
L37	p48	p47	P2	P3
L38	p48	p49	P3	P2
L39	p49	p7	P3	P2

Table 3.6 Extraction of a Polygon Outline (continued)

Stage 2 - Reorder segments to create the path topology of the outline				
L5	p5	p6	P7	P3
L6	p6	p7	P7	P3
L39	p7	p49	P2	P3
L38	p49	p48	P2	P3
L37	p48	p47	P2	P3
L36	p47	p44	P2	P3
L32	p44	p6	P4	P3

To improve some of these deficiencies, the POLYVRT (POLYgon conVERTer) system was organized around a chain structure [Peucker and Chrisman, 1975]. The same relations for each chain are given as for each DIME segment except that the endpoint of a chain is now recognized to be a node rather than a point (nodes and points being distinctly different objects). For example, Table 3.7 presents the bounding relation between chains and nodes and the same relation between the chains and polygons presented in Figure 3.39. Additionally, the sequence of points for each chain is stored in a separate file; only a pointer to the start of the sequence was stored with the chain file. Finally, a polygon file is added where a circular list of chains comprising each polygon is recorded. The POLYVRT model is a synthesis of the chain/point dictionary model and the DIME model although the point dictionary is partitioned into separate point and node dictionaries.

All of the path and graph topological models presented thus far use either a sequential or random access file structure. Secondly, DIME and POLYVRT use a linear feature (segment or chain) as the basic unit for storing the neighborhood relations between nodes, chains, and polygons. Another approach is to organize these relations in a node structure [Brassel, 1977; Cromley, 1984]. For each node, the ID values for each adjacent node are recorded in a counter-clockwise direction. Any node is restricted to having only three adjacent node neighbors; if four or more adjacent nodes exist for any node in practice, a new node is added that occupies the same geographic location (Figure 3.40). The chain between these nodes will have a zero length. Next, the polygon ID values are recorded for the three polygons that are the right-hand polygons of the chain that cobounds the node and each of its respective adjacent nodes. Finally, the chain ID values are recorded for these cobounding chains.

The node relations for Figure 3.39 are given in Table 3.8. In addition to this file of neighborhood relations, a polygon file containing the ID value of one node on its boundary and a chain file containing its list of points are included in the model.

Table 3.7 The POLYVRT Topology of New England

Chain	From Node	To Node	Left Polygon	Right Polygon
C1	N1	N2	P7	P1
C2	N2	N1	P2	P1
C3	N5	N4	P3	P2
C4	N10	N4	P7	P3
C5	N6	N10	P7	P4
C6	N5	N10	P4	P3
C7	N5	N3	P2	P4
C8	N6	N7	P4	P6
C9	N6	N8	P6	P7
C10	N8	N7	P6	P5
C11	N9	N3	P4	P7
C12	N7	N9	P4	P5
C13	N8	N9	P5	P7
C14	N3	N2	P2	P7
C15	N4	N1	P7	P2

The node model has a linked allocation file structure. The boundary of individual polygons is retrieved by cross-referencing the node neighborhood relation file with the polygon file that contains a starting node ID for each polygon. Given the starting node ID for a polygon **P**, that node ID's record is scanned to find **P**. The next node in the polygon boundary is the adjacent node for which **P** is the right-hand polygon. The first chain of the boundary is the corresponding cobounding chain. The next chain and new pointer node ID is found by scanning the contents of the current node to determine the location of **P**. The entire sequence of nodes and chains that comprise the boundary of **P** has been enumerated when the next node ID is the same as the original node ID.

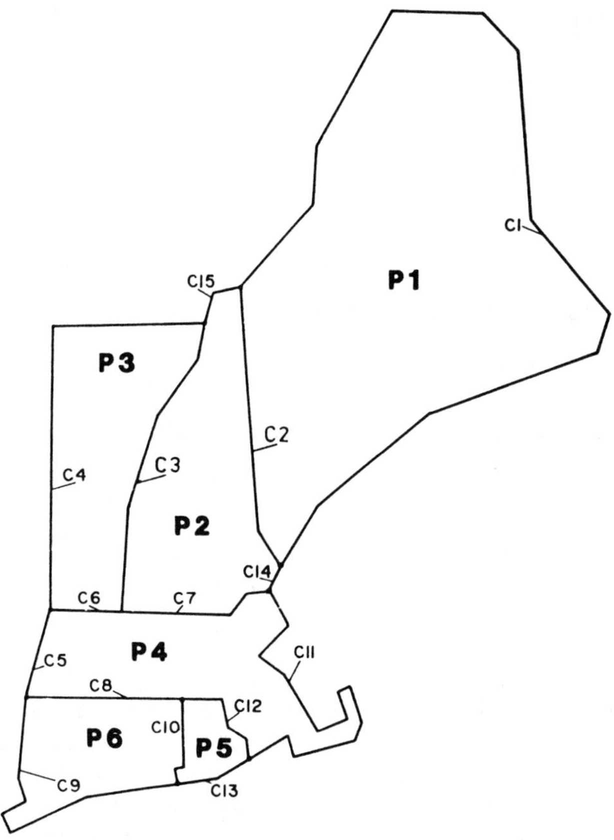

Figure 3.39 The Node Locations for New England.

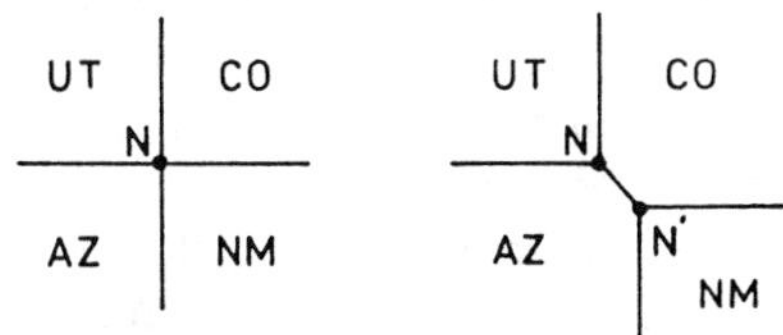

Figure 3.40 The Four Corner Situation.

Table 3.8 A Node Model Representation of New England

Node	Cobounding Chains			Right-Hand Polygons			Adjoining Nodes		
N1	C15	C2	C1	P7	P2	P1	N4	N2	N2
N2	C14	C1	C2	P2	P7	P1	N3	N1	N1
N3	C7	C11	C14	P2	P4	P7	N5	N9	N2
N4	C15	C4	C3	P2	P7	P3	N1	N10	N5
N5	C3	C6	C7	P2	P3	P4	N4	N10	N3
N6	C5	C9	C8	P4	P7	P6	N10	N8	N7
N7	C8	C10	C12	P4	P6	P5	N6	N8	N9
N8	C9	C13	C10	P6	P7	P5	N6	N9	N7
N9	C11	C12	C13	P7	P4	P5	N3	N7	N8
N10	C4	C5	C6	P3	P7	P4	N4	N6	N5

Polygon	Node	Polygon	Node
P1	N1	P4	N5
P2	N3	P5	N8
P3	N4	P6	N8

For example, in Table 3.8 the boundary of polygon **P3** is retrieved by accessing the polygon file to find an initial node ID value of **N10**; **P3** is the right-hand polygon for adjacent node **N4** and cobounding chain **C4**. Next, **P3** is the right-hand polygon for adjacent node **N5** and chain **C3**. Finally, it is the right-hand polygon for adjacent node **N10** and chain **C6**.

Another linked allocation model is the extended chain model that is a modification of the DIME and POLYVRT structures. The DIME file is deficient because it lacks any cobounding relations between DIME segments. The POLYVRT also lacks an explicit description of these connections; the connections between chains are implied by a chain's position in the circular list of chains comprising a polygon outline. The neighborhood of a chain can be extended to include the chain ID of the next counter-clockwise chain about an node in either direction (refer to Figure 3.31) [Marx, 1986; Herring, 1987]. As one would walk clockwise around the outline of an individual polygon, these chains would be the next chain in order.

The neighborhood relation for each chain **C** now includes the first and last nodes, the right and left polygons, and the corresponding right chain **rC** and left chain **lC**. The right chain is the next chain in order for the right polygon and the left chain is the next chain in sequence for the left polygon. In addition, a polygon file containing the ID of one chain on its boundary and a chain file containing its list of points are included. Such a system has been used to create extended DIME segments [Annitto and Cromley, 1987] to facilitate the retrieval of block group or census tract outlines in metropolitan areas. The new TIGER system of the U.S. Census uses this extended chain framework for storing their 1-cell relationships and retrieving the outlines of 2-cells [see Marx, 1986].

Table 3.9 The Extended Chain Model

Chain	From Node	To Node	Left Polygon	Right Polygon	Left Chain	Right Chain
C1	N1	N2	P7	P1	C15	C2
C2	N2	N1	P2	P1	C14	C1
C3	N5	N4	P3	P3	C6	C15
C4	N10	N4	P7	P3	C5	C3
C5	N6	N10	P7	P4	C9	C6
C6	N5	N10	P4	P3	C7	C4
C7	N5	N3	P2	P4	C3	C11
C8	N6	N7	P4	P6	C5	C10
C9	N6	N8	P6	P7	C8	C13
C10	N8	N7	P6	P5	C9	C12
C11	N9	N3	P4	P7	C12	C14
C12	N7	N9	P4	P5	C8	C13
C13	N8	N9	P5	P7	C10	C11
C14	N3	N2	P2	P7	C7	C1
C15	N4	N1	P7	P2	C4	C2

The extended chain relation for Figure 3.39 is presented in Table 3.9. To retrieve the boundary for polygon **P3**, chain ID **C3** is retrieved as the starting chain from the polygon file. Its contents are scanned in the chain relation to see if **P3** is its left or right polygon; because it is the right polygon, chain **C6** is the next chain in sequence. Next, the contents of **C6** are examined and because **P3** is its left polygon, **C4** is the next chain. Finally, upon examining the contents of **C4**, **P3** is its right polygon and the corresponding right chain is the same as the first chain.

The discussion here is not exhaustive of every possible method for organizing the basic geographical data elements found in a map (for further examples including hierarchical structures, see Brassel, 1977; Cook, 1977; Cooke, 1977; Morehouse, 1985). The most appropriate model to use depends on the functions needed by the cartographic processing system. Certain functions need explicit pointers between different data elements in other to link the components together in an efficient manner. To facilitate an understanding of these relationships, Gold [1988] has developed PAN (Polygons, Arcs, Nodes) graphs as an aid in developing the requisite data structure for a particular purpose. In a PAN graph, each class of objects is given a vertex in the graph. In Figure 3.41, the vertex labelled as **P** denotes the vertex associated with polygons, **A** is the vertex associated with arcs (it could be labelled **C** for chains), and **N** is the vertex associated with nodes. An arrow connecting one vertex to another in the graph indicates that objects in one class have points either to objects in another class or other objects within the same class. For example, in the node structure, nodes have pointers to other nodes, to polygons, and to arcs (chains) so there would be arrows connecting nodes to each of these classes of objects (Figure 3.41a). In addition, polygons have pointers to nodes and there is an arrow connecting vertex **P** to vertex **N**. From this diagram, it is easy to see that if the boundary of a polygon is to be retrieved it would be a two-step process involving the node set as an intermediary. Alternatively, in the extended chain structure, chains (arcs) are connected to another chains, polygons, and nodes (Figure 3.41b). If pointers also existed between polygons and chains, then an arrow would connect polyons to chains also. With this connection the boundary of a polygon is directly retrieved; without it the chain set would be searched first to establish which polygons are associated with which chains.

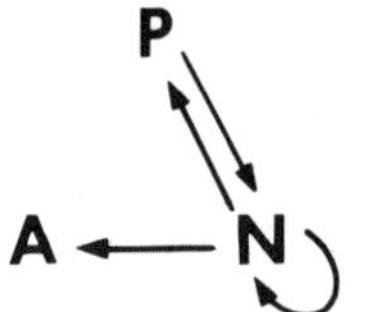

(a) the node structure

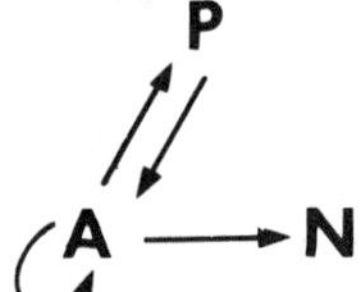

(b) the extended chain structure

Figure 3.41 Example PAN Graphs.

Other approaches have been used to sort out the most efficient structure for data organization. Van Roessel [1986; 1987] has provided a useful theoretical perspective on spatial data structures based on principles from relational database management theory (see Date [1985] for more details regarding the relational model). The organizational unit of a relational database is a relation. However, to be efficient every relation should be normalized. Normalized relations have the property that the relation is really a function; instead of a many-to-many correspondence between objects there is a one-to-many correspondence.

An inspection of a point dictionary relation would show a many-to-many correspondence between polygons and points. This correspondence for Figure 3.42 is presented in Figure 3.43a. Such a relation has low informational content as confusion can easily occur regarding which polygon matches which point. The potential for slivers is much higher in such a situation as slivers are caused by the independent digitizing of each polygon containing the points. The informational content is increased in the chain/point dictionary model as the chain-point relation is almost one-to-many except for the endpoints (the nodes) of each chain (Figure 3.43b). This confusion is removed by recognizing nodes as being distinct from points (Figure 3.43c).

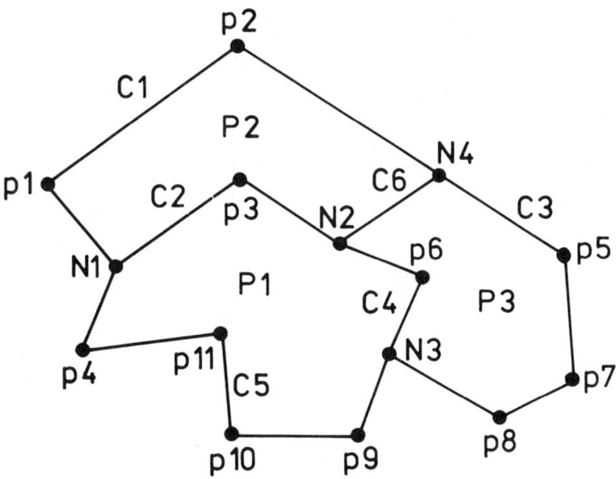

Figure 3.42 An Example Digital Caricature.

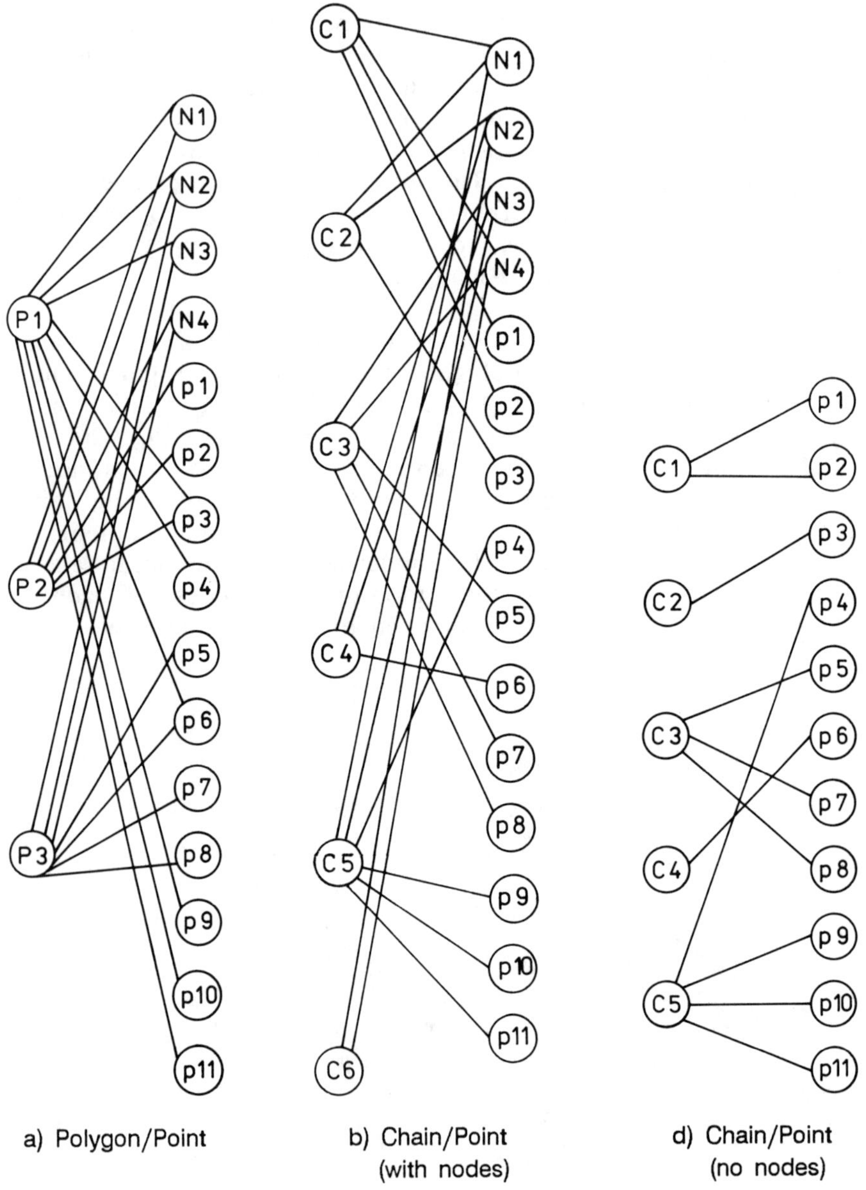

Figure 3.43 Differing Relations Between Spatial Objects.

The same analysis is appropriate for examining the structure of the graph topology. For example, for each chain there is only one right polygon given a 'from' node; this (node,polygon) pair forms a unique unit that is associated with the given chain (see Figure 3.44a) in the same manner that (x,y) is a unique coordinate unit associated with a point or node. The other node that cobounds the chain also forms a unique (node,polygon) pair with the other polygon that the chain bounds (Figure 3.44b). Given a (node,polygon) pair, the corresponding chain is immediately known; conversely, given a chain, a small degree of confusion exists as one of two (node,polygon) pairs could be retrieved. This fact enables data structures based on the chain as the primary object to be more efficient than ones where the polygon is the organizing object because the polygon/chain relation has a many-to-many correspondence (Figure 3.45).

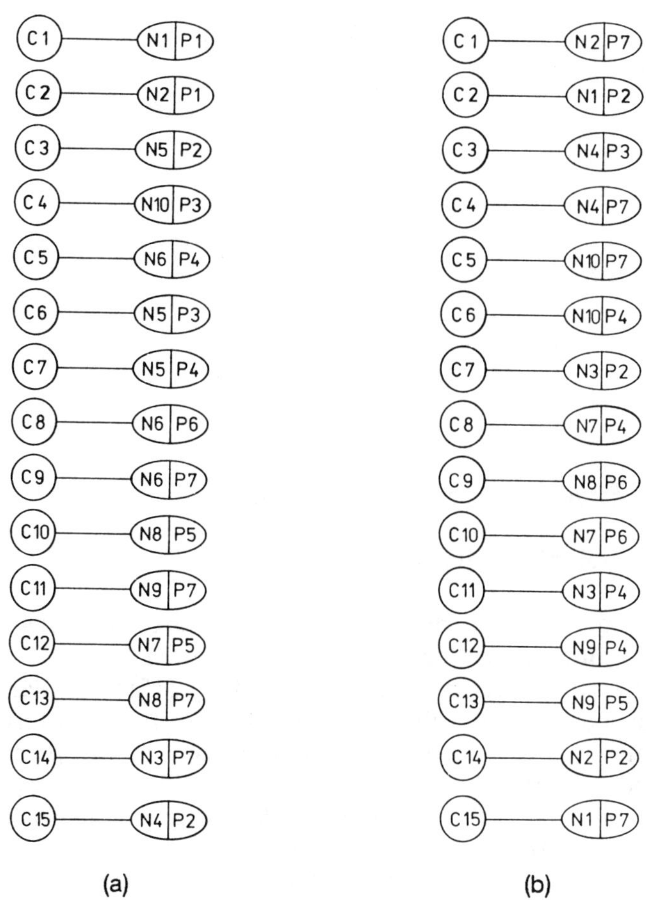

Figure 3.44 Chain/(Node-Polygon) Relations for New England.

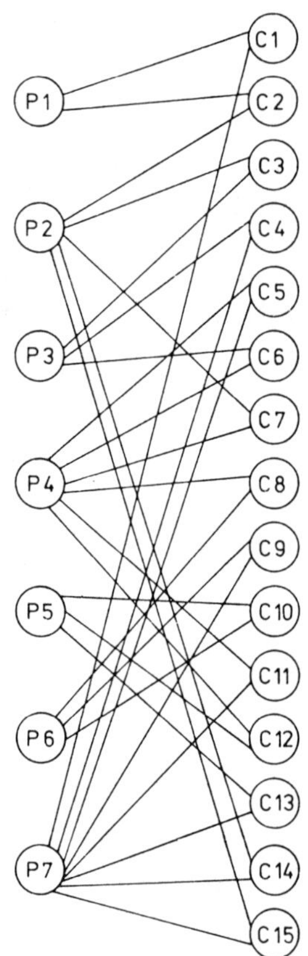

Figure 3.45 Polygon/Chain Relation for New England.

3.4.3 Other Topological Models

Frequently, geographic data for surfaces are not aggregated into polygonal units but are collected at control points located at irregularly spaced intervals that reflect changes in the surface. Earlier in this chapter, it was noted that a duality exists between the structure of incident cells. The dual object of a 2-cell (polygon) in the primal structure is a 0-cell (node) in the dual (see Figure 3.4). The control points represent the dual nodes of this network. A triangular mesh results from connecting each control point on the surface to its neighboring points (Figure 3.46). The orientation of the triangles (the 2-cell duals of the 0-cell nodes in the primal) do not remain constant but change to correspond to changes in the orientation of the surface. An imaginary control point **C8** is added in Figure 3.46 to the original seven control points to represent the background area; dashed lines represent connections to this point. The basic objects of the resulting triangular irregular network (TIN) are the control points themselves which are now vertices of triangles, the triangles formed by the connections between control points, and the connections themselves representing the sides of the triangles.

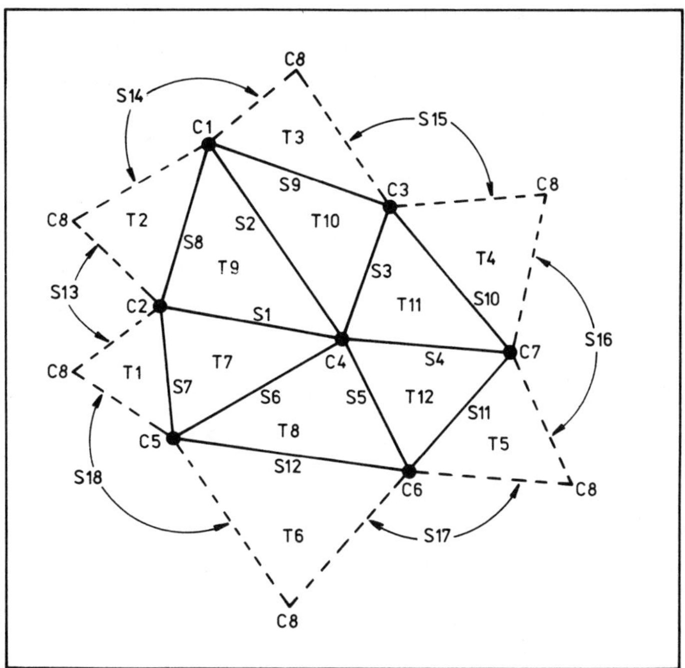

Figure 3.46 A Triangulation of Irregularly Spaced Control Points.

This information is organized into a data structure based on the bounding and cobounding relations of the network [Peucker, 1975; Elfick, 1978; Gold, 1978; Mark, 1978]. Normally, the organizational unit of this structure is the triangle. For each triangle, the IDs of the three triangles that share a common side are recorded [Elfick, 1978]. Next, the control point ID corresponding to the point that is to the right of a line from the given triangle to respective cobounding triangle. The corresponding side IDs can also be recorded but the location of each side is implicit in the location of the two control points that are its endpoints. Therefore, the sides are frequently omitted. The triangle data structure for Figure 3.46 is presented in Table 3.10. Gold [1988] has shown how the data structure of the dual model corresponds to that of the primal using the PAN graph construct; each vertex of the primal network is replaced by its dual object while the orientation of the arrow pointers remains the same. The TIN data structure presented here is the dual of the node model given in the previous section because the triangles, control points, and triangle sides in a triangulated network are the dual objects to nodes, polygons and chains respectively in a vector-based digital geographic base map.

One problem associated with an irregular triangulated network is that there are many different triangulations that can be created from the same point distribution [Elfick, 1978; Peuquet, 1985]. One special TIN is based on a Delaunay triangulation of the point distribution. A Delaunay triangulation is based on the connecting of each control point to its respective Thiessen or Voronoi neighbors.

Table 3.10 A TIN Representation

Triangles	Bounding Connections			Cobounding Control Points			Adjacent Triangles		
T1	S13	S18	S7	C2	C8	C5	T2	T6	T7
T2	S14	S13	S8	C1	C8	C2	T3	T1	T9
T3	S15	S14	S9	C3	C8	C1	T4	T2	T10
T4	S16	S15	S10	C7	C8	C3	T5	T3	T11
T5	S17	S16	S11	C6	C8	C7	T6	T4	T12
T6	S18	S17	S12	C5	C8	C6	T1	T5	T8
T7	S7	S6	S1	C2	C5	C4	T1	T8	T9
T8	S6	S12	S5	C4	C5	C6	T7	T6	T12
T9	S8	S1	S2	C1	C2	C4	T2	T7	T10
T10	S9	S2	S3	C3	C1	C4	T3	T9	T11
T11	S10	S3	S4	C7	C3	C4	T4	T10	T12
T12	S11	S4	S5	C6	C7	C4	T5	T11	T8

A Thiessen or Voronoi diagram is a partitioning of space based on proximity regions. Given a set of n control points or Thiessen centroids on a plane bounded by a convex polygon, each centroid can be used to generate a Thiessen polygon such that all points contained in the interior of the polygon are closer to that polygon's centroid than to any centroid [Brassel and Reif, 1979; Cromley and Grogan, 1985] (Figure 3.47). A Thiessen polygon is a connected set. The convex bounding polygon **P** is defined by a set of **m** edges that separate of points enclosed by **P** from those of its unbounded complement **P′** (the background polygon). The problem of delineating these polygons is equivalent to finding a set of **p** points that are equidistant and closest to three centroids; these points are called Thiessen vertices. Each Thiessen vertex that lies on the convex bounding polygon is called a boundary Thiessen vertex; all others are known as interior Thiessen vertices. A Thiessen edge is a line segment equidistant and closest to two centroids.

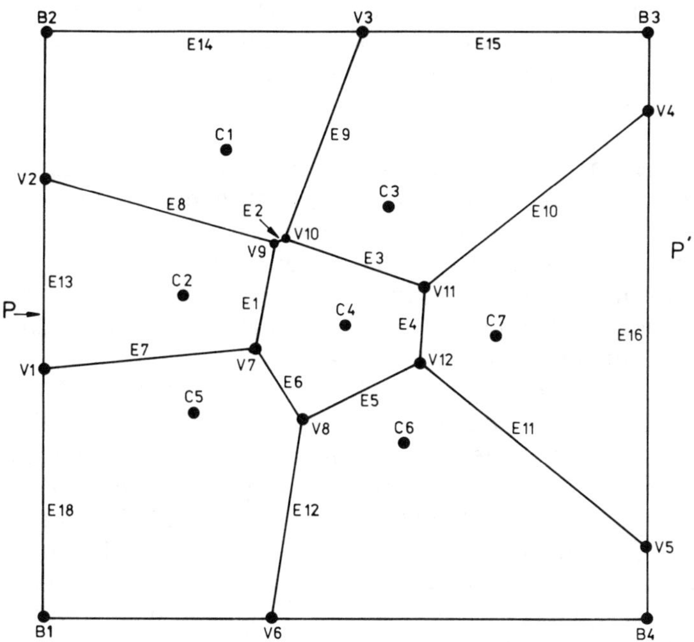

Figure 3.47 An Example Thiessen Diagram.

A backgound Thiessen centroid exists such that each bounding edge is equidistant between it and the respective interior centroids. Each portion of the convex boundary that is connected by two boundary Thiessen vertices is called a boundary Thiessen edge. Each Thiessen vertex is directly connected to three other Thiessen vertices by either a boundary or interior Thiessen edge. Alternatively, each Thiessen vertex is formed by the intersection of three Thiessen edges. Each boundary Thiessen vertex lies on a bounding edge that connects two sequentially numbered bounding vertices ({**B1**, **B2**, **B3**, **B4**} in Figure 3.47).

One centroid is called a Thiessen neighbor of another centroid if the polygons associated with the two centroids cobound a common Thiessen edge. If two centroids only cobound a common Thiessen vertex (a degenerate edge), they are called Thiessen half-neighbors. However, as in the node model, an additional vertex having the same location can be added so that each vertex will cobound exactly three Thiessen edges although an edge may have a length of zero.

It is important to enumerate each Thiessen vertex and edge because an exact number of them exist as a transformation of the number of centroids. For a Thiessen diagram containing **n** centroids, there are **3(n-2)** Thiessen edges and **2(n-2)** Thiessen vertices. Given a bounding polygon, there are **n+1** centroids resulting in **3(n-1)** edges and **2(n-1)** vertices. For the Thiessen diagram presented in Figure 3.44, there are **3(7-1)** or **18** edges and **2(7-1)** or **12** vertices.

The Thiessen diagram is the dual of the Delaunay triangulation. Each Thiessen vertex is also the circumcenter of a circle that enscribes each Delaunay triangle (see Figure 3.48). One can again construct a Thiessen data structure that parallels the TIN model (and the node model) because Thiessen centroids, vertices, and edges are the dual objects of control points, triangles, and sides in the triangulation. If the Thiessen vertex lies on the boundary, the next element is the reference value of the lower number boundary vertex of the bounding edge on which that Thiessen vertex lies. In Figure 3.47, the reference value for **V1** is **B1** as it lies on the bounding edge connecting **B1** and **B2**, while the reference value for **V5** is **B3** as it lies on the bounding edge connecting **B3** and **B4**. Table 3.11 contains the full data structure for the Thiessen diagram in Figure 3.47. The outlines of individual Thiessen polygons can also be retrieved in the same manner as the outlines of polygons in the node model if one also records the reference value of one vertex that lies on the boundary of respective Thiessen polygons.

Another partitioning of area within a closed polygon is to subdivide the space within a polygon into subpolygons such that the interior points of each subpolygon are closer to one edge of the polygon than any other edge in the polygon outline (Figure 3.49a). Such a partition is called a bimedial skeleton [Montanori, 1969]. A modification of this problem is to partition the space into subpolygons whose area is closer to one edge of the polygon or its internal linear extension than to any other edge or their corresponding internal extension; this partition is called the bisector skeleton of the polygon [Brassel, Heller and Jones, 1984] (Figure 3.49b). In these situations the subpolygons are not necessarily convex. However if the polygon is convex, then the bimedial and bisector skeletons will coincide and each subpolygon will be convex (Figure 3.50).

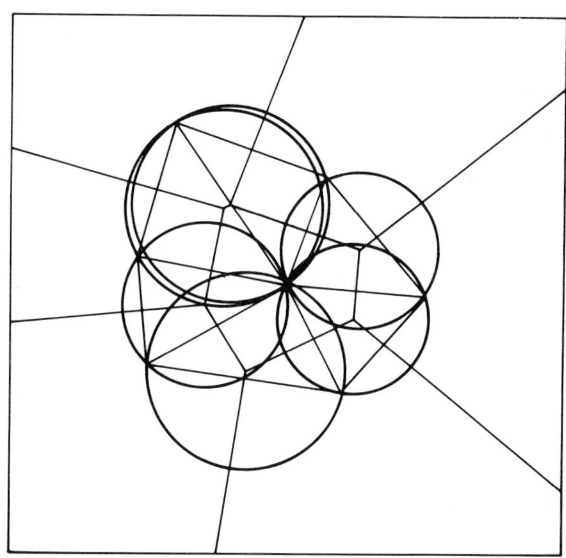

Figure 3.48 The Thiessen Vertex Circles Enscribing Delaunay Triangles.

Table 3.11 A Thiessen Diagram Representation

Vertices	Cobounding Edges			Cobounding Control Points			Adjoining Vertices			Boundary Vertex
V1	E13	E18	E7	C2	C8	C5	V2	V6	V7	B1
V2	E14	E13	E8	C1	C8	C2	V3	V1	V9	B1
V3	E15	E14	E9	C3	C8	C1	V4	V2	V10	B2
V4	E16	E15	E10	C7	C8	C3	V5	V3	V11	B2
V5	E17	E16	E11	C6	C8	C7	V6	V4	V12	B3
V6	E18	E17	E12	C5	C8	C6	V1	V5	V8	B4
V7	E7	E6	E1	C2	C5	C4	V1	V8	V9	0
V8	E6	E12	E5	C4	C5	C6	V7	V6	V12	0
V9	E8	E1	E2	C1	C2	C4	V2	V7	V10	0
V10	E9	E2	E3	C3	C1	C4	V3	V9	V11	0
V11	E10	E3	E4	C7	C3	C4	V4	V10	V12	0
V12	E11	E4	E5	C6	C7	C4	V5	V11	V8	0

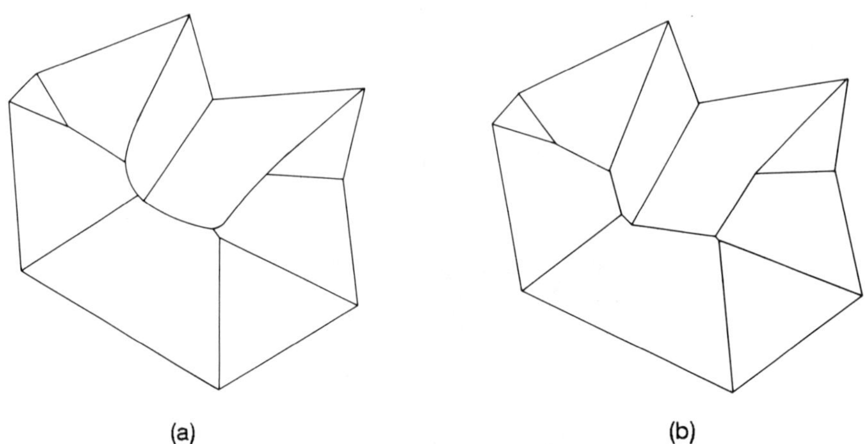

Figure 3.49 Bimedial and Bisector Skeletons.

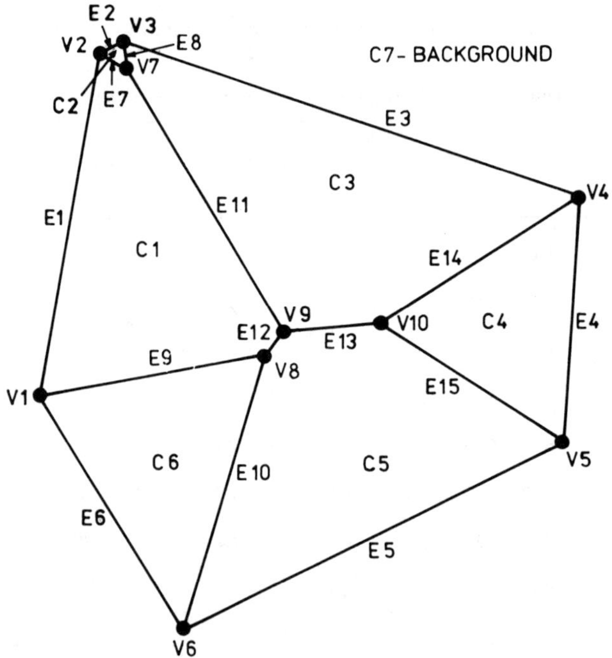

Figure 3.50 The Bimedial and Bisector Skeleton of a Convex Polygon.

There is a clear correspondence between Thiessen diagrams and skeleton diagrams. Just as each Thiessen vertex is equidistant to three centroids polygon, a skeleton vertex is one that is equidistant and closest to either three polygons' edges (Figure 3.51a) or three polygons' edges and their interior linear extension (Figure 3.51b.) The set of skeleton vertices can also be partitioned into interior and boundary subsets. The boundary vertices are equivalent to the endpoints of each polygon edge. Thus, a data structure for a Thiessen diagram can be transformed into one for a skeleton diagram. Table 3.12 presents the corresponding vertex data structure for the skeletons in Figure 3.50.

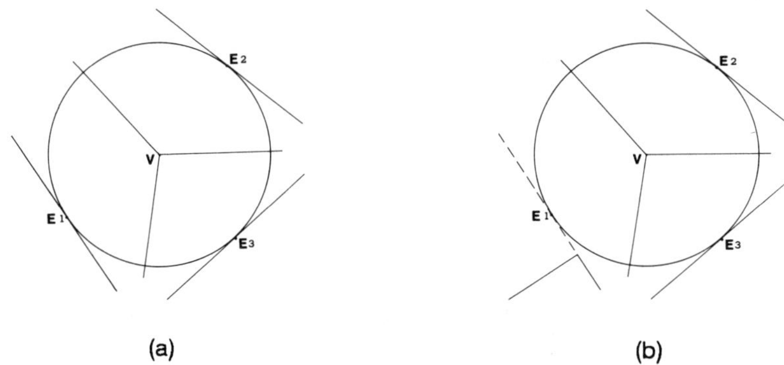

Figure 3.51 Skeleton Vertices and Their Nearest Edges.

Table 3.12 A Vertex Data Structure for Storing a Skeleton Diagram

Vertices	Cobounding Edges			Cobounding Subpolygon			Adjoining Vertices		
V1	E6	E9	E1	C7	C6	C1	V6	V8	V2
V2	E1	E7	E2	C7	C1	C2	V1	V7	V3
V3	E2	E8	E3	C7	C2	C3	V2	V7	V4
V4	E3	E14	E4	C7	C3	C4	V3	V10	V5
V5	E4	E15	E5	C7	C4	C5	V4	V10	V6
V6	E5	E10	E6	C7	C5	C6	V5	V8	V1
V7	E8	E7	E11	C3	C2	C1	V3	V2	V9
V8	E9	E10	E12	C1	C6	C5	V1	V6	V9
V9	E13	E11	E12	C5	C3	C1	V10	V7	V8
V10	E14	E13	E15	C4	C3	C5	V4	V9	V5

However, for polygons with no interior ring(s), the graph topology of a skeleton is a tree once the edges of the original polygon are removed and can be also represented in a tree data structure. For example, Figure 3.52 is the tree associated with Figure 3.50.

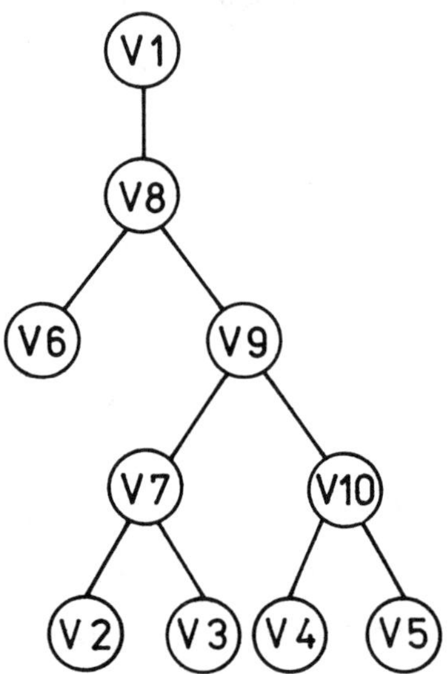

Figure 5.52 A Skeleton Tree Diagram.

Bimedial and bisector skeleton diagrams are used in Chapter Five to identify center points within polygonal outlines.

3.5 TESSELLATION DATA STRUCTURES

Tessellation models are an alternative to the vector approach. The basic data unit in a tessellation model is a unit of area corresponding to the interior of a region. The three basic areal units that have been used in regular tessellations are squares, triangles, and hexagons. Each shape has different geometric properties that distinguish it from the others. One characteristic is orientation; objects in both square and hexagonal patterns have the same orientation while, in a triangular mesh, objects have a different orientation (see Figure 3.53). A second characteristic is whether two-dimensional space can be recursively subdivided using that shape; both squares and triangles can be subdivided infinitely while a hexagon cannot. Hexagons however have the property of radial symmetry; all neighboring cells of a given cell are the same distance to the center-point of that cell (Figure 3.54). Hexagons also form the most compact shape good for spatial sampling. The square mesh on the other hand is most compatible with array data structures and a cartesian coordinate system. Digital remotely sensed data from LANDSAT (see Chapter Four) and output devices such as line printers and color raster terminals also favor the grid cell structure. The advantages of the square mesh sufficiently outweigh the other two so that it is the most frequently used.

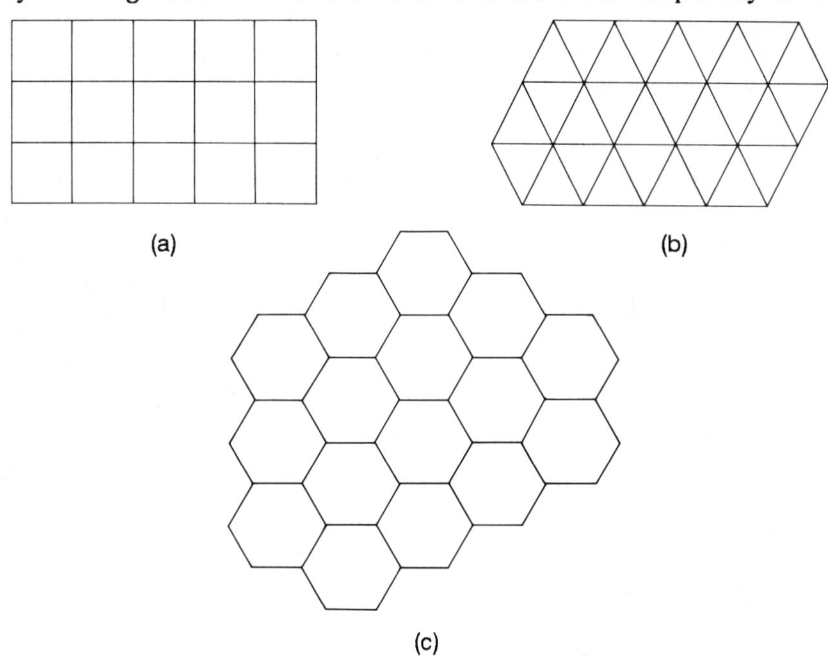

Figure 3.53 The Orientation Property.
(after Peuquet, 1984)

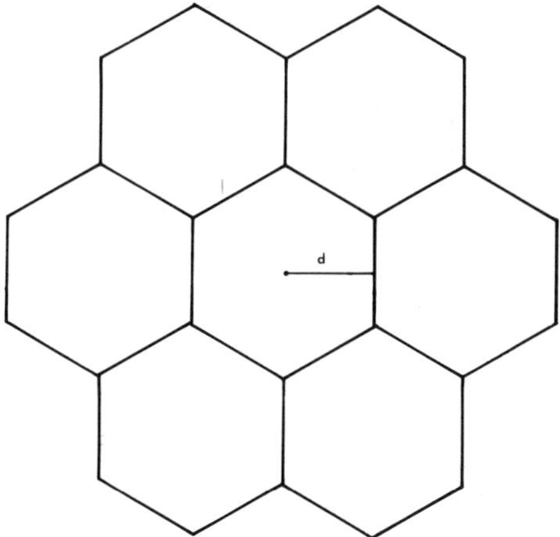

Figure 3.54 The Radial Symmetry Property.

The simplest data structure for encoding a map in a square tessellation is a rasterization of the map. The area of the map is converted into a grid cell overlay (Figure 3.55a); each cell (pixel) is assigned to a region based on some rule (see section 4.2.1). This information is then stored as a matrix of data (P7 is added for the background) (Figure 3.55b). Depending on the size of the raster units, the stylized representation of the map can be very crude (Figure 3.55c); the representation can be improved by making the pixels smaller but this increases the volume of data that is stored in the digital representation.

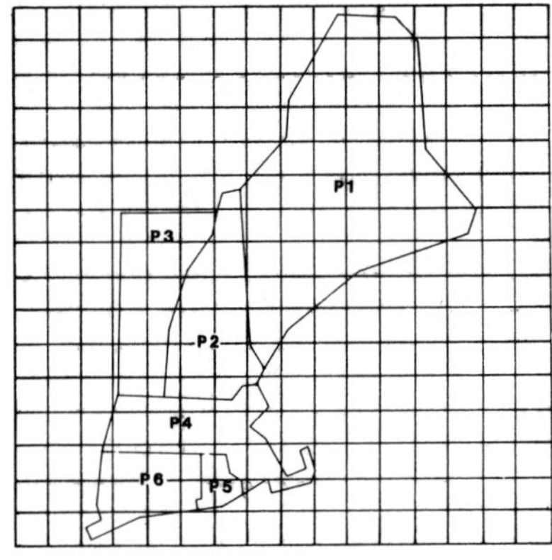

(a) a grid cell overlay

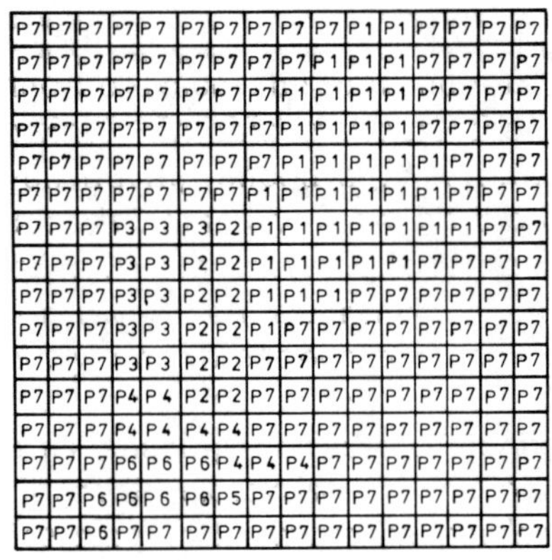

P7	P7	P7	P7	P7	P7	P7	P7	P7	P7	P1	P1	P7	P7	P7	P7
P7	P7	P7	P7	P7	P7	P7	P7	P7	P1	P1	P1	P7	P7	P7	P7
P7	P7	P7	P7	P7	P7	P7	P7	P1	P1	P1	P1	P7	P7	P7	P7
P7	P7	P7	P7	P7	P7	P7	P7	P1	P1	P1	P1	P7	P7	P7	P7
P7	P7	P7	P7	P7	P7	P7	P7	P1	P1	P1	P1	P1	P7	P7	P7
P7	P7	P7	P7	P7	P7	P7	P1	P1	P1	P1	P1	P1	P7	P7	P7
P7	P7	P7	P3	P3	P3	P2	P1	P1	P1	P1	P1	P1	P1	P7	P7
P7	P7	P7	P3	P3	P2	P2	P1	P1	P1	P1	P1	P7	P7	P7	P7
P7	P7	P7	P3	P3	P2	P2	P1	P1	P1	P7	P7	P7	P7	P7	P7
P7	P7	P7	P3	P3	P2	P2	P1	P7	P7	P7	P7	P7	P7	P7	P7
P7	P7	P7	P3	P3	P2	P2	P7	P7	P7	P7	P7	P7	P7	P7	P7
P7	P7	P7	P4	P4	P2	P2	P7	P7	P7	P7	P7	P7	P7	P7	P7
P7	P7	P7	P4	P4	P4	P4	P7	P7	P7	P7	P7	P7	P7	P7	P7
P7	P7	P7	P6	P6	P6	P4	P4	P4	P7	P7	P7	P7	P7	P7	P7
P7	P7	P6	P6	P6	P6	P5	P7	P7	P7	P7	P7	P7	P7	P7	P7
P7	P7	P6	P7	P7	P7	P7	P7	P7	P7	P7	P7	P7	P7	P7	P7

b) a matrix representation

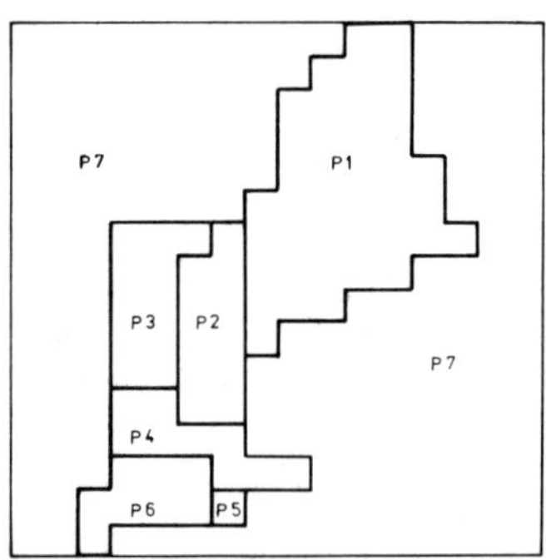

c) the raster caricature of New England

Figure 3.55 The Rasterization Process.

These data can easily be retrieved and a display formed. However, in a rasterization the integrity of a region and the graph topology between regions is lost; only connections between pixels are implicitly retained by their row and column index. A second disadvantage of this approach is that the matrix of data values has very little informational content. A large homogeneous region is now replaced by many pixels having the same value as the original region.

To increase the informational content and thereby reduce storage requirements, the scan line concept was introduced [Scripter, 1969]. A scan line is one row of the matrix. Instead of stopping at individual pixels, region segments were identified. The only items recorded for each scan line were the number of regions transversed by the scan line, the region ID value for each region crossed and the column where a region segment ended on the line (Figure 3.56). This structure is more compact for storing regionalized categories. In many applications only a single scan line must be processed at once so that storage requirements are reduced.

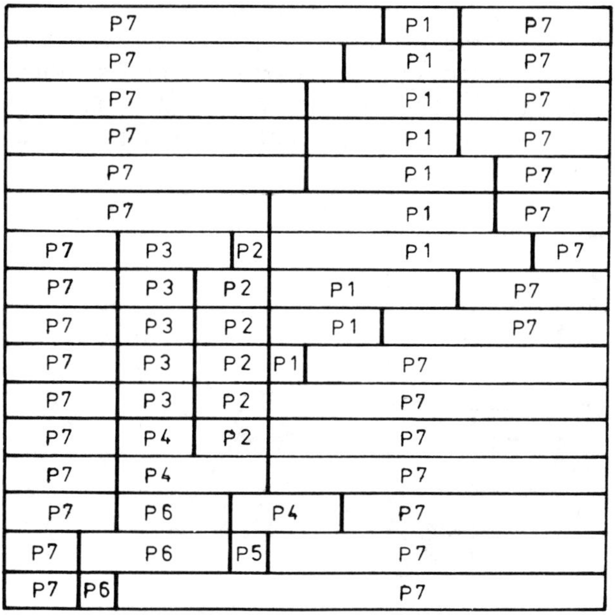

P7 P1 P7
P7 P1 P7
P7 P1 P7
P7 P1 P7
P7 P1 P7
P7 P1 P7
P7 P3 P2 P1 P7
P7 P3 P2 P1 P7
P7 P3 P2 P1 P7
P7 P3 P2 P1 P7
P7 P3 P2 P7
P7 P4 P2 P7
P7 P4 P7
P7 P6 P4 P7
P7 P6 P5 P7
P7 P6 P7

Figure 3.56 A Scan Line Structure.

Scan lines, however, only improve compactness in one direction. The encoding of areas still includes a lot of redundant data. To improve the overall informational content of objects present in the data model, maximal blocks are used. A maximal block is the largest square block that contains a homogeneous area. A region also can be represented by the recursive subdivision of two-dimensional space into quadrants stored in a tree structure. Each vertex of the a tree corresponds to the notion of a maximal block [Rosenfeld and Samet, 1979; Samet, 1985]. The recursive units are not necessarily maximal due to the imposed divisions. The root vertex of the tree represents the geographic domain of the mapping space. If the entire space of the root vertex is not occupied by the region, it is subdivided into quadrants; each quadrant is a leaf of the root vertex and the eldest sibling is the northwest quadrant followed in turn by the northeast, southwest, and southeast quadrants. If the region fully occupies one of these leafs, subdivision of that leaf is terminated and is colored black (signifying it's an element of the region). If none of the region is contained within the area of a leaf, subdivision of that leaf is also terminated and colored white to signify that it is not an element of the region but of its complement. If only part of the leaf area is occupied by the region, then the leaf is colored gray and must be further subdivided to find smaller maximal blocks.

In Figure 3.57a, a given region (shaded gray) does not occupy the entire mapping area and the mapping area is first divided into four quadrants. Of these four quadrants, the northwest and southeast ones are not homogeneous and must be further subdivided into smaller quadrants which are homogeneous. Figure 3.57b presents the quad-tree representation of this region.

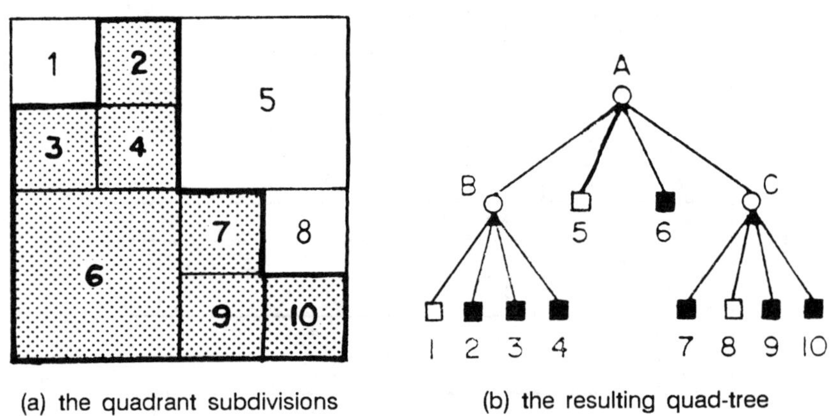

(a) the quadrant subdivisions

(b) the resulting quad-tree

Figure 3.57 A Quad-tree Representation of a Region. (after Samet, 1985)

If more than one region is being encoded, black leafs are given different colors that correspond to the appropriate region and white leafs correspond to the background. For example, Figure 3.58 presents the multi-colored quad-tree for New England.

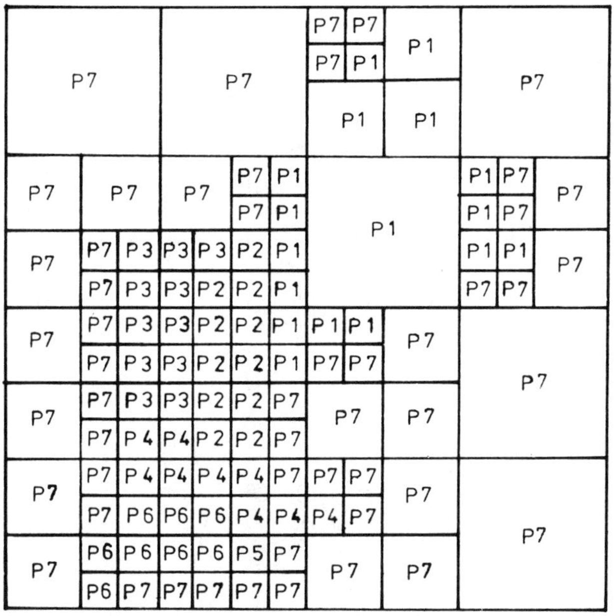

(a) the quadrant subdivisions for New England

Figure 3.58 A Quad-tree Data Structure for New England.

Quad-trees have several important properties in addition to their compactness of space. First, spatial detail can rapidly be attained by recursive division by a power of four. This division can proceed until the resolution of the image being encoded is reached. Secondly, it is possible to perform union and intersection operations on quad-trees as leaf operations (see Samet, 1985). Third, the neighbors of a particular block can easily be retrieved.

3.6 LINEAR INDEXING TRANSFORMATIONS

There has been recent interest in the transformation of a graph topology (which may be a tree) into a path topology. The purpose of this transformation is to order the objects of the data model in a linear sequence while preserving some of the spatial connections between objects. A space transformation can be applied to any set of spatial units, either polygons, irregularly spaced control point data or regular tessellations. Space-filling curves, also known as Peano scans, have several properties [Peuquet, 1984]. First, the curve must pass once through every object in

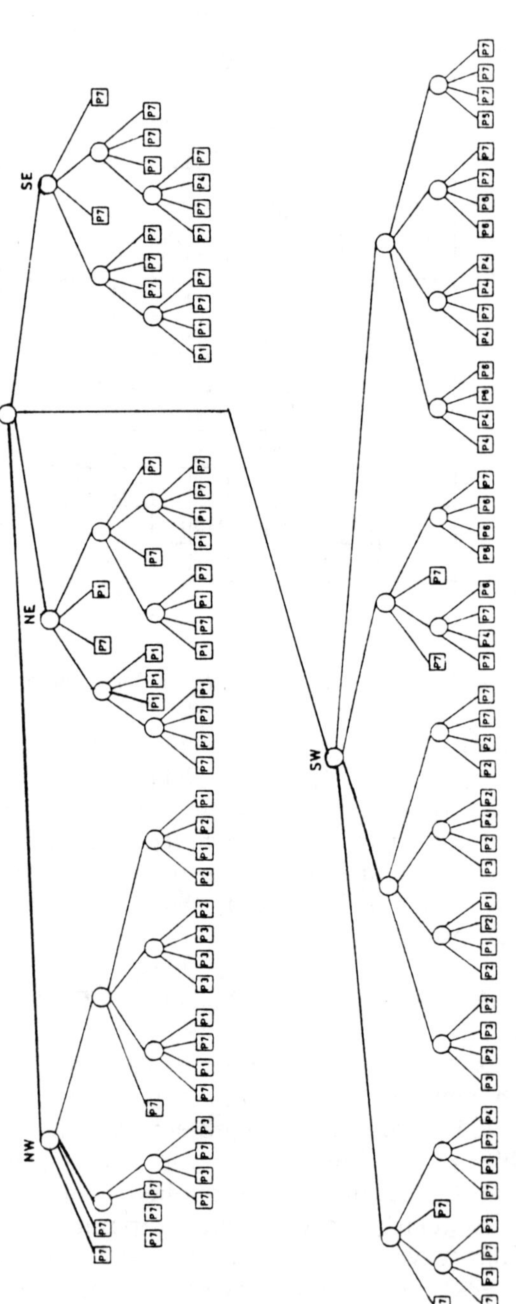

(b) the resulting quad-tree for New England

Figure 3.58 A Quad-tree Data Structure for New England.

the space. Secondly, objects close to one another in the original space should be near one another in the path transform. Finally, the curve is a transformation of space such that an inverse operation exists to recover the original space. The first and third properties are constraints or requirements imposed upon the construction of the curve. The second property is a goal that can have different interpretations of how to define it. Thus there are alternative curves to represent the same original space.

For an irregular distribution of points, one path topology would be to connect the points based on their Y-coordinate value in a descending manner (Figure 3.59). Such a curve would preserve the nearness of points based on the projection of their Y-coordinate.

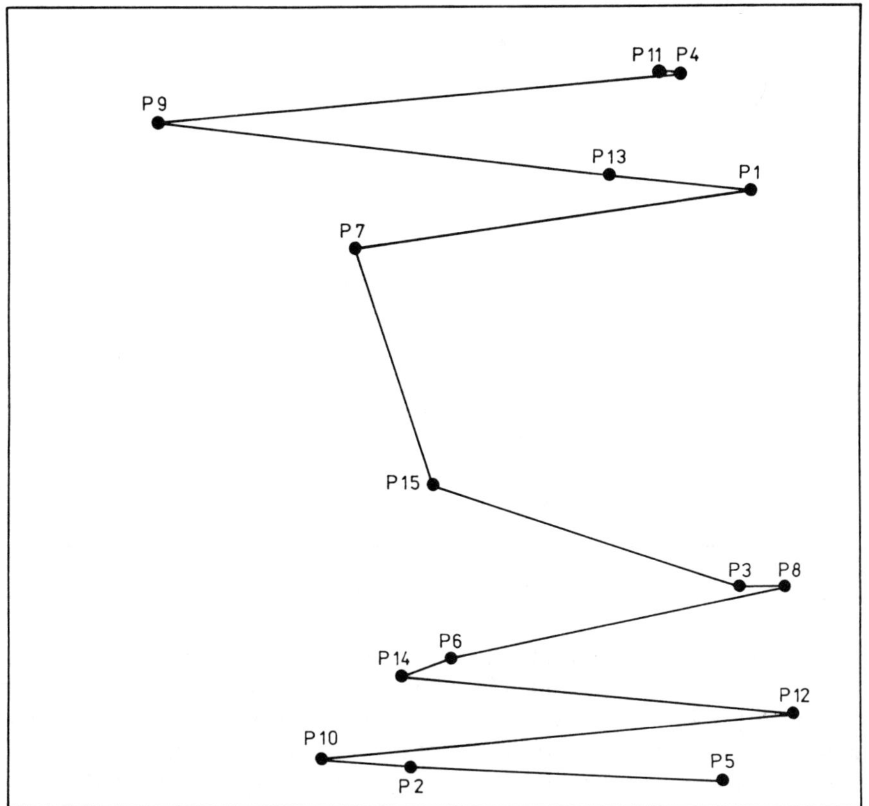

Figure 3.59 A Y-Coordinate Projection Path Transformation.

An alternative would be a minimal distance path. The minimal distance path passes through every object in space once given an origin and a final destination such that the total distance travelled between the orign and destination is minimized. However, no exact efficient algorithm exists to determine this path and different heuristics are normally used to find a close approximation to the true minimal distance path (see Chapter Four). Figure 3.60 is a minimal path approximation for the same point distribution given in Figure 3.59.

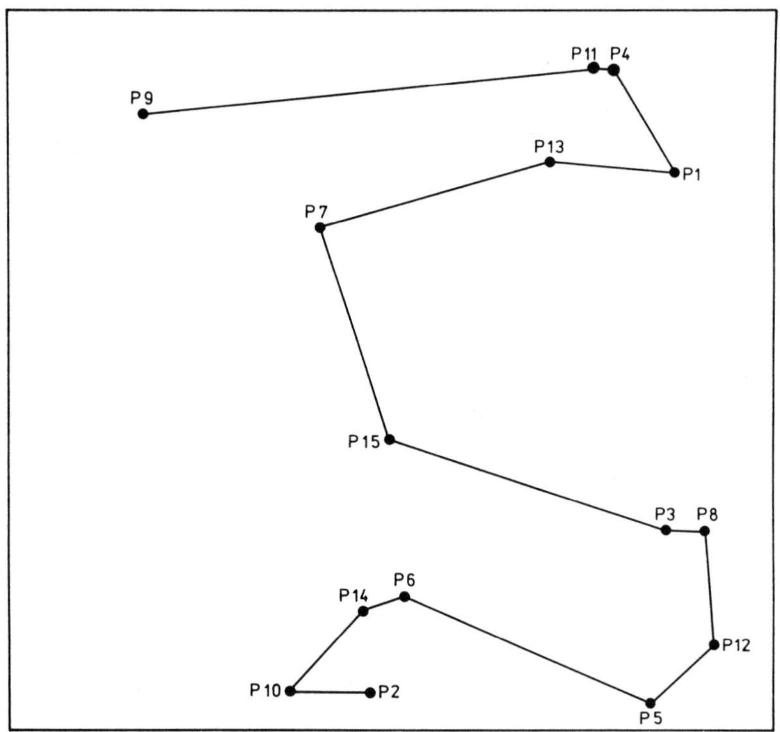

Figure 3.60 A Minimal Distance Path Transformation.

More interest has been shown in the space transformation of tessellations. A number of Peano scans have been proposed to transform a square mesh [Goodchild and Grandfield, 1983] (see Figure 3.61). Each of these scans has certain desirable properties. The Morton (Figure 3.61a) and pi orders (Figure 3.61b) recursively subdivide the original space and are related to quad-trees in this manner. Secondly, the address or sequence number of each object (given in base four) in the Morton and row orders (Figure 3.61c) can be easily computed from the X- and Y-coordinates of each object. Finally, the pi and the row-prime (Figure 3.61d) orders minimize the total distance associated with the entire path.

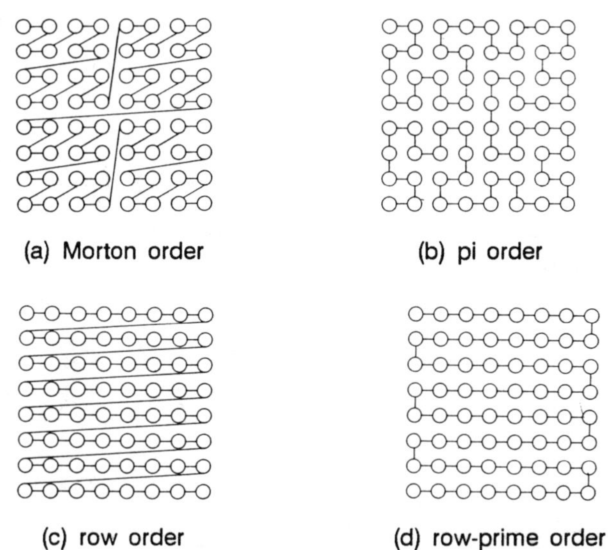

(a) Morton order (b) pi order

(c) row order (d) row-prime order

Figure 3.61 Different Space Orders.

For the Morton order, the binary digits of the X- and Y-coordinates are interleaved and the resulting bit string is partitioned into digit pairs (see Figure 3.62). For example the address of a point at coordinate **(3,4)** in the original space is found by interleaving the binary strings **011** and **100** to form the string **100101**. This digit string is next partitioned into **10-01-01** or **211** which is the base four representation of address **37**. The ability to compute this address permits the back and forth transformation between the space-filling curve and the original space. These two properties have enabled the Morton order to be used in conjunction with quad-tree structures to construct linear quad-trees [Mark and Lauzon, 1984]. For the row order, the binary string of the Y-coordinate is simply adjoined to the binary string of the X-coordinate. The address of the point at the coordinate **(3,4)** is found by adjoining **100** to **011** to form the binary string **100011** which is the binary representation of address **35**.

The ability to organize objects in a linear manner facilitates their storage and retrieval in a sequential machine. The subsequent ability to reconstruct their two-dimensional position in relation to other objects enables other spatial operators to manipulate them.

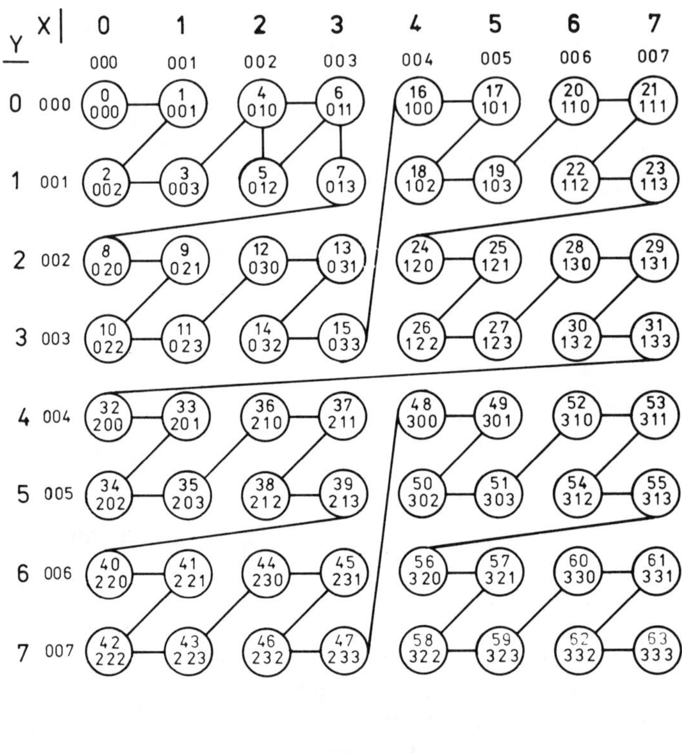

X 0 1 1

1 0 0 1 0 1

Y 1 0 0

Figure 3.62 Address Computation.

3.7 SUMMARY

Data organization remains an important topic in digital cartography. The alternative approaches to the organization and storage of digital images have advantages and disadvantages although some are inherently better than another. The structure that is chosen depends on the type of base map being stored and the purpose of the digital cartographic information processing system. Whichever structure is chosen does impact on the way spatial information is encoded and subsequently processed. The next chapter covers the different ways in which cartographic information is acquired and initially processed.

3.8 REFERENCES

Annitto, R. and R. Cromley. [1987]. "MARKMAP: A GIS for Small Scale Market Area Analysis," **Proceedings**, International GIS Conference, Vol. III, 37-44.

Brassel, K. [1978]. "A Topological Data Structure for Multi-Element Map Processing," **Harvard Papers on Geographic Information Systems**, G. Dutton (ed.), Vol. 4.

Brassel, K. and D. Reif. [1979]. "A Procedure to Generate Thiessen Polygons," **Geographical Analysis**, 11, 289-303.

Brassel, K., M. Heller, and P. Jones. [1984]. "The Construction of Bisector Skeletons for Polygonal Networks," **Proceedings**, First International Symposium on Spatial Data Handling, 117-26.

Burrough, P. [1986]. **Principles of Geographical Information Systems for Land Resources Assessment**, Oxford: Clarendon Press.

Cairns, S. [1961]. **Introductory Topology**, New York: Ronald Press Co.

Chrisman, N. [1977]. "Impact of Data Structure on Geographic Information Processing," Internal Report No. 74-4, Laboratory for Computer Graphics and Spatial Analysis.

Cooke, D. [1978]. "DIME Variants for Curvilinear Networks," **Harvard Papers on Geographic Information Systems**, G. Dutton (ed.), Vol 4.

Cooke, D. and W. Maxfield. [1967]. "The Development of a Geographic Base File and Its Uses for Mapping," **Proceedings**, URISA, 207-18.

Corbett, J. [1979]. **Topological Principles in Cartography**, Washington, D.C.: Bureau of the Census.

Cromley, R. [1984]. "A Triangulation Data Structure for Storing Choropleth Base Maps," **The Cartographic Journal**, 21,19-22.

Cromley, R. and D. Grogan. [1985]. "An Algorithm for Identifying and Storing a Thiessen Diagram within a Convex Boundary," **Geographical Analysis**, 167-75.

Date, C. [1985]. **An Introduction to Database Systems**, Reading, Massachusetts: Addison-Wesley.

Elfick, M. [1979]. "Contouring by Use of a Triangular Mesh," **The Cartographic Journal**, 16, 24-29.

Gold, C. [1978]. "The Practical Generation and Use of Geographic Triangular Element Data," **Harvard Papers on Geographic Information Systems**, G. Dutton (ed.), Vol. 5.

Gold, C. [1988]. "PAN Graphs, An Aid to GIS Analysis," **International Journal of Geographical Information Systems**, 2, 29-41.

Goodchild, M. and A. Grandfield. [1983]. "Optmizing Raster Storage: An Examination of Four Alternatives," **Proceedings**, AUTO-CARTO VI, 400-07.

Herring, J. [1987]. "TIGRIS: Topologically Integrated Geographic Information System," **Proceedings**, AUTO-CARTO 8, 282-91.

Knuth, D. [1973]. **The Art of Computer Programming: Fundamental Algorithms**, 1, Reading, Massachusetts: Addison-Wesley.

Males, R. [1978]. "ADAPT - A Spatial Data Structure for Use with Planning and Design Models," **Harvard Papers on Geographic Information Systems**, Vol. 3.

Mark, D. and J. Lauzon. [1984]. "Linear Quadtrees for Geographic Information Systems," **Proceedings**, First International Symposium on Spatial Data Handling, 412-30.

Marx, R. [1986]. "The TIGER System: Automating the Geographic Structure of the United States Census," **Government Publications Review**, 13, 181-201.

McCarty, G. [1961]. **Topology: An Introduction with Application to Topological Groups**, New York: McGraw Hill Book Co.

Montanori, U. [1969]. "Continuous Skeletons from Digitized Images," **Journal of the Association for Computing Machinery**, 16, 534-49.

Morehouse, S. [1985] "ARC/INFO: A Geo-Relational Model for Spatial Information," **Proceedings**, AUTO-CARTO 7, 388-97.

Munkres, J. [1975]. **Topology: A First Course**, Englewood Cliffs, New Jersey: Prentice-Hall.

Perkal, J. [1966]. "An Attempt at Objective Generalization," **Michigan Inter-University Community of Mathematical Geographers, Discussion Paper No. 10.**

Peucker, T. and N. Chrisman. [1975]. "Cartographic Data Structures," **The American Cartographer**, 2, 55-69.

Peuquet, D. [1984]. "A Conceptual Framework and Comparison of Spatial Data Models," **Cartographica**, 21, 66-113.

Rosenfeld, A. and H. Samet. [1979]. "Tree Structures for Region Representation," **Proceedings**, AUTO-CARTO IV, 108-18.

Samet, H. [1984]. "The Quadtree and Related Hierarchical Data Structures," **Computing Surveys**, 16, 187-260.

Scripter, M. [1969]. "Choropleth Maps on Small Digital Computers," **Proceedings**, Association of American Geographers, 133-36.

Tarjan, R. [1983]. **Data Structures and Network Algorithms**, Philadelphia: SIAM.

Van Roessel, J. [1987]. "Design of a Spatial Data Structure Using Relational Normal Forms," **International Journal of Geographical Information Systems**, 1, 33-50.

White, M. [1979]. "A Survey of the Mathematics of Maps," **Proceedings**, AUTO-CARTO IV, 1, 82-96.

White, M. [1984a]. "Technical Requirements and Standards for a Multipurpose Geographic Data System," **The American Cartographer**, 11, 15-26.

White, M. [1984b]. "Tribulations of Automated Cartography and How Mathematics Helps," **Cartographica**, 21, 148-59.

Chapter 4
Data Acquisition and Preprocessing

Cartographic data are the basis for generating cartographic information. Although the result of cartographic information processing often is some form of map product, data are the primary ingredients of that product [Kennedy and Meyers, 1977]. Which data are needed and what the characteristics of those data should be, come after an analysis of the type of cartographic information needed by the map user. In digital cartography, the emphasis is on the production of many maps and other graphical products from a single cartographic database, rather than producing only one map for each set of data collected. In an automated system, the primary cost and time in production are associated with the compilation of the digital database. The strength of digital cartographic systems lies in their ability to manipulate and display cartographic data to the satisfaction of the information user.

Because collecting data can be the most expensive component in the entire cartographic process, special care must be given to the conversion of real world entities into their cartographic object counterparts. Data selection is the initial generalization of cartographic entities in constructing a map model. Determining what data are needed is not a simple process. The ideal order of matching data to needs is from the specification of the information product back to data acquisition. Data collection requires an analysis of information flow in the opposite direction of the actual production process.

Secondly, because digital databases are expensive to compile, data collection is often influenced by the availability of existing data sets. A very common practice is encoding a digital geographic base file from existing real maps. In any situation involving existing data, one must be careful not to allow inappropriate data to dictate the nature of subsequent digital forms. This chapter is an introduction to the principles of data collection and preprocessing which form the basis for the acquisition and compilation of cartographic objects that are stored in digital form.

4.1 ENCODING STRATEGIES

Encoding is the conversion of cartographic features into digital objects. The manner in which encoding is performed will affect the nature of subsequent digital display and measurement operators. Thus the form of encoding should reflect the objectives of the cartographic process. The form of encoding chosen is also influenced by the hardware system, as certain encoding strategies are better suited to some hardware than others.

4.1.1 Line Encoding

Because digital computers have finite numerical/arithmetic precision, lines cannot be directly represented in their analog form. Instead, they are approximated as mathematical functions such as splines (see Chapter Six) or by coordinate strings. There are two primary methods for encoding the digital caricature of a one-dimensional feature as a string. The first method represents a line by a string consisting of line segments of fixed orientation and length. An example of this is chain encoding [Freeman, 1961]. In chain encoding, each new line segment takes one of eight different positions with respect to the endpoint of the previous line segment (Figure 4.1a). Because the positions are invariant from segment to segment, it is only necessary to record the orientation value of successive segments relative to previous ones. This results in compact storage requirements. However in this approach, segment endpoints can deviate from the original line and it is possible for no point other than the starting node to correspond to the original line. Better approximations are possible by reducing the fixed unit of length (although this increases storage), but even in this approach only the starting node is guaranteed to be part of the original line. This encoding approach is suitable for raster hardware devices because of their fixed resolution.

The second method represents a line by a string consisting of line segments having variable orientation and/or lengths. Each point location in this string is given an absolute coordinate reference in a cartesian coordinate system (Figure 4.1b).

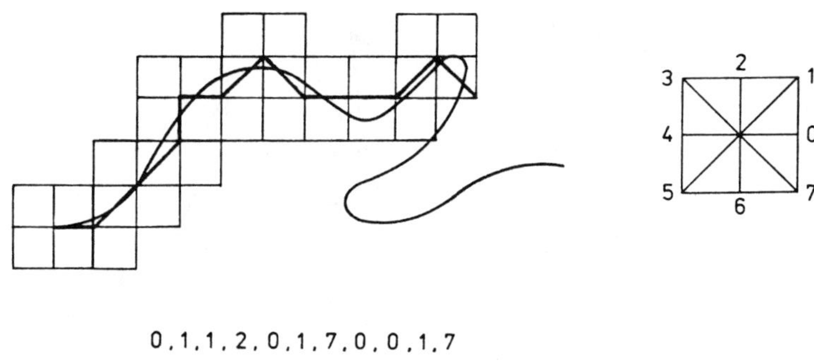

a) fixed orientation and length

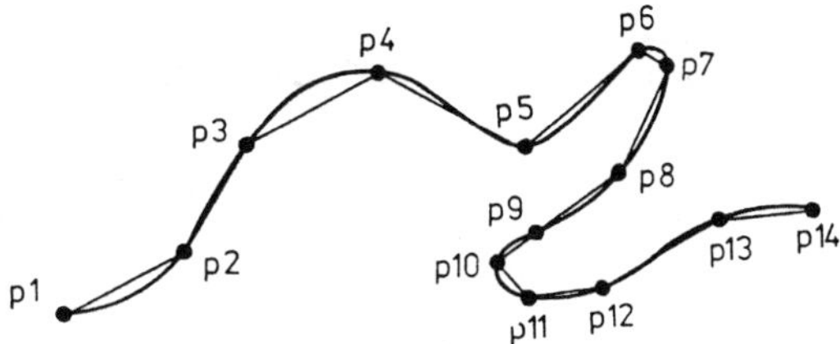

p1, p2, p3, p4, p5, p6, p7, p8, p9, p10, p11, p12, p13, p14

b) variable orientation and/or length

Figure 4.1 Alternative Methods for Encoding a Line.

There are many alternative ways for selecting which points to retain in the string. A fixed length sampling interval for each segment can be used to determine the approximating string (Figure 4.2a). Another approach is to approximate a line with a string having a fixed bandwidth; the maximum perpendicular distance between any point on the original line and the approximating string is fixed as ϵ. Every point on the orignal line is contained in a rectangle having a width of 2ϵ (Figure 4.2b). The bandwidth approach has been used by Poiker (formerly Peucker) [1976] to formulate a theory of the line. Another method is to select the "most characteristic" points from the original line. Jenks [1981] defines characteristic points as those that either have significant economic or political importance such as the intersection of political boundaries or those psychologically perceived as being important to line structure. Freeman [1978] would include important mathematical points such as local maxima and minima, discontinuities and inflections as characteristic points.

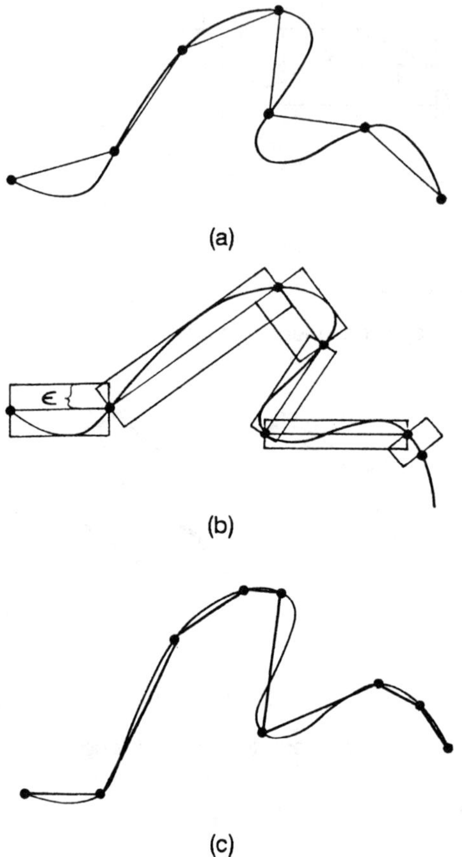

Figure 4.2 Alternative Approximating Strings.

In each case, the amount of error between the original feature and its encoded form is a function of the length of the sampling interval. In section 4.2 we will see that the sampling interval in turn is dependent on map scale.

4.1.2 Area Encoding

The regular tessellation data structures presented in Chapter Three all required that the resolution grid cell, the pixel, have an assigned value.

There are four basic techniques for encoding the pixel values. Assume that the mesh presented in Figure 4.3 represents the resolution of the encoding grid. The first approach is to encode the value at each grid cell center to represent the area within its pixel (Figure 4.3a) [MacDougall, 1976]. The second method passes a transversing line through the middle of each cell and encodes the value that comprises the plurality of the length within each pixel (Figure 4.3b). Another approach is the modal cell method. In this method the value is encoded corresponding to the feature that occupies the plurality of the area of the pixel (Figure 4.3c). Although the modal cell method should give a better area representation of the original map, it is numerically more difficult to compute area than either line lengths or center point values. If greater accuracy is required in the retrieval of area information for the study region, then the percentage of each polygon type occupying a portion of the cell could be stored (Figure 4.3d). This allows more flexibility in the retrieval of the original polygon areas at the expense of more storage requirements.

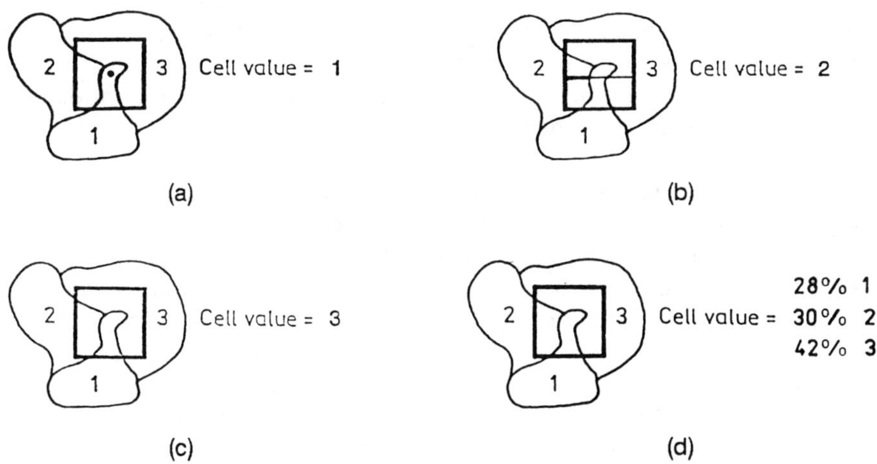

Figure 4.3 Alternative Methods for Encoding a Pixel.

If some ordinal ranking is established among the cartographic features being encoded, a priority could be established so that if a higher order feature occupies any portion of the cell, the entire cell is encoded as that feature. For example, if any wetland occupies a cell in a land use map, the cell is encoded as being wetland. Alternatively, separate features could be represented as bit-planes. Every cell in which a feature is present is assigned a value of one and every cell in which it is absent is assigned a zero. For categorical data, there will be one bit-plane for each category.

For both line and area encoding, the sampling interval is critical to the stylized representation of cartographic features. The sampling interval acts as a *spatial filter* to eliminate detail. This filtering should eliminate only unwanted data redundancy and not information. In the next section we shall see that sampling intervals are interconnected with the geographic scale of the encoded image.

4.2 MEASUREMENT AND SCALE

All geographic base file data are acquired at a certain scale. *Scale* is the number of metric units in the space of the real world that are represented by a unit in the space of the map model. It is impractical or functionally impossible to collect data using a one-to-one correspondence between cartographic entities and objects; resulting maps would be a replication of the real world, not a model of it. Data acquisition is therefore a functional relation between the real world and the digital representation rather than a transformation of the real world. The particular scale chosen to collect data must reflect the objectives of the map determined at the outset. The scale should also match the precision of the instruments used in data collection. Because all instruments have a finite resolution for distinguishing between features, it is impossible to collect data at a precision finer than an instrument's resolution.

As the scale is reduced, the level of detail in the data is reduced. Although the scaling operator was presented in the abstract in Chapter Two as a point transformation, in practice it is not always possible to shrink and then enlarge a map image and have the inverse image of the process remain an identity image with the original if the reduction was beyond the resolution of the storage medium. Figure 4.4a presents a pattern of sixteen dots that are either black or white. Let's assume that during reduction four dots in the original coalesce into one dot on the reduced image given the resolution of the recording instrument and the level of reduction. The original sixteen dots are converted into four dots during reduction. However, none of these four dots is black or white. They are different shades of gray depending on the number of black and white dots in each of the four original sets of four dots each (see Figure 4.4b). An inverse enlargement of the reduced image recaptures the size of the original scale but not the finer detail of the original image. It is impossible during the enlarging operator to know both the number of black and white dots (some could have been gray) and which dots were originally black or white (see Figure 4.4c).

Similarly, once attribute data have been aggregated they cannot be disaggregated completely (unless the original data were also retained). If we know only the average age of a population, we can almost never know the ages of individual members of that population. One strategy for a general purpose database (the system objectives are not fully known in advance) with respect to encoding would be to record the data at the finest scale that is possible. A recommendation given by the Committee of Enquiry in Great Britain [Chorley, 1987] for handling geographic information is that "data suppliers should both keep and release their data in as unaggregated a form as possible." In a digital system, scale changes involving the removal of detail (aggregation) can easily be handled during cartographic generalization and analysis (see Chapter Five) in a virtual environment so that none of the integrity of the original database is lost.

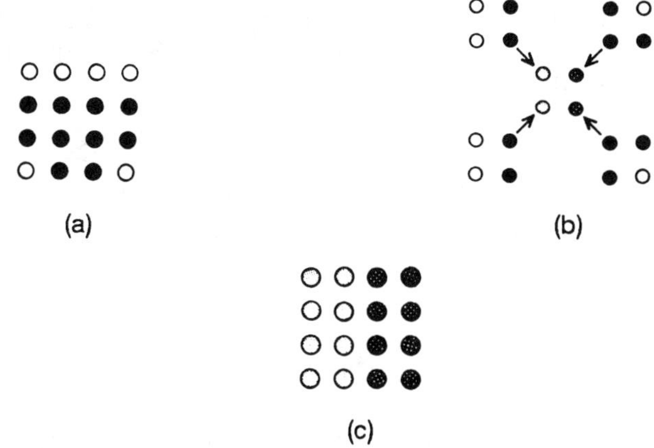

Figure 4.4 Information Loss in Scale Change at Pixel Resolution Limits.

Once attribute and spatial data have been encoded at a particular scale, the resolution of the database has been established and finer detail can only be introduced as an approximation (see enhancement procedures in Chapter Six). One advantage of vector data structures over raster is that scale changes can be performed over a continuum of values rather than for discrete multiples. However, no matter how much a map is enlarged, no more detail will be present in the display than what exists in the resolution of the original digital database.

All derived spatial measurements of cartographic entities such as line length and area are scale dependent. Suppose that the line given in Figure 4.5a is represented digitally by a string having line segments of equal length **L** (Figure 4.5b). The length of this string is **7L.** If the length of an individual segment was reduced to **L/2** the length of the resulting string representation of the line would be **16.5(L/2)** or **8.25L** (see Figure 4.5c). The measured length of any linear cartographic feature is a function of the sampling interval of the recording instrument.

As the length of the measuring segment is successively subdivided, the total length of the resulting string will continuously increase without bound [Steinhaus, 1954]. Assume that the shape of the line is invariant with respect to scale changes; if the scale were changed, its length would only change by the scaling ratio. However, the shape of a cartographic entity is not invariant to scale; its shape is scale-dependent [Buttenfield, 1985]. Only cartographic objects may be invariant. As resolution becomes finer, more detail would be introduced into the cartographic feature. Each segment in an approximating string at coarser resolutions would be replaced by its own string (see Figure 4.6). For entities in the real world, their measured lengths would increase to the limit of the instrument measuring the length.

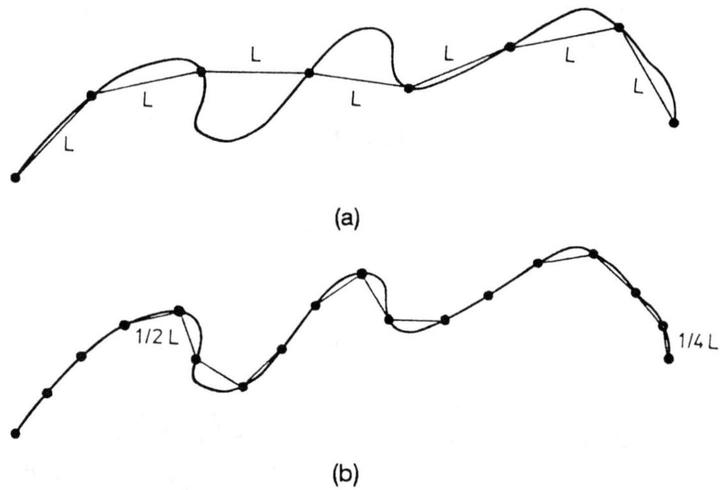

Figure 4.5 Measurement Changes with Sampling Interval Change.

Perkal [1966] attempted to measure the length of a line by calculating the area of its ϵ-halo (Figure 4.7). The ϵ-halo of a line is an extension of the ϵ-ball concept for points; the ϵ-halo is the locus of ϵ-balls associated with each point of the line. The length of a line is measured the area of the ϵ-halo minus the area of one ϵ-ball (to compensate for the portion of the halo area beyond the endpoints of the line divided by the diameter of the ϵ-ball, 2ϵ. The area of an ϵ-halo is estimated empirically by counting the number of tangential circles having a radius of ϵ arranged in either a square or triangular lattice that the line passes through multiplied by their area.

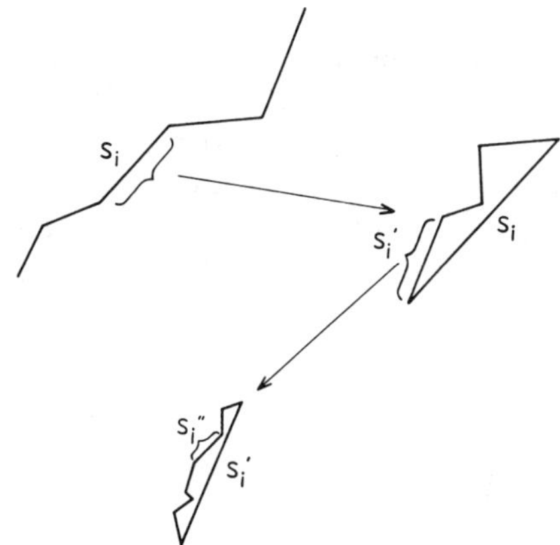

Figure 4.6 The Introduction of More Detail as Scale Increases.

Figure 4.7 The ε-Halo of a Line.

Richardson [1961] also has evaluated the relationship between cartographic line length and scale by measuring the length of various coastlines and national frontiers. Based on empirical observations, Richardson noticed that the plot of the logarithm of total length against the logarithm of the length of the measuring segment was a straight line (Figure 4.8). He therefore hypothesized the following relation between the total length of a cartographic feature and the length of the measuring segment:

$$L(x) = A\ x^{1-D}; \tag{4.1}$$

where, **L(x)** is the length of the feature;
A is a proportionality constant;
x is the length of the measuring segment;
D is a power factor.

Mandelbrot [1977, 1982] interprets the exponent **D** as a decimal value that represents the *fractal dimension* of a cartographic object. The topological dimensions of points, lines, and areas are defined as zero, one and two respectively. In Euclidean measurement, the magnitude of any object, **M**, is calculated as the number of units, **n**, multiplied by the unit length raised to the power of its appropriate dimension. Thus given a unit length **L**, the length of a straight line is measured as the number of units times **L** raised to the power of one. The area of an enclosed polygon is the number of unit squares times **L** raised to the power of two.

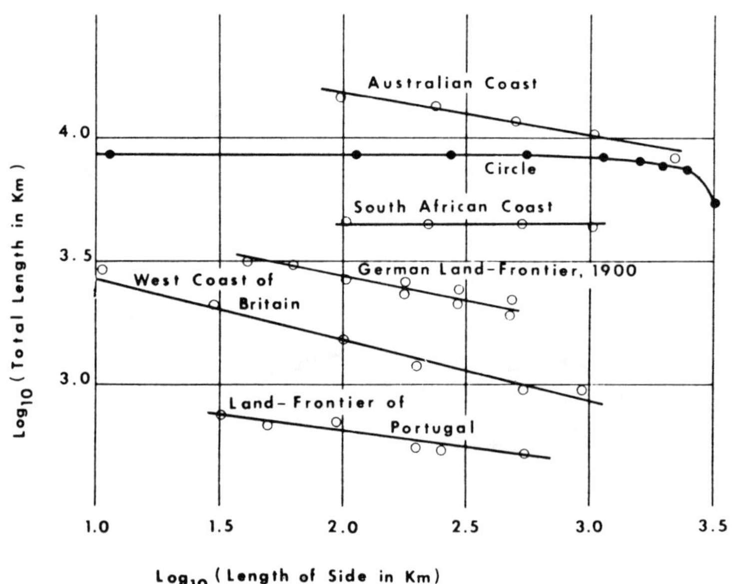

Figure 4.8 Richardson's Coastline and Frontier Analysis.
(Source: Richardson, 1961)

Every time the unit length **L** is halved, the number of linear units must double to retain the same length ($\mathbf{M} = (2\mathbf{n})(\mathbf{L}/2)^1$) and the number of square units is quadrupled ($\mathbf{M} = (4\mathbf{n})(\mathbf{L}/2)^2$). The dimension exponent **D** can also be calculated:

$$D = \log (n_2/n_1) \; / \; \log (L_1/L_2); \qquad (4.2)$$

where $\mathbf{n_2}$ is the number of units for the second unit length;
$\mathbf{n_1}$ is the number of units for the first unit length;
$\mathbf{L_2}$ is the second unit length;
$\mathbf{L_1}$ is the first unit length.

For straight lines the value of **D** will equal one, the topological dimension. However for lines in general, **D** will be greater than one or a fractal dimension between one and two. Similarly, a planar surface will have a **D** value equal to two; indulating surfaces will have a fractal dimension between two and three.

Goodchild and Mark [1987] note that **D** may be the most important parameter to describe irregular cartographic features. The fractal dimension of digitally encoded lines has been estimated by using equal chord lengths as dividers to measure the length of the originally encoded line [Shelburg, Moellering, and Lam, 1982]. The logarithm of total line length is plotted against the logarithm of the length of one chord, as in Richardson's study, to calculate fractal dimension. Alternatively, the original encoded line can be successively generalized using a line simplification algorithm (see Chapter Five) and the logarithm of the total length of the resulting lines is plotted against the logarithm of the average length of a chord to estimate the fractal dimension [Buttenfield,1989].

An underlying premise of fractals is the concept of *self-similarity*. Any portion of a self-similar object is either exactly or statistically similar to the object as a whole. However, for many cartographic features **D** may not stay constant over a wide range of sampling intervals and may be scale-dependent [Goodchild, 1980; Buttenfield, 1989]. Therefore, the sampling interval should correspond to the fractal dimension at these different scales; it should be smaller as the dimensionality becomes higher. Once the sampling interval is set, data acquisition can actually begin.

4.3 DATA ACQUISITION

For digital mapping two different data sets must be acquired, the spatial data forming the geographic base file and the attribute data for the thematic overlays. The discussion here concerns only the acquisition of the spatial component of the overall database. Spatial data can either be directly acquired through instrumentation or encoded from existing map documents.

4.3.1 Digital Remotely Sensed Data

An important source of data for cartographic processing is remotely sensed data. Remote sensing is the science and art of acquiring information about an entity through the analysis of data acquired by a sensor that is not in contact with the entity under study [Lillesand and Kiefer, 1979]. Of direct interest here are data acquired by sensors that detect variability in reflected electromagnetic energy distributions. All entities on the earth's surface may be quantified by measuring the portion of incident electromagnetic radiation at different wavelengths that is reflected. The amount of energy reflected by each entity is a function of the energy's wavelength. Different entities exhibit different spectral signatures with respect to the amount of reflectance at varying wavelength bands. For example in Figure 4.9, water absorbs most energy in the infrared portions of the electromagnetic spectrum (above 0.8 μm), while vegetation reflects much higher amounts between 0.8 and 1.2 μm; soil reflects the most in the bands between 1.4 and 2.6 μm. The uniqueness of these spectral reflectance properties forms the basis for the identification of entities from their reflectance values at different wavelengths.

Cartographers have relied heavily on remotely sensed images from aerial photographs for the measurement and mapping of earth surface features. Air photo interpretation has formed the basis for the construction and updating of topographic and land use maps. However, the manual processing of remotely sensed data through direct human interpretation is limited by the resolution of the human eye (humans can only differentiate eight to sixteen gray tones when interpreting black-and-white aerial photography) [Jensen, 1986]. Digital processing of remotely sensed data can retain the radiometric precision of the data captured by a sensor whereas visual interpretation filters the data (although it should be noted that any sensor itself filters the data in both the radiometric and spatial dimensions).

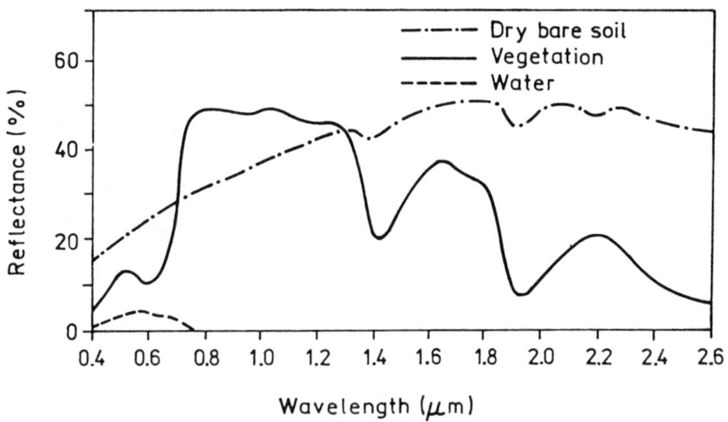

Figure 4.9 Example Spectral Signatures.
(After Lillesand and Kiefer, 1979)

The Landsat series of satellites (initiated as the Earth Resource Technology Satellite program in 1972) was designed to observe earth resources.

These satellites carry sensors which record reflected and emitted radiation in several wavelength bands of the electromagnetic spectrum. A multispectral scanner system (MSS) has been on board each of the five satellites. The scanning sensors detect reflectance over a 185 km swath on each orbit; six parallel detectors sensitive to four spectral bands - bands 4, 5, 6, and 7 (see Table 4.1) - capture an analog signal that is converted into a digital signal having ground resolution units (picture elements or pixels) of approximately 56x79 meters [Jensen, 1986]. Each pixel is represented by a digital number (DN) with higher values indicating higher reflectance [Sabins, 1978]; the brightness values range between 0 to 127 for bands 4, 5, and 6 and between 0 to 63 for band 7. Each row of pixels radiance values is called a scan line.

Table 4.1 Landsat and SPOT Sensor Wavelengths[a]

Sensor	Spectral Range (μm)
Landsat MSS (56x79 m pixel)	
Band 4	0.5-0.6 (green)
Band 5	0.6-0.7 (red)
Band 6	0.7-0.8 (reflective infrared)
Band 7	0.8-1.1 (reflective infrared)
Landsat TM (30x30 m pixel)	
Band 1	0.45-0.52 (blue)
Band 2	0.52-0.60 (green)
Band 3	0.63-0.69 (red)
Band 4	0.76-0.90 (reflective infrared)
Band 5	1.55-1.75 (mid-infrared)
Band 6	2.08-2.35 (mid-infrared)
Band 7	10.4-12.5 (thermal infrared)
SPOT Panchromatic (10x10 m pixel)	0.51-0.73 (visible)
SPOT Multispectral (20x20 m pixel)	0.50-0.59 (green)
	0.61-0.68 (red)
	0.79-0.89 (reflective infrared)

[a] Source: Jensen [1986], Tables 2-4, 2-6, and 2-7

The Thematic Mapper (TM), a second generation multispectral scanner, was placed on board Landsats 4 and 5. The TM has seven bands and detects radiance for 30x30 meter pixels in the six reflective wavelength bands and 120x120 meter pixels in the single thermal infrared (emitted) band (see Table 4.1). Even higher spatial resolution became available with the French SPOT sensor system. The SPOT satellite sensors detect radiance for 10x10 meter pixels in a single panchromatic spectral band and for 20x20 meter pixels in three narrower reflective visible and infrared bands (see Table 4.1).

Once data have been received, several image processing operations are performed. Image restoration operations attempt to remove radiometric and geometric distortions introduced into the data at the time of capture and transmission. Image enhancement procedures accentuate contrast between features to aid primarily in visual interpretation while image classification techniques attempt to interpret the digital image data directly and transform reflectance values into land cover types or other environmental characteristics. Enhancement and classification procedures are covered in the next chapter because they are operations performed on the database once it has been stored as a digital image.

Radiometric corrections are needed to rectify malfunctions by sensors and the impact of atmospheric scattering on reflectance values. Occasional sensor failures result in periodic scan lines having a value of zero for all pixels. This failure is generally corrected by taking the average value of the DN values for the scan lines preceding and succeeding the defective scan line. Aside from total failure, some detectors may deviate from their initial calibration causing some scan lines to be brighter or darker than their neighboring scan lines. One correction method is to compute the mean or median value for each detector over a homogeneous radiance area. Significant differences in these mean or median values are used to identify a malfunctioning detector and to establish a correction factor that is added or subtracted (or multiplied) to the DN values of the defective scan lines.

Finally, because the atmosphere selectively scatters shorter wavelengths, MSS and TM bands at the shorter wavelengths will have more brightness added to their DN values. To determine the bias caused by scattering (a haze correction), the pixel DN value in a visible band is plotted against the DN value in an infrared band for an area in shadows or an area of deep water (see Figure 4.10). Ordinary least squares regression (see Chapter Five) is used to fit a straight line through the data plot. If no haze is present, then the line should intercept the visible band's axis at the origin; the amount of offset from the origin is the additive effect of haze on that band. This intercept value is then subtracted from the DN values for that band.

Geometric corrections are used to remove a number of nonsystematic and systematic distortions introduced into the data and to register the image with a given reference map. Nonsystematic distortions result from variations in the satellite's altitude, velocity, and attitude and are monitored from tracking and ground control point (GCP) data (see Figure 4.11 and Table 4.2). Systematic distortions are predictable and result from scan skew, scanner distortion, and variations in mirror velocity (see Figure 4.11 and Table 4.2).

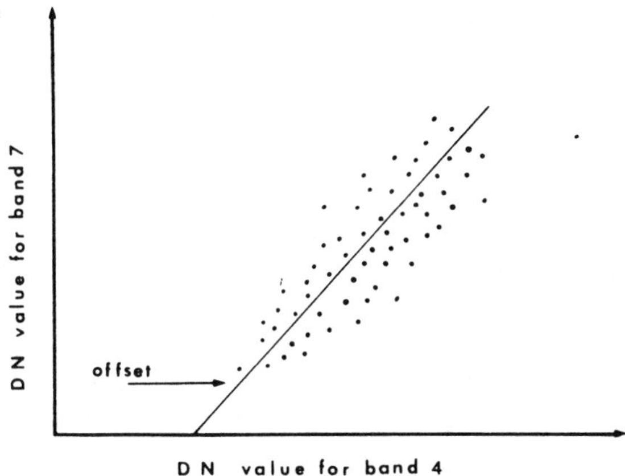

Figure 4.10 The Additive Correction for Atmospheric Scattering.

Nonsystematic distortions are corrected by analyzing distortions between GCPs in the original imagery and on a reference map. The geometric rectification of image coordinates **(x,y)** to ground coordinates (x_g, y_g) is performed by the following affine transformations:

$$x = a_0 + a_1 x_g + a_2 y_g \; ; \qquad (4.3)$$
$$y = b_0 + b_1 x_g + b_2 y_g \; ;$$

where $\mathbf{a_0}$, $\mathbf{a_1}$, $\mathbf{a_2}$, $\mathbf{b_0}$, $\mathbf{b_1}$, and $\mathbf{b_2}$ are estimated from least squares regression models interrelating the respective **x** and **y** positions of identifiable features on the image with their geographic position on a ground oriented coordinate system (see Jensen [1986]).

When the geometrically corrected output matrix is superimposed on the original image matrix, cells in the output matrix do not exactly match with cells in the original image (Figure 4.12). The radiance values of the rectified image must be estimated by a spatial interpolation function (see Chapter Six). The net result of all these radiometric and geometric corrections may be to create pixels values that have not occurred on the ground. Extensive ground truthing is necessary to establish the quality of the data before it is used in later analyses.

Table 4.2 Sources of Geometric Distortion[a]

Earth Rotation - the earth's rotation during scanning causes along-scan distortion.

Spacecraft Velocity - Departures from nominal spacecraft velocity during scanning cause a cross-scan distortion.

Altitude - Departures from nominal spacecraft altitude cause scale distortions.

Attitude - One axis of the sensor system is normal to the earth's surface and another is aligned with the spacecraft's velocity. Departures from this attitude cause geometric distortion.

Perspective Projection - MSS images may be used to represent the projection of points on the earth onto a plane tangent to the earth, resulting in along-scan distortion.

Scan Skew - As the MSS mirror completes one scan, the movement of the spacecraft along the ground track causes cross-scan distortion.

Panoramic Distortion - Nominally, data are sampled at regular spatial intervals on the ground but the ground area imaged is proportional to the tangent of the scan angle rather than to the angle itself., causing along-scan distortion.

Mirror Velocity - Departures from the constant angular rate of the scanning mirror causes along-scan distortion.

Map Projection - Although not a direct geometric distortion, output in a specific map projection requires a geometric transformation that can be accomplished simultaneously with other corrections for actual distortions.

[a]Source: Bernstein and Ferneyhough [1975], p. 1469.

4.3.2 Digitizing

Although digital remote sensing devices are generating large volumes of spatial data, most compilations of digital geographic base files involve the conversion of an analog map into a digital image through the digitizing process. Because the expense of digitizing is so high compared with other cartographic processing (it is inexpensive compared to the true cost of satellite remote sensing), great care should be given to outlining the digitizing procedure in advance.

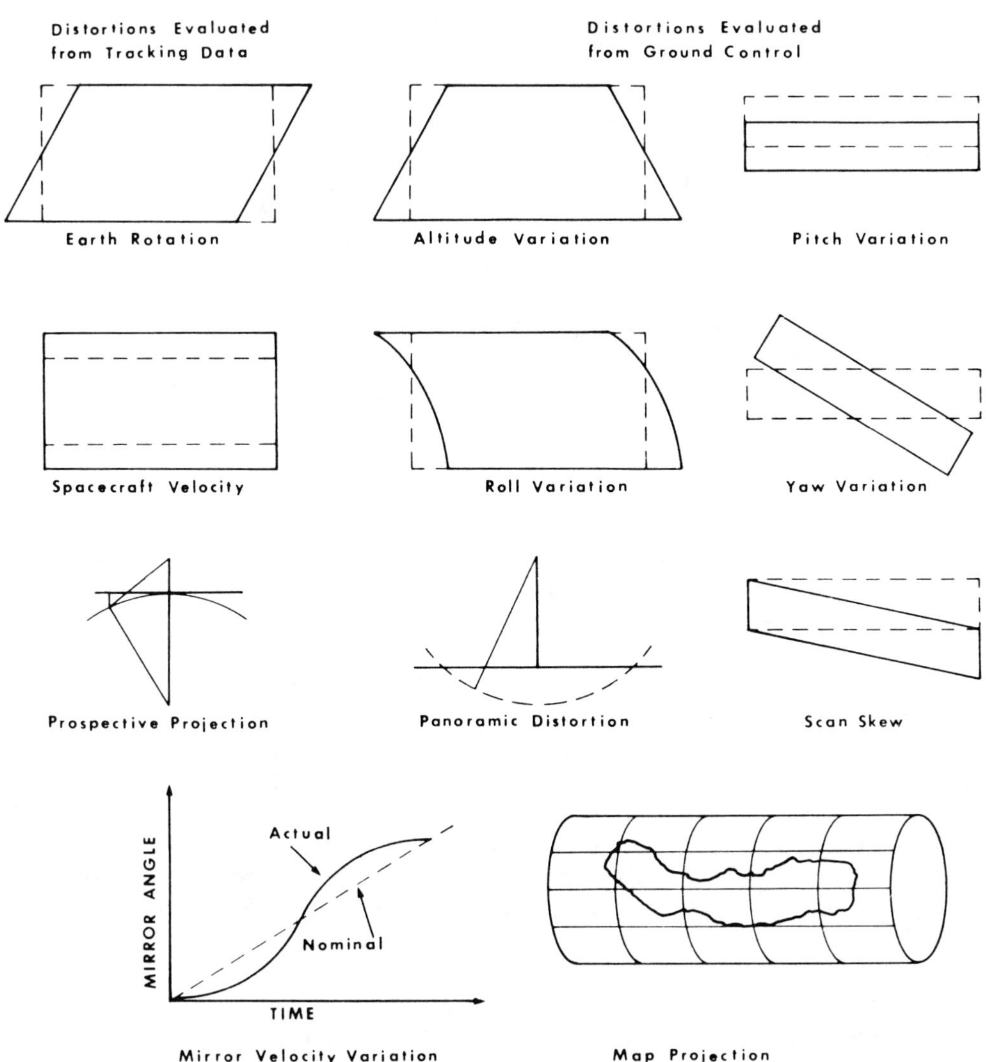

Figure 4.11 Geometric Distortions of Landsat Images.
(Source: Bernstein and Ferneyhough, 1975)

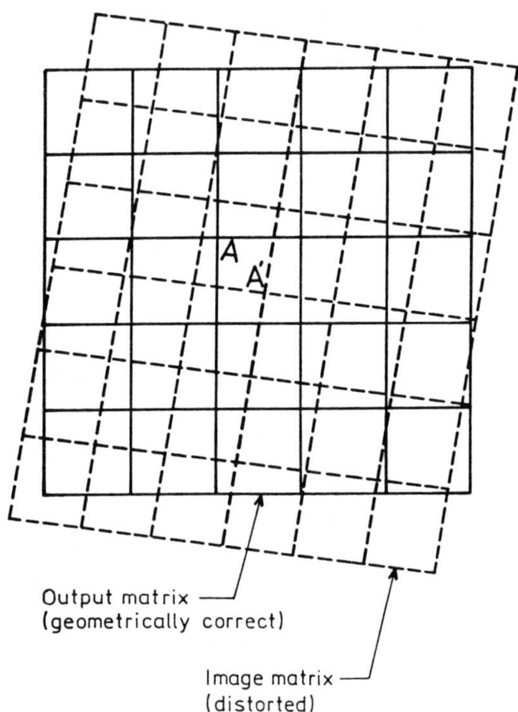

Figure 4.12 Geometric Rectification of a Landsat Image.
(Source: Lillesand and Kiefer, 1979)

The entry of maps into digital form can be divided into four stages: feasibility and requirements analysis, map preparation, digitizing, and editing [Marble, *et al.*, 1984]. Before actual digitizing can proceed, depending on the scale of the project and its integration with other ongoing projects, a feasibility report should determine if it is even worthwhile to create a digital database, and, if it is, what the goals and standards of the digital database should be. Next the map documents must be acquired and inspected and, if necessary, reformatted for compatibility and quality control.

After a document has been preprocessed, it is ready to be encoded. Digital encoding can range from a fully automated process using scanner technology to a completely manual one using transparent grid overlays. The former is better suited to projects requiring massive amounts of encoding while the latter is relegated to classroom or small individual projects. Most digitizing, however, is performed in a man/machine environment using a graphic tablet. There are several important considerations in the design of such a digitizing system. First, it is desirable to minimize the likelihood of operator-induced errors in capturing the data. A balance must be maintained between manual operations and machine processing. In a production mode, the operator is required to perform as few tasks as possible. However, the less effort required by the operator, the more complex the software system must be. Because the graphics tablet is used to capture lines as strings (a sequence of points), the topology between polygon objects must be subsequently constructed. Although topological data structures for storing the digital representation require more preprocessing operations, recent digitizing packages such as ROOTS [Corson-Rikert, 1988] construct the topology as the operator digitizes.

How the graph topology is constructed involves trade-offs between software and human decisions. In a production mode, an operator is only asked to enter the linear features of a map as spaghetti strings. Polygons' ID points are entered separately and the corresponding polygon outlines are attached using point-in-polygon tests during the editing stage [see Fegeas, 1978; Dougenik, 1979; Ericksen, 1983; Corson-Rikert, 1988]. The compilation of polygon outlines from spaghetti data requires considerable calculation of intersections between lines. Usually, the lines will be sorted first by the **YMIN** value of their bounding rectangles (see the next section) established for initial rectangle intersection checks.

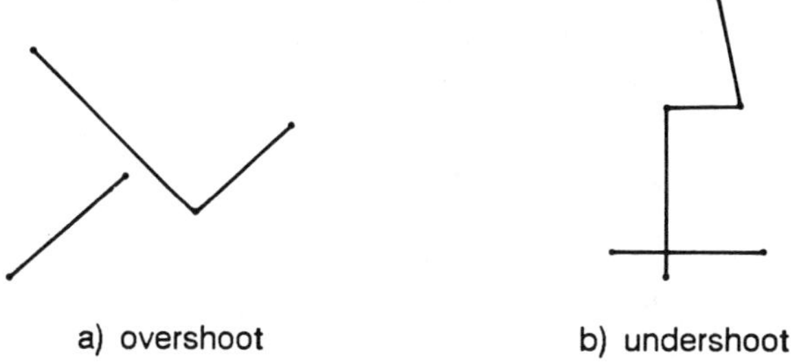

Figure 4.13 Dangling Chains.

Secondly, during editing a number of errors in the data input may be detected including switchback dangling chains as the result of either over- or undershoots (Figure 4.13), unlabelled polygons, conflicting names for polygons or chains with the same left/right polygon IDs [Chrisman, 1987]. Because it is impossible to expect the operator to match lines encoded at independent times exactly, tolerances are given for determining intersections rather than exact points. One point is defined to be within the neighborhood of another point if the first point is within a preselected distance of the second. If this tolerance is exceeded by a careless operator, then many unlabelled polygons will result from the slivers created by the mismatching of points along a common boundary (Figure 4.14).

A strategy requiring more attention on the part of the operator would be to trace directly the outline of each polygon in order (including the background polygon). The polygon outlines are explicitly identified and each chain is found by the intersection of its cobounding polygons. In this approach, the outlines can be sorted by the YMAX value of their corresponding bounding rectangle. Since one polygon ID is known for each chain at the time of encoding, both left and right polygon IDs are known for each chain once the common intersection of two polygons is found.

Further operator involvement is needed to trace the outline of each polygon breaking at each node in the outline. In this manner, the geometric location of individual chains is given during encoding. Again, one polygon ID is initially known for each chain. Chains can now be matched by matching just their endpoints (the nodes). No intersections need to be calculated, just point-in-circle tests for the given tolerance. Finally, the chains themselves can be traced directly and the operator can input the corresponding polygon and node IDs as input [Cromley, 1984]. This only requires that the endpoints of chains sharing the same nodes be "snapped" together, but does require considerable expertise on the part of the operator. Many more manual preprocessing tasks must be performed before digitizing, making it less adaptable to a production environment.

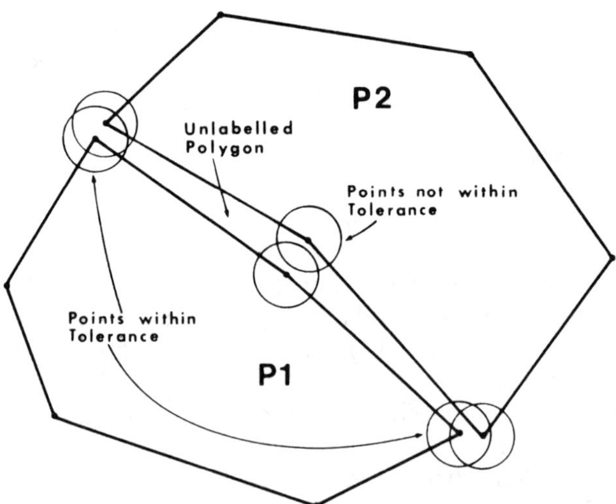

Figure 4.14 Unlabelled Polygons Resulting from Slivers.

4.4 PREPROCESSING

Preprocessing is the manipulation of recently acquired data to establish associations between cartographic objects and their spatial and non-spatial attributes or to uncover order within the values of an attribute. Certain preprocessing operators assist in the organization of data elements into structures, while others facilitate the execution of subsequent functions.

4.4.1 Searching

One basic preprocessing operation is *searching*. There are two primary motives for performing a search. One reason is to determine which objects satisfy certain criteria. For example, one special search is to find the object having the minimum or maximum value with respect to either locational coordinates or a thematic attribute. When processing polygons or chains it is sometimes important to know the minimum bounding rectangle about either a polygon (Figure 4.15a) or a chain (Figure 4.15b).

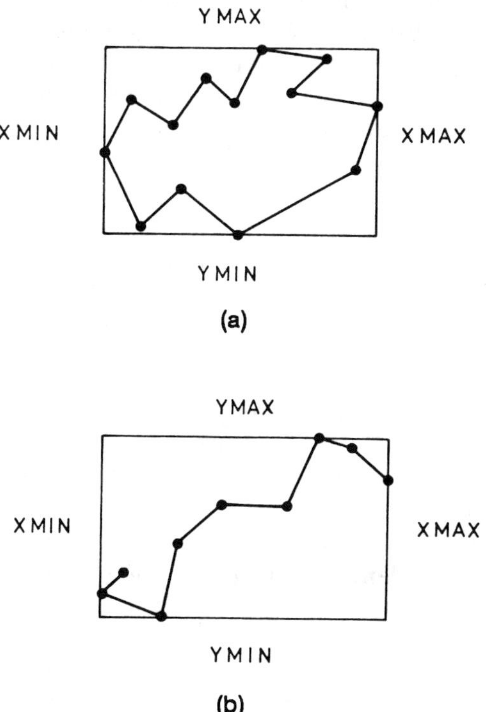

Figure 4.15 The Minimum Bounding Rectangle.

This rectangle may be used in subsequent operations involving polygons and chains such as labelling polygons during digitizing. The minimum bounding rectangle is found by determining the maximum and minimum X- and Y-coordinates for the respective polygons or chains.

Because **(x,y)** coordinates of a polygon outline or a chain are encoded sequentially, the **x** and **y** values will be in separate unordered lists with respect to these spatial attributes after the initial encoding stage is completed. The maximum and minimum **x** (**XMAX** and **XMIN** respectively) and **y** (**YMAX** and **YMIN** respectively) values can be found by the comparing the **x** and y value of each coordinate against the respective current minimums and maximums. The search for each minimum or maximum value requires **(n-1)** comparisons.

A second motive for searching is to establish the relative position of a new object (point), **Pn**, within an existing one-dimensional or two-dimensional distribution of objects (points) with respect to either the coordinate locations or non-spatial attributes of the objects. The problem is to find the nearest neighbor of the new object in all directions from among the existing objects. For a one-dimensional distribution, this means finding the next higher and next lower objects in value from the new object. For example, the next higher and lower neighbors of point **Pn** in Figure 4.16 are **P9** and **P1** respectively.

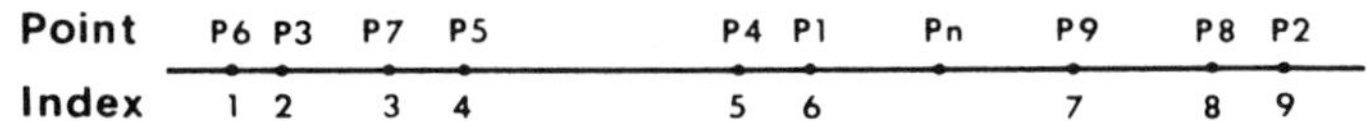

Figure 4.16 One-Dimensional Nearest Neighbors.

For a two-dimensional distribution, finding the nearest neighbors in all directions corresponds to finding the Thiessen neighbors of the new point. For example in Figure 4.17, the Thiessen neighbors of point **Pn** are points **P7**, **P13**, **P1**, **P6** and **P15**. Because the order among the existing objects has already been established before the relative position of the new object is found, this problem is solved in the context of an existing data structure.

For one-dimensional distributions organized as lists that have a sequential or random access allocation, a frequently used strategy is to perform a binary search. In a binary search, the strategy is to reduce the size of the search interval by one-half in each iteration. Assume that the attribute value of the new object and the *ith* object in the list are **Bn** and **Bi** respectively; the index of the next lower object is *l* and the index of the next higher object is *h*. The indices of the next higher and lower objects can be found by the following binary search:

```
BEGIN
   l = 1
   h = m (the highest index)
   WHILE h - l ≠ 1 DO
   i = [ (l + h)/2 ]
   IF Bn < Bi THEN
      h = i
   ELSEIF Bn > Bi THEN
      l = i
   ELSEIF Bn = Bi THEN
      h = l = i
   END IF
   END WHILE
END
```

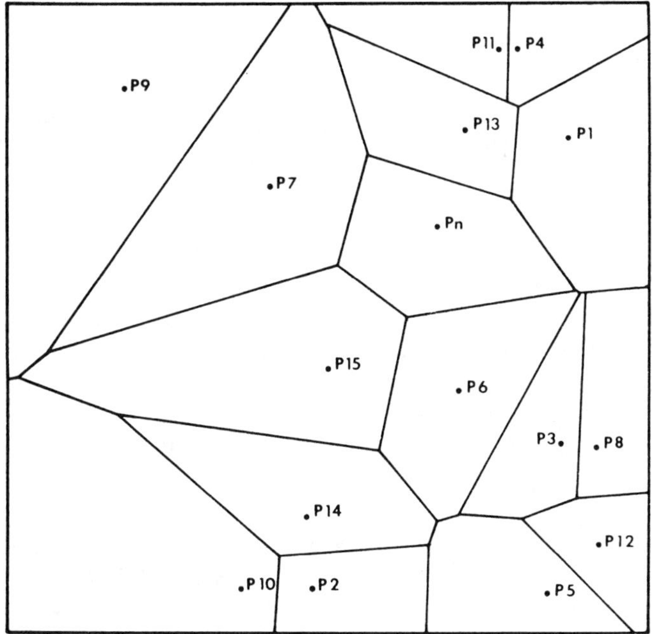

Figure 4.17 Two-Dimensional Nearest Neighbors.

For the situation in Figure 4.16, the initial values of *l* and *h* are **1** and **9** respectively. The initial value of **i** is **5**. Because **Bn** is greater than **B5**, the value of *l* is updated to **5**; the new value for **i** is **7**. In this case, **Bn** is less than **B7** and the value of *h* is updated to **7**. The new value for **i** is **6**. Because (*h*-*l*) now equals **1** the search stops and **Pn** lies between the points having index **6** and **7** respectively. Binary searches are possible in a linked allocation by first converting the interval into a binary tree (see Preparata and Shamos [1985], p. 13) where each segment between two neighboring points is represented as a vertex in the tree.

Binary searches are not possible for two-dimensional distributions because the search interval involves more than one direction. One strategy in this case is first to find the nearest neighbor of the new object within the existing distribution. Fowler [1978] has devised such a method by walking through a Thiessen diagram moving from some initial object to the nearest neighbor of the new object. The index *l* for the nearest neighbor of a new object **Pn** can be found by the following algorithm:

```
BEGIN
   l = the index of some existing object (i.e. the point
         closest to the lower left corner of the diagram.)
   h = the index of the object closest to Pn from among
         l and the Thiessen neighbors of l.
   WHILE l ≠ h DO
      l = h
      h = the index of the object closest to Pn from among
            l and the Thiessen neighbors of l.
   END WHILE
END
```

Figure 4.18a shows the track of potential nearest neighbors for point **Pn**. Initially, **P10** is chosen as the nearest neighbor of **Pn**. However among the Thiessen neighbors of **P10** and point **P10** itself, point **P15** was found to be the nearest neighbor of **Pn**. Next, point **P13** was determined to be nearest neighbor of **Pn** from among the Thiessen neighbors of **P15**. The search for the nearest neighbor of **Pn** now stops, as no Thiessen neighbor of **P13** is closer to **Pn** than **P13** itself.

The nearest neighbor **P***l* is also always a Thiessen neighbor of the **Pn**. The problem now is to find the remaining Thiessen neighbors of **Pn**. Next, each Thiessen vertex of **P***l* is checked to determine which ones are closer to point **Pn** than to point **P***l*. This is easily done by moving around the boundary of **P***l* in a clockwise manner using the vertex data structure presented in section 3.4.3. In Figure 4.18b vertices **V1**, **V2** and **V3** are nearer to point **Pn** than to point **P13**. The Thiessen centroids sharing these three vertices are also Thiessen neighbors of **Pn**.

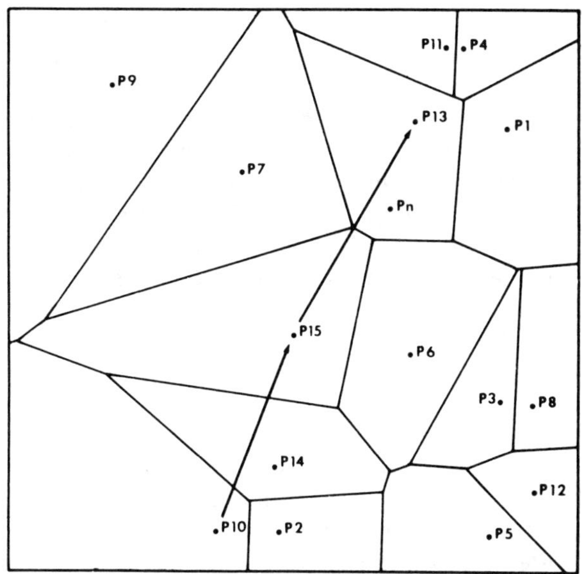

a) the nearest neighbor search

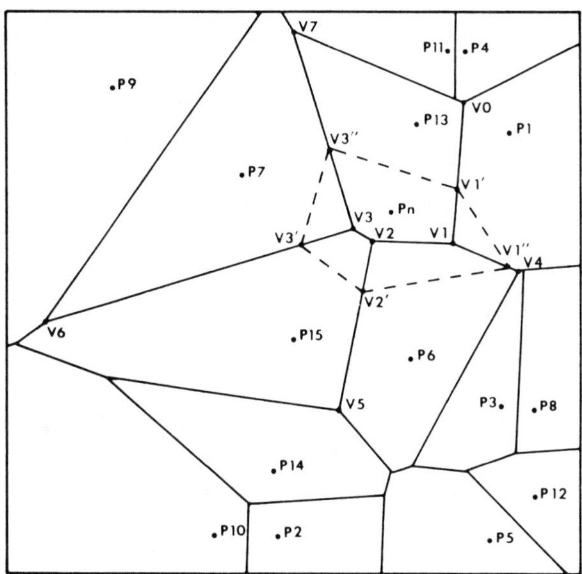

b) finding the remaining Thiessen neighbors

Figure 4.18 Finding the Relative Position of a Point.

In this example, points **P1**, **P6**, **P15** and **P7** are the centroids sharing **V1**, **V2** and **V3**. Next the outlines of these Thiessen centroid neighbors are examined to determine if any other of their vertices lie closer to **Pn** than to the existing centroid. If they do, the Thiessen centroids sharing these vertices are also Thiessen neighbors of **Pn**. This process continues until no more current Thiessen vertices are closer to $\mathbf{P_n}$ than their current centroid neighbors. In the current example, no other vertices associated with **P1**, **P6**, **P15** or **P7** lie closer to **Pn** than their respective centroids. At this juncture, all Thiessen neighbors of $\mathbf{P_n}$ have been enumerated and this point can now be inserted into the diagram (Figure 4.18b).

4.4.2 Sorting

Another major preprocessing operator related to searching is *sorting*. The sorting operator is performed on one- and two-dimensional distributions of points to find the existing order among the points. There are many different sorting strategies that can be used to find this order. Knuth [1973] provides a thorough examination of the differing approaches; only a few are covered here.

For one-dimensional distributions, sorting generates a list structure from an unordered list of points. Sorts are performed to establish either ascending (lowest to highest) or descending (highest to lowest) order. One basic sorting strategy is based on the principle of insertion. Each successive point is inserted in its appropriate location within the sub-distribution of preceding points. For example, suppose that seven points have the following attribute values - **17, 24, 30, 5, 7, 12, 19** - respectively. These values would be sorted in ascending order on each iteration in the following manner:

S1| 17 : 24, 30, 5, 7, 12, 19
S2| 17, 24 : 30, 5, 7, 12, 19
S3| 17, 24, 30 : 5, 7, 12, 19
S4| 5, 17, 24, 30 : 7, 12, 19
S5| 5, 7, 17, 24, 30 : 12, 19
S6| 5, 7, 12, 17, 24, 30 : 19
S7| 5, 7, 12, 17, 19, 24, 30:

(note: the symbol ":" separates the sorted from the unsorted portion of the distribution.)

On iteration **S1**, the first value in sequence, **17**, is the only element of the initial list. On iteration **S2**, the next value in sequence, **24**, is inserted into its proper location with respect to the current list **{17}**. Next the value, **30**, is inserted into the list **{17, 24}**. This process continues until on iteration **S7**, the value, **19**, is inserted into the list **{5, 7, 12, 17,**

24, 30}. If a binary search is used on each iteration, then $log_2\mathbf{m}$ comparisons are needed to insert the next point where **m** is the number of points in the current list. For **n** unordered points, a total of $log_2[(\mathbf{n}-1)!]$ comparisons are needed to sort the points into a list.

An alternative approach is to search successively for the minimum value of the point set, reducing the size of the unordered subset on each iteration. For the example above, the sort sequence would be:

S1| 5 : 17, 24, 30, 7, 12, 19
S2| 5, 7 : 17, 24, 30, 12, 19
S3| 5, 7, 12 : 17, 24, 30, 19
S4| 5, 7, 12, 17 : 24, 30, 19
S5| 5, 7, 12, 17, 19 : 24, 30
S6| 5, 7, 12, 17, 19, 24 : 30

On iteration **S1**, the value **5** is the minimum value of the entire set. This point is moved to the first position of the new list. On iteration S2, the value 7 is the minimum of the subset **{17, 24, 30, 7, 12, 19}**. On each iteration **(m-1)** comparisons are made to find the minimum value where **m** is the number of points in the current unordered subset. For **n** unordered points, a total of **[(n-1)(n-2)/2]** comparisons are needed to sort the points into a list.

Although both of the above sorting procedures are easy to implement, they are not very computationally efficient. Neither takes advantage of any numerical order that may already be present in the unordered list. Another approach is to merge smaller lists hierarchically into larger lists by interleaving the respective points of each list based on numerical order. The initial lists to be merged can be determined in a number of different ways. One way is to let each point be its own list. In our example the subsequent merging of lists would be performed as follows:

S1| 17, 24 : 5, 30 : 7, 12 : 19
S2| 5, 17, 24, 30 : 7, 12, 19
S3| 5, 7, 12, 17, 19, 24, 30

On iteration S1, pairs of the initial lists are merged together into four larger lists. The list **{19}** is not merged with any other list at this stage because there are an odd number of initial lists; the last list is never merged on any iteration in which there are an odd number of lists. On iteration **S2**, the four lists from **S1** are now merged into two lists and finally into one list on iteration **S3**. For **n** unordered points, only $log_2\mathbf{n}$

iterations are needed to perform the sort. Overall **[nlog_2n-(n-1)]** comparisons are required at most for sorting.

Another way to find the initial lists is to partition the initial sequence of points into a set of lists based on any natural order present in the sequence. In our example, the merging sequence is as follows:

S1| 17, 24, 30 : 5, 7, 12, 19
S2| 5, 7, 12, 17, 19, 24, 30

Only two iterations were necessary because of the high level of order that occurred naturally in the sequence. On iteration **S1**, **(n-1)** comparisons are necessary to establish the initial set of **m** lists. The total number of additional iterations is a function of the number of initial lists. Overall at most **(n-1)(log_2m+1)** comparisons are necessary for sorting. In section 4.6 we will see how merge sorts are easily integrated with cartographic data structures in processing cartographic objects.

For two-dimensional distributions, one sorting strategy is to order the points based on a Peano sequence. The easiest ordering of two-dimensional points for a Peano list discussed in section 3.6 is to list the points with respect to the numerical order of one of the two dimensions (frequently the Y-dimension) (see Figure 3.59). Such an ordering of points is frequently used in conjunction with many cartographic operations. However, this path topology does not retain the same efficiency property that a path topology does for a true one-dimensional distribution of points. In a one-dimensional metric space, a path topology should express the minimal distance path between two extreme objects of the set that includes all objects of the set. Any line possesses this property and a sort creates such a path for a one-dimensional set of objects.

This property should also hold for a path topology of a two-dimensional set of points. The solution to this problem, a planar subset of the Traveling Salesman problem, is computationally infeasible for more large problems (see Lawler *et al.*, [1985]). One approximation is to insert points into the Peano list sequentially such that on each iteration, the increase in the length of the path is minimized. For example in Figure 3.51a, the sequence of points based on a sort of the Y-coordinates is:

{P_{11}, P_4, P_9, P_{13}, P1, P7, P15, P3, P8, P6, P14, P12, P10, P2, P5}.

Using this order to form the initial list, the points are inserted into the current list on each iteration in sequence to minimize the increase in path length:

S1| P11, P4
S2| P9, P11, P4
S3| P9, P11, P4, P13
S4| P9, P11, P4, P1, P13
S5| P9, P11, P4, P1, P13, P7
S6| P9, P11, P4, P1, P13, P7, P15
S7| P9, P11, P4, P1, P13, P7, P15, P3
S8| P9, P11, P4, P1, P13, P7, P15, P3, P8
S9| P9, P11, P4, P1, P13, P7, P15, P3, P8, P6
S10| P9, P11, P4, P1, P13, P7, P15, P3, P8, P6, P14
S11| P9, P11, P4, P1, P13, P7, P15, P3, P8, P12, P6, P14
S12| P9, P11, P4, P1, P13, P7, P15, P3, P8, P12, P6, P14, P10
S13| P9, P11, P4, P1, P13, P7, P15, P3, P8, P12, P6, P14, P10, P2
S14| P9, P11, P4, P1, P13, P7, P15, P3, P8, P12, P5, P6, P14, P10, P2

Although the final list cannot be guaranteed to be the minimal path, it gives a reasonable approximation (see Figure 3.60).

Another strategy for sorting two-dimensional sets of points is to order the points into a tree structure. Samet [1985] provides a summary of point tree structures. Two such trees are discussed here. A point quad-tree recursively subdivides the point space into four quadrants as new points are added sequentially into the tree (Figure 4.19a). Each new point forms a successor to a previous point. For example in Figure 4.19b, point **P2** is the SW successor to point **P1** as its X- and Y-coordinates are less than that of **P1**. Point quad-trees are an efficient organization for search operators as many branches of the tree are pruned away during a search. The order that new points are added can be arbitrary as in Figure 4.17 but this can lead to an unbalanced tree (see Figure 4.19b) which can increase the search computation of later operators.

Another way to enter subsequent points is to first sort the points by both their X- and Y-coordinates to establish the ranking of each point in both dimensions. Next the absolute value of each point's deviation from the midpoint ranking in each dimension is calculated:

$$D_x = |(n+1)/2 - R_x| + 1;$$
$$D_y = |(n+1)/2 - R_y| + 1; \qquad (4.4)$$

where $\mathbf{D_x}$ and $\mathbf{D_y}$ are the ranking deviations from the midpoint ranking, **n** is the number of points, and, $\mathbf{R_x}$ and $\mathbf{R_y}$ are a point's ranking in the respective dimensions. The product $\mathbf{D_x \cdot D_y}$ is a measure of the rank centrality of a point with respect to both dimensions. This product is recalculated for the points in each subquadrant during the recursive subdivision of space (see Figure 4.20a). The result is a more balanced tree structure (Figure 4.20b).

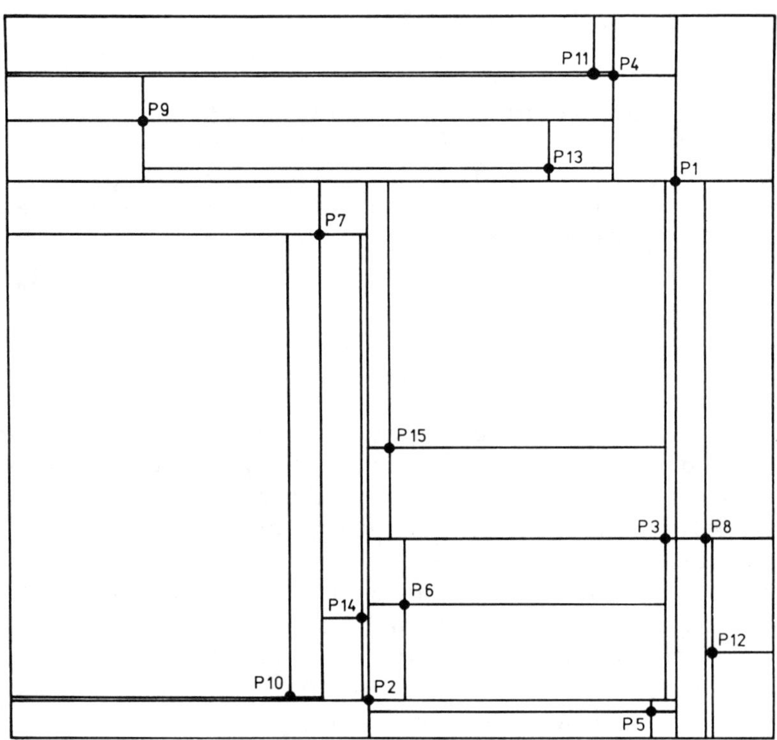

a) a natural order recursive partition

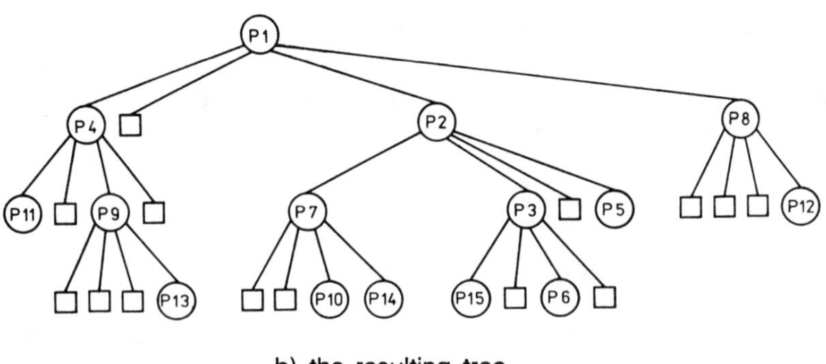

b) the resulting tree

Figure 4.19 A Point Quad-tree Sort.

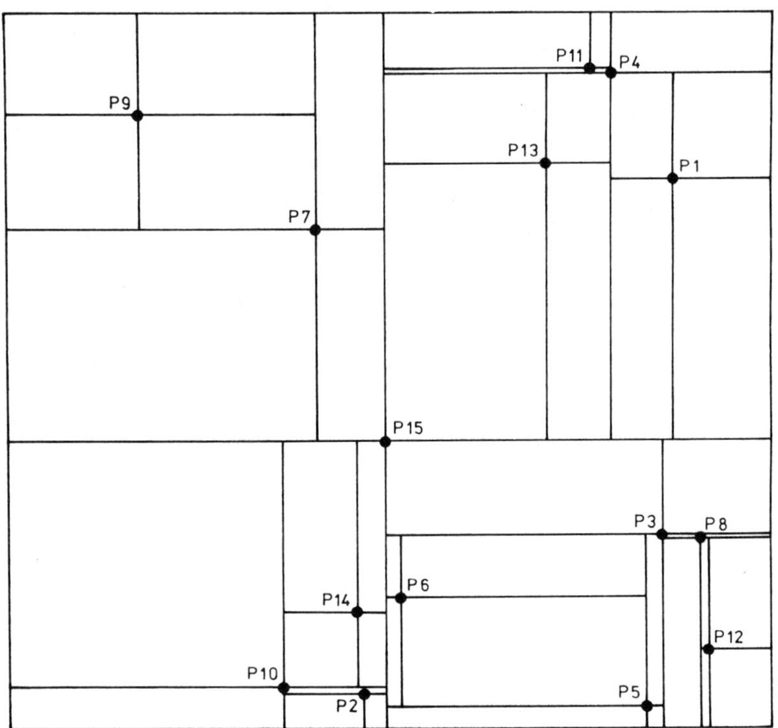

a) an ordered recursive partition

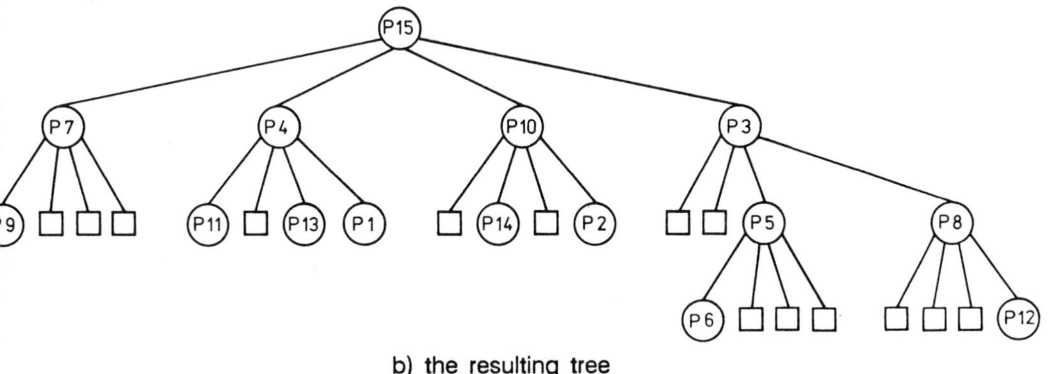

b) the resulting tree

Figure 4.20 A Point Quad-tree Ordered by $D_x \cdot D_y$.

A different tree sort is to order the points in a *k-d tree*. A k-d tree subdivides the point space in half alternating partitions by the X- and the Y-dimensions (see Figure 4.21a). The sequence by which points enter the tree is optional. In Figure 4.21a, points enter in their natural sequence; the initial partition is of the X-dimension. Again the natural sequence of points can result in an unbalanced tree structure (Figure 4.21b) thus increasing the number of search operations.

Alternatively, the points can be sorted first by their X- and Y-coordinates respectively. The initial point of the tree is that point having the midranking in the X-dimension. The successors of this point are the two points having the midranking in the Y-dimension for the respective subsets formed by the initial partition in the X-dimension. This process is repeated until each subset contains only one point (see Figure 4.22a). The resulting tree (Figure 4.22b) usually is more balanced than one created by the natural order of points.

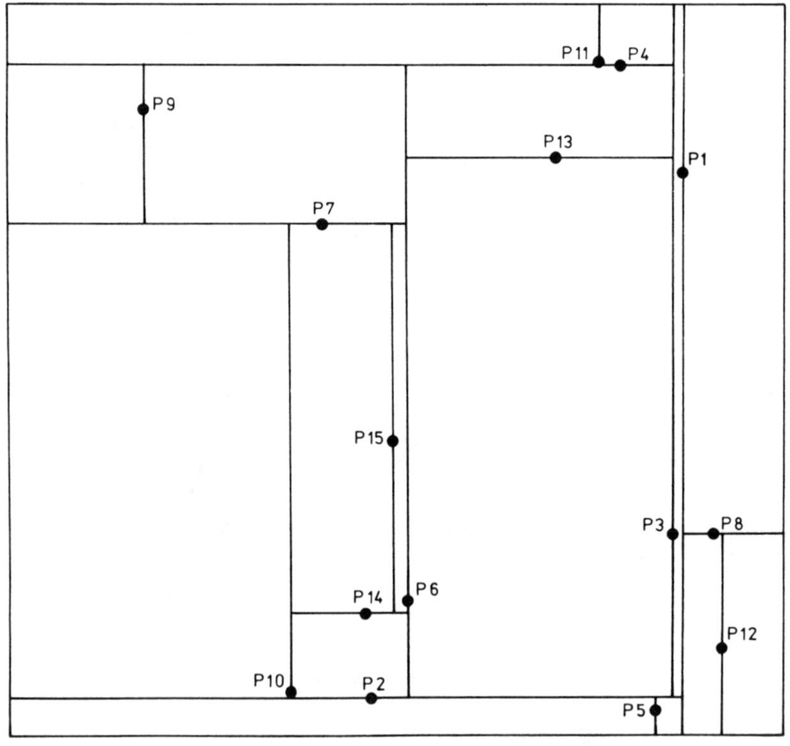

a) a natural order k-d partition

Figure 4.21 A k-d Tree Sort.

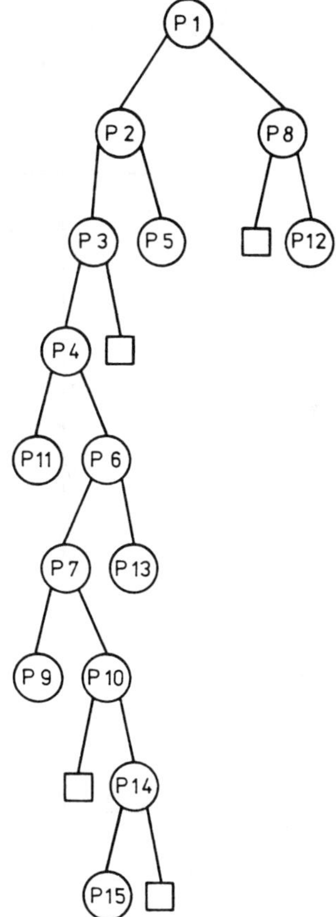

b) the resulting tree

Figure 4.21 A k-d Tree Sort (continued).

A different approach is to sort a two-dimensional set of points into a graph structure of nearest neighbors in Thiessen diagram. This strategy is covered in section 4.5.

4.4.3 Point-in-Polygon Tests

Another preprocessing search operator is a point-in-polygon test. The purpose of point-in-polygon tests is to identify within which polygon a given point lies. The ability to identify numerically a polygon ID using graphic input is a critical operation in many cartographic problems, especially in an interactive environment. Point-in-polygon tests are used to attach labels to polygons during the digitizing process. Point-in-polygon tests rely on the function between interior polygon points and the polygon ID. In order to uniquely identify a polygon ID, the point selected must be a polygon interior point and not a polygon boundary point.

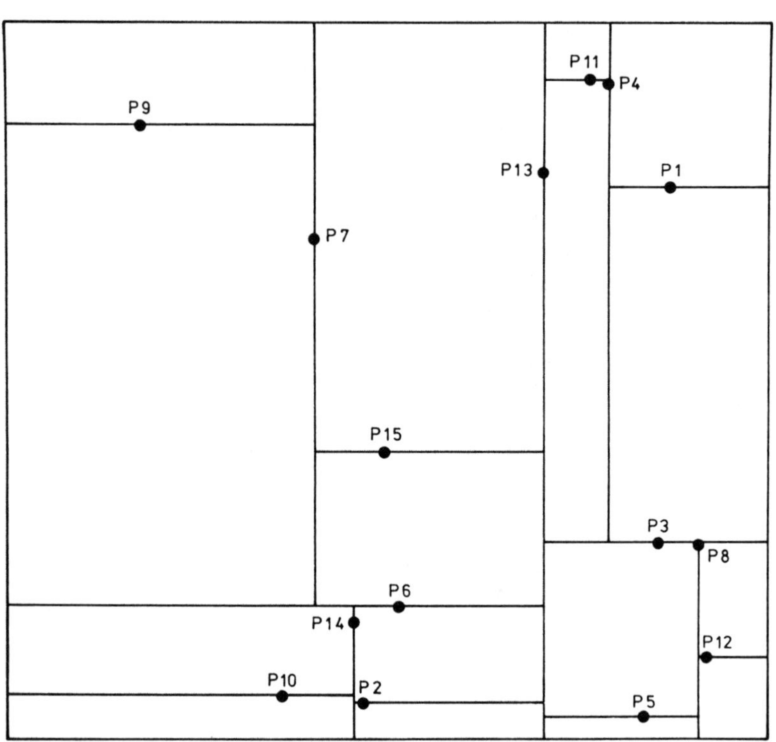

a) an ordered k-d partition

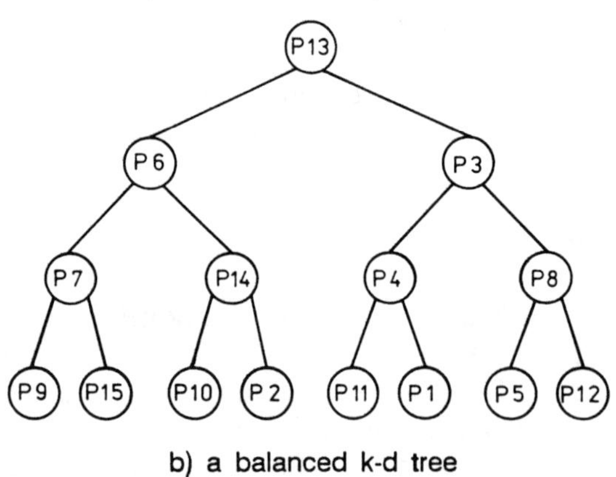

b) a balanced k-d tree

Figure 4.22 A k-d Tree Ordered by Alternating Midrankings.

One basic point-in-polygon test proceeds as follows. Given an interior point, (x_p,y_p), create a vertical line from the top of the mapping area that terminates at the point in question (see Figure 4.23). For each polygon, calculate the number of intersections that its outline makes with the vertical line. The point will lie inside the polygon that has a odd number of intersections; therefore terminate the search once an odd number of intersections is found for any polygon.

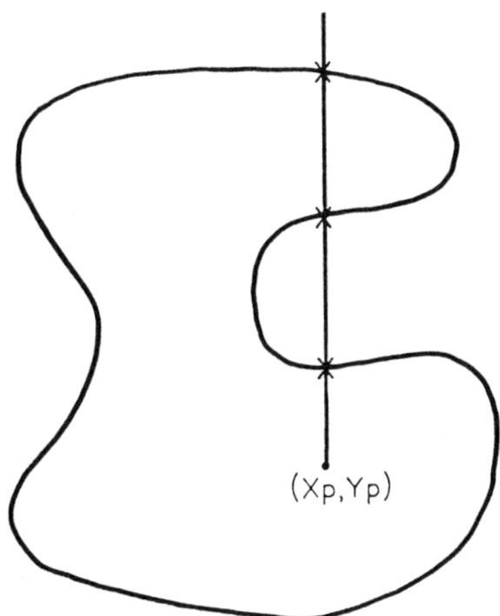

Figure 4.23 A Point-in-Polygon Test.

This search will require an exhaustive number of calculations. Several improvements can be made to this basic strategy. For each polygon, first determine if the point lies within its minimum bounding rectangle. This check does not involve any line intersection calculations but only comparisions against the bounds of the rectangle. It can quickly eliminate a polygon from further tests for outline intersections. A second improvement is first to sort the polygons by their **YMAX** value in a descending order and their **YMIN** value in an ascending order. The rectangle checks would either end with the polygon whose **YMIN** value is just above the point's Y-coordinate or with the polygon whose **YMAX** value is just below the point's Y-coordinate. In Figure 4.24 based on the **YMIN** value, the testing would end with polygon **P2**; based on the **YMAX** value, the testing would end with polygon **P7**.

Polygons can also be searched in a nested hierarchy [Brassel, 1978; Monmonier, 1982]. This requires that polygons be organized in a tree structure (see Figure 4.25a). The point-in-polygon test is performed at each successive level of the tree; however, there are many fewer polygons to be evaluated at the upper levels. For example, suppose that in Figure

4.25b the point was found in polygon A_2; the next set of tests would only be performed on its successors. At the next level, the point was found inside polygon B_4; further testing then passes to its successors until the bottom of the tree is reached.

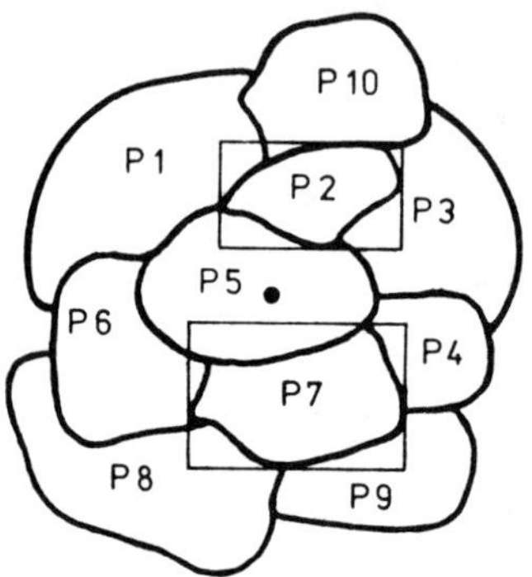

YMAX	YMIN
P10	P8
P1	P9
P3	P7
P2	P6
P5	P4
P6	P5
P4	P3
P7	P1
P8	P2
P9	P10

Figure 4.24 A Sorted Point-in-Polygon Test.

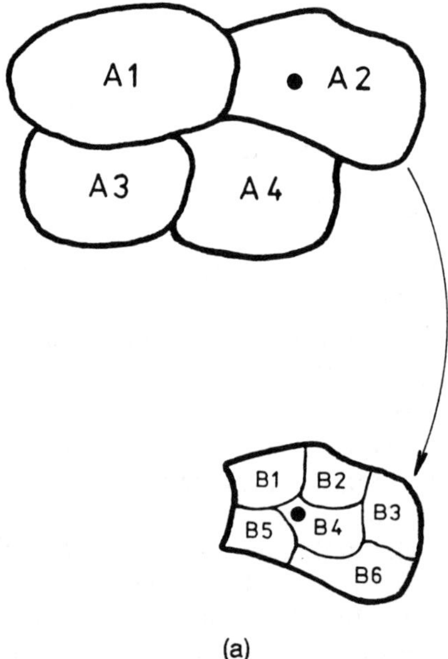

Figure 4.25 A Hierarchical Point-in-Polygon Test.

4.5 DETERMINING PROXIMAL POLYGONS

Just as it is necessary to build topological data structures from spaghetti strings for polygon outlines during digitizing, it is also necessary to generate the topological data structure for proximal polygon diagrams. In these cases part of the path topological data must also be created in the process.

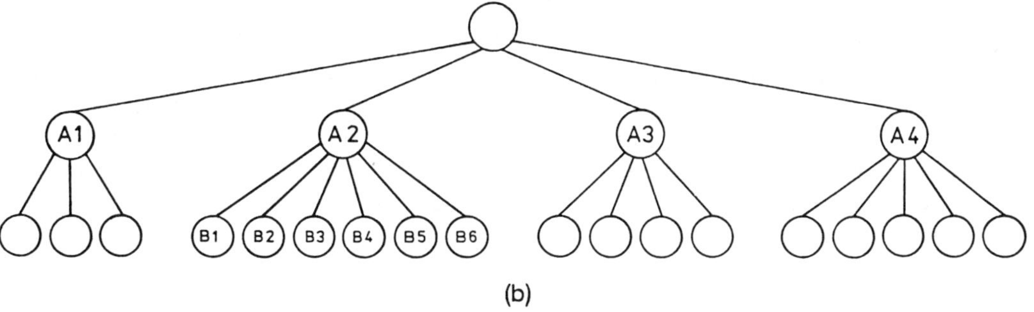

Figure 4.25 A Hierarchical Point-in-Polygon Test (continued).

The data input for a Thiessen diagram is much simpler than that for region outlines. The operator inputs only a set of Thiessen centroids (points) and the outline of the background polygon. This backgound polygon is frequently given as a rectangle although any convex polygon can be used [see Cromley and Grogan, 1985]. There are many different strategies for enumerating the boundaries of Thiessen polygons [Rhynsburger, 1973; Shamos and Bentley, 1978; Brassel and Reif, 1979; Cromley and Grogan, 1985]. One method is to extend the two-dimensional search algorithm given in section 4.4.1 for inserting a new point into an existing diagram; in this case, the initial diagram consists of one point and all other points are sequentially inserted.

Another approach is to identify Thiessen vertices in an ordered sequence after the chain digitizing approach given in the section 4.4.2. This method simulates the encoding of polygon outlines by their chain segments (Thiessen edge segments in this case) as one traverses the perimeter of each polygon. The problem is to identify the location of the Thiessen vertices that separate the outline into edges. Initially all Thiessen vertices that lie on the background polygon are enumerated. The boundary Thiessen vertices are found using Brassel and Reif's circle test (Figure 4.26) [Brassel and Reif, 1979]. A Thiessen vertex exists on a boundary line segment between boundary vertices $\mathbf{B}_i$ and $\mathbf{B}_{i+1}$ whenever a Thiessen centroid lies closer to the next clockwise boundary vertex $\mathbf{B}_{i+1}$ than the current centroid $\mathbf{C}_k$.

Initially, the next potential Thiessen vertex $\mathbf{V}_j$ is set equal to $\mathbf{B}_{i+1}$. A circle is inscribed around this vertex having a radius equal to the distance between $\mathbf{V}_j$ and $\mathbf{C}_k$. If no other centroid lies within the circle, then no Thiessen vertex exists on the edge between $\mathbf{B}_i$ and $\mathbf{B}_{i+1}$. If another centroid **C′** does lie within the circle (Figure 4.24) then the location of $\mathbf{V}_j$ is recomputed as the intersection of the perpendicular bisector between $\mathbf{C}_k$ and **C′** and the line segment between $\mathbf{B}_i$ and $\mathbf{B}_{i+1}$. A new circle is inscribed around the new $\mathbf{V}_j$ having a radius equal to the distance between $\mathbf{V}_j$ and $\mathbf{C}_k$ (Figure 4.26). This process is repeated until no other centroid is found to lie inside the circle. The coordinates of Thiessen vertex $\mathbf{V}_j$ are found and its record in the vertex topological file (see section 3.5.3) is updated. $\mathbf{C}_k$ is set equal to **C′** and the process is repeated until the locations of all Thiessen vertices on the background outline have been found.

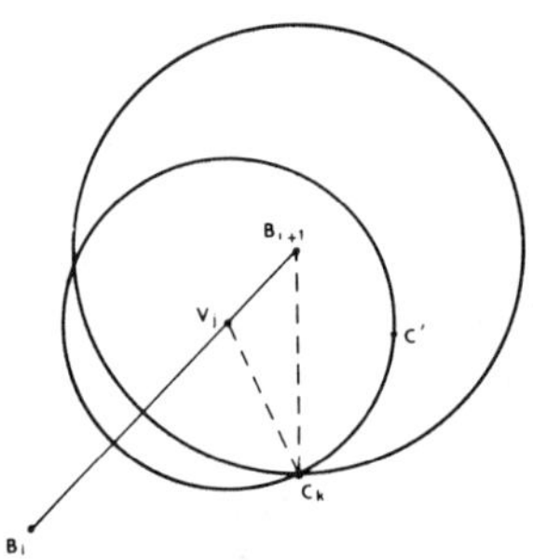

Figure 4.26 The Circle Test.

During this process all centroid neighbors - $\mathbf{C}_k$, **C′**, and $\mathbf{C}_B$ (the backgound centroid) - of each boundary Thiessen vertex and two of its adjoining Thiessen vertices are found and recorded in the vertex topological file (Table 4.3). Next the interior Thiessen vertices are identified in a similar manner by traversing the outline of each Thiessen polygon in a clockwise manner. This is done by completing the vertex record for each boundary Thiessen vertex in order. The first interior Thiessen vertex to be identified is the third adjoining vertex of the first boundary Thiessen vertex. In Figure 4.27, **V11** is the third adjoining vertex of **V1**; consequently the outline around centroid **C10** is traversed first. In completing the Thiessen polygon around centroid **C10**, vertices **V12** and **V13** are also identified.

Next the third adjoining vertex of **V2** is determined; in this example **V14** is the adjoining vertex of **V2** and the polygon around **C9**. By the time all Thiessen boundary vertex records have been completed, a set of interior Thiessen vertices have been identified - in Figure 4.27, vertices **V11-V26**. These vertices are processed in order next to determine their third adjoining vertex. It should be noted that some interior vertices like **V11**, **V13**, **V15**, **V17**, **V18**, **V19**, **V22**, **V23** and **V24** will have completed records at this time. These records are skipped over in the sequence. In this manner all interior vertices eventually will be identified. Once all interior vertices have been enumerated, the full vertex topological file is complete and all vertex coordinates have been found.

Table 4.3 The Boundary Vertex Topological File

Vertex	Adjoining Vertices			Right-Hand Centroids		
V1	V2	V10	?	C9	CB	C10
V2	V3	V1	?	C7	CB	C9
V3	V4	V2	?	C11	CB	C7
V4	V5	V3	?	C4	CB	C11
V5	V6	V4	?	C1	CB	C4
V6	V7	V5	?	C8	CB	C1
V7	V8	V6	?	C12	CB	C8
V8	V9	V7	?	C5	CB	C12
V9	V10	V8	?	C2	CB	C12
V10	V1	V9	?	C10	CB	C2

4.6 CHAIN PREPROCESSING AND MEASUREMENT PROCEDURES

In the last chapter, the polygon and spaghetti models were found to be inferior to graph topological models in part because of the data redundancy involved in recording the boundaries between polygons twice. Although there has been a strong effort to develop digital cartographic data structures that eliminate this redundancy, less effort has been made to integrate the topological models into preprocessing and other measurement functions.

Graph topological data structures store explicitly only the path topology of the chains between polygons and not the topology of the polygons themselves; retrieval of an individual polygon's outline is a composite operation. Similarly, many preprocessing and measurement operations involving polygons can be performed as a composite function.

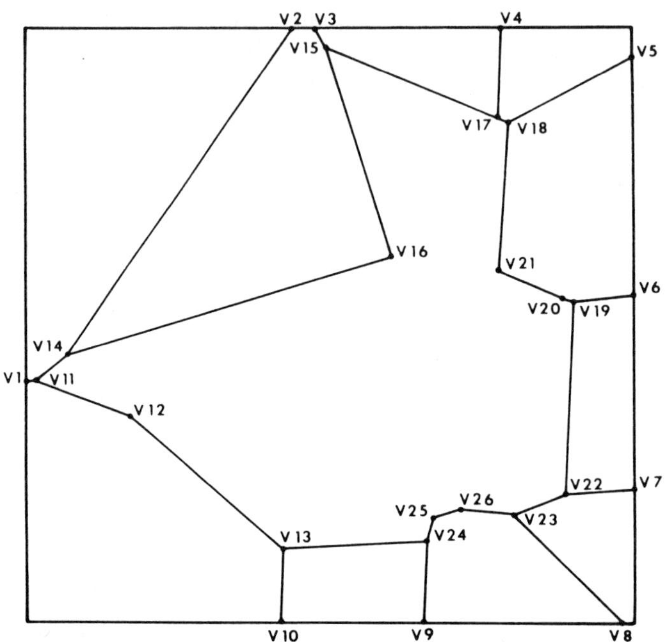

Figure 4.27 The Thiessen Polygons Sharing a Boundary Vertex.

4.6.1 Bounding Rectangles

Suppose that a given map contains **50** polygons having no external or internal islands. There are **147** chains forming the boundaries between polygons, of which **37** lie on the exterior perimeter of the body of the map and **110** lie in the interior of the map body. Additionally, there are **98** nodes of which **37** nodes lie on the exterior perimeter and **61** lie in the interior. Finally, there are **2543** points that comprise the chain lists; **518** of these points lie on the exterior perimeter and **2025** lie in the interior of the map body. To find the maximum Y-coordinate of the bounding rectangle for each polygon would entail **(N_i-1)** comparisons where N_i is the number of coordinates in the ith polygon. For the entire map, this would require:

$$\sum_{i=1}^{50} (N_i-1) \quad \text{or} \quad \sum_{i=1}^{50} N_i - 50 \quad \text{comparisons.}$$

Because each interior point appears twice, each exterior point appears once, each interior node appears three times, and each exterior node appears twice in the outlines of polygons, a total of **4675 (4050+518+183 +74-50)** comparisons would be made to find the **50** maximum points.

However, to find the maximum Y-coordinate of each chain requires far fewer comparisons (the reduction is not quite one-half because only interior chain points are duplicated in the former approach). Because every interior and exterior point appears once and every interior and exterior node appears three times in the outlines of chains, a total of **2693 (2543+297-147)** comparisons would be required to find the **147** maximum points. The maximum Y-coordinate of each polygon is found as the maximum of the maximal points associated with the chains comprising its outline. Because each interior chain appears twice and each exterior chain appears once in the outlines of polygons, an extra **207 (220+37-50)** comparisons are necessary for a grand total of **2900 (2693+207)** comparisons to find the **50** points having the maximum Y-coordinate for the respective polygons. It is far more efficient to calculate and store the bounding rectangles for each chain rather than each polygon; bounding rectangles for polygons can be subsequently compiled at a relatively minor additional time cost.

4.6.2 Polygon Sorting

An operation related to the bounding rectangle problem is the sorting of the coordinates of a polygon with respect to either the Y- or X-dimension. If this operation is performed polygon-by-polygon, then the coordinates of each interior chain are sorted twice. To reduce the number of comparisons required to sort the coordinates of each polygon, the coordinates of each chain are sorted first. The sorted outline of an individual polygon can be retrieved by performing a merge sort on the respective chains comprising its outline. Given **m** chains and **n** points in the total outline, at most $[n \log_2 m - (\log_2 m)(\log_2 m+1)/2]$ comparisons are required to sort chains into a polygon.

4.6.3 Point-in-Polygon Tests Using Chains

Point-in-polygon tests can also be performed directly on chains rather than polygon outlines. The two rationales for doing this are again the fact that interior points are only processed once and secondly that chains on average have smaller bounding rectangles than polygons and thus more chains are likely to fail a point-in-rectangle test. In this approach, the problem is now to find the chain, C^*, that intersects the plumb line at a point (x_p,y^*) that lies above and nearest to the point **p** (see Figure 4.28). The values of C^* and y^* are iteratively determined as new intersections with the plumb line are found.

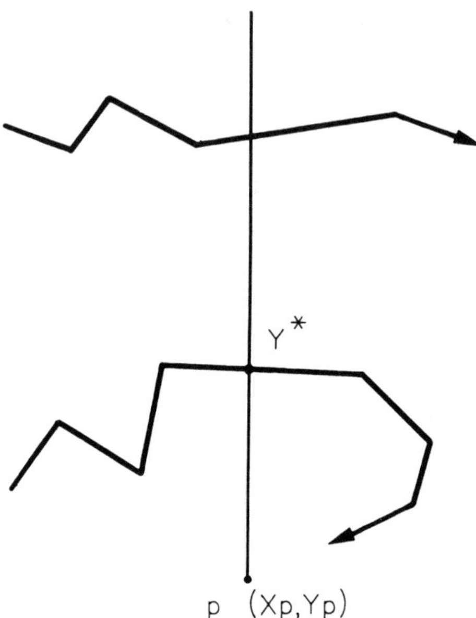

Figure 4.28 Point-in-Polygon Test by Nearest Intersection.

In processing the list of chains, any chain can be weeded whose bounding rectangle lies to the left or right of the plumb line or below p or above the current value of **y***. Each time an intersection **(x,y)** is found between chain **C** and the plumb line, the current values of **C*** and **y*** are updated to **y** and **C** respectively if $y>y_p$ and $y<y^*$. Finally, once **C*** has been found, a check is made to see if the point **p** lies in the left or the right halfplane of the line segment in **C*** that intersects with the plumb line (see Figure 4.29); if **p** lies to the right, it lies inside the right-hand polygon of **C*** while if it lies to the left it lies inside the left-hand polygon of **C***. In Figure 4.29, given the direction of chain **C***, the point **p** lies in the left halfplane of the intersected segment. Thus, point **p** lies inside polygon **P2**.

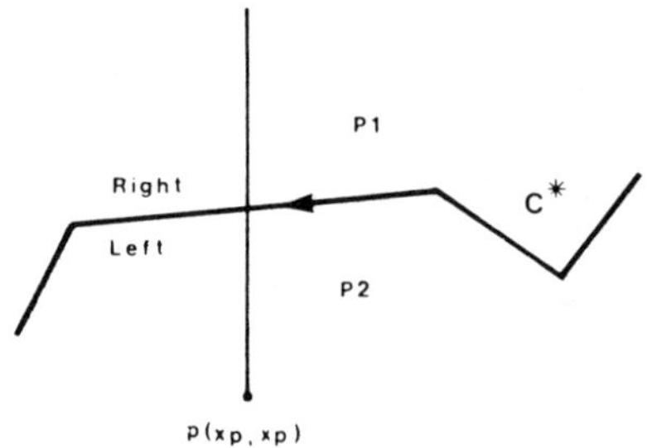

Figure 4.29 Chain Halfplane Check.

4.6.4 Area Measurement

The area of a polygon can be calculated using triangular or trapezoidal decompositions expressed in equations (2.33) and (2.34) respectively. Given that the area of a polygon is the summation of triangles or trapezoids associated with individual line segments, the polygon can be partitioned into areal components associated with individual chains that comprise the outline of a given polygon [Cromley, 1986]. Thus an areal component can be directly computed for each chain. This areal component value may be negative for certain chains if the prevailing direction of the chain is right to left. The area of a polygon is then calculated by summing all chain areal components for which the polygon is the right-hand neighbor and then subtracting the sum of all areal components for which the polygon in question is the left-hand neighbor.

By using a graph topological structure to calculate polygon area, it is not necessary to calculate areal components twice. Once calculated, the areal component associated with each chain is added in the area measurement of its right-hand polygon and subtracted in the area measurement of its left-hand polygon. For the example set of polygons given in section 4.6.1, the triangle or trapezoid areas associated with 4725 line segments would have been computed if area measurements are performed directly on the individual polygon outlines; conversely, the triangle or trapezoid areas associated with only 2693 segments would have been calculated in the chain approach.

Finally, many graphic tablets provide firmware that will calculate the areas of polygons as their outlines are digitized. Although these measurements are accurate to the precision of the hardware and reliability of the trace, they are inherently inaccurate for a system of congruent polygons comprising a map because of the slivering problem associated with retracings of previously digitized lines. Area measurements should not be computed until after the full data structure has been compiled and sliver confusion eliminated.

4.7 SUMMARY

Cartographic data acquisition and preprocessing create the digital database that will be used to compile any map product from a system. Although the advantage of a digital cartographic system is the relative ease in creating many maps from one database, the cartographic objects displayed on many maps must first be compiled from the database. The next chapter covers classification and simplification operators related to this compilation.

4.8 REFERENCES

Bernstein, R. and Ferneyhough, D.,Jr. [1975]. "Digital Image Processing," **Photogrammetric Engineering and Remote Sensing**, 41, 1465-76.

Brassel, K. [1978]. "A Topological Data Structure for Multi-Element Map Processing," **Harvard Papers on Geographic Information Systems**, G. Dutton (ed.), Vol. 4.

Brassel, K. and D. Reif. [1979]. "A Procedure to Generate Thiessen Polygons," **Geographical Analysis**, 11, 289-303.

Buttenfield, B. [1985]. "Treatment of the Cartographic Line," **Cartographica**, 22, 1-26.

Buttenfield, B. [1989]. "Scale-Dependence and Self-Similarity in Cartographic Lines," **Cartographica**, 79-100.

Chorley, R. [1987]. **Handling Geographic Information**, Report of the Committee of Enquiry into the Handling of Geographic Information, London: Her Majesty's Stationery Office.

Chrisman, N. [1987]. "Efficient Digitizing through the Combination of Appropriate Hardware and Software for Error Detection and Editing," **International Journal of Geographical Information Systems**, 1, 265-78.

Corson-Rikert, J. **The ROOTS Draft Manual**, Cambridge, Massachusetts: Laboratory for Computer Graphics and Spatial Analysis, Harvard University Graduate School of Design.

Cromley, R. [1984]. "An Efficient Digitizing System for Encoding Conformant Zone Maps on a Vector Mode Device," **Proceedings**, First International Symposium on Spatial Data Handling, 181-88.

Cromley, R. [1986]. "A Topological Approach to Area Measurement in an Automated System," **Surveying and Mapping**, 46, 269-78.

Cromley, R. and D. Grogan. [1985]. "An Algorithm for Identifying and Storing a Thiessen Diagram Within a Convex Boundary," **Geographical Analysis**, 167-75.

Dougenik, J. [1979]. "WHIRLPOOL: A Geometric Processor for Polygon Coverage Data," **Proceedings**, AUTO-CARTO IV, Vol. 2, 304-11.

Ericksen, R. [1984]. "A Polygon Chaining Algorithm to Simplify Area Encoding," **Computing Environ. Urban Systems**, 9, 237-45.

Fegeas, R. [1978]. "The Graphic Input Procedure: An Operational Line Segment/Polygon Graphic to Digital Conversion," **Harvard Papers on Geographic Information Systems**, G. Dutton (ed.), Vol. 7.

Fowler, R. [1978]. "Approaches in Multi-Dimensional Searching," **Harvard Papers on Geographic Information Systems**, G. Dutton (ed.), Vol. 6.

Freeman, H. [1961]. "Techniques for Digital Computer Analysis of Chain Encoded Arbitrary Plane Curves," **Proceedings**, National Electronic Conference, 17, 421-32.

Freeman, H. [1978]. "Shape Description via the use of Critical Points," **Pattern Recognition**, 10:159-66.

Goodchild, M. [1980]. "Fractals and the Accuracy of Geographical Measures," **Mathematical Geology**, 12, 85-98.

Goodchild, M. and D. Mark. [1987]. "The Fractal Nature of Geographic Phenomena," **Annals Association of American Geographers**, 77, 265-78.

Jenks, G. [1981]. "Lines, Computers, and Human Frailties," **Annals Association of American Geographers**, 71, 1-10.

Jensen, J. [1986]. **Introductory Digital Image Processing**, Englewood Cliffs, New Jersey: Prentice-Hall.

Kennedy, M. and C. Meyers. [1977]. **Spatial Information Systems: An Introduction**, Louisville, Kentucky: Urban Studies Center, University of Louisville.

Knuth, D. [1973]. **The Art of Computer Programming: Sorting and Searching**, 3, Reading, Massachusetts: Addison-Wesley.

Lawler,E.L., J.K. Lenstra, A.H.G. Rinnooy Kan, and D.B. Shmoys. [1985]. **The Traveling Salesman Problem: A Guided Tour of Combinatorial Optimization**, New York: John Wiley.

Lillesand, T. and R. Kiefer. [1979]. **Remote Sensing and Image Interpretation**, New York: John Wiley.

MacDougall, E.B. [1976]. **Computer Programming for Spatial Problems,** New York: Halsted Press.

Mandelbrot, B. [1977]. **Fractals: Form, Chance and Dimension,** San Francisco: Freeman.

Mandelbrot, B. [1982]. **The Fractal Geometry of Nature,** San Francisco: Freeman.

Marble, D., J. Lauzon, and M. McGranaghan. [1984]. "Development of a Conceptual Model of the Manual Digitizing Process," **Proceedings,** First International Symposium on Spatial Data Handling, 146-71.

Monmonier, M. [1982]. **Computer-Assisted Cartography: Principles and Prospects**, Englewood Cliffs, New Jersey: Prentice-Hall.

Perkal, J. [1966]. (Trans. R. Jackowski) "On the Length of Empirical Lines," **Michigan Inter-University Community of Mathematical Geographers**, Discussion Paper No. 10.

Peucker, T. [1976]. "A Theory of the Cartographic Line," **International Yearbook of Cartography**, 16, 134-43.

Preparata, F.P. and M.I. Shamos [1985]. **Computational Geometry: An Introduction**, New York: Springer-Verlag.

Rhynsburger, D. [1973]. "Analytic Delineation of Thiessen Polygons," **Geographical Analysis**, 5, 133-44.

Richardson, L. [1961]. "The Problem of Contiguity," **General Systems Yearbook**, 9, 139-87.

Sabins, F. [1978]. **Remote Sensing, Principles and Interpretation,** San Francisco: Freeman.

Samet, H. [1984]. "The Quadtree and Related Hierarchical Data Structures," **ACM Computing Surveys**, 16.

Shamos, M. and J. Bentley. [1978]. "Optimal Algorithms for Structuring Geographic Data," **Harvard Papers on Geographic Information Systems**, G. Dutton (ed.), Vol. 7.

Shelburg, M., H. Moellering, and N. Lam. [1982]. "Measuring the Fractal Dimension of Empirical Curves," **Proceedings**, AUTO-CARTO 5, 481-90.

Steinhaus, H. [1954]. "Length, Shape and Area," **Colloquium Mathematicum**, 1-13.

Chapter 5

Generalization: Classification and Simplification

Once the digital representation has been compiled, many different manipulations can be performed on the data. These manipulations are variant forms of cartographic generalization. Map generalization is a complex process that includes many different types of generalization operators [see Shea and McMaster, 1989]. This chapter focuses on two basic generalization operators - classification and simplification. These operators generate "new" digital objects from existing ones within the digital database.

The primary goal of generalization is to reduce the complexity of a compiled map product while maintaining the salient elements subject to a set of controls. In this process, important features are selected for retention and unimportant features are disregarded [Brassel and Weibel, 1988]. The controls of generalization include the map's objective, its scale, the quality of database, and the graphic limits of the cartographic system [Robinson *et al.*, 1984]. This goal is achieved by representing a set of cartographic objects by a single parameter or a set of parameters. In Figure 5.1a, the sets of objects **{s1, s2,...,sn}** and **{t1, t2,...,tm}** are associated with the respective parameters **S** and **T**, while in Figure 5.1b the same sets of objects are associated with the respective parameter pairs {S, σ} and {S, θ}. In the latter instance, a parameter pair is necessary to differentiate between the generalization of the two original sets of objects.

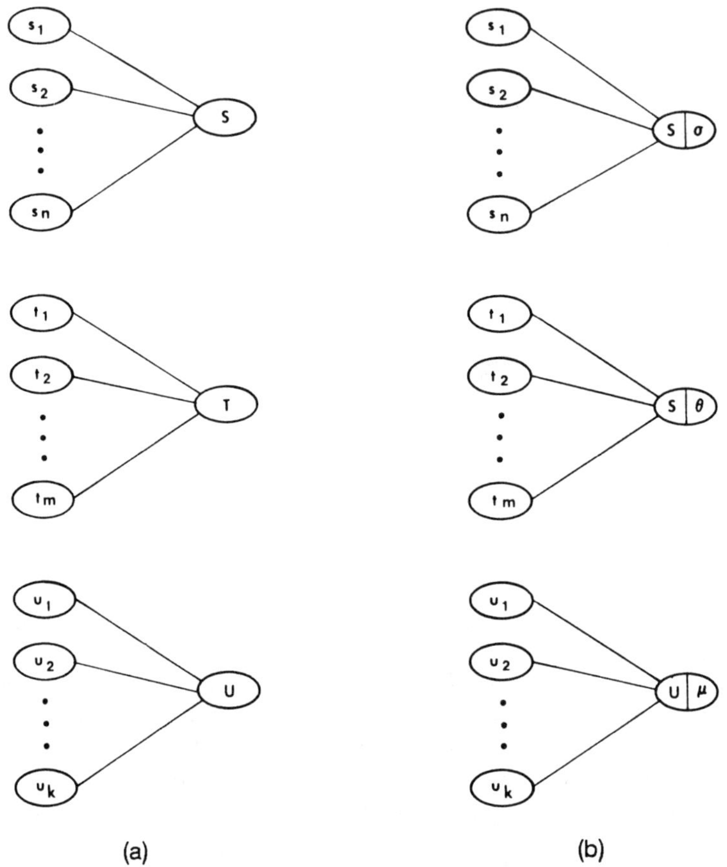

Figure 5.1 The Generalization Operator.

In the first chapter, classification was distinguished from simplification with the former defined as a grouping of objects having similar values while the latter was defined as the elimination of unneccessary detail. This difference is illustrated by the following example, modified from Robinson *et al.* [1984, p. 131]. In Figure 5.2a, the original three clusters of points are simplified by retaining only the middle point of each cluster. On the other hand, in Figure 5.2b, the same distribution is first grouped into three point clusters each represented by a new point located at the "typical" position of each group. However, this distinction does not always hold in practice; a middle position that might be retained by simplification can also correspond to the typical position. Both simplification and classification operators are designed to reduce the level of cartographic data while maintaining the level of cartographic information.

Both usually replace a set of values with a single parameter which may or may not be an element of the original database.

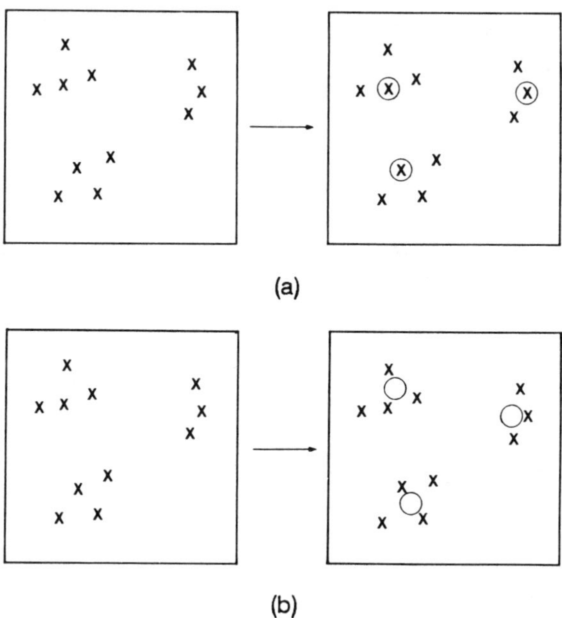

Figure 5.2 The Generalization of a Point Distribution.

The major distinction between these two forms of generalization is that classification generalizes the attributes of the thematic overlay while simplification generalizes the geometry of the geographic base file [Brassel and Weibel, 1988]. The techniques employed may often be the same. Because the purpose of classification and simplification operators is to improve the communication of the map by removing noise or redundant data from a spatial distribution of cartographic objects, the degree to which a resulting map reflects the underlying characteristics or properties of the original spatial distribution is an important measure of map accuracy. Therefore, it is first necessary to discuss the important characteristics of spatial distributions.

5.1 SPATIAL MEASURES OF CENTRAL TENDENCY

One of the most fundamental concepts in geographic analysis is that of *central tendency*. Measures of central tendency are at once both descriptive in the sense that a central tendency measure is a parameter used to summarize a distribution, and normative in the sense that an optimal location is defined with respect to some criterion. Therefore, the objective again must be clearly defined before the appropriate measure can be used. In general, the notion of a spatial measure of central tendency is to find a *center* object with respect to some set of cartographic objects. Spatial interaction, intervening distance and equity of representation are several constructs that have been used to determine what notion of centrality is being investigated. Central tendency operators are defined for point, linear and areal objects.

5.1.1 Point Sets

Suppose that one is given a set of **N** points. In choosing another point as a parameter to represent the entire set, one would expect that this point somehow resembles each member of the set. If the value of the parameter did exactly equal each of the values in the original set then there is no information loss in the generalization. However, this can only occur if the value of each of the original points is the same. Most often a certain amount of incorrect information is transmitted by this generalization function. We would like to select a parameter that minimizes the total amount of misinformation associated with its use as a replacement for the original data values.

We shall assume that such a point must lie within the *convex hull* of the original distribution, $\{\mathbf{P}_j\}$ (see Figure 5.3). A convex hull of a set of points is the boundary of the minimum convex domain that contains the set of points. Points that lie outside the convex hull lie farther away from the original distribution of points than points inside the hull do. For one-dimensional distributions, the convex hull is easy to determine and is the portion of the number scale between the minimum and maximum data points (Figure 5.3a). Although the convex hull of a two-dimensional distribution is numerically more difficult to determine, a variety of algorithms for calculating it are available [see Preparata and Shamos, 1985, pp. 98-125]. Any point within the convex hull of distribution can be written as the convex combination of any set of points contained within the hull.

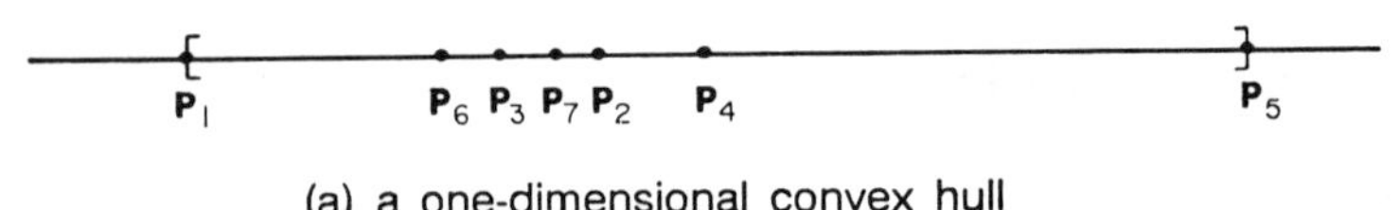

(a) a one-dimensional convex hull

Figure 5.3 The Convex Hull of Point Sets.

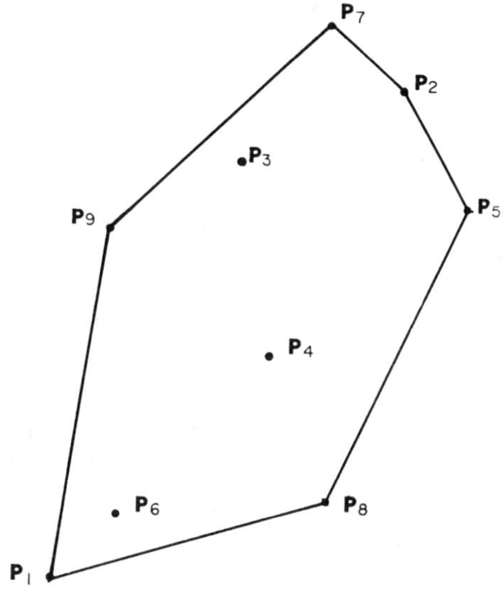

(b) a two-dimensional convex hull

Figure 5.3 The Convex Hull of Point Sets (continued).

A point measure of central tendency, $\mathbf{P}_c$, is the convex combination of this distribution of points:

$$P_c = \sum_{j=1}^{N} \beta_j P_j \quad ; \tag{5.1}$$

where
$$\sum_{j=1}^{N} \beta_j = 1 \; ; \tag{5.2}$$

and
$$\beta_j \geq 0 \; . \quad \text{for all } j \tag{5.3}$$

The set $\{\beta_j\}$ are weights associated with each point in the original distribution. The relative magnitude of the weights will pull the point of central tendency toward one point or another.

Assume that the amount of misinformation is directly related to some function of the distance between each of the actual values and the parameter. For a one-dimensional distribution of points, then find the coordinate (or attribute value), x_c, of point $\mathbf{P}_c$ that:

$$\text{minimizes or maximizes} \quad \sum_{j=1}^{N} w_j \, [(x_j - x_c)^2]^{K/2} \; ; \qquad (5.4)$$

where x_j is the value of the jth point, w_j is a weight signifying either the importance or the relative contribution of the jth point, and **K** is a distance exponent. If all points are equally important, w_j is equal to one; often when $\mathbf{P}_j$ represents geographic location, w_j is assigned one of the attribute values associated with $\mathbf{P}_j$ such as population or elevation. If $\mathbf{K} < \mathbf{0}$, then the objective is to maximize equation **(5.4)**; if $\mathbf{K} > \mathbf{0}$, the objective is to minimize equation **(5.4)**.

Unconstrained optimization problems such as the one expressed in **(5.4)** are solved using differential calculus by first finding the derivative of a relation with respect to the unknown variable(s) and then setting the derivative(s) equal to zero. This process will be referred to as finding the *normal equation(s)* of the problem; there is one normal equation for each unknown variable.

The normal equation for **(5.4)** is:

$$\sum_{j=1}^{N} w_j \, D_{cj} \, (x_j - x_c) = 0 \; ; \qquad (5.5)$$

$$\text{where} \quad D_{cj} = [(x_j - x_c)^2]^{(K-2)/2}. \qquad (5.6)$$

$\mathbf{D}_{cj}$ expresses the distance relationship between the center and the jth point.

Rearranging terms:

$$x_c = \frac{\sum_{j=1}^{N} w_j \, D_{cj} \, x_j}{\sum_{j=1}^{N} w_j \, D_{cj}} \; . \qquad (5.7)$$

If $\mathbf{K} = \mathbf{2}$, then $\mathbf{D}_{cj} = \mathbf{1}$. If $w_j = 1$, then x_c is the location, $\bar{x}$, of the *mean center*, $\bar{\mathbf{P}}$, within the distribution:

$$\bar{x} = \frac{\sum_{j=1}^{N} x_j}{N} \quad . \tag{5.8}$$

For any other value of **K**, the value of x_c is found by an iterative process, where the value of the mean center is used as an initial approximation of x_c [see Cooper, 1967]. At each iteration, the current value of x_c is used to calculate D_{cj} in **(5.6)**; the new approximation of x_c is then found by solving **(5.7)**. The algorithm terminates whenever the number of iterations exceeds some predetermined value or the distance between the old and new values of x_c is less than some preset tolerance. If $K \leq -1$, x_c will gravitate toward a value in the center of a cluster of points (see Figure 5.4) because x_c represents a location that maximizes spatial interaction within the point set. Interaction is greatest in the center of the highest density of points. In this case, x_c represents the location, x_p, of the *modal center (or potential center)*, P_p, within the distribution.

If $K = 1$, then x_c will move toward a value representing the center of gravity within the distribution. A center of gravity minimizes total aggregate distance between the center and each point of the distribution. This is the location, x_m, of the *median center*, P_m, within the distribution. For a one-dimensional distribution, the median location can also be found analytically by sorting the points by value and selecting any point that half of the points lie below in the list and half lie above in the list (see Figure 5.4). For one-dimensional distributions, the median center can always correspond to an object of the original distribution.

Finally as $K \rightarrow \infty$, x_c will move toward a location that minimizes the maximum distance between the center and any individual point. This is the location, x_e, of the *minimax center*, P_e, within the point set. Because every point in the distribution is as close to the minimax center as possible (the center cannot be moved closer to one point without increasing its distance to another point), it represents an equity location within the distribution. For a one-dimensional distribution of points, the minimax location can also be found as the midpoint of the range between the minimum and maximum data values.

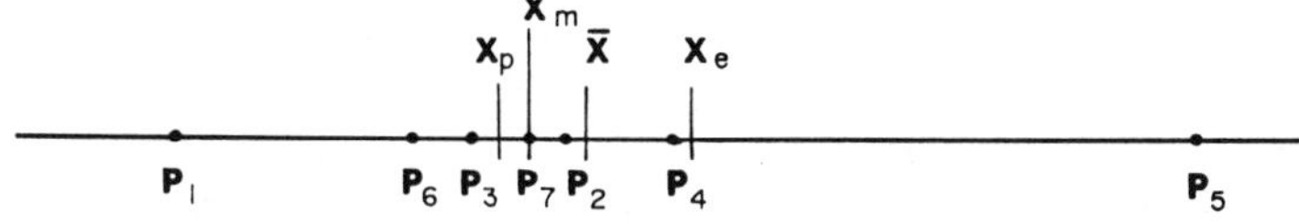

Figure 5.4 The Location of Different One-Dimensional Point Centers.

These central tendency measures are easily extended to two-dimensional point distributions. The coordinate location, (x_c,y_c), of the *bivariate center*, P_c, for a two-dimensional distribution is:

$$x_c = \frac{\sum_{j=1}^{N} w_j D_{cj} x_j}{\sum_{j=1}^{N} w_j D_{cj}} ; \tag{5.9}$$

and

$$y_c = \frac{\sum_{j=1}^{N} w_j D_{cj} y_j}{\sum_{j=1}^{N} w_j D_{cj}} ; \tag{5.10}$$

where

$$D_{cj} = [(x_j - x_c)^2 + (y_j - y_c)^2]^{(K-2)/2}. \tag{5.11}$$

If $K = 2$ and $w_j = 1$, then again $D_{cj} = 1$ and (x_c,y_c) is the location, $(\bar{x},\bar{y})$, of the *bivariate mean center (or centroid)* within the distribution:

$$\bar{x} = \frac{\sum_{j=1}^{N} x_j}{N} ; \tag{5.12}$$

and,

$$\bar{y} = \frac{\sum_{j=1}^{N} y_j}{N} . \tag{5.13}$$

For other values of K, the *bivariate median, modal,* and *minimax centers* are again found by an iterative procedure that uses the bivariate mean center as an initial approximation [see Kuhn and Kuenne, 1962; Cooper, 1963, 1967]. These bivariate centers are often used in facility location models [see Morrill and Symons, 1977]. In locational models, the w_j usually corresponds to the population at each point; the centers are then pulled closer to the points having higher populations. In Figure 5.5, higher populations are associated with points in the southwest corner of the distribution and the centers are shifted in this direction.

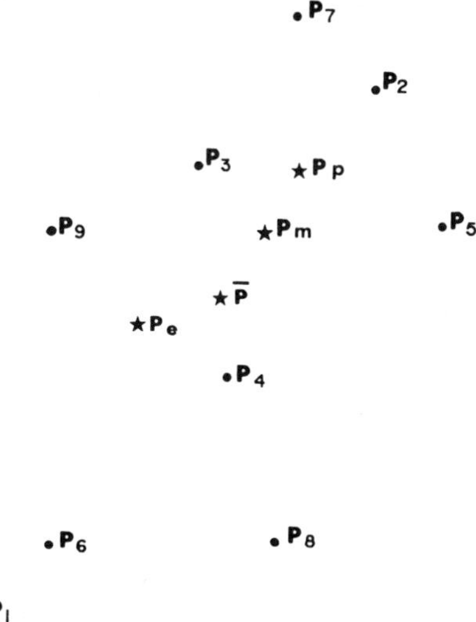

Figure 5.5 The Location of Bivariate Centers.

A two-dimensional point distribution can also be represented by linear central tendency measure, $\mathbf{A}x + \mathbf{B}y + \mathbf{C} = 0$, that passes through the distribution. One can measure the amount of misinformation associated with this straight line by measuring how far the location, (x_j,y_j), of any individual point, $\mathbf{P}_j$, deviates from this line. We know from section 2.5 that $s_j = \mathbf{A}x_j + \mathbf{B}y_j + \mathbf{C}$ measures the distance between a point and a line. Secondly, if **B** equals one, then $| s_j |$ measures the vertical distance between the point and the line; if **A** equals one, then $| s_j |$ measures the horizontal distance between the point and the line (see Figures 5.6a and 5.6b). Finally, if $\mathbf{A}^2 + \mathbf{B}^2 = 1$, then $| s_j |$ measures the perpendicular distance between the point and the line (Figure 5.6c).

The problem is to find the parameters of a line that:

$$\text{minimize} \quad \sum_{j=1}^{N} (s_j)^2 \quad . \tag{5.14}$$

Whenever **B** or **A** is set equal to one, this method corresponds to the technique of ordinary least squares (OLS) from regression analysis [see Clark and Hosking, 1986; Ebdon, 1983] (it should be emphasized that the purpose here is only to determine a line of central tendency and not inferences of population parameters from sample estimators).

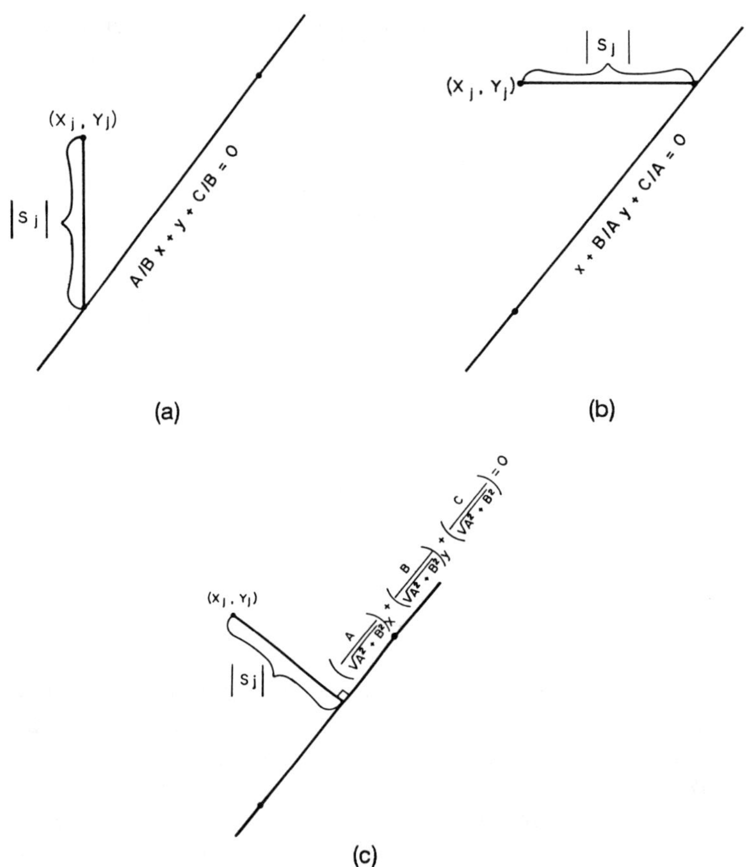

Figure 5.6 Alternate Measures of Point/Line Distance.

To minimize total vertical distance, **B** is set equal to one and the normal equations for **(5.14)** with respect to **A** and **C** result in:

$$A = - \frac{\sum_{j=1}^{N} x_j' \, y_j'}{\sum_{j=1}^{N} x_j'^2} \; ; \qquad (5.15)$$

$$\text{and} \quad C = - A \, \bar{x} - \bar{y} \; ; \qquad (5.16)$$

where x_j' and y_j' are the result of the translations:

$$x_j' = (x_j - \bar{x}) \; ;$$
$$\text{and} \quad y_j' = (y_j - \bar{y}) \; . \qquad (5.17)$$

This central tendency line will pass through the bivariate mean center of the point distribution.

Next, to minimize total horizontal distance, **A** is set equal to one and the normal equations for **(5.14)** with respect to **B** and **C** result in:

$$B = - \frac{\sum_{j=1}^{N} x_j' \, y_j'}{\sum_{j=1}^{N} y_j'^2} \; ; \qquad (5.18)$$

$$\text{and} \quad C = - \bar{x} - B \, \bar{y} \; ; \qquad (5.19)$$

where x_j' and y_j' again are the result of the translations from the bivariate mean center and this line also will pass through this point.

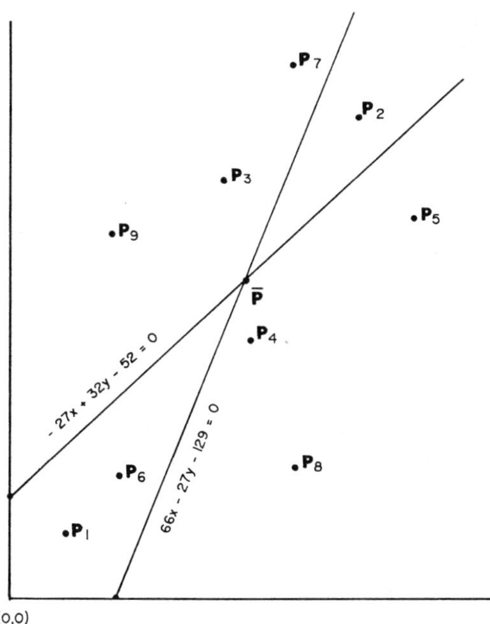

Figure 5.7 Example Central Tendency Lines.

The difference between these two central tendency lines is illustrated by the following example. Figure 5.7 presents a two-dimensional distribution of nine points. The bivariate mean center of this distribution is **(5,6)**. The central tendency line that minimizes the sum of the vertical squared distances between each point and the line is **-27x+32y-52=0** (see Figure 5.7 and Table 5.1); the central tendency line that minimizes the horizontal squared distances between each point and the line is **66x-27y-129=0** (see Figure 5.7 and Table 5.1).

Table 5.1 Calculation of Central Tendency Lines

	x	y	x'	y'	x'^2	y'^2	x'y'
P1	1	1	-3	-4	9	16	12
P2	6	8	2	3	4	9	6
P3	4	7	0	2	0	4	2
P4	4	4	0	-1	0	1	-1
P5	7	6	3	1	9	1	3
P6	2	2	-2	-3	4	9	6
P7	5	9	1	4	1	16	4
P8	5	2	1	-3	1	9	-3
P9	2	6	-2	1	4	1	-2

$\Sigma x = 36$ $\qquad \bar{x} = 36/9 = 4$

$\Sigma y = 45$

$\Sigma x'^2 = 32$ $\qquad \bar{y} = 45/9 = 5$

$\Sigma y'^2 = 66$

$\Sigma x'y' = 27$

minimize vertical distance	minimize horizontal distance
A = -27/32 ;	A = 1 ;
B = 1 ;	B = -27/66 ;
C = -(-27/32)(4) - 5 = -52/32 ;	C = -4 - (-27/66)(5) = -129/66 ;
(-27/32) x + y + (-52/32) = 0 ;	x + (-27/66) y + (-129/66) = 0;
or, -27 x + 32 y - 52 = 0 .	or, 66 x - 27 y - 129 = 0 .

Finally, the problem for minimizing the total perpendicular distance between a point set and a line (see section 2.5) is:

$$\text{minimize} \quad \sum_{j=1}^{N} (Ax_j + By_j + C)^2 \quad ; \tag{5.20}$$

$$\text{subject to:} \quad A^2 + B^2 = 1 \ . \tag{5.21}$$

This problem can be rewritten as the lagrangian:

$$\text{minimize} \sum_{j=1}^{N} (Ax_j + By_j + C)^2 - \lambda\,(1 - A^2 - B^2). \qquad (5.22)$$

where λ is the lagrangian associated with equation **(5.21)**. In constrained optimization, a lagrangian represents a weight or price that measures the rate of change in the objective function associated with an incremental change in the right-hand side constant of the constraint.

Solving the normal equations for **(5.22)** results in:

$$A = \frac{g - (g^2 + 4\,h^2)^{1/2}}{2\,h}\,B\;; \qquad (5.23)$$

$$\text{and,}\quad C = -A\,\bar{x} - B\,\bar{y}\;; \qquad (5.24)$$

$$\text{where,}\quad g = \left(\sum_{j=1}^{N} x_j'^2 - \sum_{j=1}^{N} y_j'^2\right)\;; \qquad (5.25)$$

$$\text{and,}\quad h = \left(\sum_{j=1}^{N} x_j'\,y_j'\right). \qquad (5.26)$$

(x_j',y_j') are again the translated points centered on the bivariate mean.

For the point distribution given in Figure 5.7, the equation of the line that minimizes the sum of the squared perpendicular distances to each point is **$-97.81x + 54y + 118.76 = 0$** (see Table 5.2 and Figure 5.8).

Each of these three methods for computing a generalizing line to a set of points can also be used to determine the general direction of a line. If a line is represented by a sequence of points, these points form the point set which can be used to determine a general direction. Once the general direction has been determined, a minimum bounding rectangle in this direction can be found that encloses all points of the line. The general direction, length and width of this rectangle define the basic parameters of the line [see Peucker, 1976]. The line that minimizes the squared perpendicular distances is preferred over the other two objectives because it results in a minimum bounding rectangle having a smaller area. If the set of points comprising the line are partitioned into subsets of points, a minimum bounding rectangle can be calculated for each subset in this manner. These concepts are expanded in section 5.6 to develop line simplification operators.

Table 5.2 Calculation of the Minimum Perpendicular Distance Line

$$g = 32 - 66 = -34 \;;$$

$$h = 27 \;;$$

$$A = \frac{-34 - [34^2 + (4)(27^2)]^{1/2}}{(2)(27)} = \frac{-34 - (1156 + 2916)^{1/2}}{54}$$

$$= \frac{-34 - 63.81}{54} = -97.81/54 \;;$$

$$B = 1 \;;$$

$$C = -(-97.81/54)(4) - 5 = 388.24/54 - 270/54 = 118.76/54 \;;$$

$$-97.81/54\ x + y + (118.76/54) = 0 \;;$$

$$\text{or,} \quad -97.81\ x + 54\ y + 118.76 = 0 \;.$$

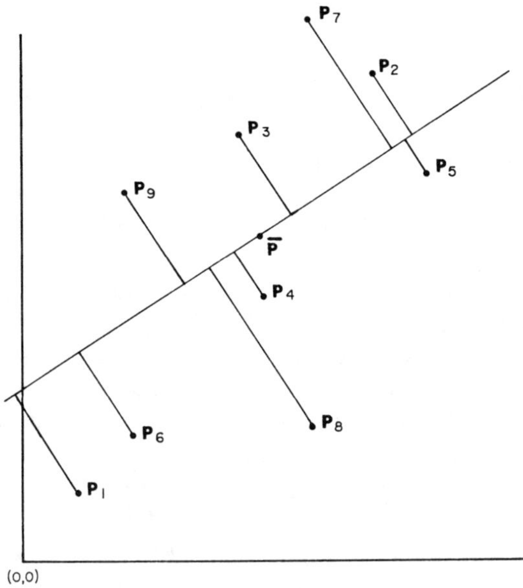

Figure 5.8 The Central Tendency Line Minimizing Perpendicular Distance.

5.1.2 Areal Sets

It is often useful to find a center point location within an areal feature such as a polygon. The simplest method to determine such a point is to calculate the bivariate mean of the coordinates that comprise the polygon's outline (Figure 5.9). However, this measure is heavily influenced by the distribution of vertices comprising the exterior ring of the polygon rather than the distribution of the polygon's interior points. For example, in Figure 5.10a, there are four vertices on the outline of the square; in Figure 5.10b, two vertices are added to the outline between points $\mathbf{P_2}$ and $\mathbf{P_3}$. Although the shape of the polygon did not change, its center was pulled toward the side that had a greater density of outline points.

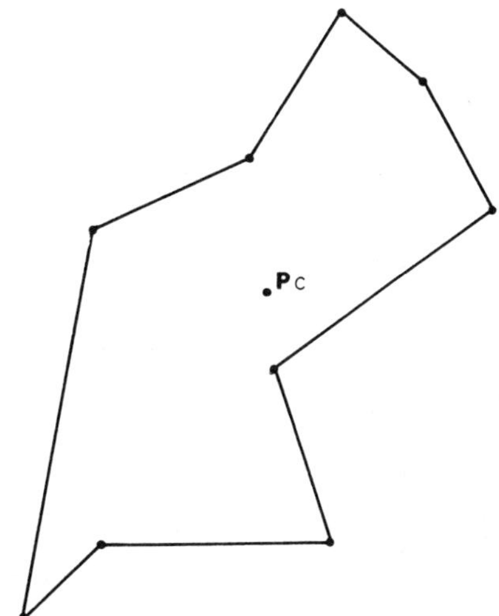

Figure 5.9 The Bivariate Mean Center of a Polygon.

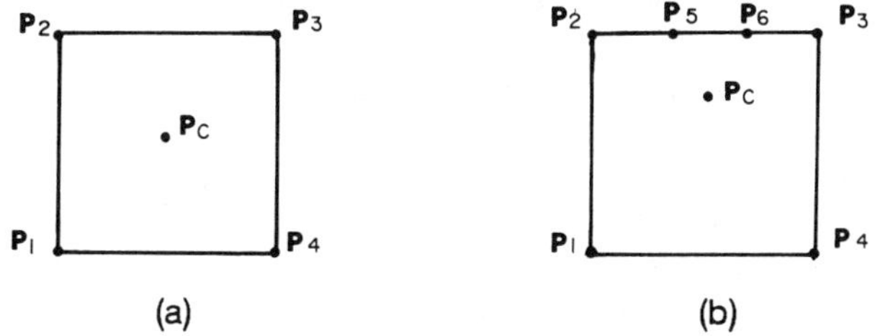

Figure 5.10 The Influence of Exterior Point Density.

An improved measure for calculating the location (x_c,y_c) of the areal center, $\mathbf{P_c}$, would be to weight each point by the area of a trapezoid formed by the line segment connecting consecutive vertices in the outline such that:

$$x_c = 1/2 \frac{\sum_{j=1}^{N} (x_{j+1} + x_j)(x_{j+1} - x_j)(y_{j+1} + y_j)}{\sum_{j=1}^{N} (x_{j+1} - x_j)(y_{j+1} + y_j)} ; \qquad (5.27)$$

$$y_c = 1/2 \frac{\sum_{j=1}^{N} (y_{j+1} + y_j)(y_{j+1} - y_j)(x_{j+1} + x_j)}{\sum_{j=1}^{N} (y_{j+1} - y_j)(x_{j+1} + x_j)} . \qquad (5.28)$$

Portions of the outline where the point density is greater will have trapezoids with smaller areas associated with individual line segments. Therefore, the weighted areal center is less variant with respect to point density than the bivariate mean center (see Figure 5.11).

However, both the simple bivariate mean and weighted areal centroid are only guaranteed to lie within the convex hull of the outline points. This is acceptable if the polygon is convex such that its outline and the convex hull of its vertices coincide. However, many polygons are concave and there is no guarantee that a point that lies within the convex hull will also lie within the boundary of such a polygon (see Figure 5.12). This is especially true if the shape of the polygon is very irregular.

One way to ensure that the center point does lie within a polygon's boundary is to restrict $\mathbf{P}_c$ to be an element of the set of points that form the bimedial or bisector skeleton of the polygon, as all skeleton points belong to the set of polygon points. Alternative properties can again be used to define which skeleton point should be the center point. For example, one property that a center point could have is that it lies in the center of the largest inscribed circle within the polygon. This is a modal concept describing the center of the greatest density of interior points within the polygon. Such a point is the interior vertex of the bimedial (or bisector) skeleton of a polygon having the maximum perpendicular distance to any polygon edge (see Figure 5.13).

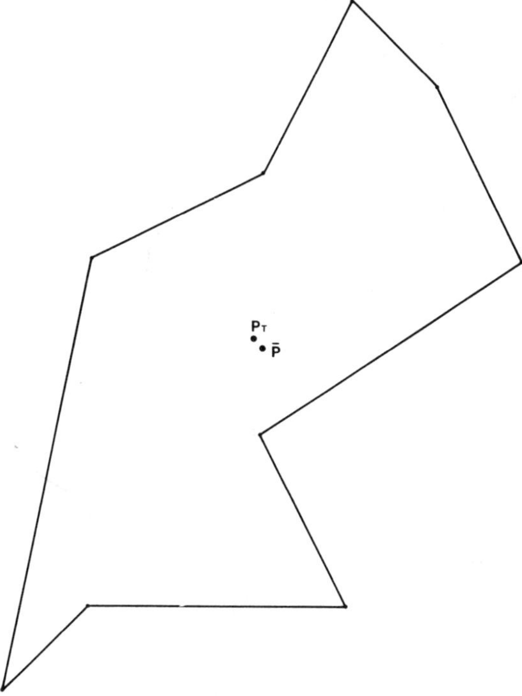

Figure 5.11 A Comparison of Bivariate Mean and Weighted Areal Centers.

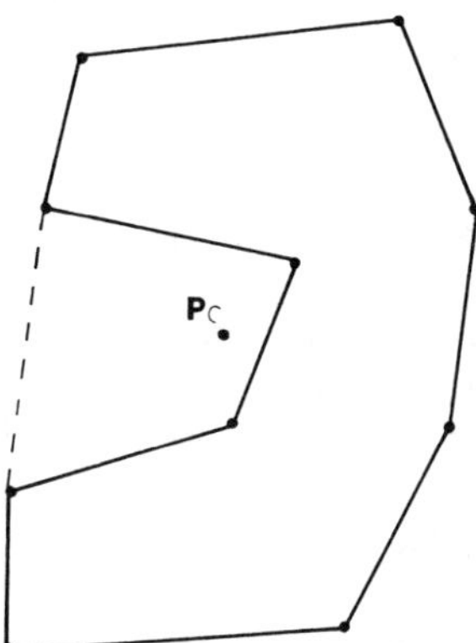

Figure 5.12 A Point within the Convex Hull but not the Polygon.

Another center measure would be to find a point that maximizes the minimum distance to any edge of the polygon. An approximation to this would be to find the path of the bimedial (or bisector) skeleton that maximizes the distance between a pair of exterior skeleton vertices. The maximin center is the midpoint of this path (Figure 5.14).

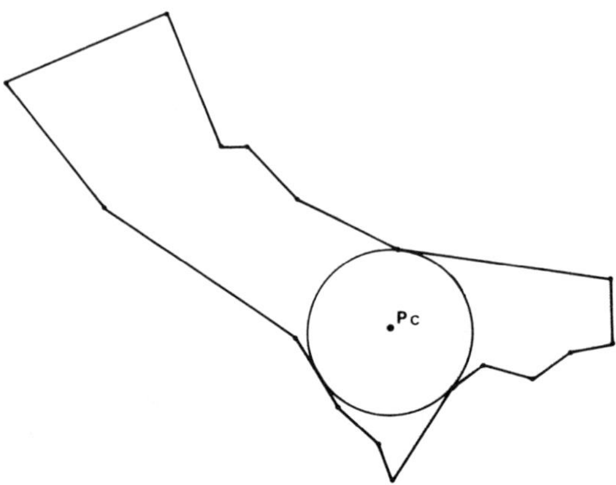

Figure 5.13 The Modal Center within a Polygon.

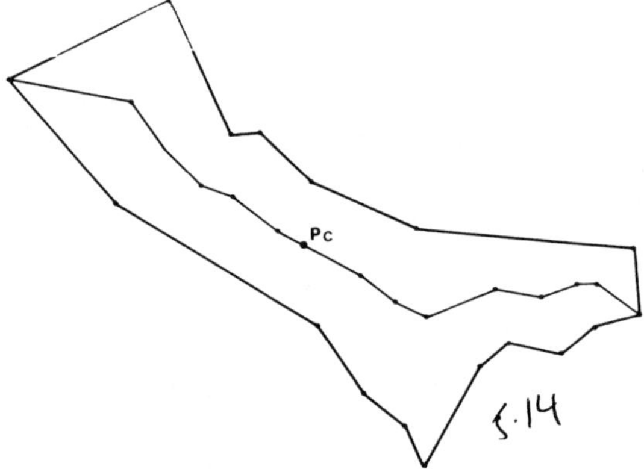

Figure 5.14 The Maximin Center within a Polygon.

Other center definitions can be composed based on some criterion of centrality. Once a central tendency measure has been calculated, the next question is how much misinformation does it communicate.

5.2 SPATIAL MEASURES OF DISPERSION

Like most other cartographic functions, there is not a one-to-one relation between the original distribution and the measure of central tendency. More than one distribution can have the same central tendency value (be it a point or a line). For example in Figure 5.15 two distributions have the bivariate mean value **(4,5)**; however, the distribution in Figure 5.15a is more dispersed around this point while the distribution in Figure 5.15b is more clustered about its bivariate mean. In each case the bivariate mean minimizes the sum of the squared distances between the set of points and the central tendency measure. However, in Figure 5.15b the total squared distance value was less. The bivariate mean is considered a more exact measure of the individual elements of the distribution in Figure 5.15b than in Figure 5.15a because the property used to determine the center point was less variant for the generalizing function. A central tendency measure can have a higher informational content for one distribution as opposed to another if it is a more exact measure of the individual elements of one distribution rather than another. *Spatial dispersion* parameters measure the level of misinformation represented by the central tendency measure and provide additional information for discriminating between point distributions.

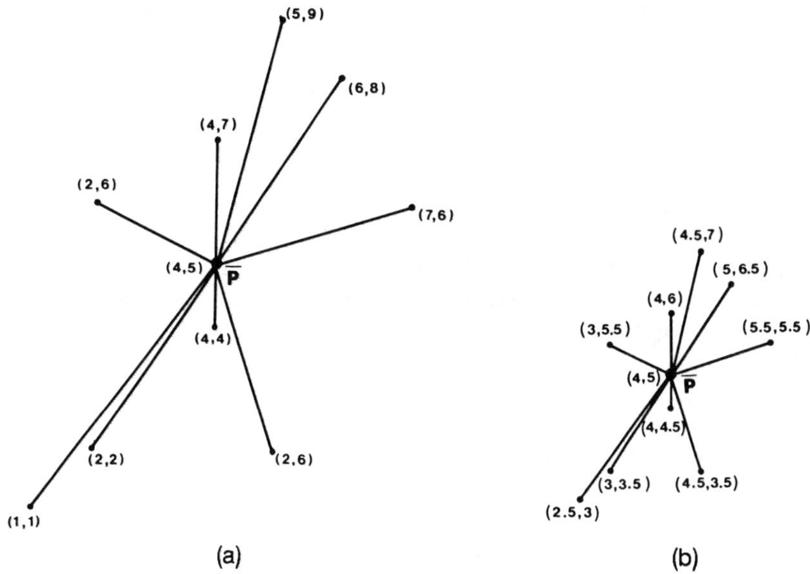

Figure 5.15 Alternative Distributions Having the Same Bivariate Mean.

Because each central tendency measure is defined in terms of the distance between it and the points of the distribution, one measure of spatial dispersion is the average distance between each point and the measure of central tendency. One method is the *mean distance* (**MD**), which is defined as:

$$MD = \frac{\sum_{j=1}^{N} w_j D_{cj}}{\sum_{j=1}^{N} w_j} ; \qquad (5.29)$$

where w_j is again a weight associated with the jth point and D_{cj} is the distance between the jth point and the center point.

Although any center measure can be used to calculate the mean distance, the median is the one that minimizes total distance; therefore, the mean distance using this center measure will always be less than using any other. In general it is preferable to use the central tendency parameter in conjunction with the dispersion parameter that measures the property used to calculate that measure of central tendency.

Another measure of spatial dispersion is based on the concept of *spatial variation* **(VAR)**. Spatial variation is the sum of the total squared distance between the center and each point:

$$VAR = \sum_{j=1}^{N} w_j \, D_{cj}^2 \quad . \tag{5.30}$$

Because the bivariate mean minimizes total squared distance, it is the most efficient center to use in conjunction with spatial variation. The *spatial variance* **(SV)** of a distribution is the spatial variation divided by the sum of the weights. The *standard distance* **(SD)** is the square root of spatial variance:

$$SD = \frac{\sum_{j=1}^{N} w_j \, D_{cj}^2}{\sum_{j=1}^{N} w_j} \quad . \tag{5.31}$$

For one-dimensional point distributions, this measure is known as the *standard deviation.*

5.3 SPATIAL ORIENTATION MEASURES

Besides central tendency and dispersion, point distributions also differ in their orientation. In Figure 5.16, two point distributions have different bivariate mean centers, standard distances, and orientations. It was noted in Chapter Two that spatial reference points such as an origin are highly arbitrary; the orientation of the X- and Y-axis for the measurement of point locations also is arbitrary. Orientation measures not only examine the prevailing direction of a point distribution in terms of the reference axes but also evaluate the informational content of the choice of axes.

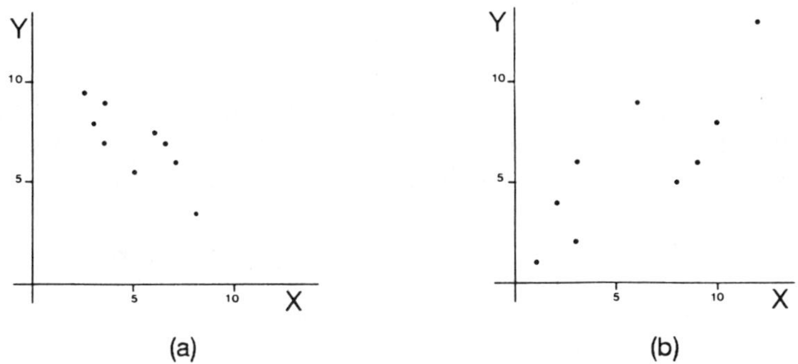

Figure 5.16 Point Distributions Having Different Orientations.

5.3.1 Spatial Covariation

Related to the notion of spatial variation is that of *spatial covariation.* Covariation **(CV)** is a measure of how points vary with respect to each dimension:

$$CV = \sum_{j=1}^{N} (x_j - x_c)(y_j - y_c) \quad . \qquad (5.32)$$

In vector notation, the covariation is the inner product of two N-dimensional vectors whose origin is the bivariate mean of the distribution (see section 2.3). The covariation of distributions whose prevailing orientation is northwest-southeast is less than zero, while the covariation of distributions having a prevailing southwest-northeast orientation is greater than zero. The covariation of Figure 5.16a is positive, **93**, while the covariation of Figure 5.16b is negative, **-23.25** (see Table 5.3).

The *correlation coefficient*, *r*, measures the cosine of the angle, θ, between the two N-dimensional vectors:

$$r = \cos\theta = \frac{\sum_{j=1}^{N} (x_j - x_c)(y_j - y_c)}{\left[\sum_{j=1}^{N} (x_j - x_c)^2\right]^{1/2} \left[\sum_{j=1}^{N} (y_j - y_c)^2\right]^{1/2}} \quad . \qquad (5.33)$$

The correlation coefficients for Figure 5.16a and 5.16b are **.8036** and **-.8036** (see Table 5.3). In this case, one distribution could be transformed into the other if the correct translation, rotation, and scaling operators were used. If the correlation coefficient equals **-1** or **1**, then the two axes are dependent and one axis is redundant. The point distribution given in Figure 5.17 is not truly two-dimensional but looks that way given the orientation of the original axes. Instead, these points could be measured using only one axis if it had the correct orientation.

Table 5.3 Calculation of Covariation and the Correlation Coefficient

	Point Distribution 5.16a						Point Distribution 5.16b				
	x	y	$(x-\bar{x})^2$	$(y-\bar{y})^2$	$(x-\bar{x})(y-\bar{y})$		x	y	$(x-\bar{x})^2$	$(y-\bar{y})^2$	$(x-\bar{x})(y-\bar{y})$
P1	1	1	$(-5)^2$	$(-5)^2$	(-5)(-5)	P1	2.5	9.5	$(-2.5)^2$	$(2.5)^2$	(-2.5)(2.5)
P2	2	4	$(-4)^2$	$(-2)^2$	(-4)(-2)	P2	3	8	$(-2)^2$	$(1)^2$	(-2)(1)
P3	3	2	$(-3)^2$	$(-4)^2$	(-3)(-4)	P3	3.5	9	$(-1.5)^2$	$(2)^2$	(-1.5)(2)
P4	3	6	$(-3)^2$	$(0)^2$	(-3)(0)	P4	3.5	7	$(-1.5)^2$	$(0)^2$	(-1.5)(0)
P5	6	9	$(0)^2$	$(3)^2$	(0)(3)	P5	5	5.5	$(0)^2$	$(-1.5)^2$	(0)(-1.5)
P6	8	5	$(2)^2$	$(-1)^2$	(2)(-1)	P6	6	7.5	$(1)^2$	$(0.5)^2$	(1)(0.5)
P7	9	6	$(3)^2$	$(0)^2$	(3)(0)	P7	6.5	7	$(1.5)^2$	$(0)^2$	(1.5)(0)
P8	10	8	$(4)^2$	$(2)^2$	(4)(2)	P8	7	6	$(2)^2$	$(-1)^2$	(2)(-1)
P9	12	13	$(6)^2$	$(7)^2$	(6)(7)	P9	8	3.5	$(3)^2$	$(-3.5)^2$	(3)(-3.5)
	54	54	124	108	CV = 93		45	63	31	27	CV = -23.25

$\bar{x} = 54/9 = 6$; $\bar{y} = 54/9 = 6$ $\bar{x} = 45/9 = 5$; $\bar{y} = 63/9 = 7$

$r = (93)/(124)^{1/2}(108)^{1/2} = .8036$ $r = (-23.25)/(31)^{1/2}(27)^{1/2} = -.8036$

Figure 5.17 A One-Dimensional Distribution Measured as Two-Dimensional.

5.3.2 Standard Deviational Ellipses

Standard deviational ellipses **(SDE)** are a centrographic construct that summarizes not only the dispersion but also the orientation of the principle direction of the distribution [Lefever, 1926]. The major axis of a **SDE** has the same orientation as the central tendency line that minimizes the sum of the squared distances between it and the members of the point set (see Figure 5.18). Given **(5.23)**, its angle of orientation, θ, is found then from the slope of this line:

$$\tan \theta = - \frac{A}{B} = - \frac{g + (g^2 + 4\, h^2)^{1/2}}{2\, h} \quad ; \qquad (5.34)$$

where **g** and **h** are defined by **(5.25)** and **(5.26)** respectively. Therefore, rotating the axes of the original point set by the angle of orientation maximizes the standard deviation of the points with respect to the major axis of the ellipse and minimizes the standard deviation with respect to the minor axis. Also the covariation of the points in the rotated space is equal to zero [Hultquist, Holmes, and Brown, 1970].

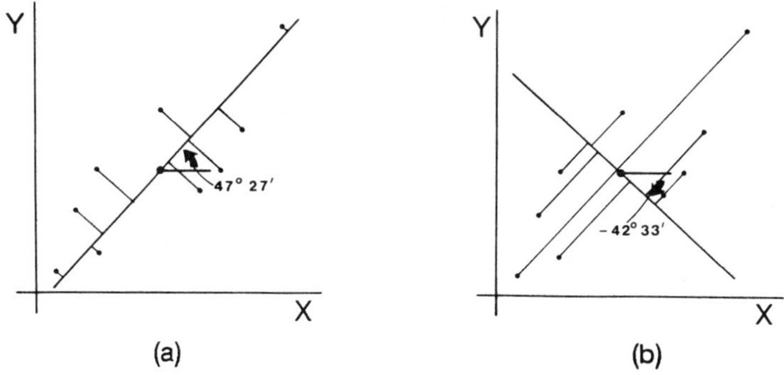

Figure 5.18 The Standard Deviation of the Major and Minor Axes.

The lengths of the major and minor axes of the ellipse are equal to the standard deviation of the point set with respect to the rotated Y- and X-axes (see section 2.3 for the rotation equations) respectively:

$$\sigma_x = \left(\frac{\sum_{j=1}^{N} (x' \cos \theta + y' \sin \theta)^2}{N} \right)^{1/2} \quad ; \qquad (5.35)$$

$$\text{and} \quad \sigma_y = \left(\frac{\sum_{j=1}^{N} (-x' \sin \theta + y' \cos \theta)^2}{N} \right)^{1/2} ; \qquad (5.36)$$

where x′ and y′ are again the translated points with respect to the bivariate mean. The respective lengths of the major and minor axes for the ellipse presented in Figure 5.19 are **4.8068** and **1.6338** (see Table 5.4). If the length of the minor axis was zero, then the ellipse would degenerate to a straight line segment because the point set could be measured and represented in only one dimension given the proper orientation.

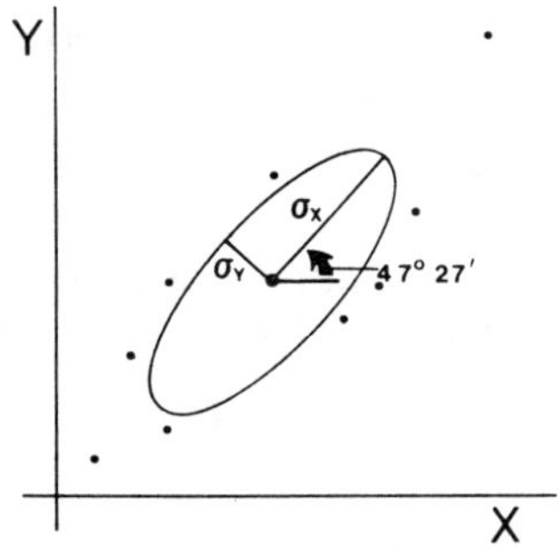

Figure 5.19 An Example Standard Deviational Ellipse.

Table 5.4 Calculation of Standard Deviational Ellipses

$$g = \Sigma (x - \bar{x})^2 - \Sigma (y - \bar{y})^2 = 124 - 108 = 16$$

$$h = \Sigma x'y' = 93$$

$$\tan \theta = \frac{16 + [16^2 + (4)(93)^2]^{1/2}}{(2)(93)} = \frac{16 + [256 + (4)(8649)]^{1/2}}{186}$$

$$= \frac{16 + (34852)}{186} = \frac{16 + 186.6869}{186} = \frac{202.6869}{186} = 1.0897$$

$$\theta = 47^\circ\ 27' \qquad \cos \theta = .67623 \qquad \sin \theta = .73669$$

$$\sigma_x = [207.9510]^{1/2}/9^{1/2} = 14.4205/3 = 4.8068$$

$$\sigma_y = [24.0258]^{1/2}/9^{1/2} = 4.9016/3 = 1.6338$$

5.4 SPATIAL PATTERN MEASURES

The spatial measures discussed thus far separate the generalization of cartographic objects into an analysis of individual thematic attributes (a one-dimensional point set) and that of the spatial attributes (a two-dimensional point set). *Spatial autocorrelation* measures examine how a thematic attribute varies over a two-dimensional surface rather than between thematic attributes. For a set of spatial objects (see Figure 5.20a), strong positive spatial autocorrelation implies that thematic values that are connected within some defined neighborhood of each other are very similar (Figure 5.20b); conversely, strong negative spatial autocorrelation means that neighboring thematic values are very dissimilar (Figure 5.20c) [Griffith, 1987]. Finally, if no spatial autocorrelation exists among the thematic values, these values are randomly arranged (Figure 5.20d). The degree of spatial autocorrelation present in a distribution has an impact on the visual complexity of maps [Olson, 1975]. Maps will communicate different messages depending on the amount and type of autocorrelation present in the distribution of cartographic objects. The notion of "texture" in remotely sensed digital images and pattern in thematic maps is directly associated with spatial autocorrelation. Maps will communicate different messages depending on the amount and type of autocorrelation present in the distribution of cartographic objects. The notion of "texture" in remotely sensed digital images and pattern in thematic maps is directly associated with spatial autocorrelation.

In order to calculate a spatial autocorrelation measure, it is necessary to know first: (1) whether the thematic data are measured in nominal, ordinal or interval scales; (2) whether the thematic data are associated with areal objects (polygons) or point objects; and, (3) how the connectivity relations are defined. Initially, we will only consider distributions of polygons and the connectivity neighborhood for each object consists only of its adjacent objects.

The most elementary nominal scale is a binary classification of data and the simplest area map using this data is a binary map [Unwin, 1981]. For each of **N** cartographic features (assume for present these features are regions) we note the occurrence of a given event for a thematic attribute. If the event has occurred in a region, the thematic attribute has a value of one and we refer to it as a "black" region; whereas if it has not occurred, the thematic attribute has a value of zero and we refer to it as a "white" region. We can classify each chain cobounded by two regions as either being a **BB** chain (both cobounding regions are coded black), a **WW** chain (both cobounding regions are coded white), or a **BW** chain (one cobounding region is black and one is white). For this analysis, the exterior chains of the study area (Figure 5.21a) cobounded by the background region are ignored (the interior chains are commonly referred to as joins in the spatial autocorrelation literature). If positive autocorrelation exists, then we would expect the black regions to be clustered together (Figure 5.21a); if negative autocorrelation exists, then the black regions should be dispersed (Figure 5.21b). Finally, if no spatial autocorrelation exists, the black regions would be randomly distributed (Figure 5.21c).

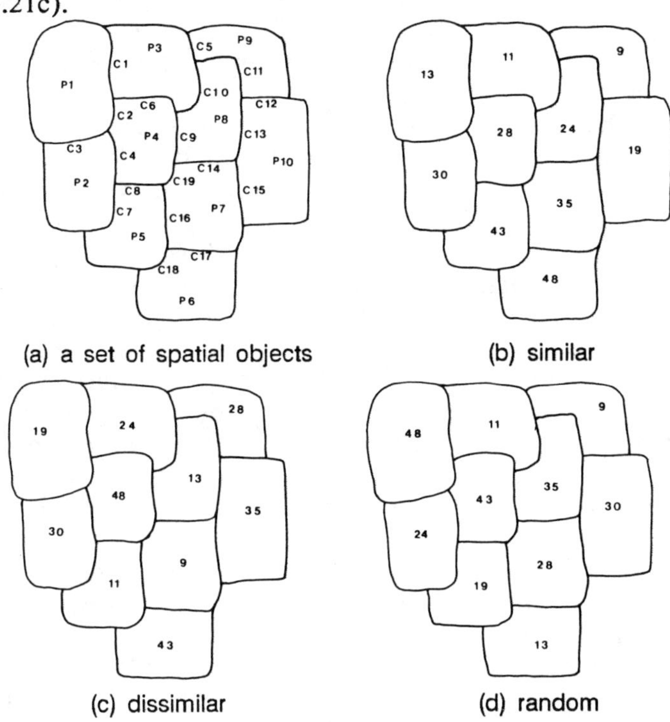

Figure 5.20 Differing Spatial Arrangements of Thematic Values.

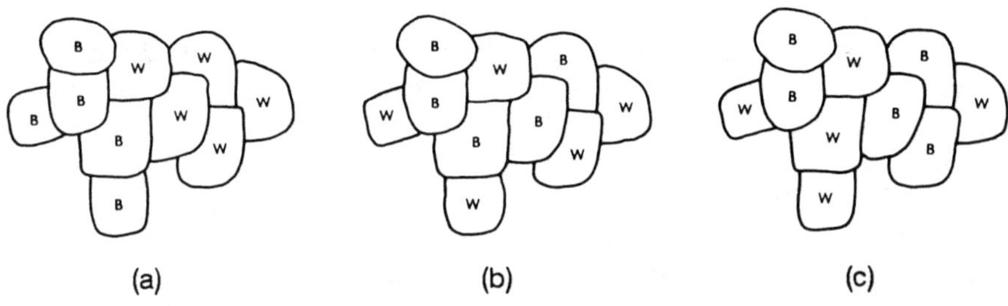

Figure 5.21 Possible Spatial Arrangements of Black and White Regions.

As black regions cluster together, the number of **BB** and **WW** chains increases and the number of **BW** chains decreases; as they disperse, the number of **BW** chains increases. A simple count of the number of **BW** chains then gives an indication of the degree of spatial autocorrelation. The maximal number (highest negative spatial autocorrelation) and minimal number of **BW** chains (highest positive spatial autocorrelation) that can be present in a spatial arrangement of regions is dependent on the number of black versus white regions and the number of internal chains that are present. The expected number of **BW** chains, $\mathbf{E_{BW}}$, associated with a random pattern (no spatial autocorrelation) assuming that the observed distribution represents a nonfree sample (sampled without replacement) is:

$$E_{BW} = \frac{2\ N_c\ N_b\ N_w}{N\ (N - 1)}\ ; \qquad (5.37)$$

where N is the number of polygons (regions); N_c is the number of interior chains; N_b is the number of black regions; and N_w is the number of white regions ($N_b + N_w = N$). The values for N_c, N_b, and N_w are easily computed within the context of a chain data structure. As each chain is processed sequentially, running totals for these parameters are updated. The value for N_c is incremented by one if neither the left nor the right polygon is the background polygon. The value for N_b is incremented by one if the values of the thematic attribute under question for both the right and left polygons associated with the chain have a value of one. Finally, the value for N_w is incremented by one if thematic values for both the right and left polygons have a value of zero.

For interval scale data, one measure of spatial autocorrelation is the Moran **I** index [Moran, 1950]. Using a chain data structure for storing the geographic base file this index can be written as:

$$I = \frac{N \sum_{i \epsilon C_I} (x_{rp(i)} - \bar{x})\ (x_{lp(i)} - \bar{x})}{N_c \sum_{j=1}^{N} (x_j - \bar{x})^2}\ ; \qquad (5.38)$$

where N is the number of polygons (regions); N_c is the number of interior chains; C_I is the set of interior chains; $x_{rp(i)}$ and $x_{lp(i)}$ are the thematic values of the right and left polygons of the ith chain respectively; x_j is the thematic value of the jth polygon; and $\bar{x}$ is the mean thematic value for the set of polygons.

The numerator of this index is a measure of the covariation between cobounding regions while the denominator is a measure of the variation within the entire set. The Moran index will have values greater than **(-1)/(N-1)** if positive spatial autocorrelation is present (similar neighboring values) and values less than **(-1)/(N-1)** if strong negative autocorrelation is present (dissimilar neighboring values) [Cliff and Ord, 1973]. Index values close to **(-1)/(N-1)** indicate the absence of any autocorrelation. The actual range of values that the Moran index can have is dependent on the structure of the connectivity relation [deJong *et al.*, 1984]. The Moran index for the thematic values given in Table 5.5 and the geographic base map presented in Figure 5.20a is **0.4203**.

Another measure of spatial autocorrelation is the Geary **c** index [Geary, 1954]. Again using a chain data structure for storing the geographic base file, this index can be written as:

$$c = \frac{(N-1) \sum_{i \in C_I} (x_{rp(i)} - x_{lp(i)})^2}{2 N_c \sum_{j=1}^{N} (x_j - \bar{x})^2} \; ; \qquad (5.39)$$

where each of the terms are the same as those defined for **(5.38)**. The numerator of the Geary **c** index measures the variation between cobounding regions, while the denominator measures the variation within the entire set. Because no term in either the numerator or the denominator is negative, the Geary **c** index is always positive. It will have values greater than one if positive spatial autocorrelation is present and values less than one if strong negative autocorrelation is present. Index values close to one indicate the absence of any autocorrelation. The Geary index for the thematic values given in Table 5.5 and the geographic base map presented in Figure 5.20a is **0.3607**. Although it is outside of the scope of this text, tests of significance can be performed on each of the indices for measuring autocorrelation among nominal, ordinal, or interval data distributions to determine if the arrangement of thematic values could have occurred by chance [see Cliff and Ord, 1981; Griffith, 1987]. The autocorrelation indices defined above are generally associated with distributions of discrete areal cartographic features such as regions. They can also be applied to point distributions once a Thiessen diagram has been constructed for the point distribution [see Griffith, 1979]. In this situation, the cobounding relations between the left and right Thiessen polygons for each interior Thiessen edge form the basis for a connectivity relation.

Table 5.5 Calculation of the Moran and Geary Indices

Polygon ID	x
P1	13
P2	30
P3	11
P4	28
P5	43
P6	48
P7	35
P8	24
P9	9
P10	19

$\Sigma\, x = 260 \quad \bar{x} = 260/10 = 26$

Chain ID	$(x_{rp(i)} - \bar{x})(x_{lp(i)} - \bar{x})$	$(x_{rp(i)} - x_{lp(i)})^2$
C1	(13-26)(11-26) = 195	$(13-11)^2 = 4$
C2	(13-26)(28-26) = -26	$(13-28)^2 = 225$
C3	(13-26)(30-26) = -52	$(13-30)^2 = 289$
C4	(30-26)(28-26) = 8	$(30-28)^2 = 4$
C5	(11-26)(9-26) = 255	$(11-9)^2 = 4$
C6	(28-26)(11-26) = -30	$(28-11)^2 = 289$
C7	(30-26)(43-26) = 68	$(30-43)^2 = 169$
C8	(43-26)(28-26) = 34	$(43-28)^2 = 225$
C9	(28-26)(24-26) = -4	$(28-24)^2 = 16$
C10	(11-26)(24-26) = 30	$(11-24)^2 = 169$
C11	(24-26)(9-26) = 34	$(24-9)^2 = 225$
C12	(19-26)(9-26) = 85	$(19-9)^2 = 100$
C13	(24-26)(19-26) = 14	$(24-19)^2 = 25$
C14	(24-26)(35-26) = -18	$(24-35)^2 = 121$
C15	(35-26)(19-26) = -63	$(35-19)^2 = 256$
C16	(43-26)(35-26) = 153	$(43-35)^2 = 64$
C17	(48-26)(35-26) = 198	$(48-35)^2 = 169$
C18	(48-26)(43-26) = 374	$(48-43)^2 = 25$
C19	(35-26)(28-26) = 18	$(35-28)^2 = 49$

$\Sigma\, (x_{rp(i)} - \bar{x})(x_{lp(i)} - \bar{x}) = 1273 \quad \Sigma\, (x_{rp(i)} - x_{lp(i)})^2 = 2428$

$I = (10)(1273)/(19)(1594) = 0.4203$

$c = (9)(2428)/(38)(1594) = 0.3607$

Thus far the connectivity relation, w_{ij}, has only been defined in terms of the presence ($w_{ij} = 1$) or absence ($w_{ij} = 0$) of a contiguous connection between (i,j) pairs of objects. One criticism of this relation is that the resulting measures are then invariant to certain transformations of the objects such as changing the size of the areal units or length of the chains [Dacey, 1965]. A more generalized form of the Moran and Geary indices is respectively [see Cliff and Ord, 1981]:

$$I = \frac{N \sum_{i=1}^{N} \sum_{j=1}^{N} w_{ij} (x_i - \bar{x})(x_j - \bar{x})}{W_t \sum_{j=1}^{N} (x_j - \bar{x})^2} \quad ; \qquad (5.40)$$

and

$$c = \frac{(N - 1) \sum_{i=1}^{N} \sum_{j=1}^{N} (x_i - x_j)^2}{2 W_t \sum_{j=1}^{N} (x_j - \bar{x})^2} \quad ; \qquad (5.41)$$

where

$$W_t = \sum_{i=1}^{N} \sum_{j=1}^{N} w_{ij} \quad . \qquad (5.42)$$

The values for the connectivity relation (or weights) can be defined in many different ways. For example, w_{ij} can express more than the presence of a chain; it can be weighted by the relative size of neighboring region and/or the relative length of the connecting chain [Dacey, 1965].

Alternatively, w_{ij} can express the presence or absence of a second- or higher-order neighbor pair (also called a lag). A second-order neighbor pair would be one where there was one intervening polygon between the pair of polygons. Higher-order pairs are used to construct *spatial correlograms.* A correlogram can be based on either the Moran (a covariogram) or the Geary (a variogram) index (see Figure 5.22). The purpose of correlogram analysis is to analyze the spatial periodicity that the distribution might possess. For example in Figure 5.22a, the spatial distribution exhibits high positive autocorrelation among first-order neighbors, then declines over successive lags until it increases again among fourth-order neighbors. This "blip" indicates that some spatial process may be operating between objects at this distance.

Finally, w_{ij} can be expressed as a continuous function of distance. Usually some negative exponential model is preferred to give more weight to closer object pairs [Gatrell, 1979]. Either,

$$w_{ij} = d_{ij}^{-\alpha} \quad \text{or} \quad w_{ij} = e^{-\alpha d_{ij}} \quad ; \tag{5.43}$$

is used where α is a friction of distance or spatial impedance factor. The distance between two objects, d_{ij}, is measured either as the distance between two areal centers in the case of polygon units or between two locations in the case of point objects. Covariograms and variograms can also be computed as a function of distance if pairs of objects are aggregated into distance bands [see Hanink, 1988].

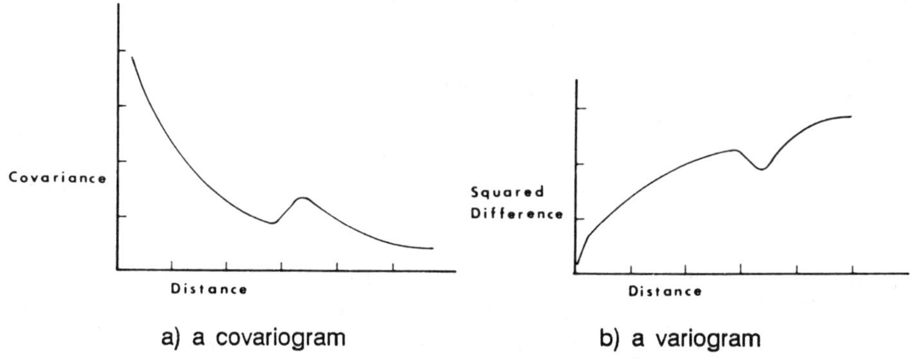

a) a covariogram b) a variogram

Figure 5.22 An Example Covariogram and Variogram.

5.5 ATTRIBUTE CLASSIFICATION

As mentioned at the outset of this chapter, classification normally is an attempt to separate the underlying structure or characterisitics of a spatial distribution from unwanted noise to ascertain the pattern of spatial variation. However, there are many different classification operators and the approach one takes toward this problem should again reflect the objectives of a cartographic project. For example, a series of maps depicting a temporal spatial process such as diffusion disease needs to be visually compared. Because symbolism is a function of classification, a reader needs to know how to interpret the symbolism when visually interpreting a map.

In large part, the classification legend serves to aid the reader in interpreting the symbolism. However, if the groupings change from map to map either with respect to the number of groups, the limits of each interval, or the type of grouping, it is difficult to compare from distribution to distribution. In Figure 5.23, fixed length intervals of 100 were chosen to display the spatial variation in the number of death occurrences. In specific time periods, especially near the onset, this classification does not capture the local variation in the number of disease deaths. However, time periods can readily be compared because the symbolism and the class intervals remain constant. In the case of a time series, it is not the structure or characteristics of an individual spatial distribution that is important but rather the structure of an entire space/time distribution.

Classification can also be set exogenously to the distribution at hand by some government agency [Evans, 1977]. The purpose here is spatial standardization. Although the spatial variation in individual localities may be poorly presented by the imposed classification, the distribution of a thematic attribute for one study area can be compared against the distribution of that variable for another study area. Exogenous classifications normally sacrifice representation of the underlying structure of a spatial distribution for other factors. *Ideographic* classifications on the other hand focus on specific characteristics of the distribution [Burrough, 1986].

Besides removing unwanted noise in preparation of graphic display, classification operators also are used to derive new data. Most classifications are performed on interval or ratio scale attributes but different classifications can result in either nominal, ordinal, interval or ratio groupings depending on how much variation is removed. For example, certain attributes like land cover cannot be measured directly by instruments, but surrogate attributes such as electromagnetic reflectance can be measured (see section 4.4.1). Electromagnetic reflectance values (ratio scale data) for a set of objects can be classified to place the objects into groups representing land cover categories (nominal scale data). In this case the classification of electromagnetic reflectance is used to identify values for a new thematic attribute, land cover. The new attribute can then be added to the digital database.

5.5.1 Quantile Classification

Quantile classifications divide the distribution so that an equal number of observations lie in each class interval. Such a classification induces a visual pattern in the distribution that may not reflect all of the character-

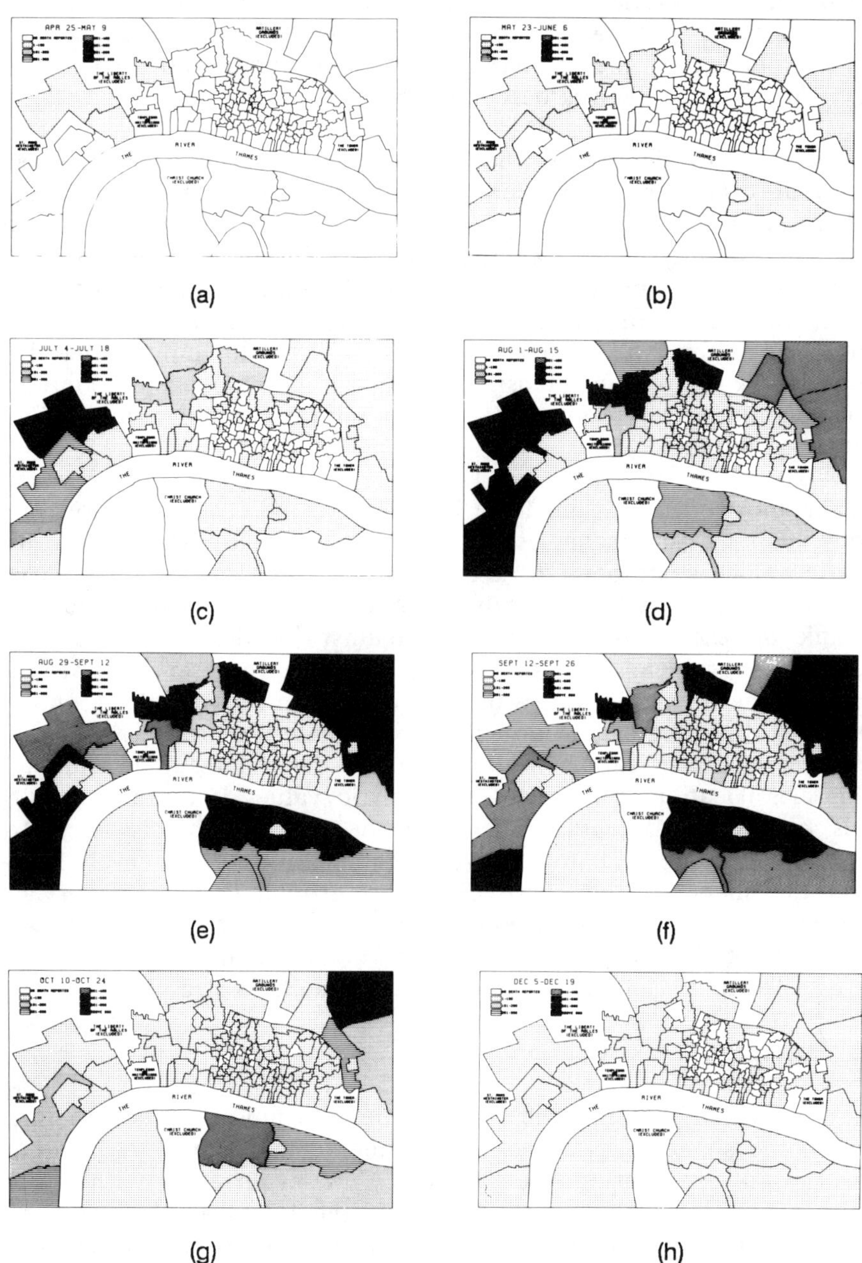

Figure 5.23 A Time Series Display of Plague Deaths.
(Source: Shannon and Cromley, 1980.)

istics of the distribution. The major advantage of this approach is ease of interpretation. The effect of a quantile classification is to perform an ordinal grouping of the thematic values; the symbolism associated with such a classification then is best interpreted as a ranking.

It is easy to determine that certain objects have higher thematic values than others, but it is more difficult to determine the magnitude of the difference. For example in a four class map, one object may belong to the highest quartile and another to the next highest quartile, but the one in the highest quartile may lie near the class limit and be closer in value to the object in the next highest interval than to any other member in its own interval. Therefore it is difficult to impute directly that differences in symbolism intensity on the map correspond to a similar difference in numerical magnitude. We can infer ordinal relationships but not interval ones.

Jenks and Coulson [1963] have investigated the conditions under which various classification schemes involving a scale transformation of the thematic values correspond to a quantile grouping of objects. First, the set of objects is sorted in ascending order by their thematic value. Next, the rank of each object is plotted against its thematic value (Figure 5.24a). The problem is to define the function representing this plot to determine the thematic intervals that result in a quantile grouping of objects. If the plot of the objects approximated a straight line, then an *equal interval* classification would have the desired result (Figure 5.24b). In this classification, the range of thematic values is divided into N intervals having equal length. Because the plot of objects is a straight line, an equal number of objects would fall within each interval. Depending on the shape of the curve either an *arithmetic progression*, a *geometric progression* or a *reciprocal hyperbolic* classification would be perferred (Figure 5.24c). In each of these classifications, an appropriate scale transformation of the thematic values results in straight line.

5.5.2 Histogram Classification

Another set of ideographic classifications groups objects into intervals based on the shape of a *histogram* of the thematic data. A histogram is a bar graph representing the frequency of occurrence within defined (usually equal) intervals (Figure 2.25). If the histogram is *unimodal* (has only one relative maximum frequency), class intervals can be defined as a multiple of the standard deviation of the distribution with the class centered on the mean. For example, the breaks for the four class intervals in Figure 5.25a could be $\mu-\sigma$, μ, and $\mu+\sigma$. Symbolism again should only imply a ranking as observations from different classes could be very similar in value.

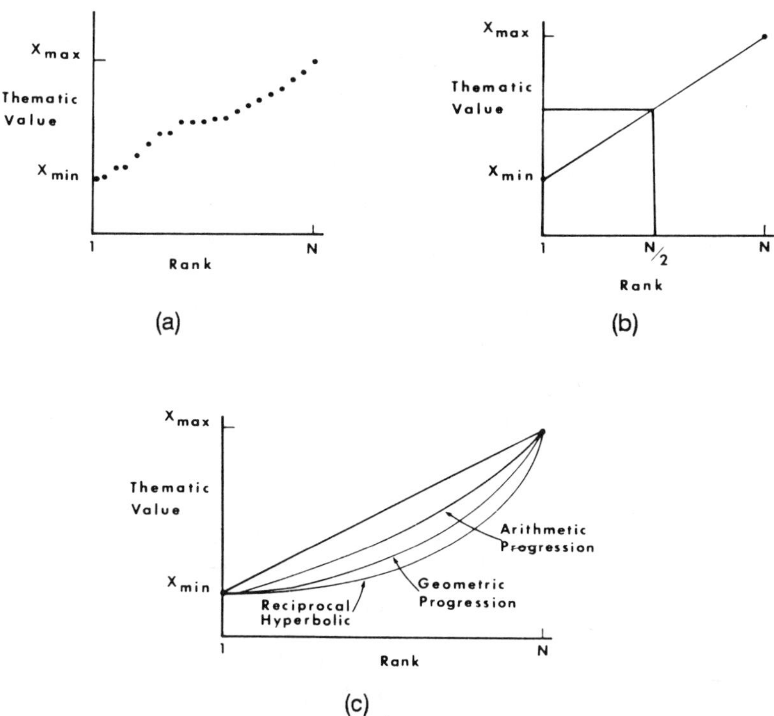

Figure 5.24 A Quantile Grouping of Objects.

If the histogram is *multi-modal* (more than one relative maximum frequency), then groupings may be determined by the "natural breaks" in the histogram (Figure 5.25b). Observations within each modal grouping are more likely to be alike than between groupings in this case. A symbolism corresponding to the mean of each modal grouping could be used.

The major drawback to classifications based on histograms is that the shape of a histogram is not invariant to transformations of the grouping interval. The same distribution that is unimodal in Figure 5.25a is multimodal in Figure 5.25c once the length of the grouping interval is reduced by one-half. The length of the grouping interval is itself a filter; the longer the length, the more local variation is removed from the histogram. Sometimes, the histogram's interval length is also exogenously determined. In this case, an ideographic classification is dependent on an exogenous one because the histogram itself is a classification.

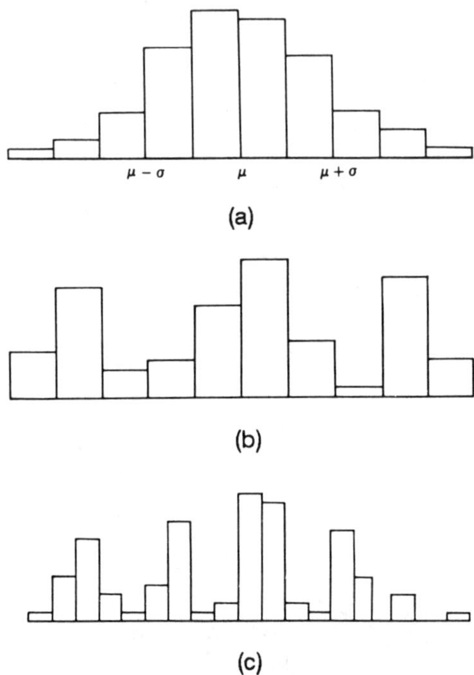

Figure 5.25 Example Histograms.

5.5.3 Optimal Classification

One definition of a "good" classification is that it should account for as much of the total variation, σ_T^2, in the thematic data set as possible in terms of differences between class means [Burrough, 1986]. As the amount of variation within each group decreases, then the informational content of the group mean as a parameter representing all members of the group increases. One way to measure the accuracy of a classification is to compute the amount of variation present within the groups, σ_w^2, and between the groups' means, σ_b^2, associated with the classification where $\sigma_w^2 + \sigma_b^2 = \sigma_T^2$. The ratio σ_b^2/σ_T^2 represents the amount of total variation "explained" by the classification; more accurate maps explain more variation.

A modification of this approach is to weight each thematic value by the size of the geographic area of the associated object [Jenks and Caspall, 1971]. The purpose of this weighting is to give more importance to larger sized regions because they visually "stand out" on the map and thus should be more accurately portrayed.

Another method for measuring the accuracy of a classification is to perform a univariate *discriminant analysis* of the groupings. Discriminant analysis fits a probability density function to each group based on the characteristics of group members. In this case, only one characteristic, the thematic attribute being classified, is used to construct this function for each group. These probability functions can then be used to classify each object into its "most probable" group. Certain objects near group boundaries are likely to be misclassified by these probability functions. For example in Figure 5.26, object **a** was originally placed in group **A** by a given classification; however, it was found to be "more probably" a member of group **B** by the discriminant analysis. For a given number of classes, the more accurate the original groupings, the fewer objects will be misclassified by the discriminant function.

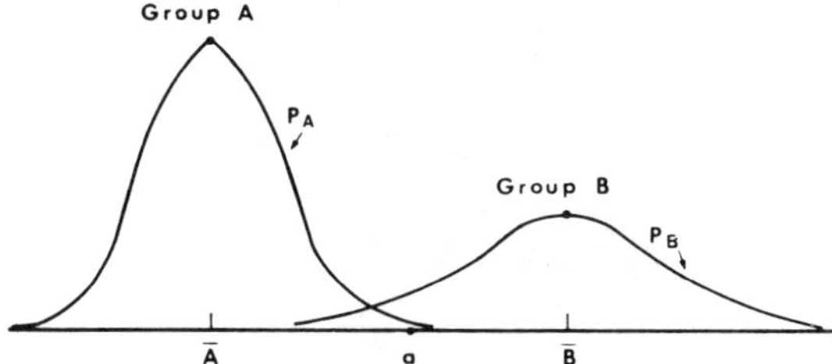

Figure 5.26 A Discriminant Analysis Evaluation of Group Membership.

Another criterion for determining the accuracy of a classification is to examine the change in spatial autocorrelation within the spatial distribution as a result of a chosen classification. In a good classification, chains between similar valued polygons will lie in the interior of the region formed by the class interval and chains between dissimilar valued regions will form the boundary between these class regions (see Figure 5.27). One can measure the accuracy of a classification as an autocorrelation index, $\mathbf{I_a}$, that is the ratio between the amount of spatial variation associated with the boundary between class regions, and that present in the unclassified distribution:

$$I_a = \frac{\sum_{i \in C_B} (x_{rp(i)} - x_{lp(i)})^2}{\sum_{i \in C_I} (x_{rp(i)} - x_{lp(i)})^2} \quad ; \qquad (5.44)$$

where $\mathbf{C_B}$ is the set of chains associated with the boundary between class regions and $\mathbf{C_I}$ is the set of interior chains defined in section 5.4 associated with the geographic base map. For a given number of classes, more accurate classifications will have a higher autocorrelation index because more spatial variation will be associated with those chains forming the boundary between class interval regions.

Because these indices all measure a classification in terms of the underlying characteristics of the distribution, natural breaks classifications usually yield higher values when compared to other standard classifications. However, natural breaks themselves are a function of the length of the histogram grouping interval. A more direct method would be to produce an "optimal" classification by maximizing some accuracy index [Jenks and Caspall, 1971].

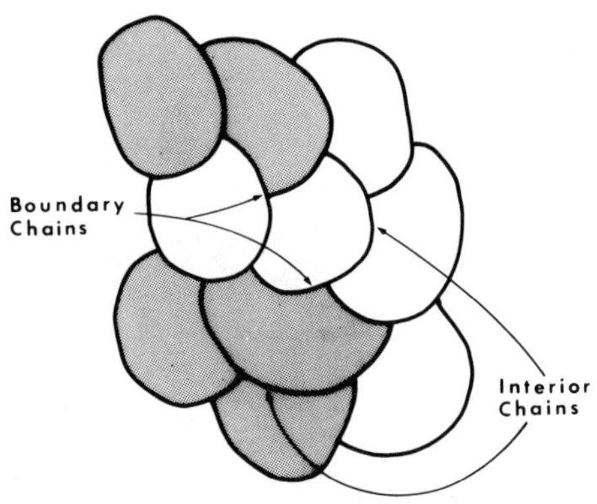

Figure 5.27 Interior and Boundary Chains of Class Regions.

Unfortunately, exact methods for optimal classification are computationally expensive. Jenks [1977] adapted Fisher's grouping algorithm [Fisher, 1958] for univariate data to the problem of data classification for mapping but the computational speed of his algorithm is relatively slow for large problems having around 1000 values. More recently, Lindberg [1990] has improved the computational time of the Fisher algorithm so that large problems run in under 500 seconds on an 80386 PC with an 80387 coprocessor at 16 mhz.

Another approach is to find an approximation of the optimal solution using an heuristic algorithm. Monmonier [1973] has shown how p-median heuristics designed to solve facility location-allocation models can be applied to the selection of class intervals. In this case the selection of N class intervals involves choosing N of the original thematic values to be the respective centers of the N class intervals and then assigning each of the remaining data values to the nearest center.

After an initial set of N centers has been selected, two general strategies can be used to converge to a final solution. One approach [Maranzana, 1964] is:

S1) Assign each noncenter value to the nearest center value.

S2) Within each grouping determine the new center object that minimizes within group variation or distance.

S3) If the set of new centers is exactly the same as the set of old centers, stop; otherwise go to step S1.

This strategy can be extended to allow the center of each group to be any central tendency value such as the mean rather than one of the thematic values in the attribute set [see Cooper, 1968].

The other approach, known as vertex substitution [Teitz and Bart, 1968], is:

S1) Assign each noncenter value to the nearest center value.

S2) Substitute the ith noncenter value for the jth center value. If this substitution results in a decrease in within group variation or distance, replace the jth center value with the ith noncenter value.

S3) If no noncenter value can replace any center values, stop; otherwise go to step S1.

This substitution approach can be applied to the problem of maximizing the spatial variation associated with class region boundaries:

S1) Given N class intervals, find an initial classification. Calculate the amount of spatial variation associated with the set of class region boundary chains measured as:

$$\sum_{i \in C_B} (x_{rp(i)} - x_{lp(i)})^2 .$$

S2) Calculate the change in spatial variation associated with the chains forming the boundaries between class regions for the respective polygons whose thematic values lie closest to a class break if the polygon were reassigned to the class on the other side of its break.

S3) If the change is less than zero for all such polygons, stop; otherwise reassign that polygon resulting in the greatest increase to its new class interval and go to step S2.

These heuristics for improving accuracy indices are only useful if the resulting map is not part of any comparison with other maps.

5.5.4 Multivariate Classification

The measurable attributes of a cartographic object are used as a surrogate for latent characteristics of the object itself. Sometimes it is difficult to measure certain characteristics by a single attribute. It may be relatively straightforward to measure the population size of a region by direct enumeration. However, it is more difficult to measure more complex concepts such as economic development by a single attribute. In this case a set of attributes is collected as the surrogate for this multivariate concept. Likewise, in digital remote sensing it is sometimes difficult to identify an object by a single wavelength band, so it is necessary to collect a set of wavelength attributes. Because the set of attributes is related to a similar characteristic, there is likely to exist a large amount of covariation between pairs of attributes. Principal component analysis can be used in this case to transform the original attribute axes into a set of uncorrelated axes or components where most of the original variation is associated with the major or principal components. The principal component(s) can then be mapped instead of each of the original attributes. Certain aspects of the distribution may appear in the resulting map(s) that were not directly observable in the original data.

Once a set of M attributes has been transformed into a set of M components, it is also possible to group the object into N clusters based on minimizing within group variation or distance (Figure 5.28). Component values rather than the original attribute values are preferred in cluster analysis because components are uncorrelated and are measured on a similar scale [Johnston, 1978]. Such a multivariate classification is useful for forming nominal groupings of objects that can then be used to help identify an underlying characteristic such as landcover classification in a digital remotely sensed image.

5.6 SIMPLIFICATION

Simplification operators generalize the geometry of objects contained in the geographic base file. Digital base files are collected at one scale but the information can be displayed at many other scales. One objective in simplification is to match the amount of information to be displayed with the capability of a map (or the resolution of a display device) to represent it at a given scale [Robinson, *et al.*, 1984]. Simplification operators are needed when one changes geographic scale and the amount of map space available for displaying cartographic features changes. When changing the scale of the source database, then the number of cartographic objects to be displayed should also change according to the *radical law* [Topfer and Pillewizer, 1966]:

$$N_c = N_s \ (S_s/S_c)^{1/2} \quad ; \qquad (5.45)$$

where N_c and N_s are the number of objects on the compiled and source databases respectively and S_c and S_s are the associated scale denominators of these databases. The ratio N_c/N_s is the relative reduction in the number of features associated with the scale change.

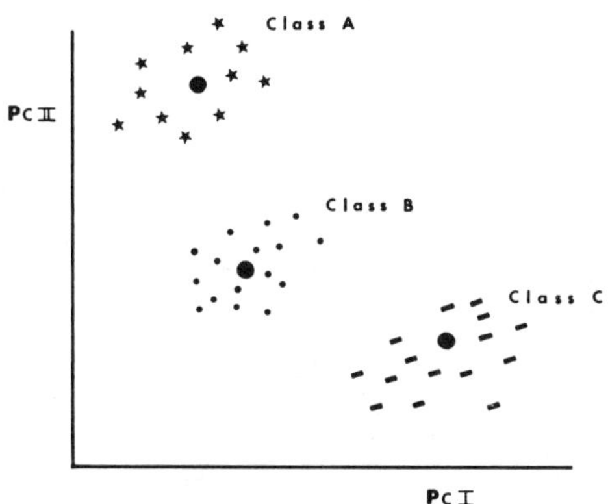

Figure 5.28 A Multivariate Classification of Objects.

5.6.1 Point Simplification

Frequently, a set of point objects collected at one scale must be reduced before display at another scale. This process requires aggregating the original set of points into N_c groups each having approximately the same number of points and choosing an appropriate center point to represent each group at the new scale (see Figure 5.29).

The optimal classification heuristics can be applied to this problem with some modifications. First, the **(x,y)** coordinates of each object rather than a thematic attribute are used to determine the groupings. Secondly, the modal center within each group should be used as the location of the generalized point. This center point is located within the area of the highest density of points in each group and is not greatly influenced by extreme point locations.

5.29 Point Simplification.

5.6.2 Line Simplification

With the technological advancements made in the electronic encoding of cartographic data, methods for performing automated line generalization have become a critical component of cartographic information processing. Line generalization is a complex task. No generalization occurs in isolation; any generalization of one line may be encumbered by its neighbors [Monmonier, 1986]. Douglas and Peucker [1973] state that there are three different ways to generalize a line by machine: 1) to delete specific features; 2) to represent a line by a mathematical function; or, 3) to reduce the number of points needed to represent it. They suggest that the first two approaches are too complex and time consuming to be performed by machine and recommend that point elimination (or conversely point selection for retention) be used to produce line caricatures.

Like classification procedures, simplification algorithms can be broadly grouped into exogenous and ideographic routines. Unlike classification, exogenously determined simplification routines are not used to permit comparison between two simplifications but exist solely for their ease of computation. *Independent point* algorithms then retain points without any consideration of their relationship to neighboring points. Retaining every nth point (Figure 5.30a) or randomly selecting 1/nth of the original points are examples of this category (Figure 5.30b). Although expedient, the resulting line simplification is frequently a poor caricature of the original line.

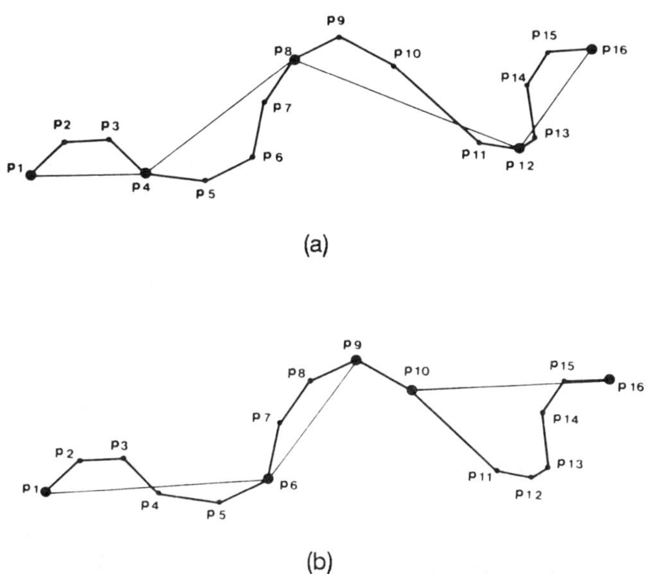

Figure 5.30 Independent Point Routines.

One should use the same criteria for retaining points in simplification that are used in an original encoding. The characteristic points of a line would include its endpoints, inflection points and local maxima and minima [Freeman, 1978]. In general, the points retained should retain the line's scale-dependent structural signature [Buttenfield, 1986]. McMaster [1987a] has made a thorough study of ideographic line simplification algorithms (his study also includes exogenous routines) and has produced a classification of them based on the geometric extent of their search domain. The following discussion of ideographic routines is drawn primarily from this study.

Local processing routines use a triad of neighboring points to determine whether to retain the middle point. One such technique is the perpendicular triad method [Jenks, 1981]; the perpendicular distance between the second point and the line segment connecting the first and third points of a point triad is calculated. If this distance exceeds a pre-specified bandwidth, the middle point is retained (Figure 5.31a). Another method uses an angular tolerance for each triad of points [McMaster, 1983]. The angle between vectors connecting the first and second and the first and third point is calculated. If this angle exceeds a pre-specified tolerance, then the middle point is retained because it represents a position on the line of acute angular change (Figure 5.31b).

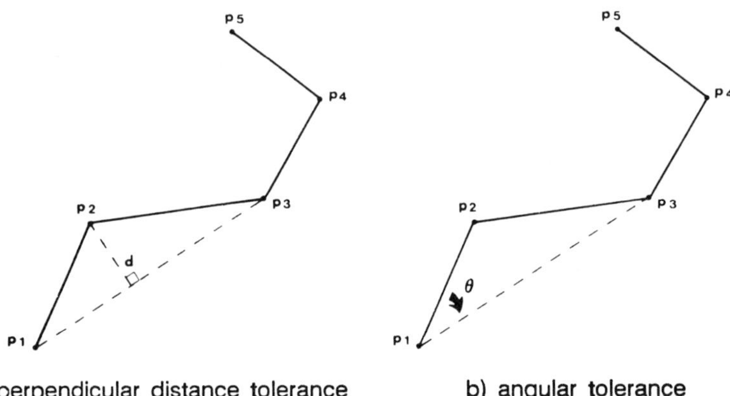

Figure 5.31 Local Processing Routines.

Extended local processing algorithms have a search domain beyond the adjacent points that examine portions of the line. These routines can be either unconstrained or somehow constrained in the search domain. One unconstrained procedure is to center a bandwidth on the first segment of the line [Reumann and Witkam, 1974]. All points along the line are eliminated until some line segment intersects the bandwidth's outer edge; the last point before this intersection is retained (see Figure 5.32a). The bandwidth is then recentered on the line segment that intersected its edge and the process is repeated. A constrained version of this routine is to impose a minimum and maximum distance check on the search region [Opheim, 1982] (see Figure 5.32b). Any points within the minimum distance are eliminated and the bandwidth is automatically repositioned once the maximum distance constraint is reached regardless of whether the line intersects the bandwidth edge or not.

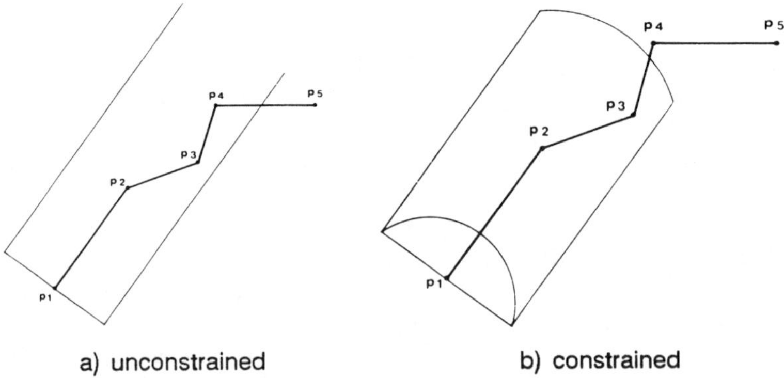

Figure 5.32 Extended Local Processing Routines.

Another extended local procedure is the Lang routine [Lang, 1969]. The Lang routine initializes the first point as an "anchor" and a point that is N points away from the the anchor as a "floater" and examines the set of intervening points between the anchor and the floater to determine if all of these points are within the bandwidth; if they are not, the point immediately preceding the current floater becomes the floater and the process is repeated until all intervening points are within the bandwidth centered on the line connecting the current anchor and floater. The anchor is now updated to the current floater and the floater is reset to be the point that is N points away from the current anchor.

Finally, *global* routines process the entire line rather than sequential sections of it. The most popular of these routines, the Douglas-Peucker algorithm [Douglas and Peucker, 1973], also uses a bandwidth approach that is an extension of the Lang routine. The first endpoint of the line is set as an initial "anchor" point and the other endpoint of the line is designated the current "floating" point. If the perpendicular distance between each intervening point and the straight line connecting the anchor and floating points is less than the tolerance, all of the intervening points are deleted and the anchor point is updated to the floating point. Otherwise, the intervening point having the maximum perpendicular distance becomes the new floating point and the intervening point check is repreated. These iterations continue until the anchor point becomes the last endpoint of the line. This sequence is illustrated in Figure 5.33.

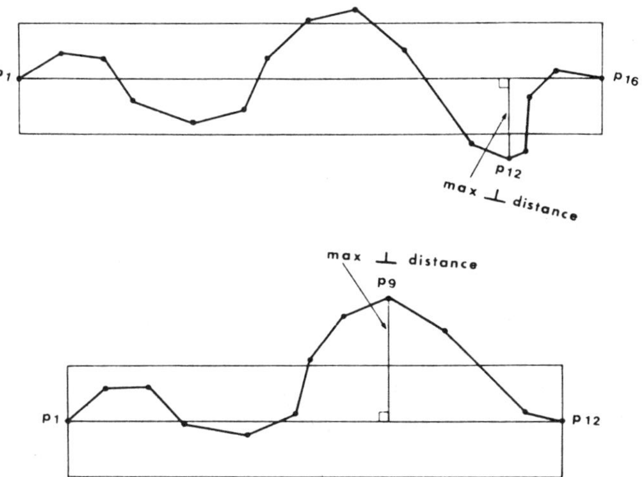

Figure 5.33 The Douglas-Peucker Algorithm.

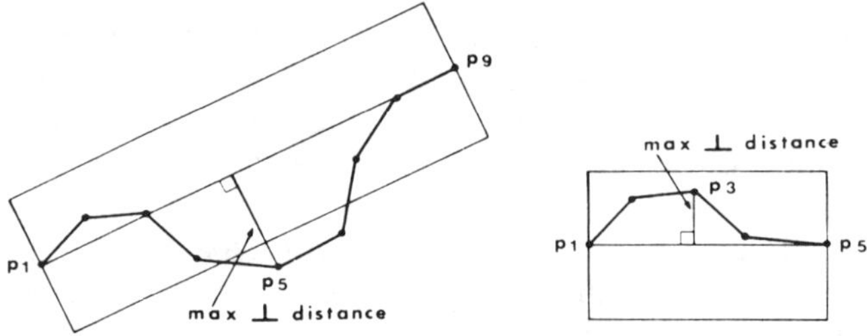

Figure 5.33 The Douglas-Peucker Algorithm (continued).

Most of these simplification algorithms have been evaluated by a variety of error measurements (see Figure 5.34) and a comparison against experimentally derived characteristic points [Marino, 1979; McMaster, 1983, 1986, 1987b; White,1985]. The consensus of these evaluations is that the Douglas algorithm, a global routine, has the overall best performance with respect to most measures. In general, the larger the search domain of the routine, the more accurate the caricature.

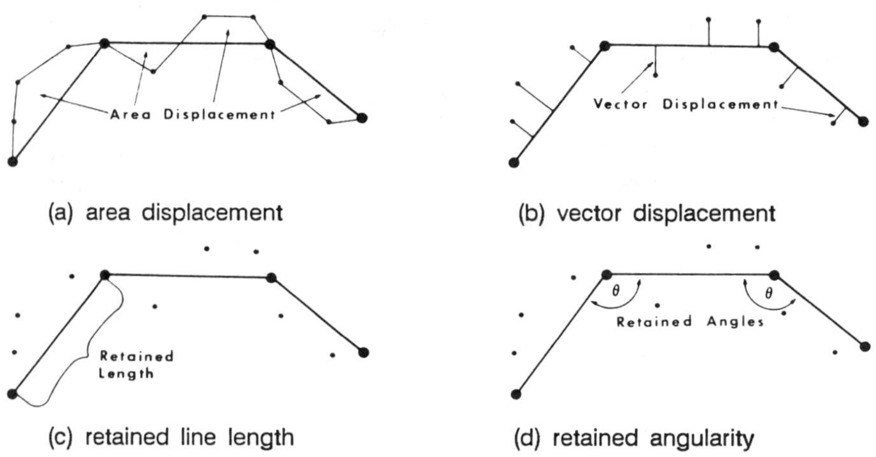

Figure 5.34 Alternate Error Measurements of a Simplified Line.

Another direction for developing global algorithms is in operations research. DeVeau [1985] has enumerated a number of objectives that a "good" simplification routine should possess including minimizing the number of retained points and ensuring that all points of the original line are within some tolerance of the simplified line. The structure of such a routine is similar to that of the point set covering problem. For a given distribution of N points, the point set covering problem selects the minimum number of points necessary to ensure that all points in the distribution are within some predetermined distance of at least one selected point [see Toregas *et al.*, 1971]. Line simplification can be modeled as a "linear" set covering problem: minimize the number of retained line segments such that all segments of the original line are within a specified perpendicular distance to a retained line segment [Cromley and Morse, 1988]. Unlike general point set covering problems, however, the segments of line are in a sequence and each original segment can be covered by only one segment in the simplified line. Bandwidth line simplification has been optimally solved by formulating it as an acyclic shortest path problem [Cromley and Campbell, 1991].

A vertex substitution heuristic has been used to solve a related problem: minimize (or maximize) a given error measurement while retaining **n** of the original **N** points [Cromley, 1988]. Given that the number of points to be retained in the simplified line has been determined either by the radical law or by application of some other simplification algorithm, vertex substitution is used to improve the caricature of the retained line with respect to some objective. For example, in Figure 3.35a the Douglas-Peucker algorithm retained five of an original twenty-three points; vertex substituion retained a slightly different set of ten points to minimize total vector displacement.

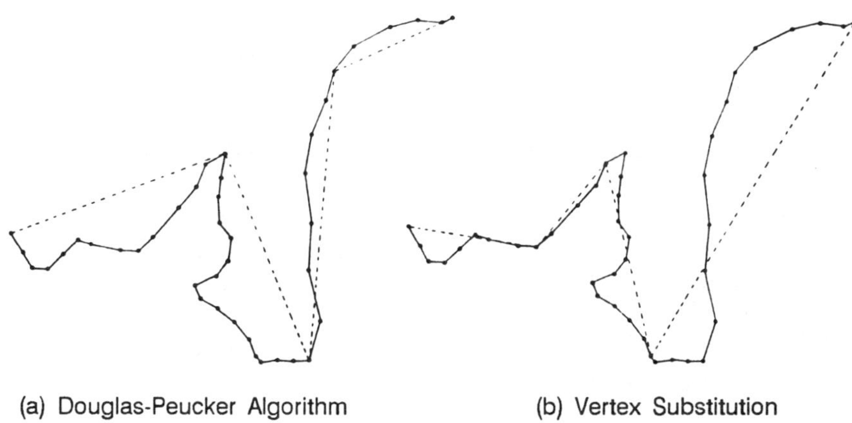

Figure 3.35 Comparison of Alternate Line Simplifications.
(Source: Cromley, 1988)

5.7 SUMMARY

Classification and simplification operators are essential manipulations of the original database for improving the communication of resulting maps. The number of cartographic objects that can be effectively communicated is scale dependent; therefore in a digital cartographic information processing system these operators must sift the kernels of information from the chaff of data. The resulting information is then transferred to display operators for conversion into graphic form.

5.8 REFERENCES

Brassel, K. and R. Weibel. [1988]. "A Review and Conceptual Framework of Automated Map Generalization," **International Journal of Geographical Information Systems**, 2, 229-244.

Burrough, P. [1986]. **Principles of Geographical Information Systems for Land Resources Assessment**, Oxford: Oxford University Press.

Buttenfield, B. [1986]. "Digital Definitions of Scale-Dependent Line Structure," **Proceedings**, AUTO CARTO London, 497-506.

Clark, W.A.V. and P. Hosking. [1986]. **Statistical Methods for Geographers**, New York: John Wiley.

Cliff, A.D. and J. Ord. [1973]. **Spatial Autocorrelation**, London: Pion.

Cliff, A.D. and J. Ord. [1981]. **Spatial Processes: Models and Application**, London: Pion.

Cooper, L. [1963]. "Location-Allocation Problems," **Operations Research**, 11, 331-43.

Cooper, L. [1967]. "Solutions of Generalized Locational Equilibrium Models," **Journal of Regional Science**, 7, 1-18.

Cooper, L. [1968]. "An Extension of the Generalized Weber Problem," **Journal of Regional Science**, 8, 181-97.

Cromley, R. [1988]. "A Vertex Substitution Approach to Numerical Line Simplification," **Proceedings**, Third International Symposium on Spatial Data Handling, 57-63.

Cromley, R. and G. Campbell. [1991]. "Noninferior Bandwidth Line Simplification: Algorithm and Structural Analysis," **Geographical Analysis**, 23.

Cromley, R. and S. Morse. [1988]. "Some Comments on Numerical Line Generalization," **Geographical Analysis**, 20, 263-69.

Dacey, M. [1965]. "A Review of Measures of Contiguity for Two and k-color Maps," in **A Reader in Statistical Geography**, B.J.L. Berry and D. Marble (eds.), Englewood Cliffs, New Jersey: Prentice-Hall, 479-95.

deJong, P., C. Sprenger, and F. Van Veen. [1984]. "On Extreme Values of Moran's I and Geary's c," **Geographical Analysis**, 16, 17-24.

DeVeau, T. [1985]. "Reducing the Number of Points in a Plane Curve Representation," **Proceedings**, AUTO-CARTO VII, 152-160.

Douglas, D. and T. Peucker. [1973]. "Algorithms for the Reduction of the Number of Points Required to Represent a Digitized Line or its Caricature," **The Canadian Cartographer**, 10, 112-22.

Ebdon, D. [1983]. **Statistics in Geography, a Practical Approach**, Oxford: Blackwell.

Evans, I. [1977]. "The Selection of Class Intervals," **Transactions Institute of British Geographers**, 2, 98-124.

Fisher, W. [1958]. "On Grouping for Maximum Homogeneity," **Journal of the American Statistical Association**, 53, 789-98.

Freeman, H. [1978]. "Shape Description via the Use of Critical Points," **Pattern Recognition**, 10, 159-66.

Gatrell, A. [1979]. "Autocorrelation in Spaces," **Environment and Planning A**, 11, 507-16.

Geary, R. [1954]. "The Contiguity Ratio and Statistical Mapping," **The Incorporated Statistician**, 5, 115-45.

Griffith, D. [1979]. "Urban Dominance, Spatial Structure, and Spatial Dymanics: Some Theoretical Conjectures and Empirical Implications," **Economic Geography**, 55, 95-113.

Griffith, D. [1987]. **Spatial Autocorrelation: A Primer**, Washington, D.C.: Association of American Geographers.

Hanink, D. [1988]. "Nonintegration of Regional Labor Markets: The Case of Large US Cities from February 1980 through December 1983," **Environment and Planning A**, 20, 1397-1410.

Hultquist, J., J. Holmes and L. Brown. [1970]. **CENTRO: A Program for Centrographic Measures**, Department of Geography, The Ohio State University, Discussion Paper No. 21.

Jenks, G. [1977]. **Optimal Data Classification for Choropleth Maps**, Department of Geography, University of Kansas, Occasional Paper No. 2.

Jenks, G. [1981]. "Lines, Computers, and Human Frailties," **Annals Association of American Geographers**, 71, 1-10.

Jenks, G. and F. Caspall. [1971]. "Error on Choroplethic Maps: Definition Measurement, Reduction," **Annals Association of American Geographers**, 61, 217-44.

Jenks, G. and M. Coulson. [1963]. "Class Intervals for Statistical Maps," **International Yearbook of Cartography**, 3, 119-34.

Johnston, R.J. [1978]. **Multivariate Statistical Analysis in Geography**, New York: Longman.

Kuhn, H. and R. Kuenne. [1962]. "An Efficient Algorithm for the Numerical Solution of the Generalized Weber Problem in Spatial Economics," **Journal of Regional Science**, 4, 21-33.

Lang, T. [1969]. "Rules for Robot Draughtsmen," **Geographical Magazine**, 22, 50-51.

Lefever, D. [1926]. "Measuring Geographic Concentration by Means of the Standard Deviational Ellipse," **American Journal of Sociology**, 32, 88-94.

Lindberg, M. [forthcoming 1990]. "FISHER: A TURBO PASCAL Unit for Optimal Univeriate Partitioning on an IBM PC," **Computers and Geosciences**.

Maranzana, F. [1964]. "On the Location of Supply Points to Minimize Transport Costs," **Operational Research Quarterly**, 15, 261-70.

Marino, J. [1979]. "Identification of Characteristic Points in Naturally Occurring Lines: An Empirical Study," **The Canadian Cartographer**, 16, 70-80.

McMaster, R. [1983]. "A Mathematical Evaluation of Simplification Algorithms," **Proceedings**, AUTO-CARTO VI, 2,267-76.

McMaster, R. [1986]. "A Statistical Analysis of Mathematical Measures for Linear Simplification," **The American Cartographer**, 13, 103-17.

McMaster, R. [1987a]. "Automated Line Generalization," **The Canadian Cartographer**, 24, 74-111.

McMaster, R. [1987b]. "The Geometric Properties of Numerical Generalization," **Geographical Analysis**, 19, 330-46.

Monmonier, M. [1973]. "Analogs Between Class-Interval Selection and Location-Allocation Models," **The Canadian Cartographer**, 10, 123-31.

Monmonier, M. [1986]. "Toward a Practical Model of Cartographic Generalization," **Proceedings**, AUTO CARTO London, 257-66.

Moran, P. [1950]. "Notes on Continuous Stochastic Phenomena," **Biometrika**, 37, 17-23.

Morrill, R. and J. Symons. [1977]. "Efficiency and Equity Aspects of Optimum Location," **Geographical Analysis**, 9, 215-25.

Olson, J. [1975]. "Autocorrelation and Visual Map Complexity," **Annals Association of American Geographers**, 65, 189-204.

Opheim, H. [1982]. "Fast Data Reduction of a Digitized Curve," **Geo-Processing**, 2, 33-40.

Peucker, T. [1976]. "A Theory of the Cartographic Line," **International Yearbook of Cartography**, 16, 134-43.

Preparata, F. and M. Shamos. [1985]. **Computational Geometry**, New York: Springer-Verlag.

Reumann, K. and A. Witkam. [1974]. "Optimizing Curve Segmentation in Computer Graphics," **International Computing Symposium**, 7, 467-72.

Robinson, A., R. Sale, J. Morrison, and P. Muehrcke. [1984]. **Elements of Cartography**, Fifth Edition, New York: John Wiley.

Shannon, G. and R. Cromley. [1980]. "The Great Plague of London," **Urban Geography**, 1, 254-70.

Shea, K. and R. McMaster. [1989]. "Cartographic Generalization in a Digital Environment," **Proceedings**, AUTO-CARTO 9, 56-67.

Teitz, M. and P. Bart. [1968]. "Heuristic Methods for Estimating the Generalized Vertex Median of a Weighted Graph," **Operations Research**, 19, 1366-73.

Topfer, F. and W. Pillewizer. [1966]. "The Principles of Selection," **The Cartographic Journal**, 3, 10-16.

Toregas, C., R. Swain, C. ReVelle, and L. Bergman [1971]. "The Location of Emergency Service Facilities," **Operations Research**, 19, 1366-73.

Unwin, D. [1981]. **Introductory Spatial Analysis**, New York: Methuen.

White, E. [1985]. "Assessment of Line-Generalization Algorithms Using Characteristic Points," **The American Cartographer**, 12, 17-27.

Chapter 6

Two-Dimensional Display

Thus far the focus of discussion has been on the encoding and storage of digital cartographic features, and the associated preprocessing and manipulation operations for these objects. Once the digital cartographic objects have been classified or simplified, the image is ready for display. Cartographic display operators are at the center of actual map production. They convert the digital representations into either softcopy or hardcopy maps. As such they are inverse operators to the data encoding operators which convert analog cartographic objects into digital cartographic objects. In cartographic display, digital objects are transformed into analog ones. This chapter covers cartographic display operators for planar representations of surfaces. Three-dimensional displays are covered in the next chapter.

Display operations cover a range of topics from symbolization and data enhancement procedures to the mechanics of map generation. Certain display functions operate primarily on the geographic base file or with thematic overlay while others integrate both. At the core of cartographic display, however, is symbolization. All features must be symbolized in some way for visual impression and interpretation. Therefore, it is first necessary to discuss the nature of cartographic symbolization.

6.1 SYMBOLIZATION

Symbolization operations involve the conversion of thematic numerical information into analog cartographic symbols. The form of symbolization depends on the nature of the thematic data. As discussed in Chapter Four the thematic attributes of cartographic objects are measured at nominal, ordinal, interval, and ratio scales. The range of symbolization corresponds to the range of measurement scales from nominal to ratio (see Figure 6.1). For an attribute measured in a nominal scale, objects are grouped into mutually exclusive and exhaustive categories. For an attribute measured in an ordinal scale, objects are ordered in either an ascending or a descending manner, but the distance between objects is not known. In an interval scale, the distance between objects is known but the location of the origin of the scale is arbitrary. Finally, ratio scaled data have an absolute zero value so that all measurements are positive. All symbolism is possible at the ratio scale, while nominal symbolism is more limited. However, mapping with symbolism below the level of measurement implicitly generalizes the data and results in a loss of information [Muehrcke, 1972].

SCALE	CARTOGRAPHIC SYMBOL		
	POINT	LINE	AREA
NOMINAL	Town	Stream Network	U R K Soil Type
ORDINAL	Large Medium Small	Interstate State Local Roads	dry wet Climate Zones
INTERVAL	70 80 60 Spot Elevations	10 20 30 10 20 30 Contours	1940 1900 1961 Date of Purchase
RATIO	Graduated Circles	Flowlines	Darkness Proportional to Data

Figure 6.1 Cartographic Symbolism and Measurement Scales.
(after Muehrcke, 1972)

Another consideration in symbolism is to define differences in symbols to represent a corresponding difference in thematic values. After objects have been classified and simplified, symbolism operators should transform the resulting digital objects into an analog representation so that there is no confusion in the interpretation of the symbolism. The *size*, *shape*, *orientation*, *color*, *value*, or *texture* of the symbolism can be used to transmit the information content of the symbolism message (see Bertin [1983] for more details on this topic). Value is the level of reflectance received by the human eye; it is produced by the spacing of elements in a shade pattern; texture is the variation in the fineness or coarseness of elements in a pattern. These attributes of the symbolism should be distinct enough so that a map reader will not receive the wrong message [Knopfli, 1982]. For example in Figure 6.2, the symbolism assigned objects **A** and **C** is similar enough that the reader might interpret object **A** to represent object **C**. As mentioned in Chapter Five, the "connectivity relation" between symbolism and the objects they represent is expressed through the map legend.

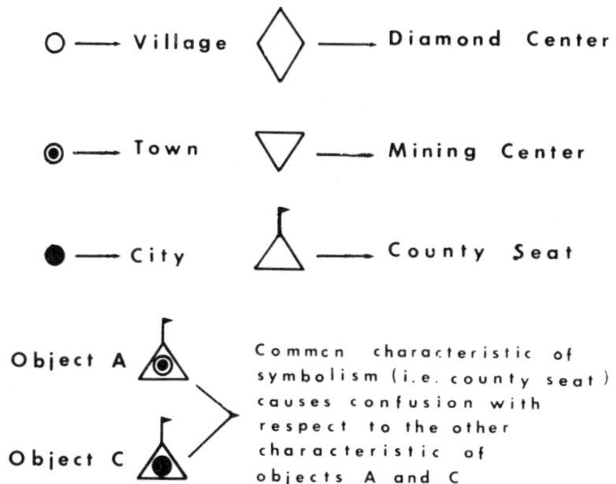

Figure 6.2 Transmission of Cartographic Information Through Symbolism.

The form of symbolism also depends on the type of geographic object associated with the thematic value. Symbolism for point objects can vary in size, shape, orientation, color, value and texture but not in its location [Bertin, 1983]. The visual center of the symbol should be located at the position of the point object. Because lines have length but no area, their symbolism also can vary in size, shape, orientation, color, value, and texture. However, because area objects represent entities that have a measurable size and a form, their symbolism should not vary in size, shape or orientation – it can vary only in value, texture and color [Bertin, 1983]. The symbolism for different objects will be some combination of the properties appropriate for the dimensionality of the object.

6.1.1 Graduated Symbols

Graduated symbols are used to denote thematic values on a ratio scale by varying the size of the symbol. The shape of the symbol can either be representative of the attribute being displayed, such as the outline of a person to represent population, or it can represent some common geometric form such as a square. The most commonly used graduated symbol is the circle. Graduated circles do not increase in size in an arithmetic progression with increases in the magnitude of the thematic value but increase as a function of the square root of the thematic value given that the area of the circle rather than its radius represents the magnitude of the thematic value (see Figure 6.3.) For graduated circles, if a standard circle having radius $\mathbf{r_s}$ represents a magnitude $\mathbf{z_s}$, the radius $\mathbf{r_i}$ for any other magnitude $\mathbf{z_i}$ is [Monmonier, 1982]:

$$r_i = \frac{r_s \cdot z_i^{1/2}}{z_s^{1/2}} \quad . \tag{6.1}$$

Because humans perceptually underestimate the true area of larger circles when viewing them, an exponent larger than one-half is frequently used to enlarge them in order to correct for this visual distortion. No single correction factor has been empirically derived but the exponent value has varied in experiments based on the research design [Dent, 1985].

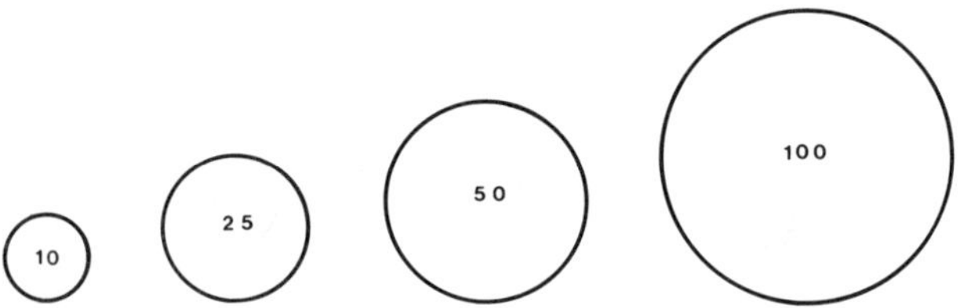

Figure 6.3 A Typical Scale of Graduated Circles.

There are several other concerns in the computer-assisted construction of a graduated symbol overlay [Rase, 1987]. First symbols will overlap one another whenever the distance separating the symbol centers is less than combined distance to the extremities of each symbol. To improve the interpretation of the overlay, the hidden portion of the symbols should be removed (Figure 6.4.) The problem of resolving the overlapping of polygons is discussed further in Chapter Eight. Secondly, legibility is enhanced if a small gap known as a "halo" is left between overlapping symbols (Figure 6.4).

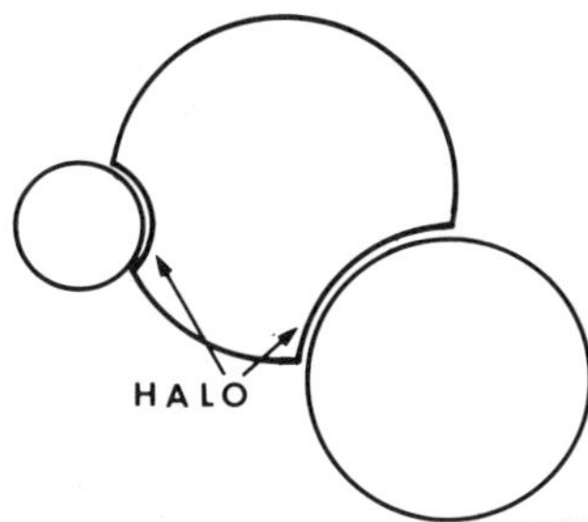

Figure 6.4 The Effect of Hidden Symbol Removal and a Halo.

Finally, it is sometimes necessary to modify the positioning of some symbols if portions of these symbols relevant to map interpretation are hidden from view. For point objects, the location of the point normally defines the center position of the symbol. For two-dimensional objects, the center point of a polygon such as the one that is the center of the largest inscribed circle is used to locate the center of the symbol. To reduce the likelihood that some symbols are completely obscured by overlap with other symbols, the symbols are drawn in order of their size with the largest symbol being drawn first (Figure 6.5.) In this manner, the smallest symbol will not be obscured by any symbol and it is less likely that the larger symbols will be totally obscured from view by the smaller ones in front.

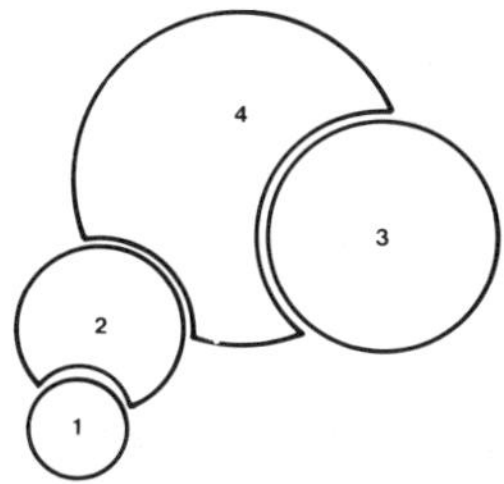

Figure 6.5 Ordering from Front to Back of Smaller to Larger Symbols.

6.1.2 Value

The magnitude of thematic values for areal units (*e.g.*, counties) is most frequently represented by value. Although a fine dot screen pattern has been shown to be the best graphical technique to depict value, the level of the prevailing technology has constrained the true objective in a digital environment (Figure 6.6a). On line printers, the tone of the shade pattern is achieved by overstriking normal alpha-numeric characters. On plotters the tone is represented by the intersection of a series of orthogonal (or sometimes parallel) straight lines spaced a constant distance apart with the polygon (Figure 6.6b). Given that line printers were not designed to produce graphics, it is difficult to represent a full continuum of gray tones. Special line printer chains have improved the tonal quality of line printer shading [see Brassel, 1974].

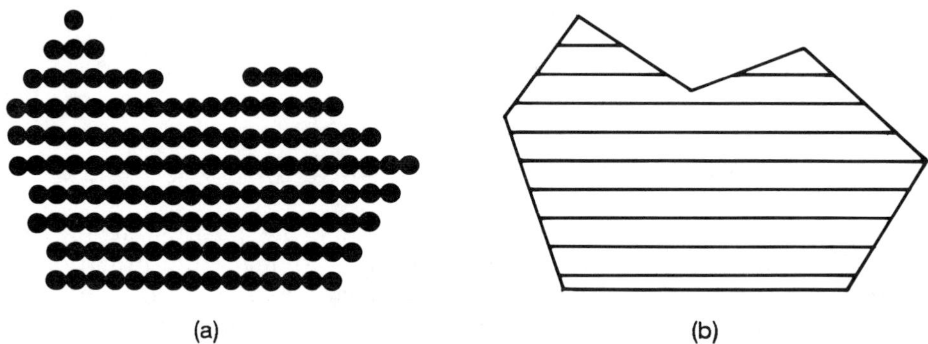

Figure 6.6 Example Area Shade Patterns.

A continuum of tones for plotters is achieved by varying the spacing between orthogonal shade lines such that there is a one-to-one correspondance between shade values and normalized thematic values (Figure 6.7) [Tobler, 1973]. Given the spacing between lines in this scheme for low thematic values, it is possible that the spacing distance can be larger than the width of small areal units. In this case an alternative shading scheme must be used. Brassel and Utano [1979] have developed a combined system that continuously dissolves the orthogonal pattern into a cross-pattern and eventually into a dot pattern (Figure 6.8.) The shading pattern is now a function of line spacing and dash length.

Figure 6.7 A Continuous Tone Legend.
(after Brassel and Utano, 1979)

Different strategies are used for assigning shade patterns to classified thematic data. One approach is to choose the shade pattern that maximizes tone contrast between classes. For line-printers, Smith [1980] has examined the intensity of various overstrike combinations by measuring the percentage of light passing through a film positive of the symbol combination using a densitometer. Adjusting the objective measurement to reflect human perception, symbols are ordered by their percent perceived grayness (or value). The differences between symbol combinations (and possibly the order), however, will vary among printers and for a printer will vary by ribbon/paper combinations. The appropriate symbolism for a map having **N** classes is achieved by selecting overstrike combinations having the maximum difference in percent perceived grayness. For standard line printer characters, this difference will not be the same between each class, but dot patterns for laser printers permit more even value. For a shade line pattern, maximum contrast is accomplished by setting the normalized thematic value in the continuous tone scheme to a multiple of **1/N**.

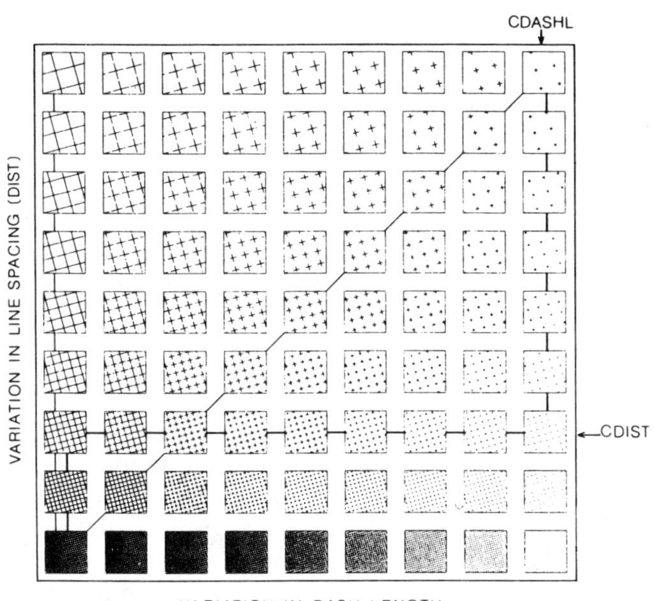

Figure 6.8 Pattern by Varying Line Spacing and Dash Length. (Source: Brassel and Utano, 1979)

A second method is to assign a shade pattern that corresponds to the mean value of each class. This would be more appropriate for optimal classifications based on minimizing within-class variation. A different approach would be to assign a shade pattern to match the original thematic value of each areal object [Tobler, 1973]. An unclassified map permits the reader to analyze spatial patterns in the data unfiltered by the classification operator (no quantification error). The trade-off is that the increased amount of information in the unclassified map may increase perceptual error in interpretation. Although the numerical values used to generate a shade pattern have a metric property, the perceptual ability to judge shading is at the bottom of our perceptual hierarchy [Cleveland and McGill, 1984]. It is easier to more accurately judge position along either a common scale or nonaligned scales, length, orientation, angle, area and volume than it is to judge shading [Cleveland and McGill, 1984]. To improve the communication of an unclassified map, Brassel and Utano [1979] suggest that the reader be provided more instructional assistance through an expanded map legend. The legend for a continous-tone map is a combination of the continuous gray-scale legend (Figure 6.7) and traditional legend boxes for selected values (Figure 6.9). The boxes aid the reader in identifying a pattern in the range between any two adjacent legend boxes.

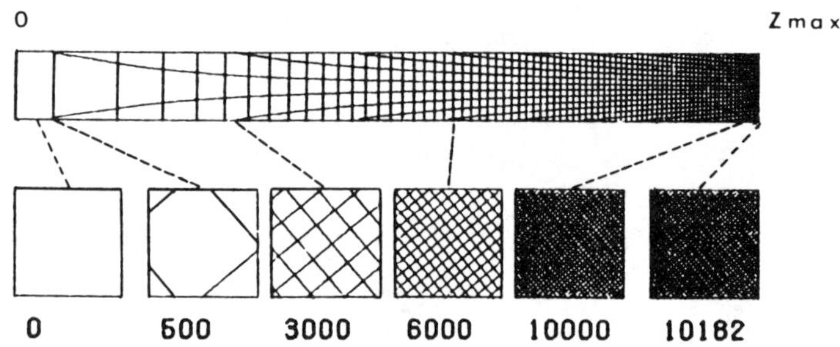

Figure 6.9 An Alternative Continuous-Tone Legend.
(Source: Brassel and Utano, 1979)

Cleveland and McGill [1984] would replace the shading of regions in a map with a *framed-rectangle chart* for each region. In a framed-rectangle chart, bars of equal length are proportionally filled to correspond to their respective attribute value. In Figure 6.10, bar **A** denotes a larger value than does bar **B** and bar **C** has the largest value of all three bars. The perceptual task in discerning the attribute value is judging position along nonaligned scales, a task much higher in the perceptual hierarchy.

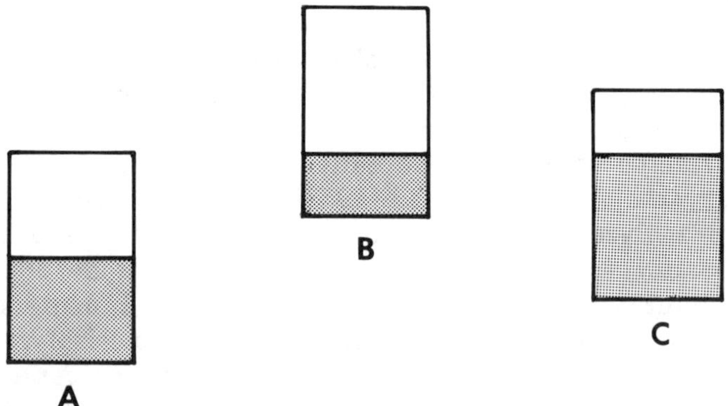

Figure 6.10 Example Framed Rectangles.

6.2 DATA ENHANCEMENT

Enhancement procedures are approximate inverses to data selection and other generalization operators. Because all generalization operators are functions and not transformations, it is impossible to perform a true inverse operation for any generalization operator. However, there is a need in cartography to add detail to linear and surface features either to improve the appearance of the display or to estimate values for locations that were not part of the data sample.

6.2.1 Linear Interpolation

Frequently in cartographic display strings are fitted by curved lines to improve the aesthetic appearance of the display (Figure 6.11a). The fitted curve can be made to either pass through the given vertices of the string (called *interpolation*) or to pass near the vertices (*approximation*) [Pavlidis,1982]. Linear interpolation can be solved by fitting a polynomial function to the string. However, a strict polynomial interpolation may intersect the individual line segments and introduce noise into the fitted curve. It is more appropriate to replace each line segment by a curve that only intersects a line segment at its endpoints. For this reason, piecewise polynomial functions produce more desirable results. To ensure that the piecewise generated curves fit together to form a smooth line, a cubic polynomial function is calculated to pass through four consecutive vertices but only the piece connecting the second and third vertices is retained (Figure 6.11b). This process is repeated for successive sets of vertices.

One method for deriving one such function is to estimate the parameters of the following cubic polynomial using least squares regression [Monmonier, 1982]:

$$Y = a + b_1 X + b_2 X^2 + b_3 X^3 . \qquad (6.2)$$

Because only four observations (coordinates in this case) are used to estimate four parameters, there are no degrees of freedom associated with the model and the cubic function must pass through the observations. A drawback to this approach is that the coordinate axes must be rotated whenever the fitted curve would result in a multi-valued function (a relation). A more general approach is to express a function in its parametric form:

$$X = f_x(t) \quad ; \qquad\qquad (6.3)$$
$$Y = f_y(t) \quad ;$$

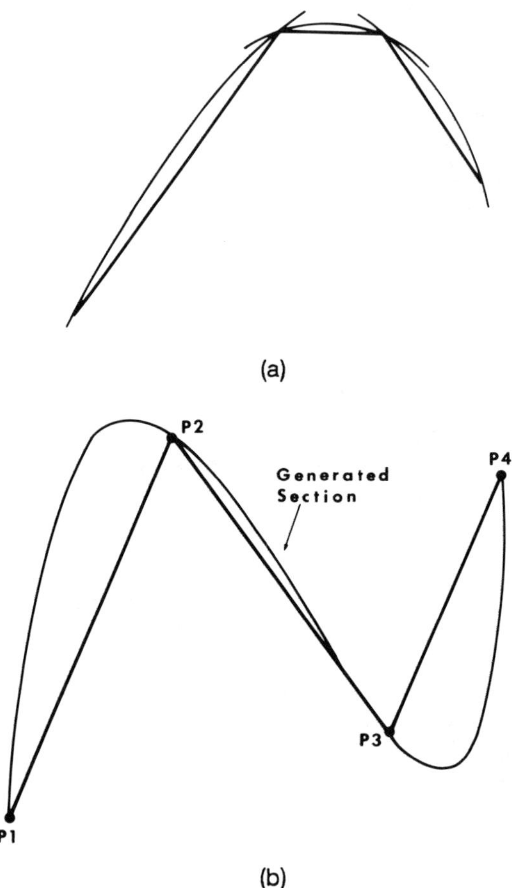

Figure 6.11 The Piecewise Construction of a Curved Line.

rather than its explicit form **Y = f(X)** [Pavlidis, 1982; Harrington, 1987]. For four points, the value of **t** ranges from minus one to two (or i-2). An interpolation function of this form is:

$$f_x(t) = \sum_{i=1}^{N} X_i \; B_i(t) \quad ; \qquad (6.4)$$

$$f_y(t) = \sum_{i=1}^{N} Y_i \; B_i(t) \quad ;$$

where $\mathbf{B_i(t)}$ are piecewise blending functions defined over different intervals of **t**. To ensure that the fitted curve passes through the ith vertex, its blending function should equal one and the blending functions for the other three vertices should equal zero. One set of blending functions for four points is [Harrington, 1987] :

$$B_1(t) = \frac{t(t-1)(t-2)}{(-1)(-2)(-3)} \; ; \; B_2(t) = \frac{(t+1)(t-1)(t-2)}{(1)(-1)(-2)} \; ;$$
$$B_3(t) = \frac{(t+1)t(t-2)}{(2)(1)(-1)} \; ; \; B_4(t) = \frac{(t+1)t(t-1)}{(3)(2)(1)} \; . \tag{6.5}$$

Although these blending functions are easy to calculate, one disadvantage is that they may not result in a smooth transition from one segment to another (Figure 6.12b). Cubic B-spline functions handle this situation (Figure 6.12c) by not forcing the approximating curve to pass through each coordinate of the original string [Harrington, 1987]. Special functions are used for the starting and ending segments and **t** only ranges from zero to one. The cubic B-spline functions for the first segment of the curve are:

$$B_1(t) = (1-t)^3 \; ; \; B_2(t) = 21t^3/12 - 9t^2/2 + 3t \; ;$$
$$B_3(t) = -11t^3/12 + 3t^2/2 \; ; \; B_4(t) = t^3/6 \; . \tag{6.6}$$

The functions for the second segment of the curve are:

$$B_1(t) = (1-t)^3/4 \; ; \; B_2(t) = 7t^3/12 - 5t^2/4 + t/4 + 7/12 \; ;$$
$$B_3(t) = -t^3/2 + t^2/2 + t/2 + 1/6 \; ; \; B_4(t) = t^3/6 \; . \tag{6.7}$$

For the last and the second to the last segments of the curve, the functions, **B**′(t), are the respective reverses of **B(t)**:

$$B'_1(t) = B_4(1-t) \; ; \; B'_2(t) = B_3(1-t) \; ;$$
$$B'_3(t) = B_2(1-t) \; ; \; B'_4(t) = B_1(1-t) \; . \tag{6.8}$$

Finally, the functions for all intermediate segments of the curve are:

$$B_1(t) = (1-t)^3/6 \; ; \; B_2(t) = t^3/2 - t^2 + 2/3 \; ;$$
$$B_3(t) = -t^3/2 + t^2/2 + t/2 + 1/6 \; ; \; B_4(t) = t^3/6 \; . \tag{6.9}$$

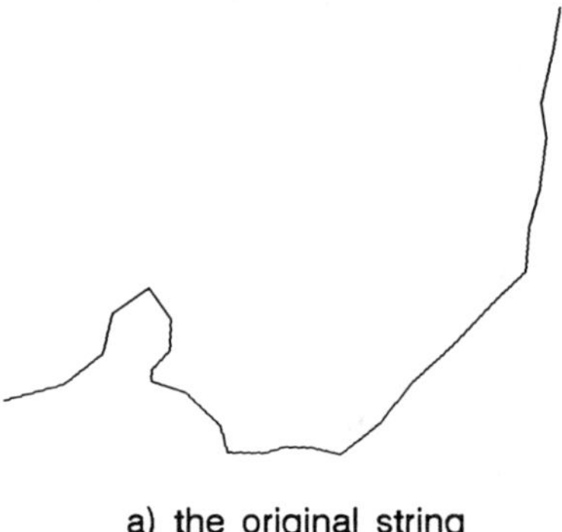

a) the original string

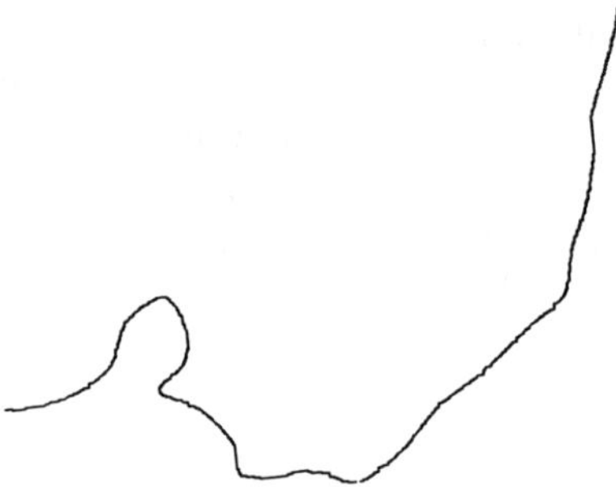

b) a blending function interpolation

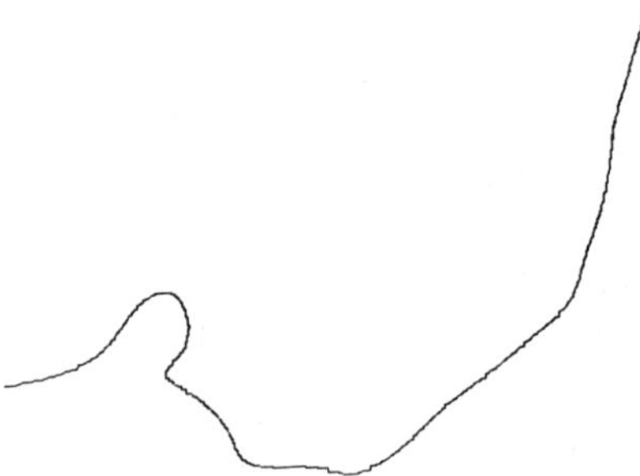

c) a cubic B-spline approximation

Figure 6.12 Interpolation and Approximation Using Blending Functions.

An alternative approach to line enhancement is fractal enhancement [Dutton, 1981]. Fractal enhancement produces a rougher appearance in the enhanced line that is more like the shape of real world objects (*e.g.*, a rugged coastline) than spline functions do. Fractal enhancement is based on the self-similarity properties of lines (see Chapter Four). Enhancement using fractals permits smaller features to be introduced into strings based on recursions of forms already present in the string. If the fractal dimension of a line was 1.0, a subdivision of each of its string segments should produce a new string that was an exact replica of the original string. However, as the fractal dimension approaches 2.0, the subdivisions should result in a new string that has many more bends than the original because the length of each pair of new segments is substantially greater than the length of the line segment they replace.

Different methods for implementing the fractal enhancement of lines have been proposed [see Dutton, 1981; Harrington, 1987]. One method computes an offset factor for the midpoint of each line segment when subdividing that is based on the fractal dimension of the line [Harrington, 1987]. If the fractal dimension is close to 1.0, the offset factor is small (see Figure 6.13).

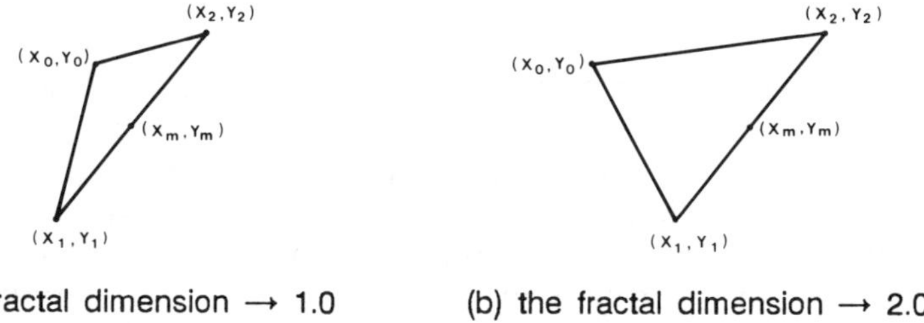

Figure 6.13 Two Offset Factors.

This concept is expressed in the following pair of equations [Harrington, 1987] :

$$X_o = X_m + L * F * R \; ; \qquad (6.10)$$
$$Y_o = Y_m + L * F * R \; ;$$

where (X_o,Y_o) is the offset location;
(X_m,Y_m) is the midpoint of the line segment;
L is a scaling factor based on the length of the segment (usually measured in euclidean or manhattan metric);
F is the fractal dimension minus one;
and **R** is a normally distributed random number with a zero mean.

Figure 6.14 shows the fractalized enhancement of a string (Figure 6.14a) based on two different self-similarity dimensions. The lower the fractal dimensionality, the smoother the appearance of the line (compare Figures 6.14b and 6.14c). For geographic lines, self-similarity properties can be altered over different portions of the line to retain certain desired shapes in local domains such as a straight line.

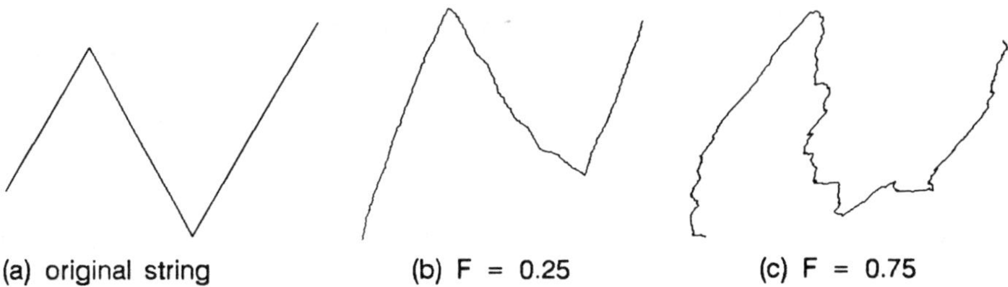

Figure 6.14 A Fractal Enhancement.

6.2.2 Spatial Interpolation

Spatial interpolation is also an approximate inverse of the data selection operator. In data selection, usually only a sample of thematic values is collected at intervals over a surface. It is impossible to know exactly what the data values are at those points on the surface that were not part of the sample. The spatial interpolation problem is to approximate thematic values at coordinates for which the value is unknown. Interpolation estimates are most reliable for points inside the convex hull of a known distribution of control points (Figure 6.15). Estimating values at positions some distance outside the convex hull is called *extrapolation*. Separate reviews of interpolation techniques are given by Ripley [1981], Lam [1983], and Burrough [1986].

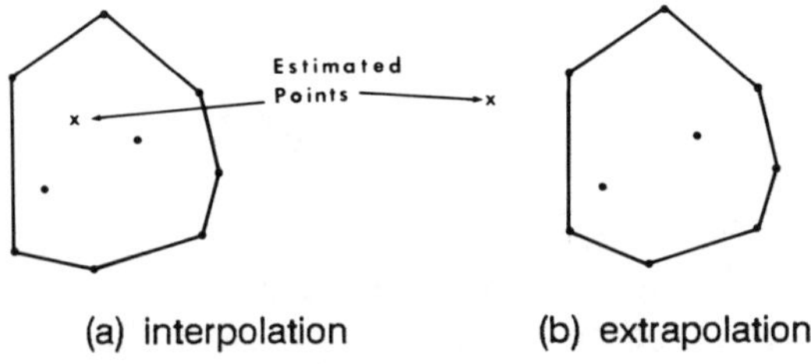

Figure 6.15 Interpolated and Extrapolated Points.

The most frequent use of spatial interpolation is to estimate thematic values for a regularly spaced distribution of points such as a square lattice from an irregularly spaced distribution of control points. Spatial interpolation is also used to estimate missing values for areal units. Besides using interpolated values directly for display purposes, these estimates are added to the database and can later be used in other forms of spatial analysis.

One approach is to assume that the unknown value at an interpolated point should be similar to (or positively autocorrelated with) its neighboring control points. Because the thematic values of a distribution are positively autocorrelated as the Geary **c** index decreases, one method for maximizing similarity is to:

$$\text{minimize} \quad \sum_{i=1}^{N} w_{ij} \, (z_i - z_j)^2 \tag{6.11}$$

where N is the number of known points in the neighborhood;
z_i is the thematic value of the ith known point;
z_j is the thematic value being estimated for the jth unknown point;
and w_{ij} is the connectivity relationship (or weight) between the ith and jth points.

The normal equation for (6.11) is:

$$\sum_{i=1}^{N} w_{ij} \, (z_i - z_j) = 0. \tag{6.12}$$

Rearranging terms:

$$z_j = \frac{\sum_{i=1}^{N} w_{ij} \, z_i}{\sum_{i=1}^{N} w_{ij}} . \tag{6.13}$$

Equation (6.13) defines a method of spatial interpolation most commonly known as a *weighted moving average* estimator because the known values are weighted by some connectivity relation and this relation is updated every time the estimator is moved to a new unknown point. As when calculating spatial autocorrelation indices, the nature of the connectivity relation between known points and the unknown point can take many forms.

The simplest relation would be to let $w_{ij}=1$ if the known point is an adjacent neighbor of the unknown point (it either shares a Thiessen edge in the case of a set of points or a chain in the case of polygons) or $w_{ij}=0$ if the objects are not adjacent (Figure 6.16). In this case the interpolated value of the unknown object is the average of its adjacent neighbors. A criticism of this weighting is that all adjacent neighbors are given equal importance. A modification of this weighting would be to let w_{ij} equal the length of the shared boundary (either the length of the shared Thiessen edge or chain) between the known and unknown objects [Kennedy and Tobler, 1983]. In this manner, more importance is given to those neighbors sharing longer boundaries and reduces the influence of a clustering of neighbors because of their shorter boundaries.

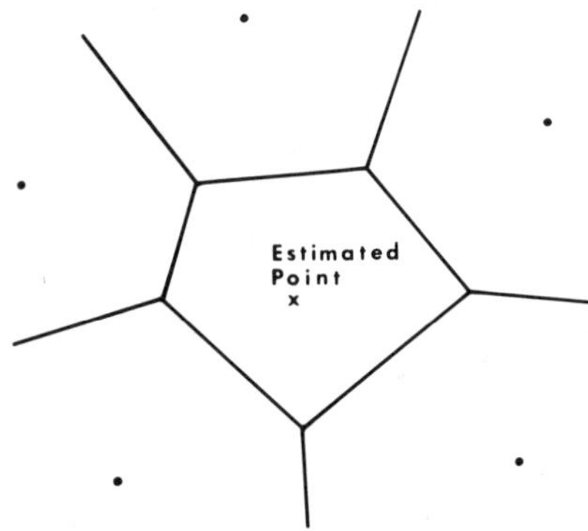

Figure 6.16 Adjacent Neighbors of an Unknown Object.

Another frequently used set of weights for point distributions are based on inverse distance. In this case the relative importance of each known object in the interpolation is a function of its distance from the unknown object, $w_{ij}=d_{ij}^{-\alpha}$, where **i** is in the neighborhood of **j**. As a friction of distance exponent, α must be greater than zero. Objects that lie closer are thus given greater weight. One inverse distance weighting is to let α be a large positive number. The effect of this weighting is to minimize the importance of any known object other than the nearest neighor of the unknown object. This weighting then is analogous to finding the Thiessen polygon associated with a Thiessen tessellation of the set of control points that contains the unknown point (Figure 6.17). Because all unknown points within the same Thiessen polygon will have the same interpolated value, the interpolated surface will be a stepped surface with breaks occurring along the Thiessen edges (Figure 6.18).

A more frequently used weighting is the inverse squared distance weighting, $w_{ij}=d_{ij}^{-2}$ [Shepard, 1968]. In this interpolation, greater weighting is given to closer objects and the interpolated surface has a smoother appearance (Figure 6.19). However, there are drawbacks of such an inverse distance function. One drawback to this function is that the spatial impedance factor was determined exogenously with respect to the surface under study.

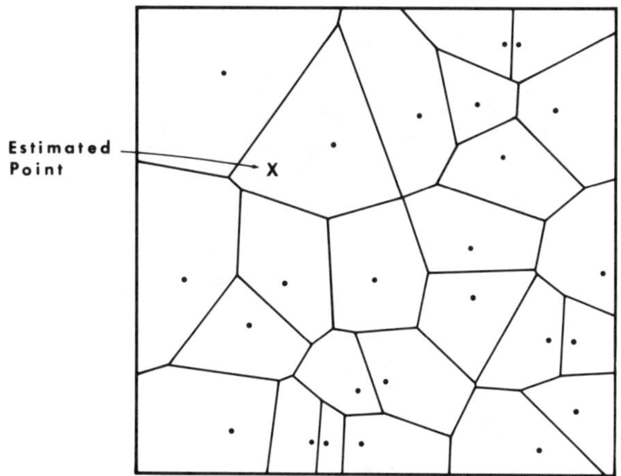

Figure 6.17 Nearest Neighbor of Estimated Point.

Figure 6.18 A Nearest Neighbor Weighting.

An alternative to this would be to estimate the weighting as a spatial impedance function, $\mathbf{w_{ij}=f(d_{ij})}$, for the local neighborhood of each unknown object. A variogram is constructed in which the variation between pairs of known points is plotted against the distance between the point pair (Figure 6.20). Regression analysis is used to approximate the form of the relationship between the two axes. If the relationship is non-linear, then logarithmic transformations of either or both axes may be applied. For a linear relationship, $w_{ij}=1/(\beta d_{ij})$, assuming the estimated line is forced to pass through the origin. For a log/linear relationship, $w_{ij}=e^{-\beta d_{ij}}$ and for a log/log relationship $w_{ij}=d_{ij}^{-\beta}$. In each case, the friction of distance value, β, is the slope of the estimated regression line.

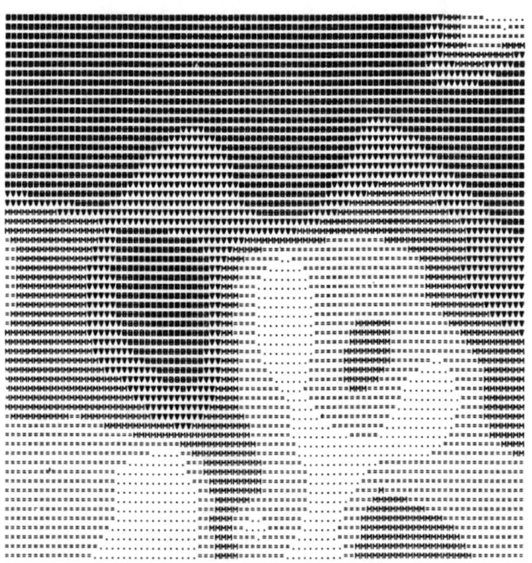

Figure 6.19 Interpolated Surface Using d_{ij}^{-2}.

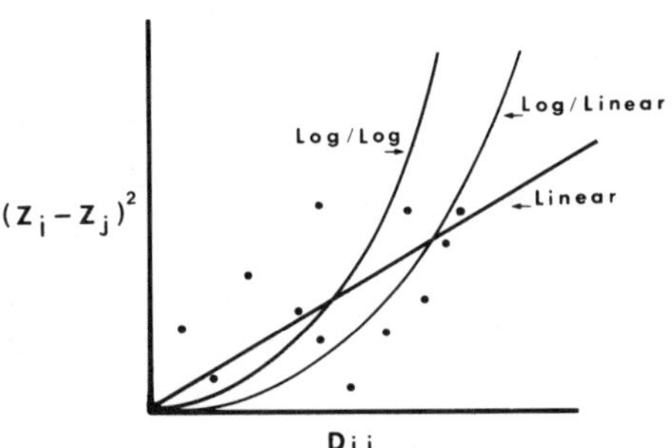

Figure 6.20 Estimating a Distance Decay Function from a Variogram.

Another criticism of inverse distance weighting is that the resulting interpolation is sensitive to the clustering of known points. To reduce the impact of clustering, Shepard [1968] suggests modifying the inverse distance weights by the incorporating the cosine of the directional angle between neighboring control points (Figure 6.21) and the unknown point.

The directional isolation of the ith control point, T_i, is measured as [Shepard, 1968] :

$$T_i = \sum_{k=1}^{N} d_{kj}^{-1} (1 - \cos \theta_{ik}) \; ; \qquad (6.14)$$

where $\cos \theta_{ik}$ is the cosine of the angle between the ith and kth control points. If the angles between the ith control point and the other control points are close to zero, the value of T_i will also be close to zero; conversely, if the angles between the ith control point and the others are all close to 180°, the value of T_i will be approximately twice the sum of the inverse distances. The resulting adjusted weight for the ith control point is :

$$w_{ij} = d_{ij}^{-2} \cdot [T_i \, / \, (\sum_{k=1}^{N} d_{kj}^{-1})] \quad . \qquad (6.15)$$

The maximum effect of directional isolation is a doubling of the value of the inverse square of distance.

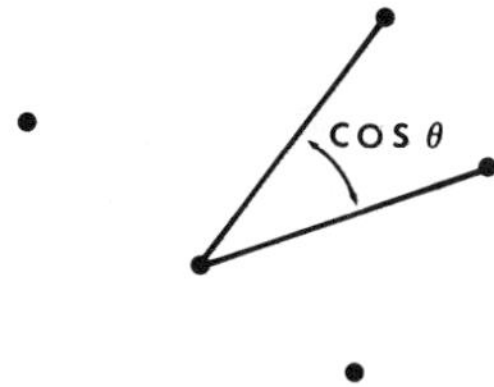

Figure 6.21 The Directional Angle Between Control Points.

A different interpolation technique using local neighborhoods is kriging. Kriging was developed as an "optimal" interpolation procedure that not only interpolates a surface but gives error estimates of the interpolated accuracy over the surface. A detailed discussion is beyond the scope of this text but the reader can find summaries in Olea [1974] and Davis [1973].

A second class of interpolation operators, called *global*, simultaneously estimates values for the entire surface. One such interpolation technique is trend surface fitting. In trend surface fitting, the x and y coordinates are assumed to be independent variables and the thematic value z is given as a polynomial function of x and y. The highest power of the polynomial function is known as the order of the trend surface. A first order trend surface fits a plane to the set of known control points (Figure 6.22); a second order surface fits a quadratic surface (see Figure 6.23). The coefficients of the polynomial are derived by least squares regression analysis which minimizes the sum of the squared deviations between the estimated values of the control points and their known value. One feature of trend surface fitting then is that the values of the control points are only approximated by the fitted function. Better approximations are achieved by raising the order of the surface, but this tends to introduce high frequency noise into the surface that may not have been in the original surface.

Figure 6.22 A First Order Trend Surface.

Figure 6.23 A Second Order Trend Surface.

Once numerical values have been derived for an interpolated grid, these values can be classified (or not classified) and displayed directly by assigning them an appropriate gray-tone symbol, or the grid of values can be used as the data for other display operators such as isoline construction (see section 6.4) or three-dimensional perspectives (see the next chapter).

6.3 CHOROPLETH MAPPING

An important type of thematic map for displaying data either aggregated into discrete zones or assigned to discrete zones is a *choropleth map*. Nominal, ordinal, interval or metric attributes can be represented by a choropleth map. For interval or metric attributes, a choropleth map is a planar representation of a discrete surface. In a conceptual model, a planar representation of the resulting surface is created by passing horizontal parallel planes through the surface at successive elevations defined by class interval limits [Jenks, 1963] (Figure 6.24). The portion of the surface between a pair of planes is then flattened into a single elevation (frequently the mean elevation of the surface between two planes). A two-dimensional representation of the surface can then be constructed by either drawing the locus of points formed by the intersection of the planes with the surface or by shading the orthographic projection of the area interval between two successive planes.

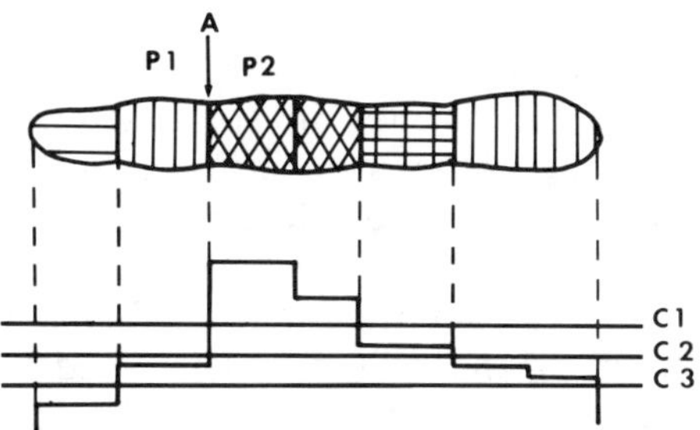

Figure 6.24 A Planar Representation of a Discrete Surface.

For a discrete surface, area shading is more appropriate than drawing the locus of intersection points because two or more class boundaries will occupy the same geographic location on the projection plane. In Figure 6.24, arc A, the boundary between polygons **P1** and **P2**, is also a portion of the boundary associated with class limit **C1** and class limit **C2**. Boundary lines can intersect because there are abrupt breaks in the surface. In this situation, the viewer's attention should be focused on the areas between the area values rather than the position of the boundaries themselves.

In a choropleth map, the boundaries between zones are determined independently of the attribute being displayed. One set of boundaries such as state outlines can be used to display a large set of attributes. In a related type of map, the *area class map*, the boundaries between zones are determined by the distribution of the attribute itself such as in a soil or vegetation classification map. The boundaries in an area class map are more ambiguous than those in a choropleth map and are unique to only one attribute. Despite these differences, the display operators are similar for both types of maps.

The steps required for choropleth mapping are 1) grouping the attribute values into class intervals (this step is not required for classless maps), 2) choosing the appropriate symbolism to represent each class (or individual values), and 3) either drawing the line-shading (or dot) pattern on a vector device or printing the symbolism on a raster device. If the attribute in question is a categorical variable, the first step is not needed. Printing symbolism on raster devices requires that the raster units associated with each region are stored explicitly in a raster data structure or that a vector-to-raster conversion is used to identify those raster units associated with each region. This conversion process is described after the procedures required for polygon line-shading.

6.3.1 Polygon Line-Shading

A frequent choropleth mapping strategy is to shade the polygons associated with individual data zones in some sequence. The sequence is often not based on a geographic ordering that minimizes total movement across a display device such as a plotter but rather on the alphabetic ordering of the data zone names. In either case, polygon line-shading algorithms need the property that the family of shade lines associated with a certain value align with the origin. The shade lines passing through two regions belonging to the same value and sharing a common boundary will align exactly (see Figure 6.25a). If the shade lines lack this common alignment, the visual impression may not maintain the one-to-one correspondence between data class and value (Figure 6.25b).

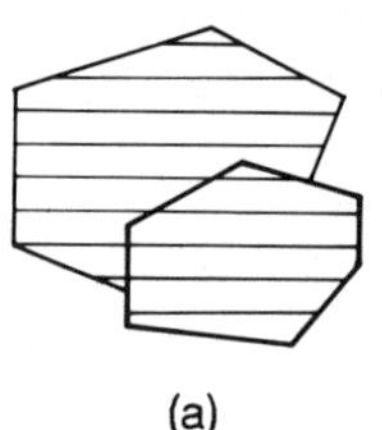

(a)

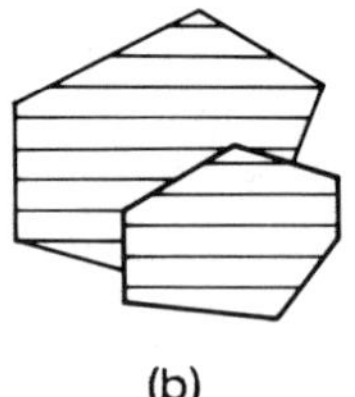

(b)

Figure 6.25 Shade Line Alignment.

This property is preserved by fixing the location of the shade lines so that they align on the X-axis. First the coordinate axes are rotated by the shade line angle of orientation (Figure 6.26). Next the maximum Y-coordinate of the polygon, **YMAX**, in the rotated space is found. The Y-coordinate, Y^*, of the highest shade line that passes through the polygon such that the shade lines are on the rotated X-axis is:

$$Y^* = \text{INT [YMAX / DELTA]} * \text{DELTA} \quad ; \qquad (6.16)$$

where **INT** is the greatest integer function;
and **DELTA** is the perpendicular distance between shade lines.

Once the Y-coordinate of the highest shade line passing through the polygon has been determined, the Y-coordinate of all others are found by incremently decreasing Y^* by the value of **DELTA** until no further shade line passes through the polygon in question.

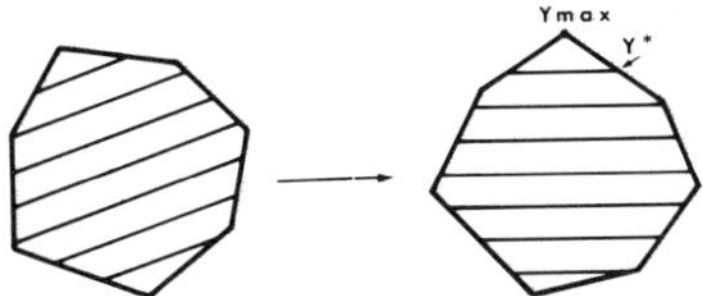

Figure 6.26 Rotation of Axes by the Angle of Orientation.

There are three basic strategies for performing the polygon line shading operator. In the "single line" approach, the polygon is first rotated by the angle of orientation and each shade line is processed independently of the next shade line in order. Next each segment of the polygon outline is checked for a possible intersection with the shade line being processed. The set of intersection points made by the shade line is stored and then sorted in the X-dimension. This sort is necessary to ensure that the shade line is properly drawn by a sequence of move and draw pairs. For example in Figure 6.27, the first intersection (X_1,Y_1) is found on the line segment connecting vertices **V4** and **V5**, and the second intersection (X_2,Y_2) is on the segment connecting vertices **V5** and **V6**. One could not move to the point (X_1,Y_1) and then draw to the point (X_2,Y_2) because this line segment would lie outside the polygon. The initial move must be to the point (X_3,Y_3) for the proper pairing of moves and draws.

Finally, all intersections are rerotated back to the original space of the polygon for display. The major advantages of the "single line" approach are its simplicity and low storage requirements. Only the intersection points of one shade line are in storage at a time. For a convex polygon, only one line segment is needed for each shade line (Figure 6.28a). For a concave polygon having **N** vertices in its outline, at most **N/2** line segments are needed for representing each shade line (Figure 6.28b). However, the amount of computation required by this approach is sensitive to the density of shade lines.

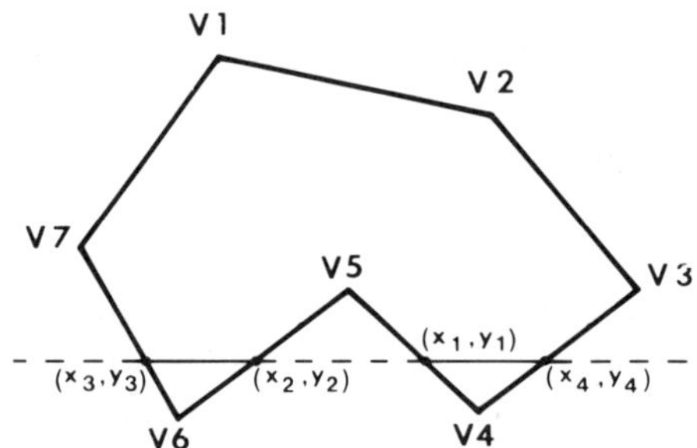

Figure 6.27 Single Line Shading.

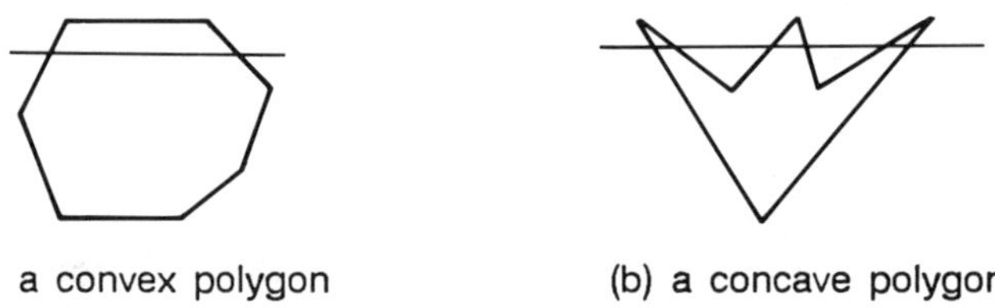

(a) a convex polygon (b) a concave polygon

Figure 6.28 Shade Line Segments.

Another approach is the "walk-around" method, in which all of the intersections made by all shade lines with the polygon outline are calculated first by moving around the polygon perimeter (see Figure 6.29). The computational efficiency is improved in this method because the polygon outline is checked only once rather than once for each shade line. Secondly, the sequence of intersections along each outline segment is computed as an **X** and **Y** displacement from the previous intersection rather than using the line intersection equations for each intersection. The major disadvantage of this method is that all intersections must be stored before any shade line can be drawn. This approach is sensitive to the density of shade lines with respect to storage and is prohibitive for polygons having a large number of coordinates.

A third strategy is to partition the polygon into trapezoidal subpolygons that are convex (Figure 6.30). Each trapezoid is then processed independently and a pair of intersections for each shade line within a trapezoid are calculated and drawn at once. Intersections are calculated using the displacement method but are not sorted because there is only one shade segment within a trapezoid.

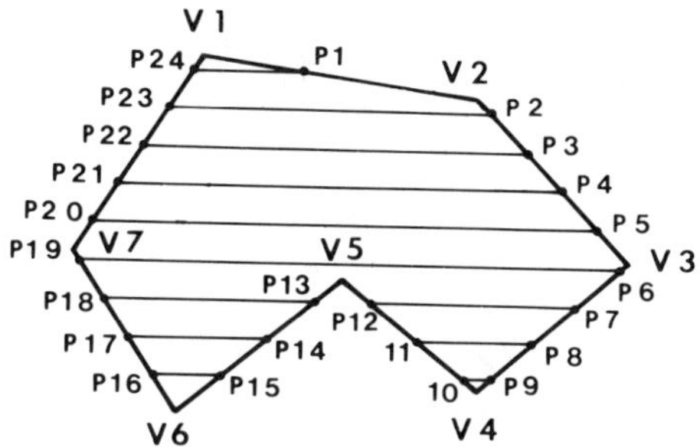

Figure 6.29 Walk-around Shading Approach.

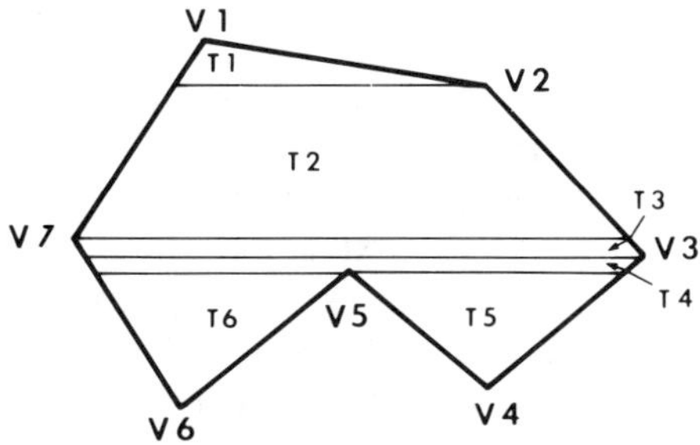

Figure 6.30 A Trapezoid Partition of a Polygon.

Because trapezoids are shaded independently of each other, the intersections can be calculated directly in the unrotated space by simply calculating the X and Y displacement values in this space:

$$DX_i = DIST * XD/XD' \quad ; \qquad DY_i = DIST * YD/YD' \quad ; \tag{6.17}$$

where **DX**$_i$ is the X displacement for the ith line segment;
DY$_i$ is the Y displacement for the ith line segment;
DIST is the perpendicular distance between shade lines;
XD and **YD** are the respective X and Y distances between the endpoints of the line segment in the unrotated space (see Figure 6.31);
XD′ and **YD′** are the respective X and Y distances between the endpoints of the line segment in the rotated space (see Figure 6.31).

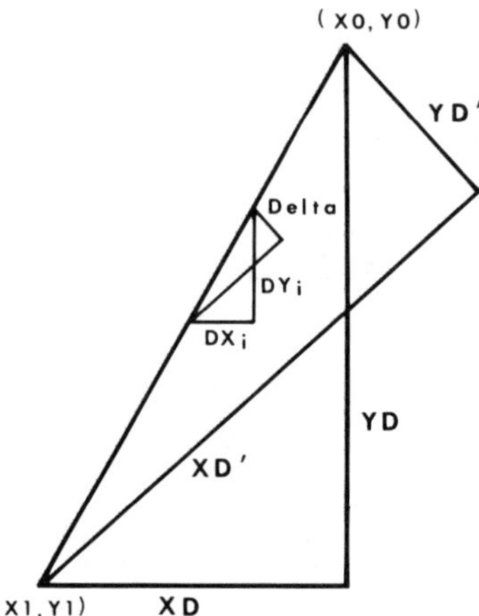

Figure 6.31 Determining the Displacement Values.
(Source: Cromley, 1984)

The set of polygon outline vertices is only processed once and the only major additional computation is that the polygon vertices must be sorted in the Y-dimension before the trapezoids can be extracted in some order. Brassel and Fegeas [1979] extracted the trapezoids using a method that shaded the polygon in a manner analogous to filling an irregularly shaped container with water. Lee [1981] and Cromley [1984] identify the trapezoids by processing each polygon vertex in a descending rank order of its Y-coordinate.

Cross-hatched patterns are generated by first passing a set of parallel lines in one direction through the polygon and then another set of parallel lines perpendicular to the first set. This involves switching the **X** and **Y** axes for the perpendicular set of shade lines. A summary of the major computational and storage requirements of each method is given in Table 6.1.

6.3.2 Region Filling

As previously mentioned, the procedures for printing symbolism on raster devices differ according to the mode of region encoding. If each region is encoded in a raster data structure, each pixel is assigned the value of the symbolism corresponding to the region it represents. For example, in a scan-line data structure, the pixels associated with each scan segment in a scan line are assigned their respective region value. If the entire set of regions comprising the choropleth map is to be displayed simultaneously, the values for one scan line are assigned and then displayed independently of the next scan line. This is a frequent strategy for line printer output devices because once the printer advances to the next line it cannot go back to a previous line [see Scripter, 1969; Monmonier, 1975]. If an individual region is to be displayed in its entirety before the next region in sequence can be displayed, then the set of scan lines is processed in order and only the scan segments for the given region are displayed. This procedure is repeated for each region.

Table 6.1 Summary Comparisons of Alternative Shade Line Methods

Method	Shade Line Coordinate Storage	Number of Times Outline is Processed	Number of Shade Line Sorts	Shade Line Intersection Method	Y-Sort
Single Line	N/2 max	M	M	Independent Intersections	Yes
Walk-Around	M*(N/2 max)	1	M	DX, DY Displacement	No
Trapezoid	N/2 max	1 plus sort cost (NlogN)	1	DX, DY Displacement	Yes

N = number of vertices M = number of shade lines

If each region is encoded in a vector data structure, then first a vector-to-raster conversion is used to identify those raster units associated with each polygon outline. This conversion process requires only a modification of the procedures used for polygon line-shading. In this case horizontal scan lines are passed through a polygon at a spacing equal to the resolution of the output device. The pixels in a three-step process [Foley and Van Dam, 1984]: 1) find the intersections of a scan line with all edges of a polygon; 2) sort the intersections in increasing X-coordinate; and 3) fill in all pixels between pairs of intersections (see Figure 6.32). The first two steps of this procedure are identical to the single line shading method discussed in the previous section. The final step just identifies the first and last pixel of a scan segment and the appropriate value assignment rather than drawing a shade segment from one intersection to the next. Each of the other shade-line procedures can be adapted to pixel identification in the same manner.

6.3.3 Hierarchical Polygon Merging

Most efforts to improve the computational efficiency of constructing choropleth maps on vector devices have focused on improving the performance of polygon line-shading algorithms. However, polygons are still shaded independently of each other. A major disadvantage of this mapping strategy is that an individual shade line is broken into a series of segments if it passes through more than one data zone. For example, shade line S in Figure 6.33 passes through polygons A and **B**. If polygon A is shaded independently of polygon **B**, then S is drawn as three segments when shading polygon A and as four segments when shading polygon **B**. If the two polygons were merged together into one polygon, then S could be drawn as just one segment.

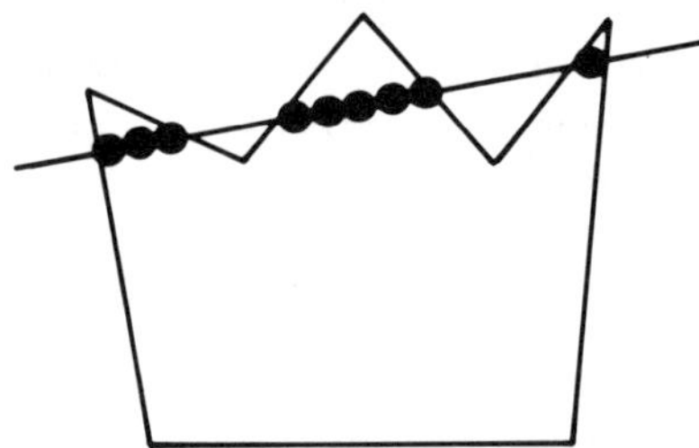

Figure 6.32 Polygon to Scan-Line Conversion.

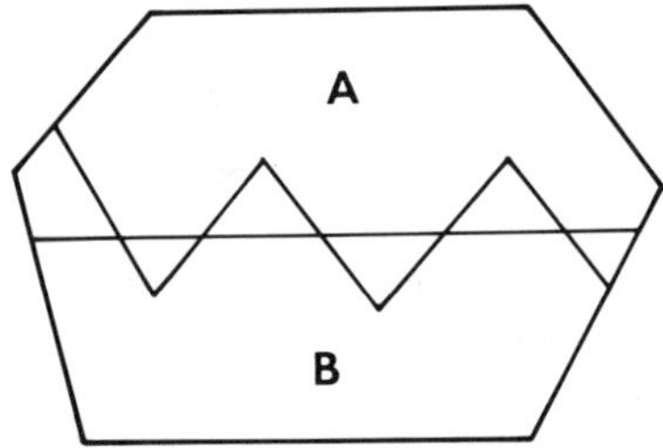

Figure 6.33 The Decomposition of a Shade Line by Polygon Boundaries.

In the process all boundaries between polygons are processed twice as part of the outline of two different polygons by line-shading algorithms. This can considerably increase the number of points that must be processed during shading calculations. An alternative mapping strategy is to eliminate all chains that lie in the interior of the area corresponding to a class interval (see Figure 6.34) before performing any shading operation [Cromley, 1983]. In this strategy, individual polygons are merged or generalized into geographical class intervals that correspond to the thematic class intervals associated with the attribute being displayed.

The gains from merging are directly proportional to the number of interior boundaries that can be deleted, which in turn is dependent on the level of first order spatial autocorrelation present in the grouping. For example, Figure 6.35a presents a highly clustered set of four spatial groupings while Figure 6.35b presents a totally unclustered set of four spatial groupings. It is impossible to delete any interior boundaries in the latter spatial grouping. In the latter case each polygon should be shaded independently. Any attempt to merge polygons would only increase the overall number of computations because a merging operator is added and no chains are eliminated.

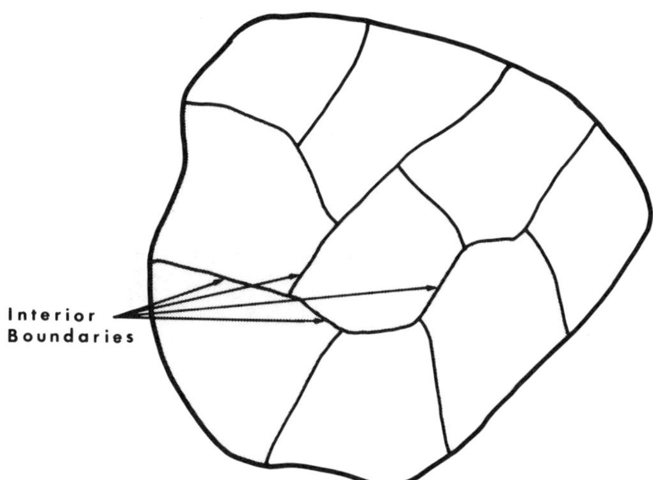

Figure 6.34 Interior Boundaries within a Class Region.

The nature of the merging procedure is dependent on the structure of the geographic base file. A polygon spaghetti model, for example, is used in **SAS/GRAPH** to compress individual polygons into larger cartographic objects. However, calculations are excessive as merging operations must first identify the string of points common to two polygons being merged. More efficient merging operators can be integrated with graph topological structures as the operations are performed on chains rather than the individual points within a chain.

In Chapter Three, the outline of an individual polygon was retrieved by cross-referencing the chain reference file with a point file containing a starting chain for each polygon. Implicit in this retrieval operation was the fact that the polygon on the other side of each chain belonged to a different grouping. For grouping polygons into larger data zones based on some criterion such as data classification, the problem is to retrieve the outline of the perimeter of each larger region. For each chain in the base map, it can either lie on the perimeter of a grouping or it can lie in the interior of a grouping (see Figure 6.34). These exterior chains are easily identified as their left- and right-hand polygons belong to different data classes. For interior chains, the left- and right-hand polygons associated with each chain either both belong to a given grouping or both do not belong to that grouping.

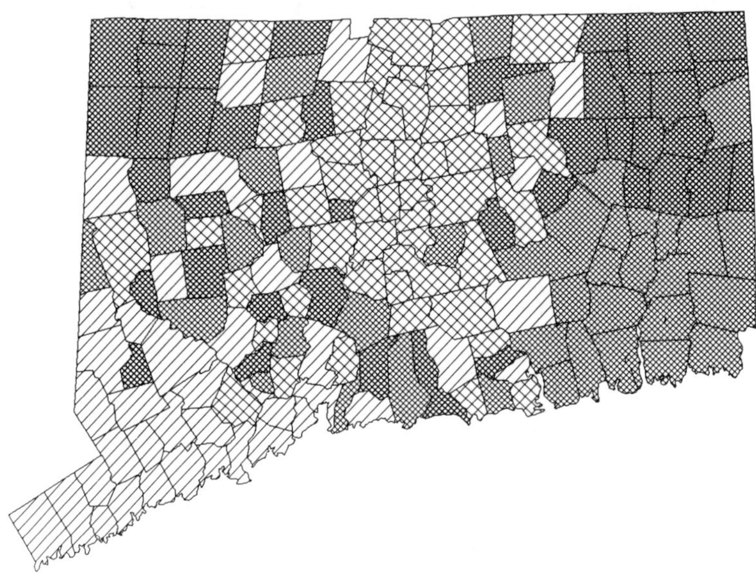

(a) positive autocorrelation

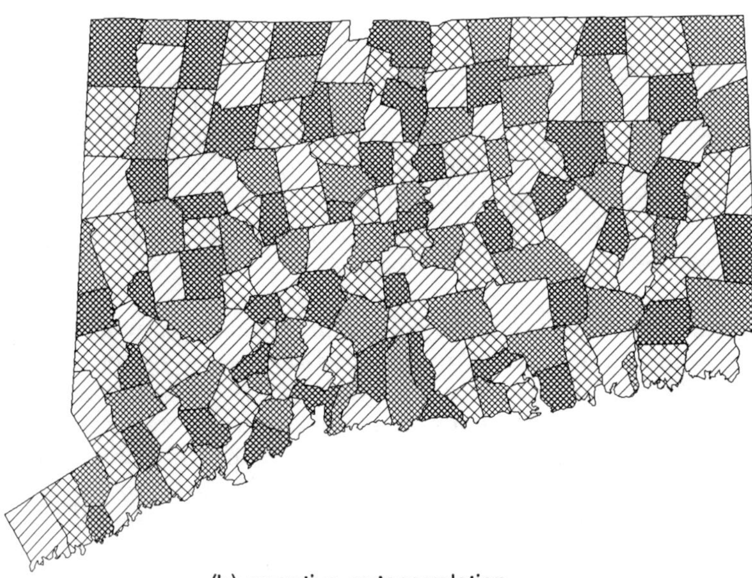

(b) negative autocorrelation

Figure 6.35 Spatially Clustered and Unclustered Groupings.

Once an initial chain is determined to be an exterior chain, one "moves" along it to the next chain for which the super-polygon lies to the right. The next exterior chain in the outline sequence will be either the right- or left-hand chain associated with the current chain depending upon whether its right- or left-hand polygon belongs to the super-polygon. For example, the polygons comprising the class interval region in Figure 6.34 are merged together by retrieving its exterior ring. Given the graph topology presented in Figure 6.36, the first chain on the exterior ring is **C2**. The next chain is **C3** in sequence because the right-hand polygon for **C2** belongs to the super-polygon. The full sequence of chains comprising the exterior ring is given in Table 6.2.

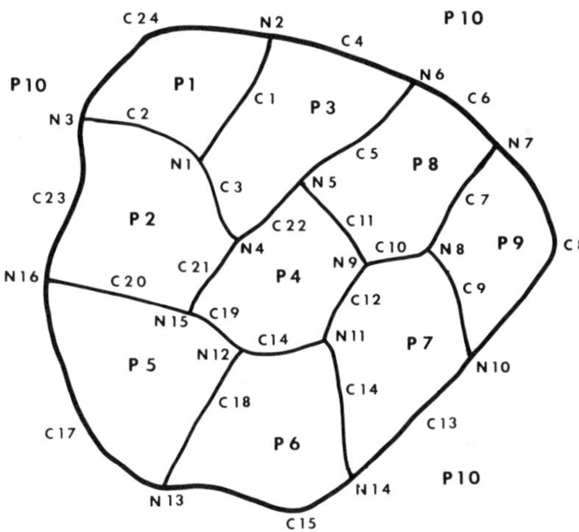

Figure 6.36 The Topological Objects.

Table 6.2 The Sequence of Extracting Perimeter Chains

Current Chain	Right-Hand Polygon	Right-Hand Chain
C2	P2	C3
C3	P2	C22
C22	P4	C11
C11	P4	C10
C10	P7	C9
C9	P7	C13
C13	P7	C14
C14	P7	C16
C16	P4	C18
C18	P5	C17
C17	P5	C23
C23	P2	C2

In the following algorithm, **K** is the total number of chains in the file; **C** is the index of the initial chain in a ring; **M** is the index of the current chain in a ring; **N** is the index of the next chain under consideration; **P** is the index of the current right-hand polygon for the ring; **rpoly, lpoly, rchain,** and **lchain** are functions for retrieving the right-hand polgon, the left-hand polygon, the right-hand chain, or the left-hand chain respectively of a given chain:

Step 1) Select a class interval; if the outlines for all groupings have been enumerated, STOP; otherwise continue.

Step 2) Set a flag for each chain to an "off" position; set the chain ID value, **C**, equal to 0 and continue.

Step 3) Update **C** = **C** + **1**; if **C** is greater than **K**, go to Step 8; otherwise continue.

Step 4) If the flag for chain **C** is "on," go to Step 3; otherwise turn its flag "on," set **M** = **C** and continue.

Step 5) If both polygons associated with chain **M** belong to the current grouping or if neither polygon associated with chain **M** belong to the current grouping, go to Step 3; otherwise continue.

Step 6) If the super-polygon lies to the right of **M**, set N = **rchain(M)** and **P** = **rpoly(M)**; otherwise set N = **lchain(M)** and **P** = **lpoly(M)**. Turn the flag for N "on" and continue.

Step 7) If both polygons associated with N belong to the super-polygon and **P** = **rpoly(N)**, set **M** = **lchain(N)** and turn the flag for **M** "on." If both polygons associated with **N** belong to the super-polygon and **P** = **lpoly(N)**, set **M** = **rchain(N)** and turn the flag for **M** "on." If only **P** belongs to the super-polygon, set **M** = **N**.

Step 8) If **M** ≠ **C**, add **M** to the set of perimeter chains and go to Step 6; otherwise one perimeter ring is complete and go to Step 3 to enumerate additional rings.

Step 9) All interior and exterior rings of the super-polygon have been enumerated; shade this outline set; go to Step 1.

This merging operator for polygons shares some elements in common with threading operators for isarithmic maps presented in the next section.

6.4 ISARITHMIC MAPPING

An isarithmic map is a planar representation of a continuous surface using isarithms (lines of equal magnitude) to depict the surface. Again, horizontal parallel planes are passed through the surface at elevations defined by class interval limits (Figure 6.37). A critical distinction between choropleth and isarithmic maps is that while the time frame for both maps is fixed, the locational variable is controlled and the thematic variable is measured in the former and the thematic variable is controlled and the locational variable is measured in the latter [Sinton, 1978]. Normally an exogenously determined equal interval classification is used in isarithmic mapping for ease of interpretation and comparison between surfaces. For a continuous surface, the isarithms formed by the intersections of the planes with the surface are drawn and labelled because numerous intervals are frequently present and do not occupy the same location on the projection plane.

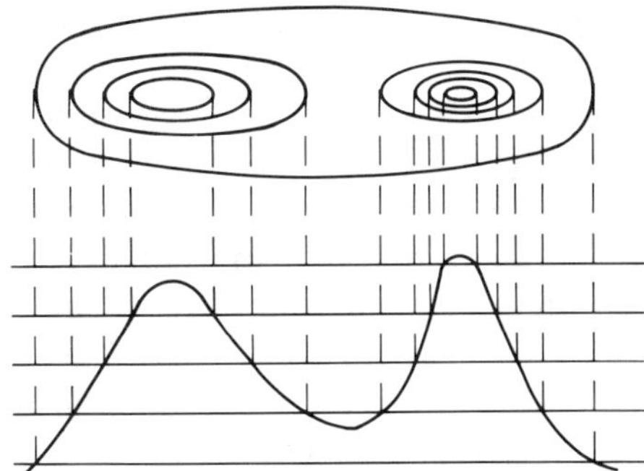

Figure 6.37 A Planar Representation of a Continuous Surface.

Although isarithmic maps represent a continuous surface, they are constructed either by using a stereoplotter to trace each contour from a pair of orthophotos in the case of measuring elevation and from a sample of control points for measuring most other continuous attributes. It is important is know how the original set of control points was selected. If the control points were purposely positioned at locations reflecting local maxima, minima, and inflection points, the point distribution is likely to exhibit a high degree of first order negative autocorrelation because neighboring locations are dissimilar. On the other hand, if the set of control points is chosen exogenously with respect to the surface under study, it is more difficult to predict the level of first order autocorrelation. In the second case, the interpolated surface is less likely to be as accurate a representation of the original surface as the former. Unfortunately, it is difficult if not impossible to know *a priori* the location of the characteristic points of many surfaces. Surfaces of continuous variables such as temperature or atmospheric pressure cannot be directly viewed before sampling.

An advantage of exogenously determined control points is that the location of sites (such as weather stations) is likely to be controlled for an array of variables. In this case, a constant geographic base file can be established for a series of isarithmic maps.

6.4.1 Grid Approaches

One method for constructing an isarithmic map is to thread the path of the respective isarithms through a regular grid of **z** values. One convention, when threading isarithms, is to move along an isarithm in a clockwise direction so that **z** values greater than that of the current isarithm z_i lie to the right of the direction of movement. If the original data were not sampled in a regular grid, the first step is to interpolate values for a regular grid from an irregular distribution (see section 6.2.2).

The advantage of threading isarithms through a grid is that a grid reference system implicitly retains neighborhood relationships between locations by row and column indexing. Once a contour line enters a grid cell **(i,j)** from one of its four neighboring cells **(i-1,j)**, **(i+1,j)**, **(i,j-1)**, or **(i,j+1)**, it should exit into one the the three remaining cells (see Figure 6.38a). The exiting side of the current cell is whichever one whose endpoints contain z_i within the range of the endpoints' **z** values. The exact position where the isarithm exits the side is usually solved by interpolation in which the **z** value is now known and the coordinate location is to be determined. Interpolation is done along the border of the cell because the corner points of the cell have known values (either given or estimated by a previous spatial interpolation step). Once the intersections of the isarithm with the grid cells have been determined (Figure 6.38b), they can either be drawn in order or passed to a linear enhancement operator to produce a curved isoline.

One disadvantage of the grid approach is that problems of indeterminacy are encountered whenever a "saddle-point" is encountered in the surface. In this situation more than one isarithm segment for a given **z** value will pass through a cell. For example, in Figure 6.39 the **50** level isarithm could connect side **S1** with **S2** and side **S3** with **S4** (Figure 6.39a) or side **S1** with **S4** and side **S2** with **S3** (Figure 6.39b). Connecting side **S1** with **S3** and **S2** with **S4** (Figure 6.39c) is numerically possible but cartographically impossible because isarithms cannot intersect.

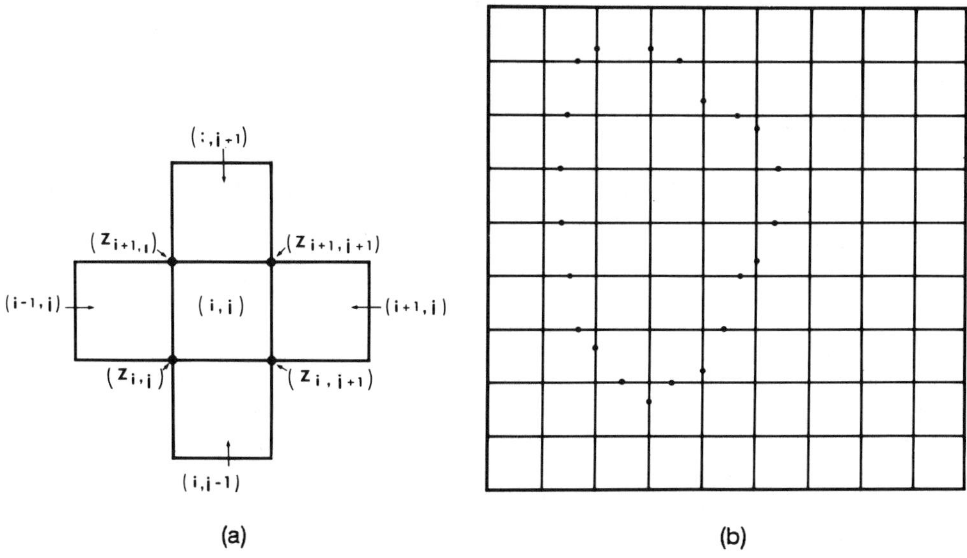

Figure 6.38 Threading an Isoline Through a Regular Grid.

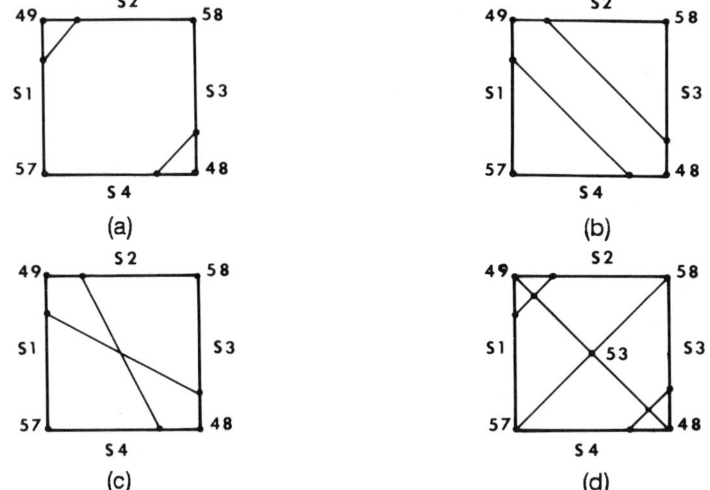

Figure 6.39 The Saddle Point Problem.

One method for resolving this indeterminacy is to interpolate a **z** value for the center of the cell based on the thematic values of the corner points and then partition the cell into four triangles (Figure 6.39d). There is no indeterminacy problem for each triangle because it has only three sides; if an isarithm enters one side of a triangle it can only exit one of the two other sides. Because the center point has a **z** value of **53**, side **S1** is connected to side **S4** and **S2** is connected to **S3**.

Another problem is that if the original data are not sampled in a regular grid, any spatial interpolation technique is likely to introduce more error into the surface. Yoeli [1983] contends that it is futile for topographic modeling to compute a set of secondary points for purposes of constructing a contour map. Instead contouring algorithms should conform to the original data point distribution.

6.4.2 Triangulation Approaches

In a triangulation approach, isarithms are threaded directly from an irregularly spaced point distribution [see Peucker *et al.*, 1978; Elfick, 1979; McCullagh and Ross, 1980; Watson, 1982; Cromley, 1986; and Gold and Cormack, 1987]. This eliminates the need to interpolate the original data points to a regular grid. Instead, a triangular mesh interconnecting the control points is calculated and stored in a topological data structure. Although more than one triangulation of the control points is possible, a frequently used one is the Delaunay triangulation (see Chapter Three). Once the triangular mesh has been computed and stored in a data structure, this structure can be used as the geographic base file for a series of maps using different interval widths or attributes (assuming the control point locations are constant for each attribute).

Different methods for threading isarithms are based on whether the underlying data structure is a tree [Gold and Cormack, 1987] or a triangle reference file [Elfick, 1979; Cromley, 1986]. In the latter case, a procedure similar to that of merging polygons can be used for threading isolines. For example, given the triangulation of control points in Figure 6.40a, a triangle reference file can be established (Table 6.3). The isarithm presented in Figure 6.40b is threaded by moving from triangle to triangle in a manner similar to the movement from chain to chain for traversing the exterior or interior ring of a class interval polygon presented in section 6.3.2. The rings of a class interval polygon are isarithms themselves.

If the intersections comprising the isarithm are computed moving in a clockwise direction, the control points with data values higher than the isarithm value will always lie to the right of the isarithm. Given the orientation of the isoline in Figure 6.40b, the first triangle that it passes through is **T1**. The next triangle is **T4** because the control point **C2** must lie to the right of the isarithm given that it has a higher data value than the value of the isarithm. Therefore, side **S3** is intersected by the isarithm. The full sequence of triangles passed through by the isarithm and the resulting intersection with each triangle side are given in Table 6.4. As the series of intersections is compiled, each set of four consecutive points can be passed to a linear enhancement operator for drawing a curved approximation of the isoline.

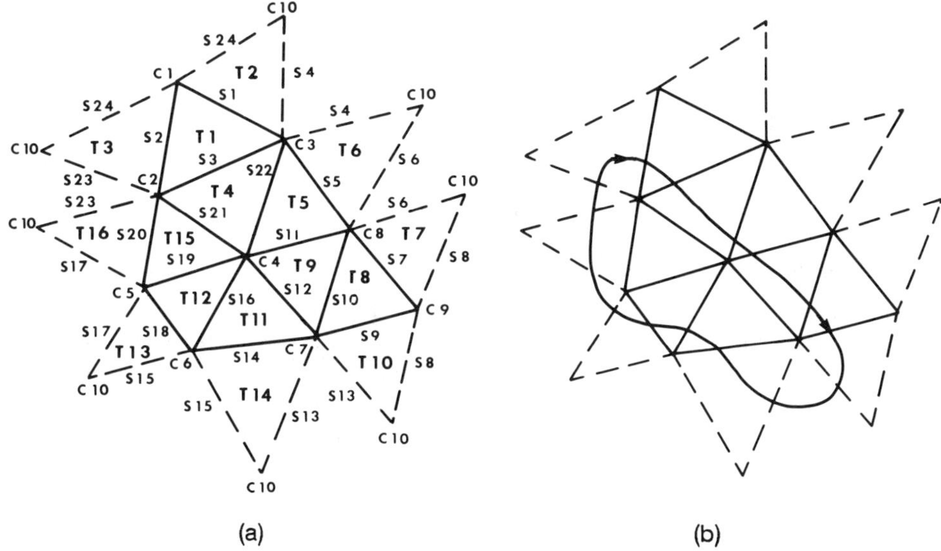

Figure 6.40 An Example Triangulation and Isarithm.

6.5 WINDOWING AND CLIPPING

The positioning, domain, and size of most cartographic displays are determined by using *windows* and *viewports*. This process involves the coordination of user and hardware spaces (see Chapter 2). Assume that the coordinates (UMINX,UMINY) and (UMAXX,UMAXY) are the respective lower and upper limits to the user space (Figure 6.41a) and (HMINX,HMAXY) and (HMAXX,HMAXY) are the respective lower and upper limits to the hardware space (see Figure 6.41b). The *window* defines that portion of the user space to be displayed and the *viewport* defines the portion of the hardware device that is used to display the user window. For example in Figure 6.41, (ULX,ULY) and (UHX,UHY) are the minimum and maximum coordinates respectively of the user window, and (HLX,HLY) and (HHX,HHY) are the minimum and maximum coordinates respectively of the hardware viewport.

Table 6.4 The Sequence of Isoline Intersections

Triangle	Next Triangle	Exiting Side	Right-Hand Control Point
T1	T4	S3	C2
T4	T5	S22	C4
T5	T9	S11	C4
T9	T8	S10	C7
T8	T10	S9	C7
T10	T14	S13	C7
T14	T11	S14	C7
T11	T12	S16	C4
T12	T13	S18	C5
T13	T16	S17	C5
T16	T3	S23	C2
T3	T1	S2	C2

In the final display, the position of the coordinate (ULX,ULY) is matched with the location of (HLX,HLY) and the position of (UHX,UHY) is matched with the hardware location of (HHX,HHY). This transformation of coordinates is performed by first translating the origin of user space to the location (ULX,ULY), then scaling the resulting coordinates into the metric of the hardware space, and finally translating these values to a new origin centered on (HLX,HLY).

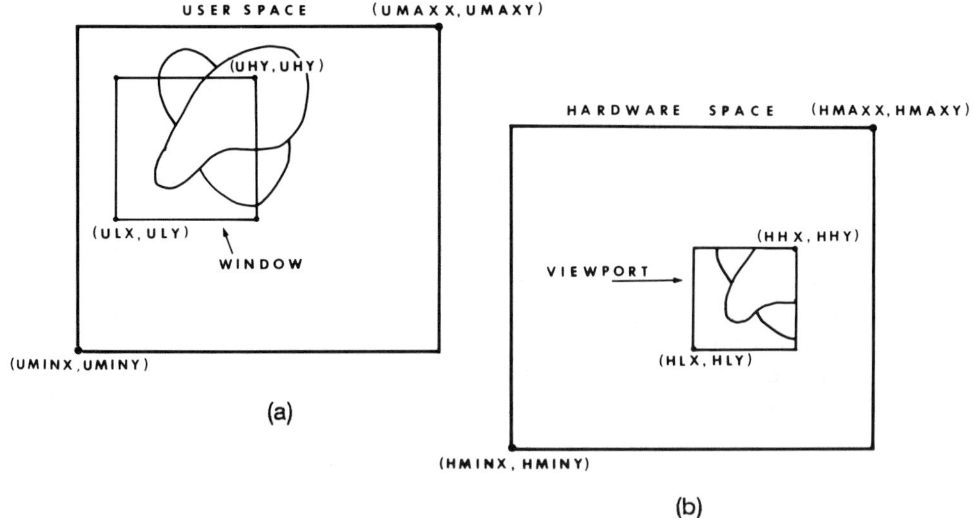

Figure 6.41 Windows and Viewports.

The scaling factors S_x and S_y for this transformation are found by the following equations:

$$S_x = (HHX - HLX) / (UHX - ULX) \quad ;$$

$$\text{and} \quad S_y = (HHY - HLY) / (UHY - ULY) \quad . \tag{6.18}$$

If no distortion is to be present in the final display, the *aspect ratio* (the ratio of height to width) of the window must equal the aspect ratio of the viewport, in which case the respective scale factors must be equal. The equations for the window transformation of each user space coordinate **(X,Y)** into each hardware coordinate **(X′,Y′)** are:

$$X' = HLX + S_x \cdot (X - ULX) \quad ;$$

$$\text{and} \quad Y' = HLY + S_y \cdot (Y - ULY) \quad . \tag{6.19}$$

Because only the portion of the map that lies inside the user window is to be displayed, the image in the window complement must next be *clipped* away. In raster mode, the operation of clipping is simple: only the rasters' locations within the hardware window are displayed. In vector mode, the clipping operator is more complex. Each line segment in user space falls within one of three cases with respect to the user window: 1) both endpoints lie inside the window, 2) one endpoint lies inside and one endpoint lies outside the window, or 3) both endpoints lie outside the user window.

If both endpoints lie inside the window (line segment A in Figure 6.42), the entire line segment is displayed. If only one endpoint lies inside the window (line segment B in Figure 6.42), then only a portion of that line segment is drawn. Finally, if both endpoints lie outside the window, then all of the line segment may lie outside the window (line segment C in Figure 6.42) or only a portion of it may lie outside the window (line segment D in Figure 6.42).

When clipping, it is necessary to restrict the sequence of device "moves" and "draws" for displaying the image inside the user window to be within the hardware viewport. If a device move is permitted outside the viewport, there is a chance that the move may be outside the physical bounds of the device itself. This is best achieved by establishing the difference between the current hardware position **(CHX,CHY)** and the current user space position **(CUX,CUY)**. Although it is necessary to evaluate positions in user space outside the domain of the user window, the current hardware position should never leave the domain of the hardware viewport.

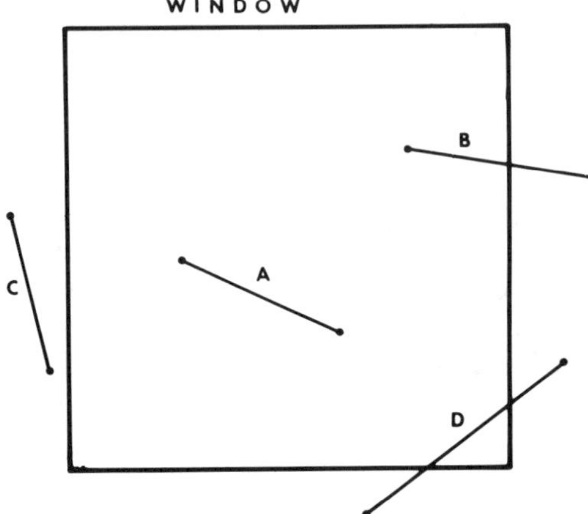

Figure 6.42 Alternative Clipping Situations.

Finally, because every object that lies outside the window is also outside the viewport, line segments can either be clipped first against the user window before the endpoints are transformed into their locations in hardware space or the line segments can be transformed first into their respective hardware space coordinates and then clipped against the viewport. For greater computational efficiency the former is preferred because fewer transformation operations are necessary. Given that a string of line segments, for which a bounding rectangle has been found, are processed in a batch, the entire string can be clipped away if the bounding rectangle of the string does not intersect with the rectangle of the window (see Figure 6.43). If the rectangle does intersect with the window, then each line segment must be examined in sequence.

Most line segment clipping algorithms are based on the Cohen-Sutherland bit-plane procedure [Newmann and Sproull, 1979]. In this method, the window is used to partition the plane into nine regions (see Figure 6.44a). Both the x and the y values of a point that lies inside any of the four corner regions are outside the range of the window. Either the x or the y value of a point that lies inside any of the four edge regions is outside the window. The remaining region corresponds to the window. As discussed above, if both endpoints of a line segment lie inside the window the entire line segment is drawn, while if both endpoints violate the same boundary of the window, the entire segment is clipped away. The line segment requires further processing only if one endpoint lies inside and the other one lies outside or if both endpoints lie outside but violate different boundaries.

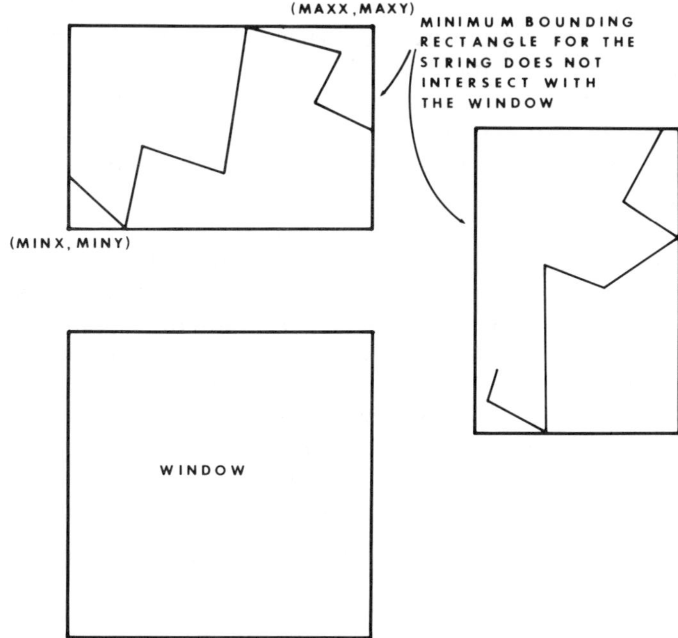

Figure 6.43 Clipping Entire Strings Outside the User Window.

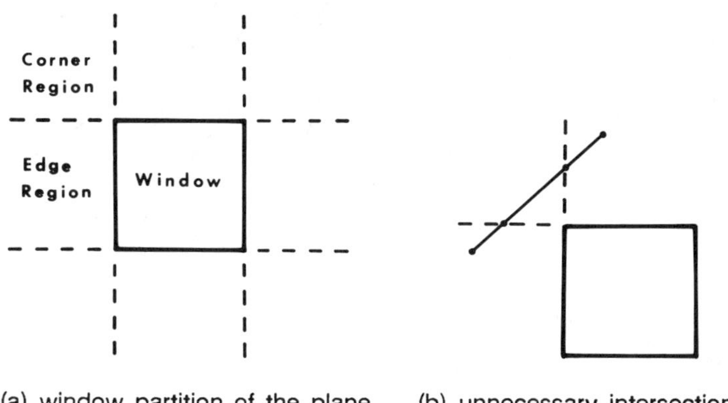

(a) window partition of the plane (b) unnecessary intersections

Figure 6.44 Window Checks.

In these last two instances, the line segment is subdivided by finding its intersection with one of the violated window boundaries. Nicholl *et al.* [1987] report that the major weakness of most clipping algorithms is that they calculate and evaluate intersection points that are not part of the final display. In Figure 6.44b, two intersections are calculated but neither is used for display because the entire line was found to be outside the window. Their approach identifies the correct boundary before an intersection operation is performed. For example, if one endpoint lies inside the window and the other outside, two situations can occur. First the second endpoint can lie in an edge region; in this case, the intersection occurs on the boundary shared between the window and the edge section.

In Figure 6.45a, point **A** lies in the edge region above the window and line segment **PA** intersects the top boundary of the window. Alternatively, the second endpoint can lie in a corner region; in this case, a halfplane check is performed to determine the correct boundary. For example, both points **B** and **C** lie in the corner region above and to the left of the window. The straight line connecting **P** to **C2** (the window corner at the upper left extremity) is calculated. If the other endpoint lies in the clockwise halfplane of this line (point **C**), the intersection is made with the left region; if the point lies in the counter-clockwise halfplane of this line (point **B**), the intersection is made with the upper region.

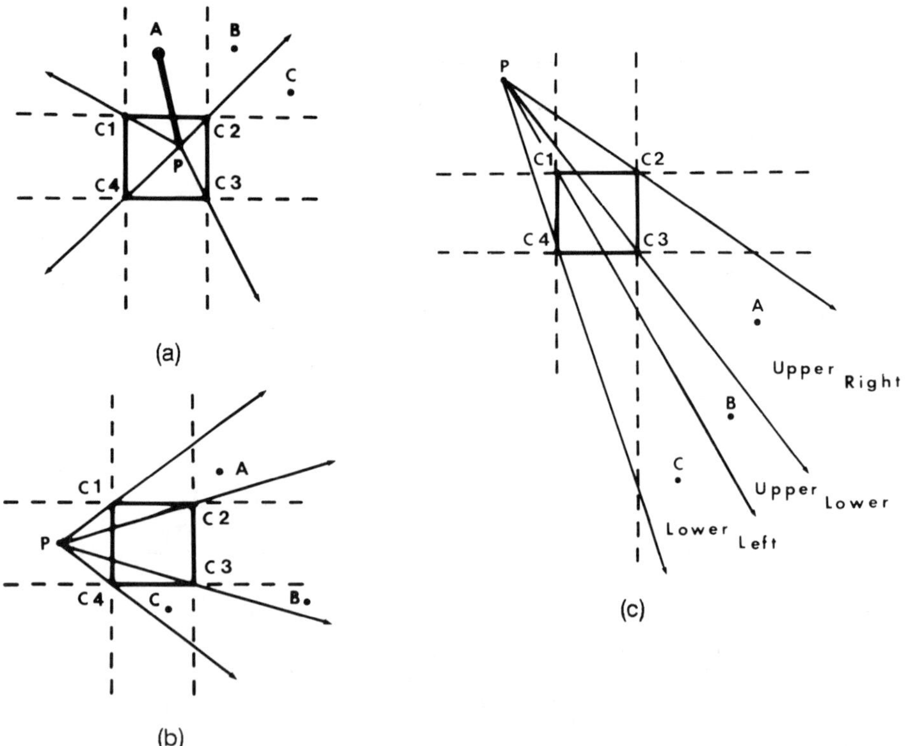

Figure 6.45 Different Line Segment Possibilities.

Next, if both endpoints lie outside the window, two situations can occur. First, one endpoint may lie in an edge region; the other endpoint must then lie in one of five other edge or corner regions not sharing the same violated boundary. The potential boundaries intersected by the line segment are again determined by a series of halfplane checks. In Figure 6.45b, point **P** lies in the edge region to the left of the window; any line segment whose other endpoint is in the counter-clockwise halfplane of the line connecting **P** to **C1** or the clockwise halfplane of the line connecting **P** to **C4** will be clipped away. If the other endpoint lies in the clockwise halfplane of **PC1** but the counter-clockwise halfplane of **PC2** (point **A**), then the line segment will intersect the left and upper boundaries. If the other endpoint lies in the clockwise halfplane of **PC2** but the counter-clockwise halfplane of **PC3** (point **B**), then the line segment will intersect the left and right boundaries. Lastly, if the other endpoint lies in the clockwise halfplane of **PC3** but the counter-clockwise halfplane of **PC4** (point **C**), then the line segment will intersect the left and lower boundaries.

Finally, both endpoints may lie in opposite corner regions (Figure 6.45c). Again halfplane checks are used to determine the boundary intersections. In Figure 6.45c, if one endpoint was located at point **P**, the line segment connecting to an endpoint lying between **PC2** and **PC3** (point A) will intersect with the upper and left window borders. A line segment connecting to an endpoint lying between **PC3** and **PC1** (point **B**) will intersect with the upper and lower window borders and one connecting to an endpoint lying between **PC1** and **PC4** will intersect with the right and lower borders.

These concepts are illustrated in the following example. In Figure 6.46, the string consisting of line segments **(L1, L2, L3, L4, L5)** passes in and out of the user space window. Because its bounding rectangle does not fall completely outside the window, the individual line segments are processed separately. The first endpoint of **L1** lies inside the left edge region; the intersection between **L1** and the lower **X** border is calculated because the other endpoint is inside the window. Because (x_a,y_a) is inside the window, the hardware cursor is moved to the corresponding position in hardware space and the current hardware position is set equal to this location. Drawing now continues until segment **L3** is processed.

Because (x_4,y_4) is inside the upper edge region, the intersection with **L3** and the upper **Y** border is calculated and a draw is made to the corresponding position of (x_b,y_b) in hardware space. No new action is taken in hardware space until segment **L5** is processed. Line segment **L4** is clipped away because (x_5,y_5) lies in the counter-clockwise halfplane of the line connecting (x_4,y_4) to the upper right-hand corner of the window. Because **L5** lies between the lines connecting (x_5,y_5) and the lower right-hand and the lower left-hand corners of the window respectively, the intersection between **L5** and the right **X** and the lower **Y** borders is calculated and the hardware cursor is now moved to the intersection (x_c,y_c) and a draw is made to the next intersection position (x_d,y_d).

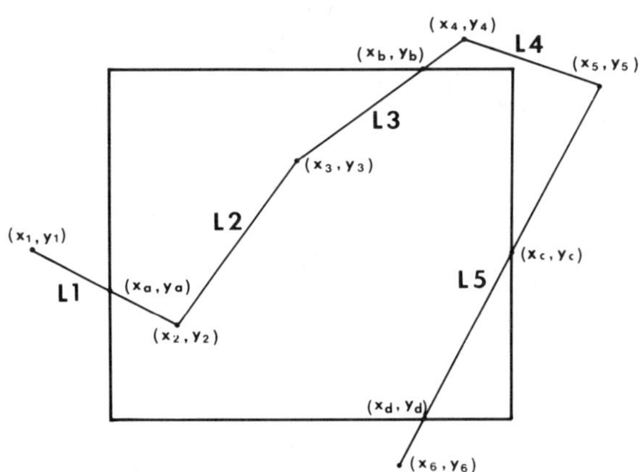

Figure 6.46 An Example of Clipping.

6.6 SUMMARY

This chapter has presented various methods for the cartographic display of digital cartographic objects in two-dimensional space. These cartographic models are representations of geographic surfaces that may be either concrete such as topography or statistical in nature such as income. However, the displays in this chapter have treated the third dimension of the surface as a thematic overlay rather than a portion of the surface. In the next chapter, procedures for directly representing cartographic objects as three-dimensional surfaces are presented.

6.7 REFERENCES

Bertin, J. [1983]. **Semiology of Graphics** (Translated by W.J. Berg), Madison, Wisconsin: University of Wisconsin Press.

Brassel, K. [1974]. "A Model for Automated Hill Shading," **The American Cartographer**, 1, 15-27.

Brassel, K. and R. Fegeas. [1979]. "An Algorithm for Shading of Regions on Vector Display Devices," **Proceedings**, SIGGRAPH, 13, 126-33.

Brassel, K. and J. Utano. [1979]. "Design Strategies for Continuous-Tone Area Mapping," **The American Cartographer**, 6, 39-50.

Burrough, P. [1986]. **Principles of Geographical Information Systems for Land Resources Assessment**, Oxford: Oxford Univeristy Press.

Cleveland M. and R. McGill [1984]. "Graphical Perception: Theory Experimentation, and Application to the Development of Graphical Methods," **Journal of the American Statistical Association**, 79, 531-54.

Cromley, R. [1983]. "A Procedure for Shading Class Interval Regions," **Proceedings**, AUTO-CARTO VI, 2, 435-42.

Cromley, R. [1984]. "The Peak-Pit-Pass Polygon Line Shading Procedure," **The American Cartographer**, 11, 70-79.

Cromley, R. [1986]. "The Commonality of Computer-Assisted Procedures for Constructing Choropleth and Isarithmic Maps," **The Cartographic Journal**, 23, 35-41.

Davis, J. [1973]. **Statistics and Data Analysis in Geology**, New York: John Wiley.

Dent, B. [1985]. **Principles of Thematic Map Design**, Reading, Massachusetts: Addison-Wesley Publishing Co.

Dutton, G. [1981]. "Fractal Enhancement of Cartographic Detail," **The American Cartographer**, 8, 23-40.

Elfick, M. [1979]. "Contouring by Use of a Triangular Mesh," **The Cartographic Journal**, 16, 24-29.

Foley, J. and A. Van Dam. [1984]. **Fundamentals of Interactive Computer Graphics**, Reading, Massachusetts: Addison-Wesley.

Gold, C. and S. Cormack. [1987]. "Spatially Ordered Networks and Topographic Reconstructions," **International Journal of Geographical Information Systems**, 1, 137-48.

Harrington, S. [1987]. **Computer Graphics: A Programming Approach**, 2nd ed., New York: McGraw Hill.

Jenks, G. [1963]. "Generalization in Statistical Mapping," **Annals of the Association of American Geographers**, 53, 15-26.

Kennedy, S. and W. Tobler. [1983]. "Geographic Interpolation," **Geographical Analysis**, 15, 151-56.

Knopfli, R. [1982]. "Generalization – A Means to Transmit Reliable Messages Through Unreliable Channels," **International Yearbook of Cartography**, 12, 83-91.

Lam, N. [1983]. "Spatial Interpolation Methods: A Review," **The American Cartographer**, 10, 129-49.

Lee, D. [1981]. "Shading of Regions on Vector Display Devices," **Computer Graphics**, 15, 37-44.

McCullagh, M. and C. Ross. [1980]. "Delaunay Triangulation of Random Data Set for Isarithmic Mapping," **The Cartographic Journal**, 17, 93-99.

Monmonier, M. [1975]. "Internally-stored Scan-lines for Line-printer Mapping," **The American Cartographer**, 2, 145-53.

Monmonier, M. [1982]. **Computer-Assisted Cartography: Principles and Prospects**, Englewood Cliffs, N.J.: Prentice-Hall.

Muehrcke, P. [1972]. **Thematic Cartography**, Commission on College Geography Resource Paper No. 19, Washington, D.C.: Association of American Geographers.

Newmann, W. and R. Sproull. [1979]. **Principles of Interactive Computer Graphics**, 2nd ed., New York: McGraw-Hill.

Nicholl, T., Lee, D., and R. Nicholl. [1987]. "An Efficient New Algorithm for 2-D Line Clipping: Its Development and Analysis," **Computer Graphics**, 21, 253-62.

Olea, R. [1974]. "Optimal Contour Mapping using Universal Kriging," **Journal of Geophysical Research**, 79, 695-702.

Pavlidis, T. [1982]. **Algorithms for Graphics and Image Processing**, Rockville, Maryland: Computer Science Press.

Peucker, T., R. Fowler, J. Little, and D. Mark. [1978]. "The Triangulated Irregular Network," **Proceedings**, Digital Terrain Models Symposium, American Society of Photogrammetry, 516-40.

Rase, W.D. [1987]. "The Evolution of a Graduated Symbol Software Package in a Changing Graphics Environment," **International Journal of Geographical Information Systems**, 1, 51-65.

Ripley, B. [1981]. **Spatial Statistics**, New York: John Wiley.

Scripter, M. [1969]. "Choropleth Maps on Small Digital Computers," **Proceedings**, Association of American Geographers, 1, 133-36.

Shepard, D. [1968]. "A Two-Dimensional Interpolation Function for Irregularly-Spaced Data," **Proceedings**, Association for Computing Machinery, Twenty-third National Conference, 517-24.

Sinton, D. [1978]. "The Inherent Structure of Information as a Constraint to Analysis: Mapped Thematic Data as a Case Study," **Harvard Papers on Geographic Information Systems**, G. Dutton (ed.), Vol. 7.

Smith, R. [1980]. "Improved Areal Symbols for Computer Line-Printed Maps," **The American Cartographer**, 7, 51-57.

Tobler, W. [1973]. "Choropleth Maps Without Class Intervals?" **Geographical Analysis**, 5, 262-65.

Watson, D. [1982]. "ACORD: Automatic Contouring of Raw Data," **Computers and Geosciences**, 8, 97-101.

Yoeli, P. [1983]. "Cartographic Contouring with Computer and Plotter," **The American Cartographer**, 11, 139-55.

Chapter 7
Three-Dimensional Cartographics

Until now thematic attributes have been displayed as a symbolic overlay for a two-dimensional geographic base map. An alternative method is to display the analog representation of the attribute as a surface rather than a symbolic representation. The attribute is treated as the third dimension of a geographic surface where the height of the surface in the third dimension is some function of the magnitude of the values being mapped. Three-dimensional representations of surfaces are difficult to construct in manual production because it is hard to know the intricacies of local relief unless a concrete object can be viewed. As mentioned in Chapter Two, three-dimensional surfaces of attributes like temperature or income have no occurrence in our visual reality and are difficult to draw.

Three-dimensional cartographics are not without some disadvantages. The viewing perspective is a critical parameter as some parts of the surface may be hidden by other portions that lie in front. Care must be taken to ensure the maximum exposure of the surface while retaining recognition of the locations being displayed. The representation of cartographic features as three-dimensional surfaces is a three-step process. First, the object is transformed into the proper viewing perspective. Second, the three-dimensional image is projected onto a viewing plane and finally, lines or portions of the surface that are hidden or obstructed from sight are removed. The discussion begins with the basics of three-dimensional analytic geometry.

7.1 THREE-DIMENSIONAL ANALYTIC GEOMETRY

The coordinate system for three-dimensional cartographics is defined in terms of an **X**, **Y**, and **Z** axis. However there are two choices of coordinate system, a right-handed and left-handed system. In a right-handed coordinate system (Figure 7.1a) the movement of direction from the positive **Z** axis to the positive **X** axis is counter-clockwise, whereas the same movement is clockwise for a left-handed coordinate system (Figure 7.1b). The right-hand system is more frequently used and the mathematics of this section are presented using this system.

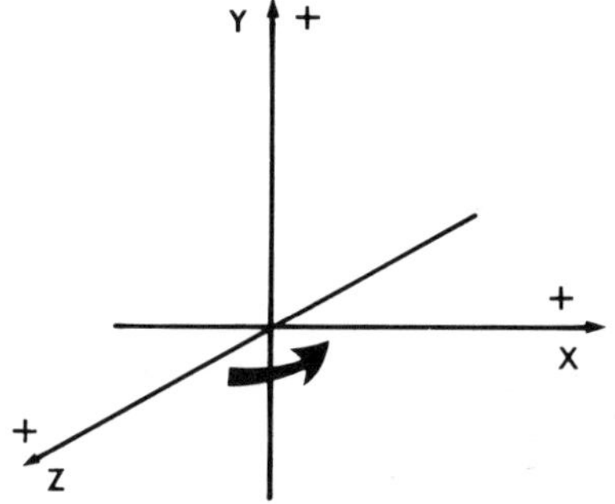

(a) a right-handed coordinate system

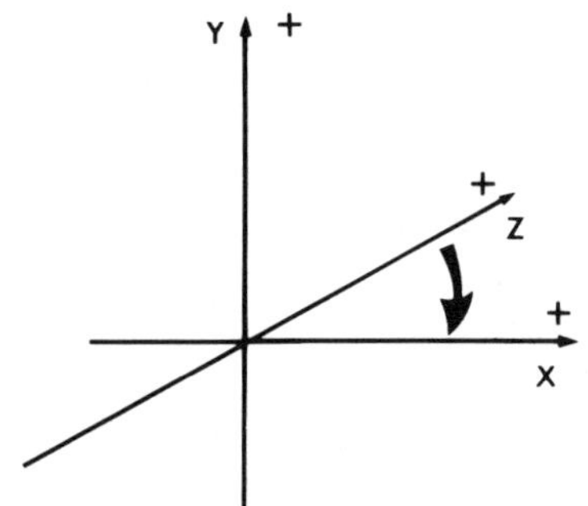

(b) a left-handed coordinate system

Figure 7.1 Three-Dimensional Coordinate Systems.

A point **p** is now represented by a **(x,y,z)** coordinate representing its projection on the respective axes. All vector and matrix operators are direct extensions of their two-dimensional counterpart. However the definition of a straight line is more complicated. Given two points

$\mathbf{p}(\mathbf{x_1},\mathbf{y_1},\mathbf{z_1})$ and $\mathbf{q}(\mathbf{x_2},\mathbf{y_2},\mathbf{z_2})$, it is easiest to express a line in a parametric form where any point on the line $(\mathbf{x},\mathbf{y},\mathbf{z})$ can be written in terms of a parameter $\mathbf{t}$ [Harrington, 1987]:

$$\begin{aligned} x &= (x_2 - x_1)\, t + x_1 \ ; \\ y &= (y_2 - y_1)\, t + y_1 \ ; \\ z &= (z_2 - z_1)\, t + z_1 \ . \end{aligned} \tag{7.1}$$

Three-dimensional surfaces can be represented as patches of polygons. Each polygon in three dimensions exists within a plane. The general equation of a plane is:

$$A\,x + B\,y + C\,z + D = 0\ . \tag{7.2}$$

Given three points $\mathbf{p}(\mathbf{x_1},\mathbf{y_1},\mathbf{z_1})$, $\mathbf{q}(\mathbf{x_2},\mathbf{y_2},\mathbf{z_2})$ and $\mathbf{r}(\mathbf{x_3},\mathbf{y_3},\mathbf{z_3})$, the parameters of the plane containing these points are found as:

$$\begin{aligned} A &= y_1\,(z_2 - z_3) + y_2\,(z_3 - z_1) + y_3\,(z_1 - z_2) \ ; \\ B &= x_1\,(z_3 - z_2) + x_2\,(z_1 - z_3) + x_3\,(z_2 - z_1) \ ; \\ C &= x_1\,(y_2 - y_3) + x_2\,(y_3 - y_1) + x_3\,(y_1 - y_2) \ ; \end{aligned} \tag{7.3}$$

$$D = x_1y_3z_2 + x_2y_1z_3 + x_3y_2z_1 - x_1y_2z_3 - x_2y_3z_1 - x_3y_1z_2 .$$

The value of **D** is the determinant of a matrix formed by the respective coordinates. The order in which the points are given is important for it establishes the orientation of the plane. A plane divides three-dimensional space into halfspaces in the same manner that a line divides a plane into halfplanes. If the points **p**, **q**, and **r** are given in a clockwise manner (Figure 7.2a), a point $\mathbf{s}(\mathbf{x},\mathbf{y},\mathbf{z})$ will lie in its clockwise halfspace if:

$$A\,x + B\,y + C\,z + D < 0\ . \tag{7.4}$$

Otherwise the point will lie in its counterclockwise halfspace. If the order of the points is counter-clockwise, these relationships are reversed (Figure 7.2b). This fact will be used later to determine which polygon patches on a surface face toward the line of sight. The parameters of a plane given by equation (7.3) are for **p**, **q**, and **r** in a clockwise order.

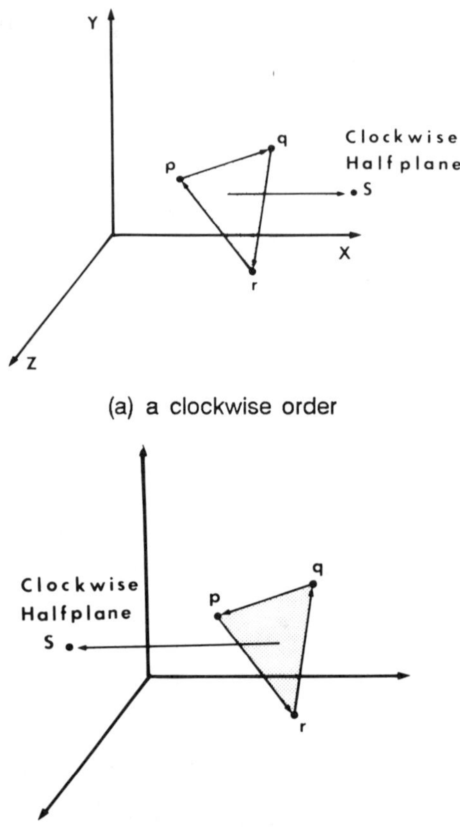

(a) a clockwise order

(b) a counter-clockwise order

Figure 7.2 The Different Directions for Defining a Plane.

Next, the *normal vector* to a plane, **N**, is a vector that is perpendicular to any line on the plane (Figure 7.3). If a plane is represented by equation (7.2), then the normal vector to the plane is:

$$\mathbf{N} = (A \quad B \quad C) \quad . \qquad (7.5)$$

The perpendicular distance, **d**, between any point **s(x,y,z)** and a plane is found as the absolute value of the inner product between the coordinates of the point and the parameters of the plane divided by the magnitude of the normal vector:

$$\mathbf{d} = |A\,x + B\,y + C\,z + D| \;/\; (A^2 + B^2 + C^2)^{1/2} \quad . \qquad (7.6)$$

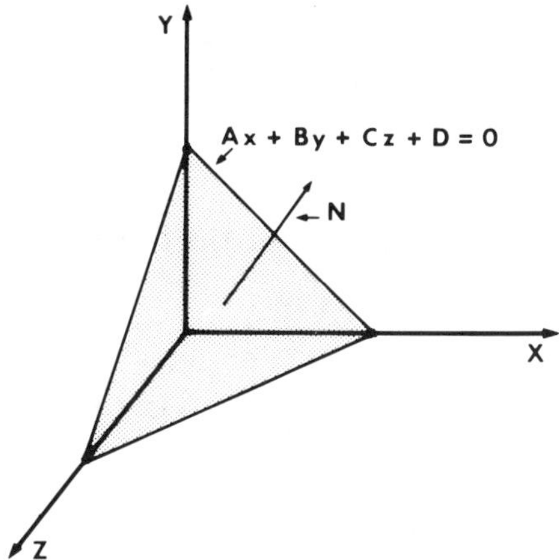

Figure 7.3 A Normal Vector to a Plane.

The homogeneous representation of a three-dimensional point **(x,y,z)** is **(hx,hy,hz,h)** where **h** is again any non-zero scalar. The homogeneous representation of coordinates is used to perform the three-dimensional point transformations of translation, rotation, and scaling for manipulating three-dimensional cartographic objects in space. The methods of translation and scaling are direct extensions of the two-dimensional case. Three dimensions requires a **4x4** transformation now rather than a **3x3**.

The translation transformation is written in matrix notation as:

$$(x' \; y' \; z' \; 1) = (x \quad y \quad z \quad 1) \begin{bmatrix} 1 & 0 & 0 & 0 \\ 0 & 1 & 0 & 0 \\ 0 & 0 & 1 & 0 \\ T_x & T_y & T_z & 1 \end{bmatrix} . \qquad (7.7)$$

The scaling transformation is written in matrix notation as:

$$(x' \; y' \; z' \; 1) = (x \quad y \quad z \quad 1) \begin{bmatrix} S_x & 0 & 0 & 0 \\ 0 & S_y & 0 & 0 \\ 0 & 0 & S_z & 0 \\ 0 & 0 & 0 & 1 \end{bmatrix} . \qquad (7.8)$$

The rotation transformation used in Chapter Two to rotate the original coordinate system about the origin by some angle α measured in a counter-clockwise direction from the X-axis is generalized now to be a counter-clockwise rotation about the **Z** axis (Figure 7.4a). This rotation transformation is defined as:

$$(x' \; y' \; z' \; 1) = (x \quad y \quad z \quad 1) \begin{bmatrix} \cos\alpha & \sin\alpha & 0 & 0 \\ -\sin\alpha & \cos\alpha & 0 & 0 \\ 0 & 0 & 1 & 0 \\ 0 & 0 & 0 & 1 \end{bmatrix} . \qquad (7.9)$$

The same rotation transformation about the **X** axis (Figure 7.4b) is:

$$(x' \; y' \; z' \; 1) = (x \quad y \quad z \quad 1) \begin{bmatrix} 1 & 0 & 0 & 0 \\ 0 & \cos\alpha & \sin\alpha & 0 \\ 0 & -\sin\alpha & \cos\alpha & 0 \\ 0 & 0 & 0 & 1 \end{bmatrix} . \qquad (7.10)$$

Finally, the rotation transformation about the **Y** axis (Figure 7.4c) is:

$$(x' \; y' \; z' \; 1) = (x \quad y \quad z \quad 1) \begin{bmatrix} \cos\alpha & 0 & -\sin\alpha & 0 \\ 0 & 1 & 0 & 0 \\ \sin\alpha & 0 & \cos\alpha & 0 \\ 0 & 0 & 0 & 1 \end{bmatrix} . \qquad (7.11)$$

These rotations define movement about the principal axes of the coordinate system. To simulate movement of an object about an arbitrary axis, a sequence of translation and principal axis rotations can be concatenated. This will give an object the desired position for viewing.

7.2 VIEWING PROJECTIONS

Once the position of the object has been determined, its image is projected onto a *view plane*. The axes of the view plane are **X′** and **Y′**. The necessary parameters to be specified besides the view plane are a view reference point, a normal vector to the view plane, and the view plane distance and the light of sight [Salmon and Slater, 1987] (see Figure 7.5). The reference point is the point on the surface being projected, and the view plane distance is the distance between the object and the view plane.

The two major types of projections are *parallel* and *perspective*. In these projections objects that are farther away from the viewing plane will appear higher on the plane. In a parallel projection the rays of sight radiating from the different points of the surface are parallel to one another. In an orthographic parallel projection, the rays are also parallel to the normal vector of the viewing plane (Figure 7.6). Parallel projections have the property that similar-sized objects will have the same size projection on the viewing plane regardless of their respective distances from the viewing plane. Given a direction of sight denoted by the vector (x_o,y_o,z_o) and the reference point (x_1,y_1,z_1), the coordinates of the reference point on the viewing plane (x',y') are found from the parametric equations of a straight line passing through (x_1,y_1,z_1) in the direction of the vector (x_o,y_o,z_o) [Harrington, 1987].

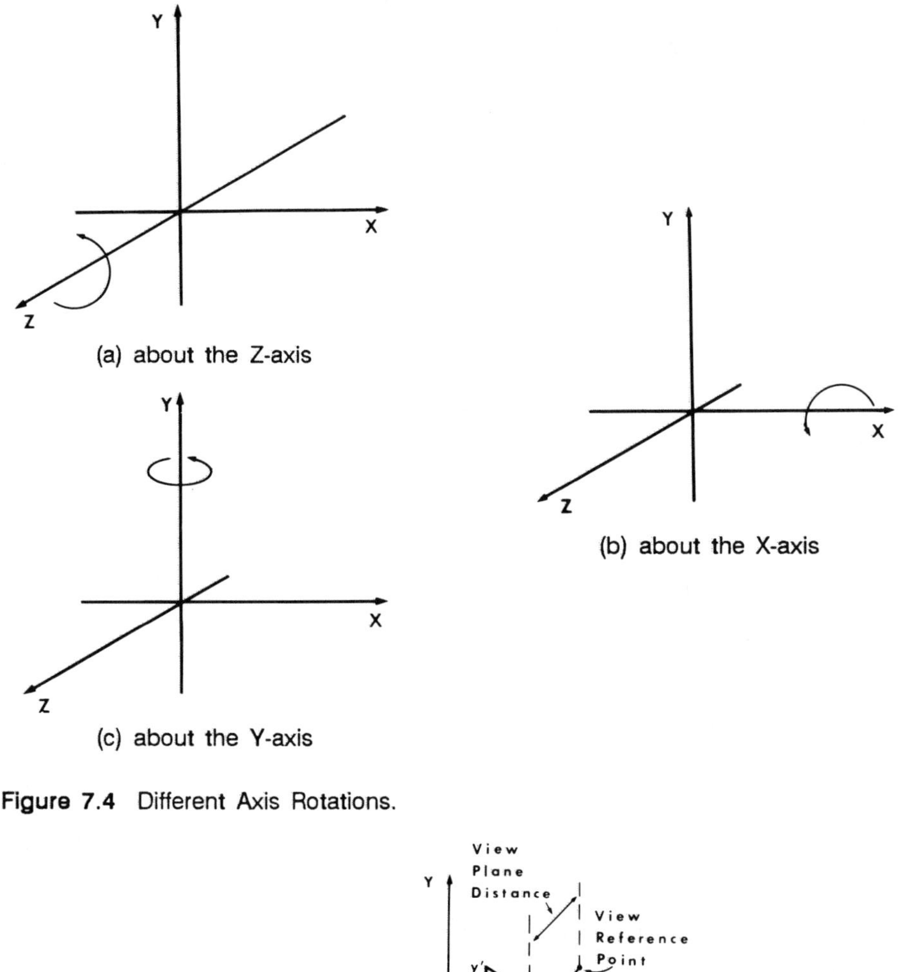

(a) about the Z-axis

(b) about the X-axis

(c) about the Y-axis

Figure 7.4 Different Axis Rotations.

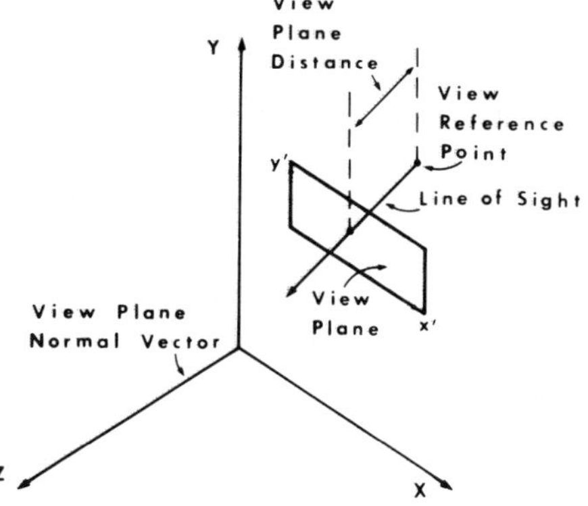

Figure 7.5 The Viewing Parameters.

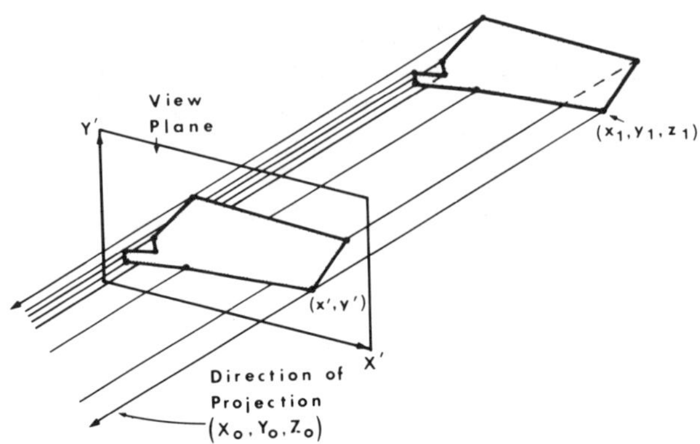

Figure 7.6 A Parallel Projection.

This line is expressed as:

$$x = x_o u + x_1 ;$$
$$y = y_o u + y_1 ; \qquad (7.12)$$
$$z = z_o u + z_1 .$$

Given that **z** is **0** when the line intersects the viewing plane, the value of **u** is:

$$u = -(z_1 / z_o) . \qquad (7.13)$$

Substituting (7.13) into (7.12), the values of **(x′,y′)** are:

$$x' = x_1 - z_1 (x_o / z_o) ;$$
$$y' = y_1 - z_1 (y_o / z_o) . \qquad (7.14)$$

In matrix notation, this projection is:

$$(x' \; y' \; 0 \; 1) = (x_1 \; y_1 \; z_1 \; 1) \begin{bmatrix} 1 & 0 & 0 & 0 \\ 0 & 1 & 0 & 0 \\ -x_o/z_o & -y_o/z_o & 0 & 0 \\ 0 & 0 & 0 & 1 \end{bmatrix} . \qquad (7.15)$$

In a perspective projection, the rays of sight focus at a point called the center of projection (see Figure 7.7). Objects that are farther away from the viewing plane in this projection appear smaller than a similar-sized object that lies closer to the plane.

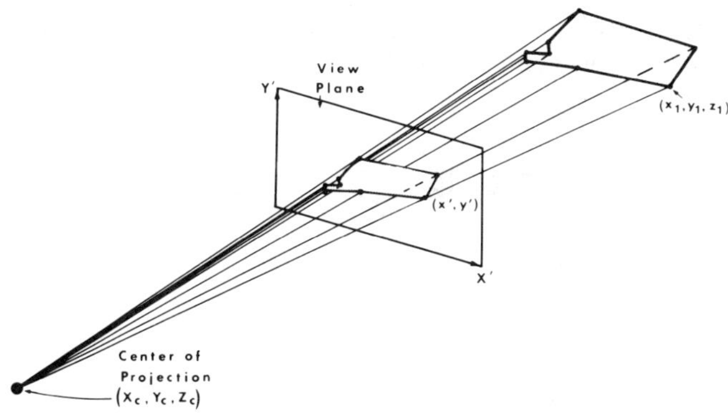

Figure 7.7 A Perspective Projection.

Given the center of projection is located at the point (x_c, y_c, z_c), the line connecting the reference point and the center point is:

$$
\begin{aligned}
x &= (x_1 - x_c)\, t + x_c \;; \\
y &= (y_1 - y_c)\, t + y_c \;; \\
z &= (z_1 - z_c)\, t + z_c \;.
\end{aligned}
\tag{7.16}
$$

Again this line will intersect with the viewing plane when **z** equals **0** and

$$
t = -\, z_c \,/\, (z_1 - z_c) \;. \tag{7.17}
$$

Substituting (7.17) into (7.16), the corresponding point on the projection plane is (see Figure 7.8):

$$
\begin{aligned}
x' &= x_c - z_c \,[\,(x_1 - x_c) \,/\, (z_1 - z_c)\,] \;; \\
y' &= y_c - z_c \,[\,(y_1 - y_c) \,/\, (z_1 - z_c)\,] \;.
\end{aligned}
\tag{7.18}
$$

After algebraic simplification, the perspective projection is expressed in matrix notation as:

$$
(hx' \;\; hy' \;\; 0 \;\; h) = (x_1 \;\; y_1 \;\; z_1 \;\; 1)
\begin{bmatrix}
-z_c & 0 & 0 & 0 \\
0 & -z_c & 0 & 0 \\
x_c & y_c & 0 & 1 \\
0 & 0 & 0 & -z_c
\end{bmatrix} . \tag{7.19}
$$

Once the surface has been projected into a two-dimensional space, it can be viewed on a virtual display terminal or drawn on a plotter. However, the resulting image will be confusing unless the portions of the surface hidden from view are removed.

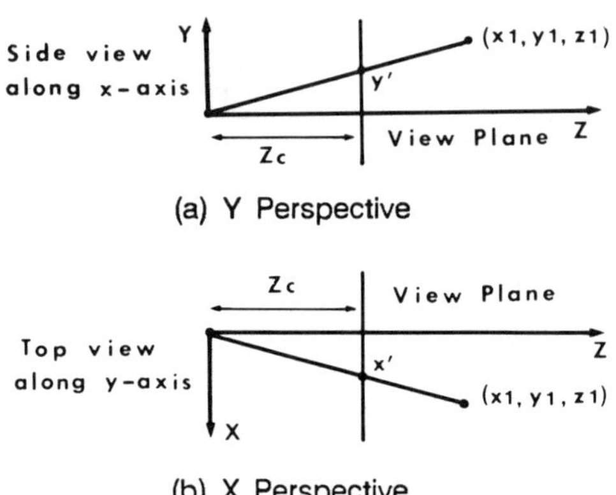

Figure 7.8 The X and Y Perspectives.

7.3 HIDDEN LINE AND SURFACE PROBLEMS

The final form of a discrete surface is usually represented either as a prism diagram [see Jenks, 1966; Tobler, 1974; Franklin, 1979] consisting of polygon patches (Figure 7.9) or by a grid diagram consisting of a series of parallel lines (Figure 7.10). The parallel lines are either a single series of profile lines [see Tobler, 1973; Schmidt and Zafft 1975] (Figure 7.11a) or an orthogonal mesh [see Sampson, 1978] (Figure 7.11b). A prism representation is associated with a polygonal or vector encoding the the geographic base file, while a grid diagram corresponds to a raster encoding of the base file. Frequently, a vector encoded base file is converted into a raster format for display as a grid diagram (see Chapter Six for a discussion of this conversion.)

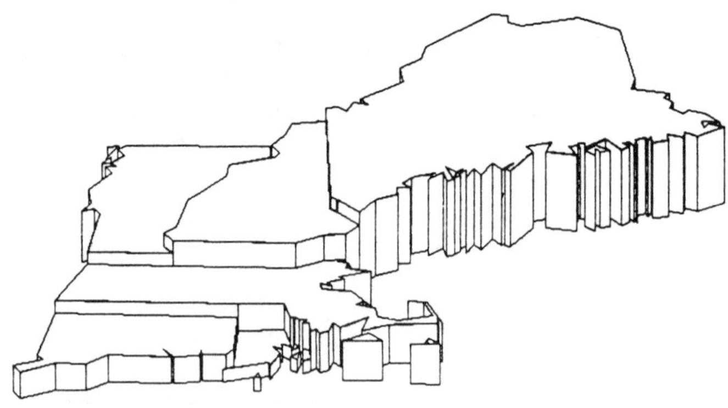

Figure 7.9 A Prism Representation.

The final form of a continuous surface is also represented by a grid diagram if the data values were encoded in a grid or interpolated to a grid (Figure 7.11). The choice of using profile lines or an orthogonal mesh depends on the density of the grid. A dense grid is better represented by profile lines while a sparse grid is better suited to an orthogonal mesh representation [Monmonier, 1982]. Alternatively, if the surface is encoded as an irregular triangulation [see Peucker *et al.*, 1978] (or TIN), it is represented as a series of profile lines or triangular patches (Figure 7.12).

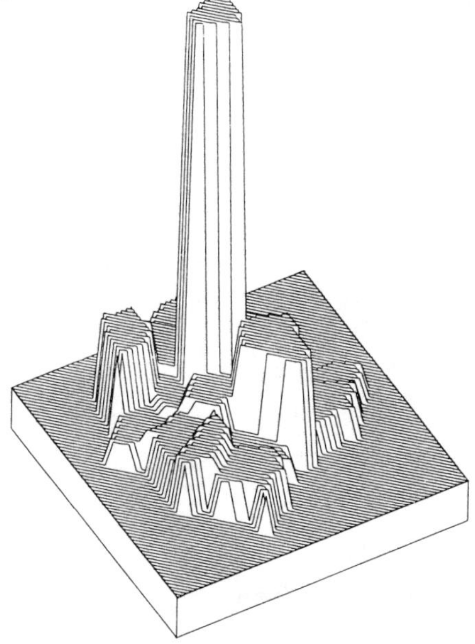

Figure 7.10 A Grid Representation of a Discrete Surface.

The form of the display influences the method of hidden line or surface removal (for a taxonomy and analysis of different hidden surface algorithms, see Sutherland *et al.* [1974]). For prisms and irregular triangulations, a series of polygons (or triangles) is processed, while in a grid approach a series of lines is processed. When constructing the diagram as a series of intersecting polygon patches, the first step is to determine whether the front-face or the back-face of the polygon faces the view plane. If back-face of the polygon faces the view plane, then that polygon is hidden from view. This view direction can be established by calculating first the normal vector associated with each polygon, assuming that the order of points in the outline of each polygon is given in a clockwise direction (Figure 7.13). If the normal vector of the polygon points away from the view plane, then its face is hidden from sight and the polygon does not need to be drawn. This test is performed by calculating the cosine of the angle, θ, between the normal vector of the polygon **(A,B,C)** and the line of sight vector (x_o,y_o,z_o) :

$$\cos\ \theta = (Ax_o+By_o+Cz_o)/[(A^2+B^2+C^2)^{1/2}(x_o^2+y_o^2+z_o^2)^{1/2}]. \quad (7.20)$$

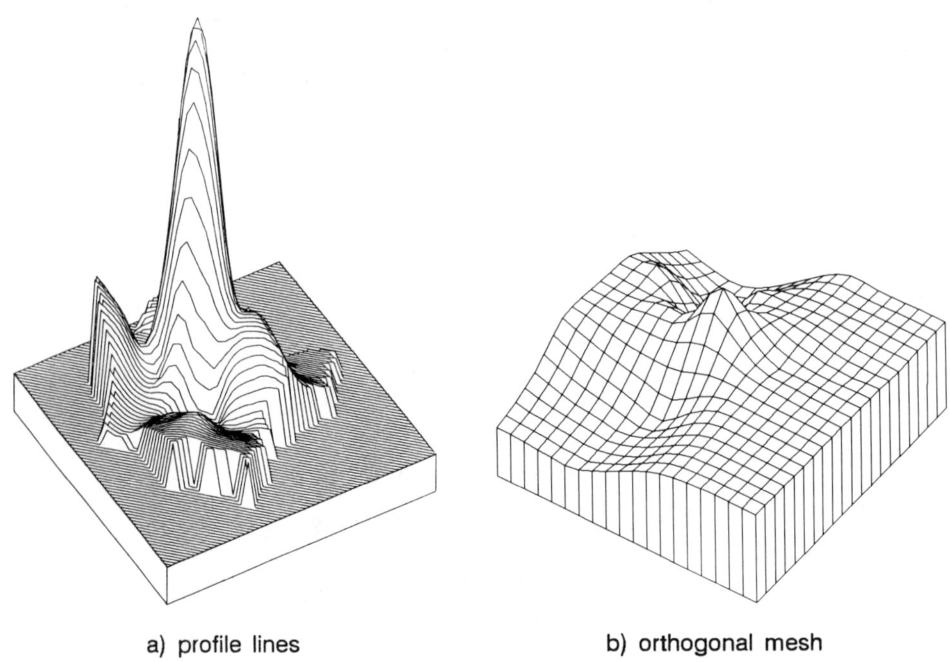

a) profile lines b) orthogonal mesh

Figure 7.11 Different Grid Representations.

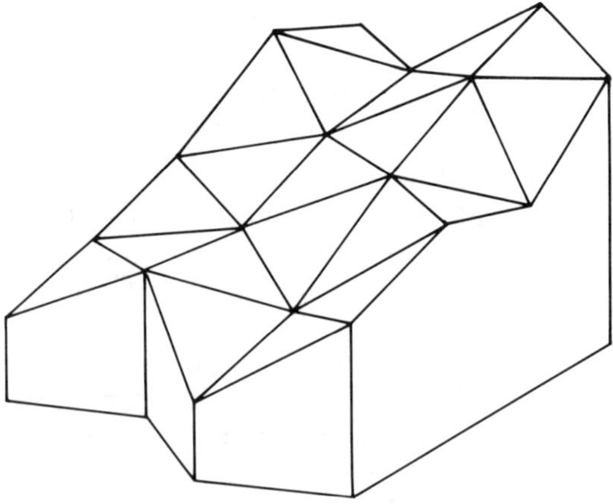

Figure 7.12 A TIN Surface as Triangular Patches.
(after Peuquet, 1984)

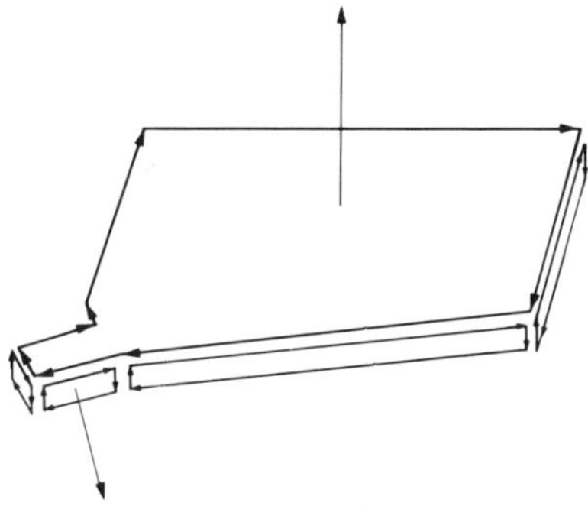

Figure 7.13 Normal Vectors to Polygon Patches.

If the cosine of the angle is less than zero, then the angle between the two vectors is greater than **90°** and the vectors are pointing away from each other (Figure 7.14) and the back-face is toward the line of sight.

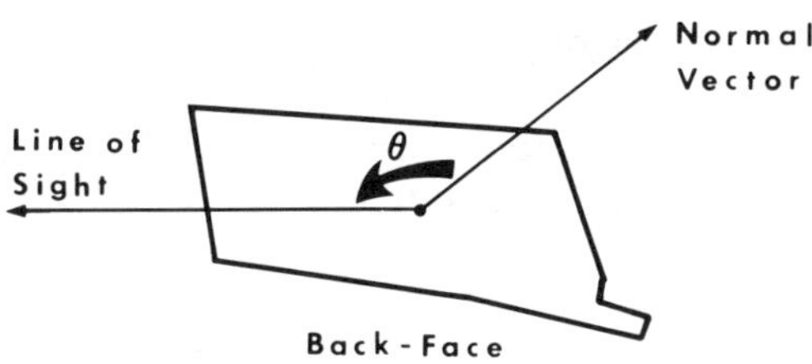

Figure 7.14 The Angle Between Two Vectors.

Next, because objects that are farther away from the viewing plane are higher on it, the general strategy of many hidden surface and line procedures is to process front-facing objects in either a front-to-back or back-to-front sequence. For example, on a virtual raster color display terminal, a polygon drawn on top of a previously drawn polygon will cover the portion of the first polygon that intersects with it (Figure 7.15). In this case, if the back-to-front sequence of polygon patches that comprise a surface can be determined, then their successive drawing on the screen will produce a surface without hidden lines. The order of front-facing polygons is determined by finding the point of each polygon that has the shortest orthogonal distance to the view plane.

For vector display devices, the actual intersections between two overlapping polygons on the view plane must be calculated. The processing of polygon intersections is improved if the minimum bounding rectangle for each polygon is computed first and sorted by the maximum Y-coordinate of each bounding rectangle. The rectangles are compared first for possible intersection (see Chapter Four for more details of this technique).

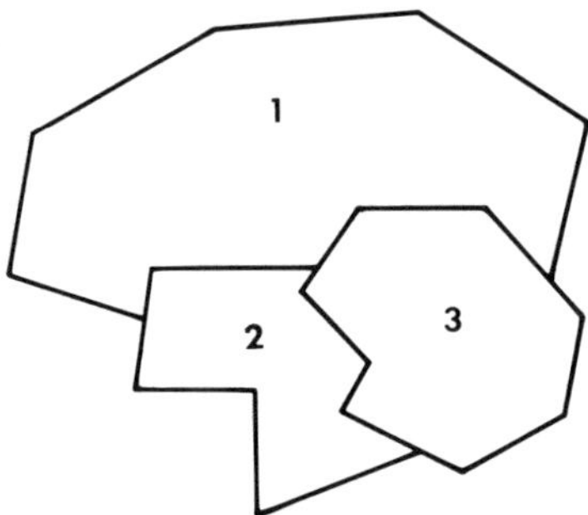

Figure 7.15 The Intersection of Polygons Back-to-Front.

The front-to-back ordering for grid diagrams is more straightforward because the parallel lines are drawn along the rows, columns or diagonals of the grid. The index number of each line gives its relative location in the front-to-back sequence. For profiles, the general strategy now is to draw lines from front to back. The first profile line will always be completely viewable because no object lies in front. Each successive profile line is processed to determine which portions of it lie above or below the current highest profile line [Monmonier, 1982] (see Figure 7.16). Each time a new line is processed the current highest profile is updated for later checks.

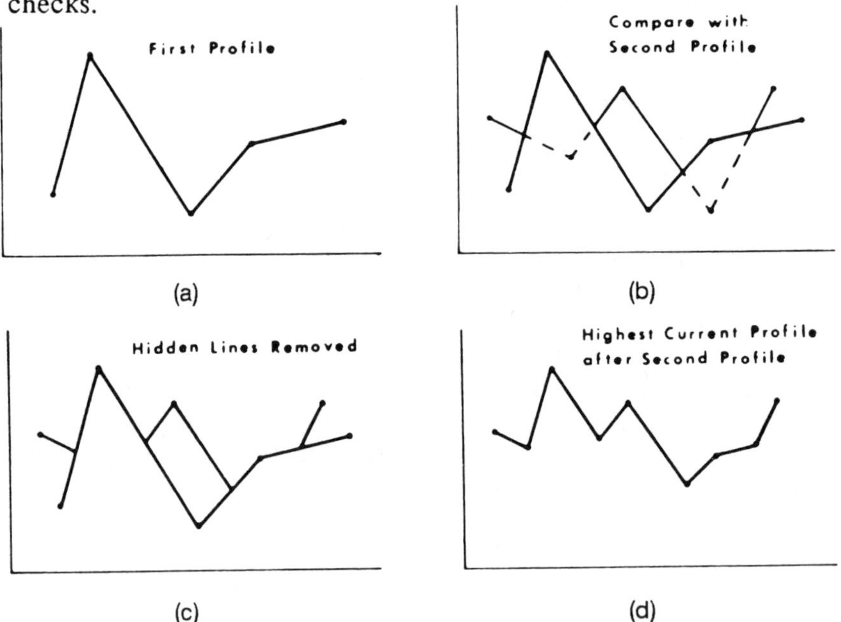

Figure 7.16 The Sequencing of Profile Lines.
(after Monmonier, 1982)

For orthogonal meshes, lines are drawn along both rows and columns and a simple overlap of the two will result in errors (Figure 7.17). One direction is chosen to be drawn first. Assume that the first row is drawn. Next the portion of each column profile that is above the current profile is drawn between the first and second rows (Figure 7.18). The current highest profile is updated and the second row is processed. Each time only the portion of a nth column's segments that lie between the nth and (n+1)st row are scanned [Penna and Patterson, 1986].

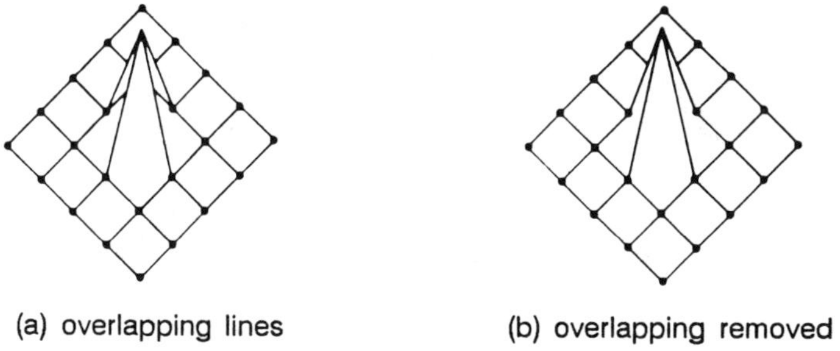

Figure 7.17 The Overlapping of Orthogonal Profile Lines.
(after Penna and Patterson, 1986)

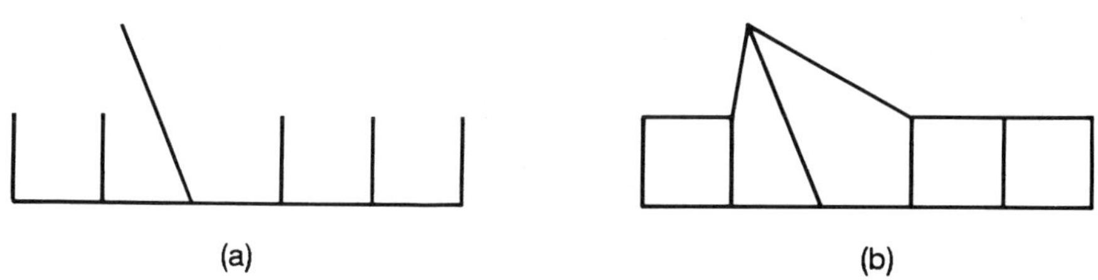

Figure 7.18 The Sequencing of Row and Column Profile Lines.

7.4 SUMMARY

Chapters Six and Seven have presented various methods for the cartographic display of digital cartographic objects. The resulting virtual or real maps can be interpreted and associated spatial distribution analyzed. However, maps can be used for more than just descriptive replications of spatial distributions. A more constructive use for cartographic information is in spatial analysis. In the next chapter, the principles of digital cartography and digital databases are examined as analytical tools for the efficient allocation of society's resources.

7.5 REFERENCES

Franklin, W.R. [1979]. "PRISM - A Prism Plotting Program," in **Mapping Software and Cartographic Data Bases**, Cambridge, Massachusetts: Harvard University.

Harrington, S. [1987]. **Computer Graphics**, New York: McGraw Hill, Inc.

Jenks, G. [1963]. "Generalization in Statistical Mapping," **Annals of the Association of American Geographers**, 53, 15-26.

Monmonier, M.S. [1982]. **Computer-Assisted Cartography: Principles and Prospects**, Englewood Cliffs, New Jersey: Prentice-Hall.

Penna, M. and R. Patterson. [1986]. **Projective Geometry and its Applications to Computer Graphics**, Englewood Cliffs, New Jersey: Prentice-Hall.

Peucker, T., R. Fowler, J. Little, and D. Mark. [1978]. "The Triangulated Irregular Network," **Proceedings**, Digital Terrain Models Symposium American Society of Photogrammetry, 516-40.

Peuquet, D. [1984]. "A Conceptual Framework and Comparison of Spatial Data Models," **Cartographica**, 21, No. 4, 66-113.

Salmon, R. and M. Slater. [1987]. **Computer Graphics: Systems and Concepts**, Reading, Massachusetts: Addison-Wesley.

Sampson, R. [1978]. **SURFACE II Graphics System**, Lawrence, Kansas: Kansas Geological Survey.

Schmidt, A. and W. Zafft. [1975]. "Programs of the Harvard University Laboratory for Computer Graphics and Spatial Analysis," in **Display and Analysis of Spatial Data**, J.C. Davis and M.J. McCullagh (eds.), New York: John Wiley & Sons, Inc.

Sutherland, I., R. Sproull, and R. Schumaker. [1974]. "A Characterization of Ten Hidden-Surface Algorithms," **Computing Surveys**, 6, 1-55.

Tobler, W. (ed.) [1973]. **Selected Computer Programs**, Ann Arbor, Michigan: Department of Geography, University of Michigan.

Tobler, W. [1974]. "A Computer Program to Draw Perspective Views of Geographical Data," **The American Cartographer**, 1, 124-90.

Chapter 8
Cartographic Analysis

Given that cartographic objects are referenced to the earth's surface, it is not surprising that cartographic displays are used daily in the evaluation of land use suitability and allocation. An important application of cartographic products is in land use analysis. The collection and synthesis of spatial data regarding the earth's surface are important for an understanding of natural and human environments. Planners, engineers, scientists, government offficals and the business community need spatial information regarding natural and socioeconomic ecosystems for making decisions that affect everyday life.

The use of maps in land use evaluation began as the overlaying of separate map sheets, each representing a different thematic coverage of the same geographic area [McHarg, 1969]. The maps were placed on a light table for better visual interpretation of the composite image. This manual overlaying had many limitations but the introduction of digital procedures for map display helped to alleviate some of the problems. This procedure in turn has led to the formulation of map analysis procedures based on a map algebra for manipulating cartographic objects [Tomlin, 1990]. Map analysis is also an important mode of investigation within a geographic information system. The discussion of these topics begins with the problem of the geometric overlay of different geographic base files.

8.1 CARTOGRAPHIC OVERLAY

A basic premise underlying the use of cartographic data in land use analysis is that different thematic coverages of the same geographic domain can be overlaid on top of one another. The overlay operator itself is a set operator involving the intersection of cartographic objects to form a new set of objects. For example in Figure 8.1, one set consists of two elements, "A" and "not A." The second cartographic set for the same domain consists of two elements, "B" and "not B." The intersection of these two sets formed by their overlay consists of four areal elements, "not A or B," "A and not B," "B and not A," and "A and B."

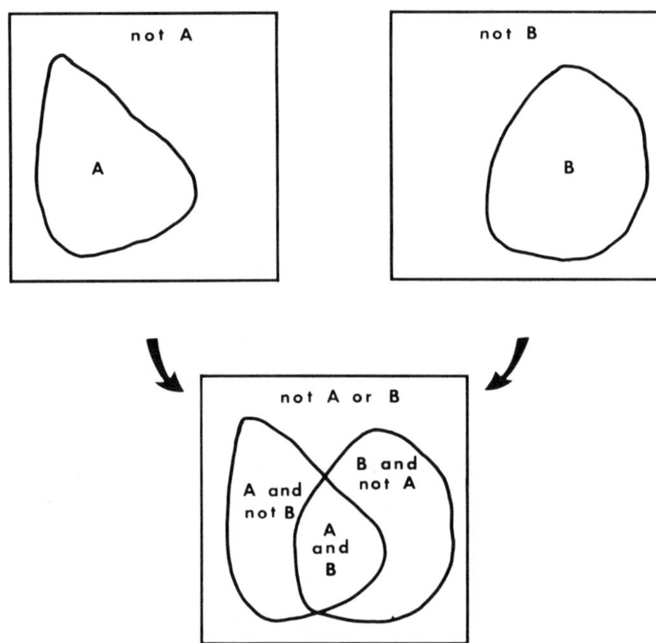

Figure 8.1 The Overlay Operation.

However, the overlay of maps is not without potential error [MacDougall, 1977]. Chrisman [1987] classifies this error into *positional* error associated with the spatial information on a map and *attribute* error related to the non-spatial information on a map. First, cartographic overlay often occurs between coverages for which distinct boundaries exist between formal regions having a common underlying thematic characteristic within each coverage. For certain socioeconomic coverages such as property parcels or zoning areas these boundaries may be easily identifiable. However, for many environmental variables such as vegetation or soils the delineation of common regions is more ambiguous and the quality of areal delineation is a concern [Goodchild and Dubuc, 1987]. Other continuous environmental attributes such as elevation or rainfall are frequently interpolated into a grid cell coverage where the interpolated thematic value represents the area within each grid cell.

Secondly, overlaying requires that coverages have a geographic registration with one another so that locations correctly align with one another. The data for each coverage should be collected at the same geographic scale to ensure accuracy in registration. Overall, overlaying requires greater locational accuracy in the positioning of cartographic objects.

Overlaying geographic base files of thematic coverages that have been encoded in a raster format is theoretically straightforward because the intersection and union of the objects involved are the same. Whenever two grid cells are overlaid their areas should exactly align so that no new cartographic object is formed. However, in practice, grid cells from one coverage may not align and the raster must be resampled (see section 4.3.1). Overlay operations are more difficult to perform on geographic base files that have been encoded in a vector format. In this case, the intersection of two polygon objects usually generates a different set of cartographic objects because the intersection and union of irregular polygons are not the same.

Several alternative methodologies exist for the overlay of vector-based objects. One common practice is to convert all coverages having a polygon structure into a raster format (see section 6.3.2). The major disadvantage of this approach is the loss of detail due to coding problems for assigning single values to pixels and the amount of area misclassified due to the rounding of area into a whole cell unit [Burrough, 1986]. Careful attention must be given to the size of the grid cell in this conversion so that it is not significantly larger than the features being converted. The amount of information loss is proportional to both grid cell size and the complexity of the boundary lines [Burrough, 1986].

Another approach is to divide the geographic domain under study into homogeneous regions. In the *gestalt* method, a trained expert determines these homogeneous units using field observation and various support documents such as aerial photographs [Hopkins, 1977]. A major limitation of this approach is the expense of delineating the units and is limited to small area analysis.

Another method is to form *greatest common geographic units* (GCGU) [Langran and Chrisman, 1987] (formerly called *least* common geographic units by Peucker and Chrisman [1975]). In this approach the various coverages are overlaid in advance and the resulting map is then encoded. Each polygon in this map is assumed to be an atomic object that cannot be subdivided further until you add a layer. In Figure 8.2, three coverages are overlaid and then encoded. Individual GCGU's can be merged in various combinations to form new objects but they cannot be split. The Census Bureau used this approach to construct the DIME files for metropolitan areas by vertically integrating separate layers of information on roads, railroads, water, other transportation lines and political boundaries into one map and has constructed the new TIGER files in the same manner [see Marx, 1986 for more discussion of creating TIGER files]. For each chain encoded in this approach, right- and left-hand polygon identifiers corresponding to each original coverage are attached to each chain.

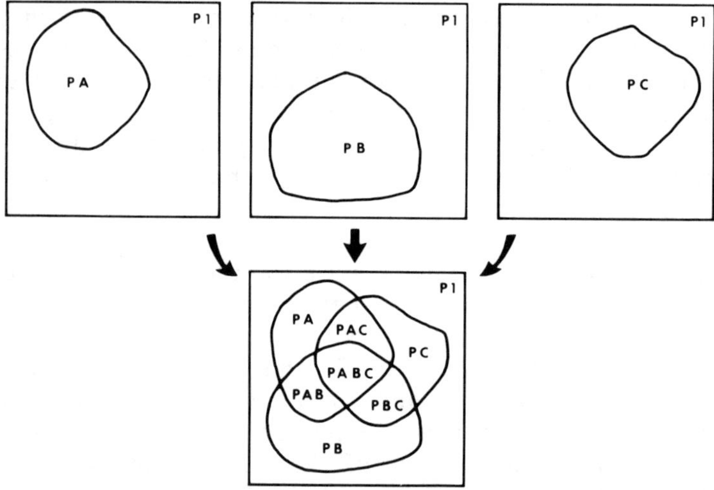

Figure 8.2 The Creation of Greatest Common Geographic Units.

Because no new attribute coverages can be added to the database without destroying the integrity of current objects unless the coverages are based on the same geographic building blocks, this approach is most easily adapted to socio-economic applications where many thematic attributes are usually associated with the same geographic aggregation unit and these units are hierarchically aggregated from the bottom up.

Whenever the addition of a new attribute does destroy the integrity of the current objects, an actual overlay of polygon sets must be performed and a new set of GSCU's are created. The polygon overlay process can be divided into three steps: 1) determining the intersecting chains and spliting them at their intersection points, 2) linking the chains together into polygons, and 3) identifying each resulting polygon as the intersection of two input polygons [White, 1978.]

In the first step, the problem is to find a new set of nodes that can be added to the nodes associated with each overlay. These nodes are found using some variant of local processing regions [White, 1978]. Assume that each coverage has been encoded in a chain data structure. The minimum bounding rectangle for each chain has been calculated and the chains in each coverage have been sorted in descending order based on the **YMAX** of their bounding rectangle. Each chain from the first coverage is processed in order; its rectangle is compared in order against the rectangles of the other coverage for a possible intersection until its **YMIN** value is greater than the **YMAX** value of the next chain in the second coverage. If two rectangles intersect, further processing is needed to find the actual intersection, if any exists (see Figures 8.3b and 8.3c). An intersection between two chains is actually an intersection between two line segments within the respective chains.

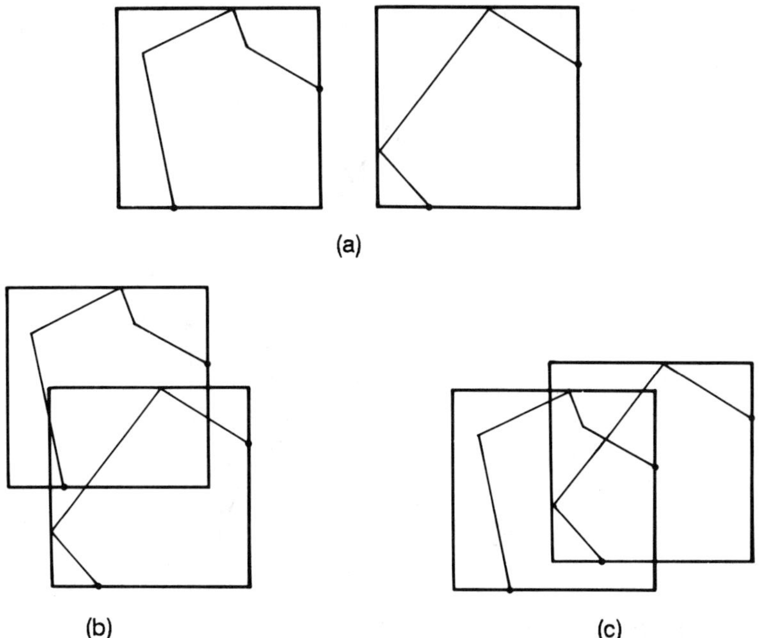

Figure 8.3 Intersection Possibilities.

If an intersection exists, the respective chains are split at their intersection which forms a new node. In Figure 8.4, chain **C1** intersects chain **C2** at node **I**; **I** is the intersection point between the line segments connecting points **p2** and **p3** in chain **C1** and points **p7** and **p8** in chain **C2**. The new chains **C1′** and **C2′** are the portions of the respective original chains that lie before the intersection given the direction of each chain, and new chains **C1"** and **C2"** are the portions that lie after the intersection. The neighborhoods for the new chains are derived from those of the original ones. Node **I** becomes the new terminus node for chains **C1′** and **C2′** and the new start node for chains **C1"** and **C2"**. The right-hand polygons for **C1′** are the right-hand polygon of **C1** and the left-hand polygon of **C2**; its left-hand polygons are the left-hand polygon of **C1** and the left-hand polygon of **C2**. The right- and left-hand polygons of the other three chains follow in a similar manner (see Table 8.1).

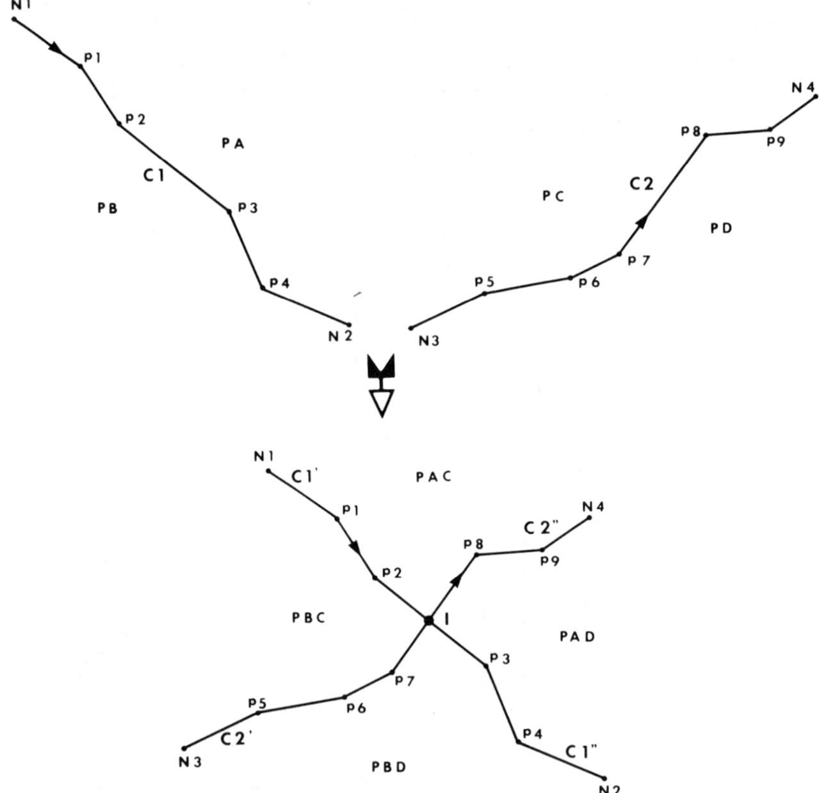

Figure 8.4 The Intersection of Two Chains.

The right and left chains for each new chain are determined next. The right chain of **C1′** is **C2′** and its left chain is the left chain of **C1**.

The right and left chains of the other new chains are similarly derived (Table 8.1). Next, chains **C1"** and **C2"** are processed to determine if there are any additional intersections between them. Each time a chain is split, the new chains, their neighborhood relations, and their new bounding rectangles replace their previous counterparts in the respective chain lists.

Table 8.1 Chain Neighborhoods Before and After Intersection

Chain	From Node	To Node	Left Polygon	Right Polygon	Point String
Before Intersection					
C1	N1	N2	PA	PB	p1,p2,p3,p4
C2	N3	N4	PC	PD	p5,p6,p7,p8,p9
After Intersection					
C1'	N1	I	PAC	PBC	p1,p2
C1"	I	N2	PAD	PBD	p3,p4
C2'	N3	I	PAC	PAD	p5,p6,p7
C2"	I	N4	PBC	PBD	p8,p9

This method for overlaying polygons assumes, however, that the respective original polygon sets are locationally accurate. In practice, the polygon overlay problem cannot be divorced from the separate problem of data error. The locations of polygon boundaries are not exact due to errors in surveys, source maps and the digitizing process [Dougenik, 1979]. The new polygons being identified by the overlay process may be degenerate polygons formed by inconsistent encoding of the original coverages (Figure 8.5). These spurious polygons are merely slivers resulting from independent encodings of the same cartographic feature rather than a real polygon and should be eliminated. To correct for this problem, the notion of line intersection is generalized to that of *fuzzy intersections* [Dougenik, 1979]. Fuzzy intersections occur if a point from one line is within some tolerance distance of a point from another. If it is, an intersection is formed and the line segments are divided at this point. The distance tolerance is also used to coalesce boundary endpoints. These problems are similar to those encountered during the digitizing process (see section 4.3.2). Fuzzy intersections also prohibit the identification of polygons at intersection time. A second pass is needed to add polygon IDs during an editing stage.

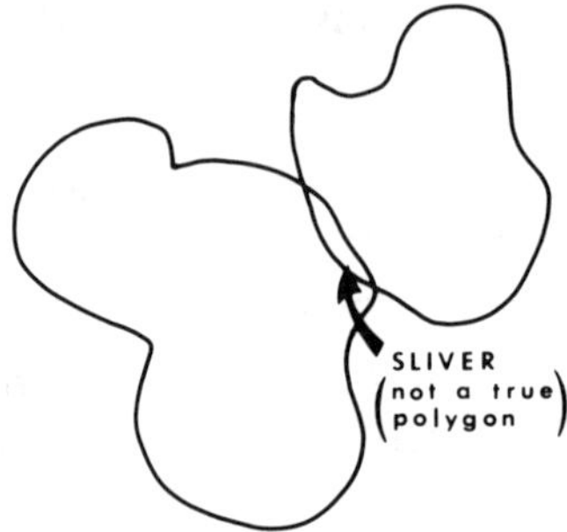

Figure 8.5 Degenerate Polygons Represented as Slivers.

8.2 THEMATIC COMPOSITING

As equally complex a problem as the geometric overlaying of polygons is the compositing of their thematic values in decision analysis. The question of how attributes are assimilated by decision-makers involves value systems and other more amorphous considerations. This question is compounded by the fact that attribute values may be misspecified as the result of misinterpretation of aerial photographs or classification error [Chrisman, 1987]. One basic problem also is that attributes may be measured on nominal, ordinal, interval or ratio scales. It is difficult to combine those values expressed in different units or even scales of measurement. For example, certain arithmetic operators are not valid with different measurement scales - one cannot add or subtract nominal attributes, nor can one multiply or divide interval attributes (see Hopkins [1977] for a brief review of the limitations of different scaled data).

Secondly, in a planning process one desires to structure environmental conditions to produce desired consequences. The decision maker must identify a set of alternative actions, the relationship between each action and consequence, and some preference for each consequence [Lee, 1972]. In evaluating the relationship between actions and consequences involving geographic objects, the attributes must be transformed into suitability levels for differing consequences. For example, land parcels may be used for two actions, housing and agriculture, that produce two desirable consequences, shelter and food. The attributes of each land parcel must be evaluated separately for each action with respect to each consequence. Besides the problem of evaluating attribute values with respect to different consequences, local policy formulation may result in a variety of perspectives associated with different user groups on how to do the evaluation.

The problem of compositing thematic attributes therefore has been handled in a variety of ways for interpretation. Hopkins [1977] has provided review and evaluation of alternative methods for determining the suitability of land use for a given activity. One method is to determine the feasible region associated with a set of constraints. In this case the geographic domain is sequentially reduced by restricting the range of permissible values for successive attributes. This approach does not require a common unit or even common scale of measurement for all variables, just a set of rules for combining the attributes. Each coverage of interest is converted into complementary subsets representing feasible and infeasible regions with respect to some activity. The coverages are overlaid to find the intersection of individual feasible regions. For example, in Figure 8.6 the feasible regions for locating a certain activity are overlaid for three relevant attributes. The feasible intersection of these coverages indicates that polygons A, B, and C possess the permissible thematic values with respect to each attribute.

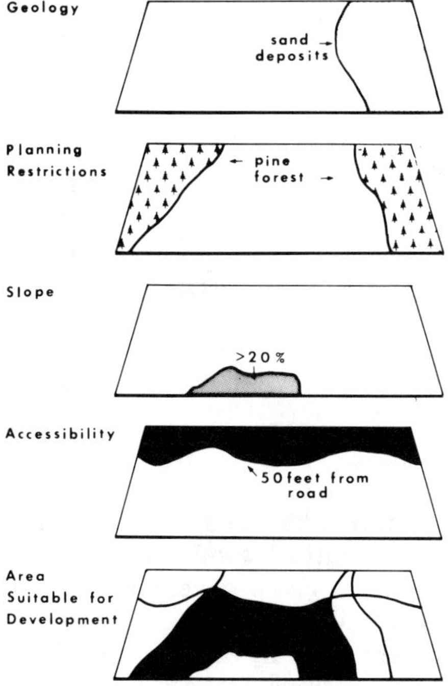

Figure 8.6 Determining a Feasible Region.
(adapted from Chorley, 1987)

Sometimes, no feasible intersection will exist. In this case, the coverages may be rank ordered in terms of their importance to the activity. The coverages are sequentially overlaid in this rank order until the next coverage added would generate no feasible solution (sometimes that nothing is feasible *is* the answer). Feasible regions are most often used in conjunction with siting problems.

If binary data are being composited, each coverage can be assigned a value of zero to denote absence of a coverage and a value of $2^{(n-1)}$ to denote the presence of the the nth coverage. For example, if three coverages are being composited, values of 1, 2 and 4 are assigned to coverages **A**, **B** and **C** respectively. When the three coverages are composited, the total will correspond to a unique combination of the coverages [Van Driel, 1980] (see Figure 8.7). At this stage, the numerical values only imply an occurrence of different combinations but not a preference or the importance of any combination for a particular activity. Each combination can now be evaluated by the gestalt method [Hopkins, 1977].

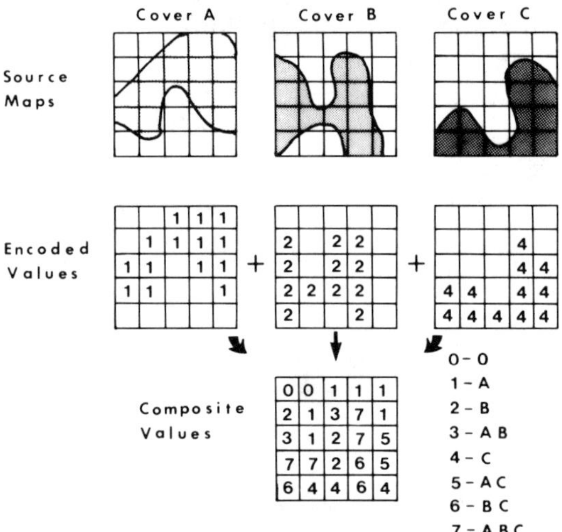

Figure 8.7 Compiling Nominal Scores.

Other methods determine the suitability of different locations for a certain activity as a mathematical combination. In an ordinal combination, the variate values for a given coverage are assigned a compatibility ranking represented as a numerical value. The overall suitability score for each location is determined by adding together the respective compatibility values for each coverage. The disadvantages of this method are that ordinal scaled numbers are not additive and the addition operator assumes that each attribute is independent of all other attributes.

The scaling problem is frequently handled by converting the variate values of the ith coverage into a compatibility index, $\mathbf{C_i}$, with the activity and then assigning the ith coverage an importance weight, $\mathbf{W_i}$. Lower compatibility indices imply the area is less suitable for the activity at hand. The weights can be used to transform all indices to the same interval scale and to reflect interdependency among the set of attributes. The suitability score for each cartographic object is the convex linear combination of its compatibility index and importance weight [Dobson, 1979]. The conversion of variate values into compatibility indices can either be determined by a local panel of experts or some predetermined value function.

Value functions have been suggested as a method for reducing the subjective nature of panel assignments [Hepner, 1984]. A value function is a transformation of attribute measurements into compatibility indices using the best available expertise (see Figure 8.8). The initial value function must be defined subjectively by a team of experts, but once it has been defined it can be imbedded into an operational system in a more objective manner. Individual value functions are defined for each association between an activity and an attribute.

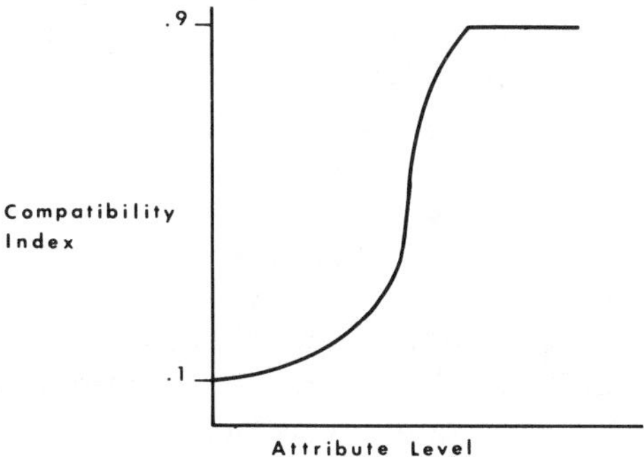

Figure 8.8 An Example of a Value Function.

Regardless of the effort used to construct compatibility indices, the utility of final suitability scores is compounded by the fact that the addition of these compatibility indices does not obey the commutative law of addition. For example, an object having a value of 8 on coverage **A** and a value of 1 on coverage **B** has the same total suitability as an object having a value of 1 on coverage **A** and a value of 8 on coverage **B**. The total masks a significant difference in the underlying structure of the phenomena being measured.

Rules of combination circumvent this problem by assigning suitabilities to sets of attribute combinations rather than to single attributes [Hopkins, 1977]. For example, places having values greater than 7 on coverage **A** and less than 2 on coverage **B** might be rated highly suitable while places having values less than 2 on coverage **A** and greater than 7 on coverage **B** are rated highly unsuitable for a certain activity. Moreover, the rules are expressed in a verbal logic rather than as an arithmetic expression. After geometrically overlaying coverages **A** and **B** to form the resulting GCGUs, the rules of combination can then be used to determine new composite attributes for these GCGUs.

8.3 MAP ANALYSIS

The notions of map overlaying and thematic compositing have been formalized into the framework of *map analysis* [Tomlin, 1983; 1990.] Map analysis is based on the notion that a cartographic or map algebra exists for cartographic objects in the same manner that traditional algebra exists for numbers. We have already seen that cartographic operators such as simplification and classification act upon cartographic objects and their attributes. In map analysis, the set of objects comprising a map is viewed as a layer having only one thematic attribute. Each object in the map has only one corresponding thematic value or coverage. Such a map is termed an overlay map [Berry, 1987]. The cartographic database contains an initial set of overlay maps having known thematic values.

A fundamental task in algebra is to solve for an unknown variable (or variables) given a relation usually expressed as an equation (or system of equations) composed of variables, constants, and operators. The cartographic model of the geographic phenomena under investigation determined exogenously establishes the system of equations relating unknowns, constants and operators. The unknowns are solved by the system while the constants and operators are predefined for the model. The constants usually represent some form of scaling or weighting determined in a manner discussed in the previous section. Existing overlays in the database also are used as constants in solving for unknown overlays. The value of an unknown overlay then is determined by sequencing map operations in a manner analogous to algebraic manipulations of equations [Berry, 1987]. For an unknown overlay, the value for each object is solved independently of all other objects although the values of many objects in a known overlay may be used in the computation.

Cartographic operators include arithmetic operators (such as addition, subtraction, multiplication, division), standard mathematical functions (such as square root, exponential, and logarithms) and special operations unique to map analysis. The set of primitive operations can be partitioned into those that: 1) reclassify maps, 2) perform overlays, 3) measure distance and connectivity, and 4) characterize neighborhoods [Berry, 1987]. Reclassification operators redefine existing values on a single coverage. Overlay operators use two or more maps to define new cartographic objects and values. Distance and connectivity operators measure shortest paths between points and proximity regions around points. Finally, neighborhood operators assign a value to an object on a new map that has been computed as a function of the values of neighboring objects.

The formulation and solution of a problem using map analysis is illustrated by the following example. Assume that there are five map operators defined in Figure 8.9 which can be used to act upon individual map layers. A new map layer, $\mathbf{MAP_g}$, is be expressed algebraically in Figure 8.10 as the composite function of these operators and six initial map layers - $\mathbf{MAP_a}$, $\mathbf{MAP_b}$, $\mathbf{MAP_c}$, $\mathbf{MAP_d}$, $\mathbf{MAP_e}$ and $\mathbf{MAP_f}$. The order in which these operations are applied must be defined in the same manner that a hierarchy of arithmetic operators has been predetermined. One cannot assume that map operators can be performed in a strict left-to-right order just as one cannot perform an addition operation before a multiplication operation solely because the addition operator was to the left of the multiplication operator in an equation.

Map Operator	Purpose
SUB	Subtract the values of the second coverage from the values of the first coverage.
MULT	Multiply the values of the second coverage by the values of the first coverage.
MIN	Find the minimum value at each location within a set of coverages
RECODE	Recode the values of a given coverage by reassigning
COVER	Replace the values at the first coverage by the nonzero values of the second coverage

Figure 8.9 An Example Set of Map Operators.

$$((\mathbf{MAP_f})\,\mathrm{SUB}\,(\mathbf{MAP_e}))\,\mathrm{COVER}\,((\mathrm{RECODE}\,(\mathbf{MAP_d}))\,\mathrm{MULT}\,(\mathrm{MIN}((\mathbf{MAP_a},\mathbf{MAP_b},\mathbf{MAP_c})))) = \mathbf{MAP_g}$$

Figure 8.10 An Example Map Equation.

A proper sequencing of map operators need not be formalized in the sense that certain types of operations must always precede other types of operations. The sequencing can be defined for each application in a flow chart showing which map layers are combined by which operators (see Figure 8.11). After each operation is performed, an intermediate map layer is generated. For example, $\mathbf{MAP_d}$ is recoded into the intermediate object $\mathbf{MAP_2}$. These intermediate maps are then combined by subsequent operators to form new intermediate map layers until all operations have been performed and the final map layer has been created.

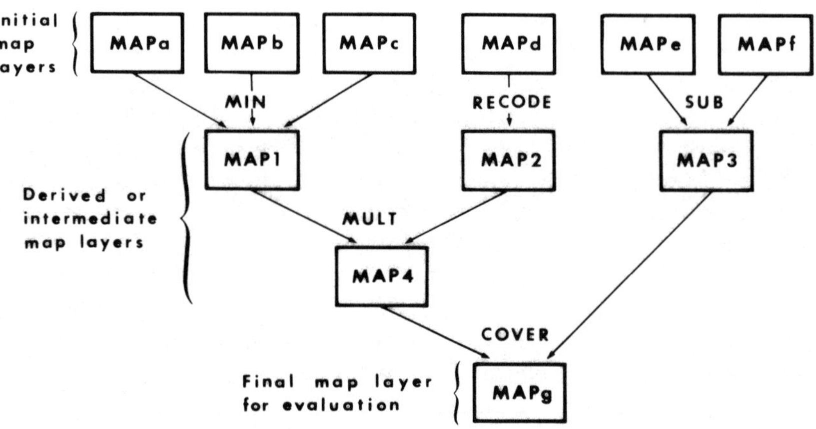

Figure 8.11 A Flowchart of the Map Operator Sequence.

The sequencing of operators has been structured in a natural language syntax by Tomlin [1983]; using verbs and nouns to denote operators and coverages, the problem of solving unknown coverages is given as verbal commands. The sequence of commands for this example is given in Figure 8.12. A lengthy list of operators and their corresponding commands are given by Burrough [1986, Table 5.2]. Map analysis has become a major mode of data analysis found in the evolving technology of geographic information systems, especially in raster based systems such as OSU Map-for-the PC [Geographic Information Systems Laboratory, 1989] and IDRISI [Eastman, 1988].

8.4 GEOGRAPHIC INFORMATION SYSTEMS

An important technique that has been developed to aid in many different forms of spatial decision making is *Geographic Information Systems* or GIS. There are many definitions of a GIS but they all share the same basic concepts. The report of the Committee of Enquiry into Handling

Geographic Information in Great Britian defines a GIS as "a system for capturing, storing, checking, integrating, manipulating, analyzing and displaying data which are spatially referenced to the Earth" [Chorley, 1987, p. 132]. A related technique is a Land Information System (LIS) that collects and analyzes data regarding land and its use, ownership and development. An LIS is considered a subset of GIS (see the taxonomy of information systems given in Figure 8.13).

```
MINimum of MAPa and MAPb and MAPc for MAP1
RECODE MAPd assigning 0 to 1 through 4,1 to 5 for MAP2
SUBtract MAPf from MAPe for MAP3
MULTiply MAP1 and MAP2 for MAP4
COVER MAP4 with MAP3 for MAPg
```

Figure 8.12 The Sequencing of Operators as Commands.

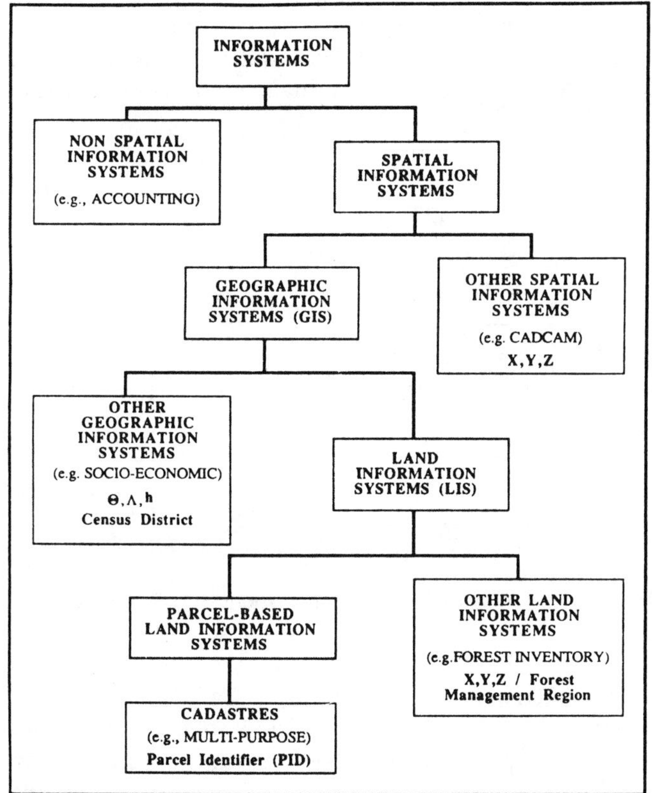

Figure 8.13 A Taxonomy of Information Systems.
(Source: McLaughlin and Nichols, 1987)

Traditionally, GIS and map analysis have been associated with maps and their interpretation. A printed multi-attribute map is a geographic information system in the same sense that other printed media are information systems in other fields of inquiry except that GIS also implies some integration process. The computer has changed the way one views GIS in the same manner that it has altered our perception of cartography and has created new GIS technologies. The computer has also brought about greater specialization in the many facets of a GIS.

GIS technology is the result of linking together parallel developments in many separate spatial data processing fields (see Figure 8.14) [Burrough, 1986]. However, it is much broader in scope than its predecessors. A wider range of data is collected in a GIS than in a computer-aided design (CAD) system. It is more than just data display as in computer-assisted mapping, and it involves more than data acquisition as in digital remote sensing. GIS is a more powerful tool for spatial analysis than other spatial data processing techniques. Abler [1987] has likened the impact of GIS technology on spatial analysis to that of the microscope and telescope in other fields. Dobson [1983] has noted that GIS will enable researchers to perform holistic analyses of geographic regions.

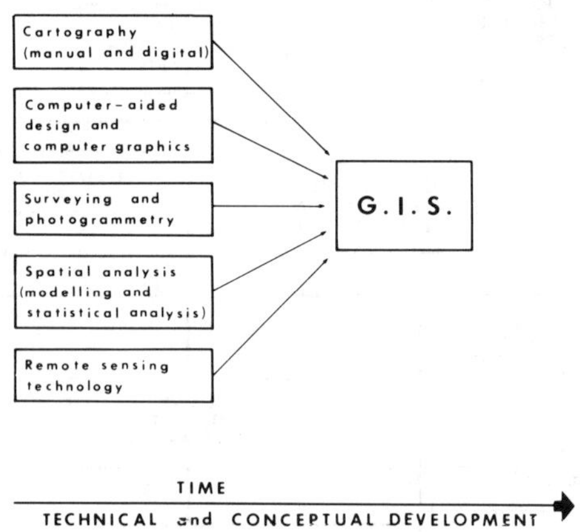

Figure 8.14 The Convergence of Spatial Data Processing Fields into GIS. (after Burrough, 1986)

For many applications, the design of a GIS is end driven. Although the flow of activity is from data acquisition to decision-making, the flow in GIS design is from the decision back to data requirements with feedback loops between the different stages of activity. As in cartographic information systems, the decision makers must first decide what type of information is useful. Then the displays and modes of analysis that will provide the necessary information are determined although, for some applications, inventories must be maintained with or without specific outputs. Finally, the data requirements are specified. Given the cost of compiling the spatial database and software system, there is a strong need for a managerial overview of system requirements. Due to lead times in digitizing there is also a need to predict uses and have the data already encoded and current. If the system has an institutional framework, then the institutional mandate is a better guide for long-term operation than either a single project or user needs study.

The major components subsystems of a GIS include: 1) managerial overview, 2) data encoding and input processing, 3) database management, 4) data retrieval, 5) data manipulation and analysis, 6) data display, and 7) information use [Tomlinson, *et al.*, 1976; Smith, *et al.*, 1987]. Each subsystem is delegated a set of tasks to ensure proper functioning of the overall system. The managment subsystem has the responsibility for supervising staff, establishing procedures, and maintaining the continuity of the system. The data encoding and input processing subsystem controls the acquisition, input and storage of the database. Many preprocessing procedures such as format conversion, line simplification, error detection and editing, edge matching, rectification and registration are included in this component. The database management subsystem provides data integrity and ensures that multiple users and databases can be supported by the system. The data retrieval subsystem performs spatial and non-spatial searches to extract attribute information about spatial objects or spatial distributions of attributes. The data manipulation and analysis and display subsystems control the mode of analysis and form of output for extracting information from the database. The modes of analysis include attribute classification, coordinate transformations, spatial and non-spatial statistics, measurements, polygon overlays, and point and line buffers [see Dangermond, 1983; Smith, *et al.*, 1987; Tomlinson and Boyle, 1981]. Finally, the information use subsystem controls the interface between different user groups and the system.

Within a GIS the spatial database occupies a central role (Figure 8.15) The data analysis and data processing subsystems are organized around the database to facilitate queries from the information use subsystem. The importance of database design for the ease of accessing information has directed the focus of recent GIS research. Database management has become the major force in GIS design, lessening the role of computer cartographics. Problems of database management are more critical to the functioning of a GIS than problems of display. Increasingly in digital cartography this is also the case -- the focus of attention is centered on the database, not the graphic form or perception of the graphic.

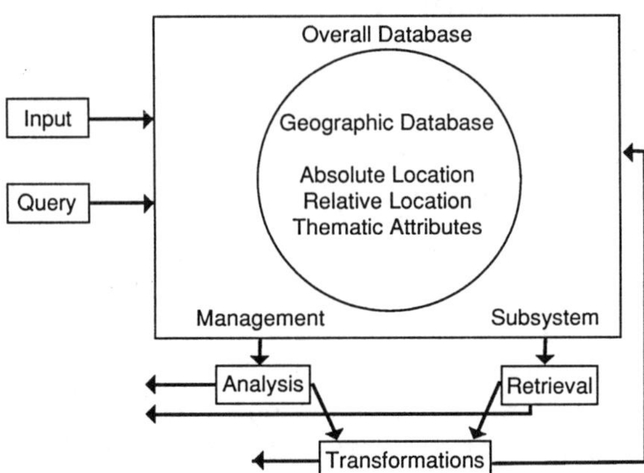

Figure 8.15 The Position of the Database within a GIS.
(Source: Burrough, 1986)

In the earlier stages of development, a GIS was tailor made for a specific purpose. The decision makers decided not only the data requirements of the system but also what the capabilities of the system should be. Most developmental work was done for the government in response to their data handling needs [Tomlinson, 1984]. Given that different government agencies in different application areas have different responsibilities, there is a need for different GIS capabilities. It was not until the 1970s that commercial vendors started to develop and market general purpose systems.

Some potential conflicts can arise from the incongruities between the need for specific information and a multipurpose system designed to meet the average needs of the marketplace. One problem is that the average needs may not satisfy the special needs of some user groups. Conversely, a multipurpose system may be overkill and provide more capabilities than certain users can ever assimilate. A system could be greatly underutilized. Given that the generic processes are present, two characteristics of a GIS should be: 1) an open architecture so that custom designed functions can be easily added to the system, and 2) modularity so that a user only has to purchase the hardware and software to satisfy his or her needs.

The future holds a high level of promise for GIS as a major instrument for geographical analysis but there are still many problems to be addressed before GIS reaches its full potential. Problems associated with data volume, quality, compatibility and timeliness must be overcome before geographic analysis reaches a mature status.

8.5 SUMMARY

The modeling of cartographic objects plays a pivotal role in many forms of geographic analysis. The spatial compositing of alternative coverages is a tool used by decision makers in every level of the public and private sectors. In Chapter One, digital cartography was defined as the study of the properties of cartographic objects that remained invariant to sets of cartographic functions. However, the utility of digital cartographic products for spatial analysis and decision making is blurring the distinction between cartographic functions and other spatial functions. The developments in digital cartography and other spatial data processing fields are being merged together in the technology of geographic information systems. Although digital cartography is still display oriented, the displays are more analytical rather than descriptive and just one of several modes of output. Spatial database design and manipulation have become more important considerations over time.

8.6 REFERENCES

Abler, R. [1987]. "What Shall We Say? To Whom Shall We Speak?," **Annals Association of American Geographers**, 77, 511-24.

Berry, J. [1987]. "Fundamental Operations in Computer-Assisted Map Analysis," **International Journal of Geographical Information Systems**, 1, 119-36.

Burrough, P. [1986]. **Principles of Geographical Information Systems for Land Resources Assessement**, Oxford: Clarendon Press.

Chorley, R. [1987]. **Handling Geographic Information, Report of the Committee of Enquiry**, London: Her Majesty's Stationery Office.

Chrisman, N. [1987] "The Accuracy of Map Overlays: A Reassessment," **Landscape and Urban Planning**," 14, 427-39.

Dangermond, J. [1983]. "A Classification of Software Components Commonly Used in Geographic Information Systems," in **Design and Implementation of Computer-Based Geographic Information Systems**, D. Peuquet and J. O'Callaghan (eds.), Amherst, New York: International Geographical Commission on Geographic Data Sensing and Processing.

Dobson, J. [1979]. "A Regional Screening Procedure for Land Use Suitability Analysis," **Geographical Review**, 69, 224-34.

Dobson, J. [1983]. "Automated Geography," **The Professional Geographer**, 35, 135-43.

Dougenik, J. [1979]. "Whirlpool: A Geometric Processor for Polygon Coverage Data," **Proceedings**, AUTO-CARTO IV, Vol. II, 304-11.

Eastman, R. [1988]. **IDRISI: A Grid-Based Geographic Analysis System**, Version 3.0, Worcester, Massachusetts: Clark University, Graduate School of Geography.

Geographic Information Systems Laboratory. [1989]. **OSU MAP-for-the-PC User's Guide**, Version 3.0, Columbus, Ohio: The Ohio State University, Department of Geography.

Goodchild, M. and O. Dubuc. [1987]. "A Model of Error for Choropleth Maps, with Application to Geographic Information Systems," **Proceedings**, Eighth International Symposium on Computer-Assisted Cartography (AUTO-CARTO 8), 165-74.

Hepner, G. [1984]. "Use of Value Functions as a Possible Suitability Scaling Procedure in Automated Composite Mapping," **The Professional Geographer**, 36, 468-72.

Hopkins, L. [1977]. "Methods for Generating Land Suitability Maps: A Comparative Evaluation," **Journal of the American Institute of Planners**, 43, 386-400.

Langran, G. and N. Chrisman. [1987]. "A Framework for Temporal Geographic Information, **Cartographica**, 24, No. 3, 1-14.

Lee, S. [1972]. **Goal Programming for Decision Analysis**, Philadelphia: Auerbach.

MacDougall, E.B. [1975]. "The Accuracy of Map Overlays," **Landscape Planning**, 2, 23-30.

Marx, R. [1986]. "The TIGER System: Automating the Geographic Structure of the United States Census," **Government Publications Review**, 13, 181-201.

McHarg, I. [1969]. **Design with Nature**, Garden City, New York: Doubleday and Company, Inc.

McLaughlin, J. and S. Nichols. [1987]. "Parcel-Based Land Information Systems," **Surveying and Mapping**, 47, 11-29.

Peucker, T. and N. Chrisman. [1975]. "Cartographic Data Structures," **The American Cartographer**, 2, 55-69.

Smith, T., S. Menon, J. Star, and J. Estes. [1987]. "Requirements and Principles for the Implementation and Construction of Large-Scale Geographic Information Systems, **International Journal of Geographical Information Systems**, 1, 13-32.

Tomlin, D. [1983]. **Digital Cartographic Modelling Techniques in Environmental Planning**, Ph.D. dissertation, Yale University.

Tomlin, D. [1990]. **Geographic Information Systems and Cartographic Modeling**, Englewood Cliffs, New Jersey: Prentice Hall, Inc.

Tomlinson, R. [1984]. "Geographic Information Systems - A New Frontier," **Proceedings**, First International Symposium on Spatial Data Handling, 1-14.

Tomlinson, R. and A.R. Boyle. [1981]. "The State of Development of Systems for Handling Natural Resources Inventory Data," **Cartographica**, 18, No. 4, 65-95.

Tomlinson, R., H. Calkins, and D. Marble. [1976]. **Computer Handling of Geographical Data**, Paris: The UNESCO Press.

Van Driel, N. [1980]. "Computer-Composite Mapping for Geologists," **Environmental Geology**, 3, 151-57.

White, D. [1978]. "A New Method of Polygon Overlay," **Harvard Papers on Geographic Information Systems**, G. Dutton (ed.), Vol. 6.

Index